Superpower Involvement
in the Middle East

Westview Special Studies

The concept of Westview Special Studies is a response to the continuing crisis in academic and informational publishing. Library budgets are being diverted from the purchase of books and used for data banks, computers, micromedia, and other methods of information retrieval. Interlibrary loan structures further reduce the edition sizes required to satisfy the needs of the scholarly community. Economic pressures on university presses and the few private scholarly publishing companies have greatly limited the capacity of the industry to properly serve the academic and research communities. As a result, many manuscripts dealing with important subjects, often representing the highest level of scholarship, are no longer economically viable publishing projects—or, if accepted for publication, are typically subject to lead times ranging from one to three years.

Westview Special Studies are our practical solution to the problem. As always, the selection criteria include the importance of the subject, the work's contribution to scholarship, and its insight, originality of thought, and excellence of exposition. We accept manuscripts in camera-ready form, typed, set, or word processed according to specifications laid out in our comprehensive manual, which contains straightforward instructions and sample pages. The responsibility for editing and proofreading lies with the author or sponsoring institution, but our editorial staff is always available to answer questions and provide guidance.

The result is a book printed on acid-free paper and bound in sturdy library-quality soft covers. We manufacture these books ourselves using equipment that does not require a lengthy make-ready process and that allows us to publish first editions of 300 to 1000 copies and to reprint even smaller quantities as needed. Thus, we can produce Special Studies quickly and can keep even very specialized books in print as long as there is a demand for them.

About the Book and Editors

The contributors to this book offer an explanation of Soviet and U.S. policy in the Middle East by exploring how the superpowers define their goals in the region, the factors that both stimulate and constrain the United States and the Soviet Union in the implementation of their objectives, and how their mutual perceptions influence behavior.

The chapters on Soviet foreign policy explore Soviet perceptions of U.S. military and political strengths and weaknesses in the region, continued fears of a superpower confrontation arising from escalating regional conflicts, the challenges posed by Islamic fundamentalism, the pressures of client demands, and the nature of internal power struggles between competing Soviet foreign policy elites.

Faulty assumptions—their content and origin—are a central theme of the chapters on U.S. foreign policy in the Middle East. Such assumptions are reflected in excessive U.S. concern with Middle East oil, inaccurate perceptions of the PLO moderation, an inappropriate transfer of Western ideals of democracy and the nation-state to the Middle East, and an unsophisticated application of the East-West ideological struggle to the conflict in the Middle East.

This volume makes a major contribution to our understanding of Soviet and U.S. policy in the 1980s, highlighting explanatory variables that are likely to persist into the next decade.

Paul Marantz is associate professor of political science at the University of British Columbia. *Blema S. Steinberg* is associate professor of political science at McGill University.

To our children
Adam, Donna, Margot, and Monica

Superpower Involvement
in the Middle East
Dynamics of Foreign Policy

edited by **Paul Marantz**
and **Blema S. Steinberg**

Westview Press / Boulder and London

Westview Special Studies in International Relations

Copyright © 1985 by Westview Press, Inc.

Published in 1985 in the United States of America by Westview Press, Inc.; Frederick A. Praeger, Publisher; 5500 Central Avenue, Boulder, Colorado 80301

Library of Congress Cataloging in Publication Data
Superpower involvement in the Middle East.
  Includes index.
  1. Near East—Foreign relations—Soviet Union—
Addresses, essays, lectures. 2. Soviet Union—
Foreign relations—Near East—Addresses, essays,
lectures. 3. Near East—Foreign relations—United
States—Addresses, essays, lectures. 4. United
States—Foreign relations—Near East—Addresses,
essays, lectures. I. Marantz, Paul. II. Steinberg,
Blema S.
DS63.2.S65S87   1985   327.56   85-13617
ISBN 0-8133-7100-7

Printed and bound in the United States of America

10   9   8   7   6   5   4   3   2   1

Contents

PART 3
THE IMPACT OF THE GREAT POWERS

Preface

The deep involvement of the United States and the Soviet Union in the Middle East has had a critical impact on both their bilateral relations and the politics of the region. This volume analyzes the role of the superpowers, paying special attention to the underlying patterns which help explain how they have perceived their options as well as the policies and goals they have chosen to pursue. The continuing sources of conflict between the superpowers as well as the limited prospects for future cooperation are also examined.

The articles in this volume are revised and up-dated versions of papers originally prepared for presentation at the annual scholarly conference of the Canadian Professors for Peace in the Middle East which was held at the University of Toronto in June 1984. The editors would like to express their appreciation to the many people who assisted in the preparation of this book. Dr. Eva Dessen, the tireless Executive Director of the CPPME, did a superb job of handling the many details of the conference and in providing highly professional editorial assistance. Ogden Gavanski and Robert Quon were ideal research assistants. Their initiative, sense of responsibility, and unfailing good cheer greatly enhanced the quality of this book and the speed with which it has appeared. Lastly, we would like to express our thanks to the Social Sciences and Humanities Research Council of Canada. Its financial support, through its program of aid to scholarly conferences, was critically important to the conference and to the publication of this volume.

P. M.   B.S.S.

Part 1

The View from Moscow

1

The Soviet View of the Utility
of Force in the Third World

S. N. MacFarlane

Introduction

Soviet military activism in the Third World since the early 1970s has become a cause of growing concern to Western policy–makers. Soviet and Cuban involvement in Third World conflicts was a significant factor in the slowing and reversal of the process of détente. It affected not only the general atmosphere of East–West relations, but also the progress of arms control negotiations. Soviet activity in the Horn of Africa, for example, delayed the conclusion of the SALT II treaty. The Soviet invasion of Afghanistan led the American government to withdraw the treaty from Senate ratification proceedings. In the current phase of tension between the superpowers, one of the more credible avenues to major war is that of escalation from confrontation in areas of the Third World where major interests of the U.S. and the USSR overlap.

The region of the Third World where this prospect is most disturbing is the Middle East. Here Soviet concerns regarding the security of their southern frontier intersect with those of the West regarding continued access to Persian Gulf oil. The Soviet quest for influence in the Arab world (a quest in which they have invested much materiel and prestige) clashes with the American commitment to the survival of Israel. This clash occurs in a region where politics are unpredictable and chronically conflictual. The region's deep–seated animosities, and the commitment of the superpowers to local actors––over whom they have little control and who seek to involve them in local conflicts––have in the past raised the prospect of superpower confrontation and in all likelihood will do so again.

In this context, it becomes important to understand how Soviet policy-makers think about conflict in the Third World and how they perceive their own role in such conflict. This paper addresses several questions:

1. How does Third World conflict impinge upon Soviet interests?
2. What constraints does the USSR face in its use of force in the Third World?
3. What do recent changes in Soviet doctrine and behavior tell us about their evolving perceptions of risk and benefit stemming from the use of force in Third World conflict?
4. How can these changes be explained?
5. What are the policy implications for the West, and particularly for the U.S., of evolving Soviet attitudes towards the use of force in the Third World?
5. What does the analysis tell us about the prospects for Soviet use of force in the near and longer term?

It is frequently assumed that whereas there existed prior to the mid-1970s a set of tacit "rules of the game" restraining superpower involvement in the Third World, Soviet behavior in the mid- and late 1970s reflected a change in Soviet attitudes towards the use of force in the Third World, and, as such, a profound challenge to established understandings. This paper argues that although in the late 1960s and early 1970s there clearly developed a greater Soviet willingness to project force in the Third World--whether directly or in the form of logistical support and supply of allied forces--the Soviet view of the utility of force remains cautious and, with respect to the U.S., risk averse and non-confrontational.

Before beginning the analysis, its parameters need to be defined. For the purposes of this paper, the "Third World" is taken to include Latin America, Africa, and Asia (excluding Japan and the Asian portions of the USSR). Chronologically, although the history of Soviet force projection in the Third World is almost as long as that of communist rule in Russia, this paper focuses on Soviet doctrine and policy during the Brezhnev years.[1]

With regard to methodology, this paper relies on official party and military sources in its analysis of Soviet doctrine and on secondary Western sources in its analysis of Soviet military behavior. It concentrates on the direct involvement of Soviet forces and those of its allies in conflict situations in the Third World, rather than on "naval diplomacy" and arms supply and military assistance to Third World states.[2] Although these latter two types of activity are important to a complete understanding of Soviet military policy in the Third World, it is the intervention of Soviet and proxy forces which most strongly affects East–West relations and raises the prospect of superpower confrontation.

The paper does not deal to any great extent with disagreements within the Soviet elite on power projection in the Third World. No doubt such disagreements exist, and in some contexts consideration of them is important.[3] But the focus here in the consideration of doctrine is on official and quasi–official statements. In this area there is little clear evidence of controversy. Moreover, the elaboration of doctrine on a number of the specific issues considered here (for example, the classification of wars) appears to be the exclusive province of a single group within the Soviet elite, the military. Moreover, our discussion of policy concentrates on patterns in Soviet behavior, that is on *outcomes*. In this context, the question of pluralism in policy *inputs* is not directly relevant.

Interests and Constraints

Force projection is one of an array of policy instruments available to Soviet policy–makers in the pursuit of the USSR's interests in the Third World. These interests are of at least three different types. The first pertains most specifically to states along the periphery of the USSR and concerns the security of the Soviet Union. To judge from their behavior at least since World War II, Soviet policy–makers view the existence of hostile or unstable states along Soviet borders as inimical to external security and internal political stability. In situations where this threat is particularly compelling while constraints on direct Soviet action to eliminate it are weak, the Soviets have used military force to rectify the situation. The Soviet invasion of Afghanistan is perhaps best explicable in these terms. Regional conflict in areas close to Soviet borders not only enhances the perceived threat, but facilitates the Soviet response by providing opportunities or pretexts for involvement.

Soviet security concerns impinge to a lesser extent on states and regions beyond the immediate periphery of the USSR. The U.S. integrates bases and deployment areas in the Third World into its strategic posture vis–à–vis the USSR. In the past, bases in Turkey, Libya, and Morocco, for example, have been used by American strategic bombers. The Indian Ocean is a potential deployment area for American strategic nuclear submarines. Soviet force projection in the Middle East and Indian Ocean zones and in particular its quest for bases along the Indian Ocean littoral as support for a naval presence in that ocean may be seen in part as attempts to reduce or counter this threat.[4] Moreover, the Indian Ocean and Suez Canal are strategic sea lanes to the USSR in the same sense that the Panama Canal is for the United States. This too gives the USSR a security incentive for military involvement in these areas.

The second interest concerns the competition with the U.S. for influence in states removed from the Soviet periphery. Soviet foreign policy in the Third World since Stalin's death seems to have been strongly affected by the desire to expand Soviet influence and to reduce Western influence in the developing world. To judge from recent official statements, one important element of this competition, from the Soviet perspective, is a desire to be recognized as an equal of the U.S. throughout the globe.[5] Soviet policy–makers have attempted to use economic instruments to win favor, particularly during the Khrushchev era. However, as the limitations on the Soviet capacity to compete with the West in these terms have become more clear, military assistance has become the dominant vehicle employed by the USSR in this competition. Regional conflict, by creating a need for what the USSR has to offer, facilitates the Soviet pursuit of influence in this competition.

The contest for influence with the West is related to a third factor, that of ideology. One should not overestimate the role of ideological commitment in explaining Soviet force projection. Yet it is true nonetheless that the domestic legitimacy of the Soviet leadership is to a degree predicated upon the credibility of its claim to being a revolutionary actor in world politics. The same is true of Moscow's claims to leadership in what is referred to as the "world revolutionary movement." Soviet influence and control over radical forces in world politics depends to some extent on the material and moral support which the USSR renders them. The use of force in Third World conflict is one means of underscoring Soviet status as a revolutionary actor in world politics and gaining influence among groups committed to revolutionary anti–Western action.

In its use of force in pursuit of these interests, the USSR is constrained in a number of ways. The first significant constraint is a physical one. Intervention in Third World conflicts requires specific military capabilities such as long range air and sea transport, naval support for land operations, long range fighter cover, and in–flight refueling capabilities. The USSR has traditionally been a continental Eurasian military power. Its military procurement programme has not historically emphasized such capabilities to the extent that a sea power like the United States does. Though considerable progress has been made in this area since the mid–1960s, Soviet force projection capabilities remain conspicuously inferior in most relevant categories to those of the U.S.

This is clear from Table 1. In particular, Soviet carrier-borne aviation is insignificant compared to its American counterpart. The tonnage of the Soviet amphibious fleet is only 24% of that of American amphibious transport. The payload of the Soviet long range air transport fleet is just over one half that of the American Military Airlift Command. Moreover, neither of the relevant Soviet aircraft (the AN22 and the IL76) can refuel in flight. Finally, the AN22, which comprises about 20% of the Soviet long range fleet is a turboprop aircraft, while all relevant American aircraft are jet.[6]

Table 1:1

Soviet and American Long Range Force Projection Capabilities (1984)

	USSR	U.S.A.
Long range air transport	280[1]	322[5]
Amphibious ships	33[2]	61[6]
Aircraft carriers	3[3]	13
Helicopter carriers	2	–[7]
Airborne forces	7 divisions[4]	1 division
Marines	16,000	196,600

[1] Includes military but not civilian IL76 and AN22.
[2] Includes Ivan Rogov, Rapucher, and Alligator classes.
[3] One more in trials.
[4] Excludes one division devoted to training. Each division approximately 7,500 men.
[5] Includes C5 and C141, excludes 218 C130.
[6] Includes Blue Ridge, Tarawa, Iwo Jima, Austin, Raleigh, Anchorage, Thomaston, Newport, and Charleston classes.
[7] Included under amphibious category.

Source: IISS, Military Balance, 1984–1985. London, IISS, 1984.

For these reasons, it is only in situations where the risk of military opposition by the U.S. is low that the USSR can safely contemplate interventionary activities. Even in those areas close to the USSR, where this imbalance is less relevant and where in fact the USSR may enjoy military superiority, if the Soviet Union expected serious military resistance (e.g. in the case of a thrust into Iran), Soviet force projection would in all likelihood involve a drawing down of land transport capabilities in other theatres, while Soviet air transport would be susceptible to considerable attrition.[7] This would affect readiness in more important theatres precisely at a time when the Soviet leadership is likely to be concerned about the consequences of heightened international tension.

The mention of the possibility of American resistance brings us to a second constraint on Soviet force projection. The Soviets, in contemplating combat use of their own forces in the Third World, or for that matter logistical support of allied forces, must consider the risk of confrontation involving the other superpower in which Soviet losses may be sufficiently large to draw into question the value of projected gains from the operation. This constraint is geographically specific, and concerns areas where the Soviets may perceive that American decision–makers consider American vital interests to be threatened by Soviet force projection. From the Soviet policy–makers' point of view, the Third World can in this context be divided into three areas: 1. countries and regions in which one superpower has vital interests while the other does not; 2. countries and regions where vital interests of the two overlap; and 3. countries and regions in which neither side's vital interests are at stake.[8] The clearest examples of the first type are states along the periphery of one superpower which do not have close ties with the other. Cases in point are Afghanistan and the nations of Central America. The most obvious case of the second is the Middle East and Persian Gulf region. Africa provides a good example of the third. The perceived constraint of possible confrontation is strongest in the first two and less compelling in the third.

The danger of confrontation is an extreme example of a more general constraint on Soviet force projection in the Third World––the potential effects of such activity on relations with the Western powers. The expansion of influence in the Third World is only one of an array of objectives of Soviet foreign policy and clearly not the most important. The attempt to expand influence at the expense of the West in the Third World can interfere with these other dimensions of Soviet foreign policy. In this context, one consideration which Soviet policy–makers must address in decisions relating to the use of force in the Third World is whether, independent of the question of success or failure in those countries, the ancillary effects of such behavior are such as to render it counterproductive.[9]

It is not only putative responses of the West which are relevant here. The USSR has expended much effort in developing an image as an anti–imperialist power sympathetic to and supportive of the struggle of the Third World against the West. The experience of Afghanistan suggests that Soviet force projection carries with it the risk of substantial damage to Soviet standing in the Third World. Again, this constraint is not constant, but varies considerably according to the specifics of the situation in which projection of force is contemplated. The defense of a Third World state at the latter's request, in the face of external threat or internal instability is less likely to involve costs of this type than the use of force to assist a Third World actor to attack a neighbor, or for that matter Soviet force projection to impose its will on a weaker state. In this regard, it is clear, for example, that the USSR paid much higher costs for its invasion of Afghanistan than for its assistance to Ethiopia, or for that matter, its defense of Angola's M.P.L.A. against what came to be perceived regionally as a South African, and to some extent American, attempt to impose a neocolonial solution in Angola.

Soviet Doctrine on the Role of Force in Third World Conflict

How does the evolution of Soviet doctrine reflect this structure of interest and constraint? What does it suggest about Soviet views concerning the utility of force? Three aspects of Soviet doctrine on conflict in the Third World concern us here. The first is Soviet doctrine on the nature of conflict in the Third World. This is a rather arcane matter which, since Khrushchev's ouster, has largely been left in the hands of military writers. The Brezhnev years witnessed considerable (in Soviet terms) debate about, and evolution of, offical doctrinal formulations concerning types of conflict in the Third World. Soviet commentators have generally classified wars according to their material–technical characteristics (e.g. means, scope, duration, etc.) and their socio–political nature (just or unjust). The traditional quadripartite classification of wars (wars between states having different social systems, civil wars between the proletariat and bourgeoisie, national liberation wars, and wars between capitalist nations)[10] was clearly an inadequate and artificial schema when it came to analyzing the nature of conflict in the Third World. In particular, it failed to address the possibility of civil wars other than those between the bourgeoisie and the proletariat and of wars between independent Third World actors, wars the origins of which were largely local or regional. But so long as such conflict was not of immediate relevance to Soviet military decision–makers, these empirical shortcomings mattered little.

The fairly rapid evolution of doctrine[11] from the mid–1960s onward, through the inclusion of additional categories of conflict specifically relevant to the Third World (e.g., civil wars between the masses and reactionary forces,[12] and, more ambiguously, wars between equal states in the Third World),[13] and the wide–ranging debate surrounding this evolution, suggest a growing sophistication and flexibility in the Soviet understanding of Third World conflict. Moreover, the fact that the debate was a relatively open one suggests that it was officially encouraged. In this sense, it is the existence of the discussion more than its substance which is intriguing. It suggests that an understanding of the origins and nature of Third World conflicts was of greater urgency to Soviet policy–makers. This may have been in part a reflection of Soviet diplomatic experience in the mid–1960s, particularly regarding the India–Pakistan War and the 1967 Middle East conflict, and the nascent Soviet involvement in the Nigerian Civil War, none of which fit easily into traditional Soviet categories of conflict. But it is reasonable to assume that the issue had become important to Soviet policy–makers for a second reason as well––their growing willingness to contemplate direct involvement in Third World conflicts.

This willingness is evident in the evolution of the Soviet discussion of their own role in Third World conflict. Before examining this evolution, several general characteristics of the Soviet discussion of their role in the Third World are worth noting. Soviet writers perceive anti–Western struggle and social revolution in the Third World to be one of the basic components of a world revolutionary process directed against imperialism and culminating in a global transition to socialism. To put this in more practical terms, anti–Western movements and governments in Asia, Africa, and Latin America are seen as important allies in the Soviet struggle against the U.S. and its Western allies. Soviet commentators have never denied their support for "anti–imperialist" struggle and their commitment to this process of transformation.

However, the Soviets have quite consistently insisted that the Soviet role in the revolutionary process in the Third World is permissive and ancillary. The rise of the USSR and the world socialist system has, in their view, created the environmental conditions which allow the consummation of the process of national liberation by giving new states an alternative to continued dependence on the world capitalist system, by deterring imperialist attempts to reverse the process, and by creating a socialist camp capable of supporting or assisting the peoples of Asia, Africa, and Latin America in repulsing such attempts as do occur.

In the official Soviet view, however, revolution is an indigenous product. The Soviet role is one of assistance in the resistance to counter-revolution rather than the export of revolution. The relevance of such principles to Soviet practice remains to be discussed. Suffice it to note here that this conception of the Soviet role in promoting "progressive" change in the Third World betrays considerable caution and restraint. As a definition of Soviet responsibilities, it is quite limited. In this sense, it reflects perhaps not only a quite orthodox Marxist–Leninist understanding of the conditions and nature of revolutionary change, but also a reluctance to contemplate open-ended commitments, particularly when these may be deemed highly provocative by the U.S.

Party statements on the question of the Soviet role show little change since the early 1960s. Soviet party spokesmen have, at least since 1961, voiced their support for wars of national liberation. However, their statements have generally remained quite unspecific. There is very little to distinguish Khrushchev's statement of 1962––to the effect that: "We recognize and approve of wars of national liberation . . . . It is the sacred duty of every people to lend assistance in this struggle for freedom and independence."––from those of Brezhnev in 1966 (when at the 23rd Party Congress he spoke of the Soviet duty to continue "all round support of the people's struggle for final liberation") and in 1976 (when at the 25th Party Congress he mentioned Soviet "support for peoples fighting for their freedom").[14]

It is in discussions by military commentators that considerable evolution in public statements on the role of Soviet forces in Third World conflict is evident. As Soviet force projection capacity grew in the late 1960s and early 1970s, one finds somewhat more explicit statements of possible Third World missions for Soviet forces. While early editions of Sokolovskii's *Military Strategy* stressed the necessity of preparing for limited as well as general wars, the 1968 edition differed from previous ones in stating flatly that "the USSR will render, when it is necessary, material support to peoples subject to imperialist aggression."[15] In a 1974 article, Defense Minister Grechko wrote that the Soviet armed forces were one of the principal means whereby the Soviet state fulfilled its duty to "purposefully oppose the export of counter-revolution and the policy of oppression, support the national liberation struggle, and *resolutely resist imperialist aggression in whatever distant region of the planet it may appear.*"[16]

One might conclude from this apparent discrepancy between party and military commentary that the military was much more sanguine and hawkish with regard to force projection in the early and mid-1970s than was the party leadership. But there is not sufficient evidence to conclude that there was a significant divergence of opinion between what you might call a pro-détente party/government/foreign policy establishment on the one hand and a more militant military establishment on the other. In the first place, these military statements may in part be explained as a form of lobbying. Such statements of the duties of the Soviet armed forces provide a rationale for the procurement of force projection capabilities. Second, it may reflect a division of labor between the party and military. It makes sense for military personnel to comment in greater detail than party functionaries about the mission of the armed forces. Third, given the care with which major statements by the party leader are read outside the USSR for clues as to the direction of Soviet policy, it is not surprising that they should be rather more circumspect than are views put forward for domestic audiences by less important people in less prominent media.

Growing Soviet frankness with regard to the use of Soviet forces in Third World conflicts was closely related to change in a third aspect of Soviet doctrine concerning Third World conflict--the treatment of the relationship between local and world wars. The closer this escalatory link is perceived to be, the higher are the perceived risks associated with the projection of force into these conflicts. Conversely, the more remote the perceived prospect of escalation, the easier it is to contemplate intervention. Change in the assessment of the risks of escalation, therefore, is directly related to the perceived utility of force.

Alternatively, and taking a more cynical view of the function of public statements on this topic, an emphasis on the risk of escalation provides an excuse for inactivity vis-à-vis such conflicts. Beyond this, Katz has suggested that when a power is incapable of effective response to an adversary's involvement in a local conflict, emphasizing the possibility of escalation may serve a deterrent purpose.[17] In these instances too, however, playing down the risks of escalation suggests an increased willingness to contemplate the use of force in local conflicts.

The standard Soviet view on this topic in the early 1960s was put succinctly by Khrushchev, when he argued that local wars should be avoided because, where they involved the superpowers, they would escalate to world war.[18] This Soviet concern over escalation faded, however, as the years passed. Military writings in the late 1960s show a considerable erosion of the proposition that local war involving the superpowers inevitably escalates to general war.[19] By the early 1970s, while they admitted the *possibility* of escalation, military commentators played it down, arguing that the great destructive capacities of the two superpowers rendered the choice of escalation improbable.[20] By 1978, the matter was put thus in the *Sovetskaya Voennaya Entsyklopedia*:

> The intensification of struggle in local wars and their tendency
> to widen in scale increases the danger of their development into

world war. At the same time, with the growth of the economic and military might of the socialist community, there develops the possibility to avert the development of local war into a world scale confrontation.[21]

Party commentary on this sensitive subject largely disappeared. Where the danger of war was treated at all, party sources betrayed a certain complacency, arguing that the mutual acceptance by both social systems of the principles of peaceful coexistence had significantly reduced the dangers of major confrontation.[22] Whatever considerations lay behind the stress on the dangers of escalation in the early 1960s, these had clearly weakened by the 1970s. The Soviet stress on their ability to avoid escalation removed a significant doctrinal constraint on their use of force in Third World local conflicts.

In summary, all three of these aspects of Soviet political–military doctrine regarding Third World conflict shifted in the late 1960s and early 1970s in such a way as to suggest that Soviet analysts considered intervention in Third World conflicts to be a more attractive option of policy.

Soviet Force Projection in the Brezhnev Years

This conclusion is supported by an examination of Soviet military behavior from the late 1960s forward. In the 1960s, Soviet policy–makers displayed little willingness to deploy regular forces in Third World conflict situations, or for that matter to provide logistical support to other external actors who might have sought to intervene in local wars. The clearest Soviet threat to use its military strength in a Third World conflict was perhaps Kosygin's warning on the last day of the 1967 war in the Middle East that the USSR would take "necessary actions, including military", if Israel moved on Damascus after its defeat of the Syrian army.[23] The only use of Soviet forces in combat in the Third World in the late 1960s was apparently in November 1967, when Soviet aircraft and pilots participated in action against Royalist forces in North Yemen while Soviet long range air transport mounted an airlift of arms and other supplies to Republican forces in that country.[24]

It was in 1970 that the Soviets first showed their willingness to commit substantial numbers of personnel in the Middle East. In that year, they deployed some twelve to fifteen thousand missile defense personnel and over two hundred pilots in Egypt. Soviet pilots engaged Israeli aircraft during the War of Attrition in the first half of 1970. In the same year, a small number of Soviet–piloted tactical aircraft and helicopters participated in a counterinsurgency campaign in southern Sudan and in a similar operation in Ceylon.[25]

In the October War of 1973, the Soviets again limited themselves to threats to intervene unilaterally in the face of the impending Egyptian collapse and the American failure to accept Soviet proposals for joint superpower intervention. This threat was backed up by raising the alert status of airborne divisions in the southern USSR and, eventually, by diverting air transport for a possible airborne operation.[26]

In 1973–1974, the Soviets committed a limited amount of air power to assist the Iraqis in putting down an Iranian–supported Kurdish rebellion.[27] In 1975–1976, Soviet air transport participated in the airlift of Cuban personnel and a substantial amount of materiel to the M.P.L.A. in Angola. In the aftermath of Angolan independence and the entry of South African troops into the Angolan conflict, some Soviet military advisers also arrived.[28] In 1977–1978, the Soviets once again intervened in a significant way in an African conflict, this time transporting Cuban personnel and Soviet military supplies to Ethiopia to assist that country in beating off a Somali attempt to seize the Ethiopian portion of the Ogaden. Apparently, Soviet officers and communications personnel took on substantial command and control responsibilities in the counter–offensive which expelled the Somalis from Ethiopian territory.[29]

In 1979, this growing use of force culminated in the Soviet invasion of Afghanistan, the first occasion during the period under consideration in which substantial elements of Soviet ground forces (ultimately more than 100,000 soldiers) were used in combat in a Third World state to determine the outcome of an internal conflict. The last Soviet action which should perhaps be mentioned in this context is the stationing of several thousand Soviet air defense personnel in Syria in the aftermath of the Israeli offensive in Lebanon in 1982, and the partial destruction of the Syrian air force.

In short, the 1970s witnessed a Soviet Union which was substantially more willing than it had been previously to use force in pursuit of its interests in the Third World. This raises the question of what shifts in the Soviet structure of interest and constraint account for this change in doctrine and policy.[30]

Détente, the International Correlation of Forces, and the Utility of Force

Three trends in the international politics of the 1970s are plausible as partial explanations for these changes in Soviet behavior: the expansion of

Soviet military capabilities, changes in the credibility of American deterrence, and the process of détente itself.

With regard to the first, it suffices to note that the late 1960s and early 1970s were years of rapid expansion in Soviet force projection capabilities. The Soviets apparently set out to back the claims of their statesmen to equal status in international affairs with tangible military assets. Robert Berman notes, for example, that between 1965 and 1977, the total lift of Soviet military air transport had grown by 132 percent.[31] This included the introduction of the Soviet Union's first two aircraft reasonably well-suited to *long range* force projection--the AN22 (in service in 1967) and the IL76 (in service by the mid-1970s). The progressive increase in Soviet airlift capacity was graphically evident in a sequence of operations, beginning with the resupply of Syria and Egypt in 1967 and 1973, the ferrying of troops and equipment to Angola in 1975-1976, and the airlift to Ethiopia in 1977-1978.

This was matched by a considerable expansion in Soviet long range amphibious transport capabilities. This included the introduction of two new classes of ships (the Ivan Rogov transport dock, of which two have entered service, and the Ropucha tank landing vessel, of which some 16 have been commissioned).[32] Thus, quite simply, by the mid and late 1970s, the USSR had acquired important capabilities that it did not previously enjoy.

In a previous section it was noted that Soviet military writings from the late 1960s onwards began to play down the danger of a Soviet-American confrontation in the Third World. This may be accounted for not only in terms of enhanced Soviet conventional capabilities (and hence a reduced need for verbal deterrence of unilateral American actions through an emphasis on the possibility of escalation), but also by reference to the American failure in Vietnam, and the subsequent obvious disillusionment of the American public with adventures in little known backwaters.

Moreover, the period of 1968-1978 was one of considerable attrition in American military capabilities. The Vietnam war consumed some $200 billion, much of which would otherwise have been used for training, re-equipment, and weapons development. In the aftermath of the withdrawal from Indochina, congressional and popular opposition to defense spending caused further atrophy of American conventional forces. The defeat in Vietnam, the budgetary squeeze, and the manifest unpopularity of the military with the public fostered a serious morale problem in the American armed forces. None of this was lost on the Soviets.[33] In short, as Soviet capabilities increased, the credibility of American conventional deterrence in the Third World declined.

This was occurring in the context of the rapid buildup in Soviet strategic nuclear forces, which began in the aftermath of the Cuban missile crisis (the relationship to the Cuban affair is probably more chronological than causal) and which brought the USSR to approximate parity with the United States by the early 1970s.[34] To the extent that American "escalation dominance" had ever been a restraint on Soviet military activity in the Third World, this factor lost much of its strength with the attainment of parity.

This brings us to the third issue--détente. In assessing the impact of détente on Soviet perceptions of the utility of force, it is important first of all to understand the Soviet view of why détente occurred. The dominant view in the early and mid-1970s was that détente was not a choice on the part of the West, but was a historical necessity, given gradual shifts in the "international correlation of forces" in favor of world socialism, of which the developments noted earlier in this section were a part. If détente were a necessity for the West, then it could not be reversed by Soviet activities in non-central theaters. And indeed, as noted above, Soviet commentary from the mid-1970s displays little awareness that Soviet or Soviet-sponsored military activities could undermine the process of improvement in East-West relations. Beyond this, the tangible Western economic interest in détente in Soviet eyes may have rendered it unlikely that the West would jeopardize gains from trade by creating crises over Soviet behavior in the Third World.

The effect of détente was not merely permissive, however. As was noted earlier, the domestic legitimacy of the Communist Party of the Soviet Union rests to some extent on the credibility of its claim to be a revolutionary force in world politics. Its position among anti-Western forces in the Third World also depends to some degree on the credibility of this claim. Détente at least superficially appears to be a policy of accommodation with the class enemy and an abandonment of revolution, and hence it is corrosive of this source of legitimacy and influence. Indeed, in the early 1970s, the Soviets were heavily criticized, particularly by the Chinese, for having made their peace with imperialism and having become an imperialist hegemonist in their own right, while in the Third World, the USSR had come to be commonly viewed as another status quo northern power. Soviet commentary from the early and mid-1970s displays considerable sensitivity to this kind of criticism. A sustained effort was made to refute the argument that détente implied an abandonment of class struggle.[35] In this sense, the pursuit of a policy of détente toward the U.S. and Europe pushes the USSR into "revolutionary" behavior in peripheral arenas in order to defend its revolutionary credentials. This effect was particularly strong in the early and mid-1970s as a result of an active Chinese challenge to Soviet influence among liberation movements in Africa. It is not too farfetched to suggest that détente contained the seeds of its own destruction. It compelled the USSR to undertake actions which, in Western eyes, drew into question the nature and extent of the Soviet commitment to the process.

Dimensions of Soviet Use of Force in the Third World

Yet in assessing Soviet perspectives on the utility of force in their foreign policy in the Third World, it is not sufficient to note that they appear to attach a greater utility to it than they did previously and to account for this in terms of changes in their own capabilities and in the international environment they face. It is also necessary to look at how force is used. What do the dimensions of Soviet force projection tell us about their view of its utility?

To judge from the specific instances mentioned earlier, despite their growing confidence in the use of force in the Third World, Soviet policy-makers continue to display considerable caution and moderation. In the first place, leaving Afghanistan aside for the moment, the USSR shows little if any inclination to become involved in *offensive* operations mounted by clients. The two major deployments of Soviet forces other than Afghanistan--those in Egypt in 1970-1971 and in Syria currently--were in defense of established regimes facing serious military threats and in situations where inaction would have resulted in serious damage to Soviet credibility. In Ethiopia, Soviet command personnel and Cuban troops were deployed to defend the territorial integrity of a friendly state which was under attack from a neighbor. In Angola, Cuban forces intervened with Soviet assistance to support one contender for power in a situation where no clear governmental authority existed. Soviet personnel did not enter in any significant number until after independence had been declared and South African intervention had severely damaged the standing of the M.P.L.A.'s rivals for power. The Iraqi, Sri Lankan, and Sudanese affairs were again all instances of support for established governments faced with internal insurgency problems. This is not to say that the Soviets have any special regard for the niceties of international law, but only that they are politically intelligent. The use of force by a superpower for offensive purposes against a small state carries far more significant political costs than does intervention in support of established governments.

The Afghan case does not conform to this generalization, except in the sense that, although it involved the overthrow of the current ruler and the military subjugation of an independent country, it was apparently a defense of established Soviet interests in the country. It supports the view that Soviet attitudes towards the use of force in contiguous states where Soviet interests are asymmetrically strong compared to American interests differs from Soviet perspectives on force projection in areas far removed from the Soviet periphery. In this sense, Afghanistan is perhaps better grouped with Berlin (1953), Hungary (1956), and Czechoslovakia (1968) than with Angola, Ethiopia, or Egypt.[36]

Secondly, the Soviet use of force has tended to be low risk. The Soviet leadership continues to sidestep commitments in areas where a high risk of confrontation with American armed forces exists, as, for example in Central America. Indeed, despite their rejection of the concept of spheres of influence, they appear to recognize that such a sphere exists in Central America and the Caribbean Basin, and, at least since 1962, they have avoided provocative new involvements. Although they have occasionally tested in a quiet way the American resolve to enforce the agreement over Cuba, when the U.S. has protested Soviet violations, these violations have ceased. It is in regions where it is Soviet and not American critical interests that are at stake and where the probability of American response is low (as in Afghanistan) that Soviet forces have been used aggressively.

While Moscow has also deployed force in the Middle East, where major interests overlap, the dimensions of the involvement in Egypt and Syria have been clearly limited and defensive. Indeed, one might argue that the principal reason that *Soviet* rather than Syrian troops are manning air defense batteries in Syria is to ensure that these weapons are not used provocatively by Moscow's less than totally reliable local client.[37] The Soviets have been careful to avoid behavior on the ground which might be construed as seriously threatening to Israel or to American interests in the region.[38] Where upgrading their involvement carried the potential for serious superpower confrontation in the region, they have behaved cautiously even at the risk of alienating local clients such as Egypt and Syria. This is evident, for example, in their reluctance in the early and mid–1970s to give Egypt the wherewithal to attempt a military solution to the Arab–Israeli problem.[39] In crises such as the War of Attrition, they have counseled caution and negotiation.[40]

The occasional threats to intervene in Middle Eastern wars, as in 1967 and 1973, appear to have been pressure tactics rather than serious military propositions. The 1967 threat, for example, occurred on the last day of the war, and was not made public. Nor was it accompanied by any demonstration of force or obvious military preparations.[41] Again, the 1973 alert of Soviet paratroopers was not apparently accompanied by any provocative behavior by Soviet forces in the war zone and the U.S. did not "perceive a substantial danger of Soviet intervention."[42]

Although the interventions in Angola and Ethiopia may have indicated a qualitative shift in Soviet attitudes towards the use of force in areas where the critical interests of neither superpower were at stake, they too displayed a low risk character. Soviet units did not become involved in combat. Instead, the Soviet role was largely one of logistical support for the Cubans and for the M.P.L.A. and the Dergue. Presumably one reason for the use of allied forces is that it renders disengagement easier should an unforeseen confrontation emerge.

Moreover, in the Angolan case, the Soviets had just witnessed a striking demonstration of American withdrawal from a Third World conflict in May of 1975, when, despite the twenty-year investment of blood and treasure in Vietnam, the U.S. failed to provide even air support for the beleaguered Saigon regime during North Vietnam's final offensive. Nonetheless, when Kissinger threatened significant reprisals in December of 1975 if the Soviets continued their interference in the conflict, the Soviets temporarily suspended their airlift of materiel to the M.P.L.A. It was apparently only after Congress prohibited further American involvement in Angola that the airlift resumed, that Soviet advisers arrived in significant numbers, and that the Soviet Union became involved in a substantial airlift of Cuban troops.[43]

In the case of the involvement in the Horn, the Soviets again had a relatively clear demonstration of American caution when the Carter Administration limited its involvement in the Shaban affair to the provision of non-lethal military supplies. Moreover, the structure of the situation in the Horn was such as to make American counterintervention quite difficult. To intervene against the USSR would have meant supporting the Somalis in their offensive and thereby alienating a significant portion of the African community, notably the Americans' most prominent client in the area--Kenya.

It should also be noted that the use of *Soviet* regular units appears to be viewed by Moscow as a last resort in the defense of critical interests. The three major deployments of Soviet forces in the Third World since the fall of Khrushchev (Egypt, Afghanistan, and Syria) were all situations in which the USSR faced a crisis in relations with its local client and nothing short of the deployment of Soviet forces promised to resolve or contain that crisis. In Egypt, Soviet forces were apparently deployed during the War of Attrition after the Egyptians had threatened to terminate their connection with the USSR and seek an accommodation with the U.S.[44] In Syria, Soviet credibility had been severely damaged by the Soviet Union's failure to act in any significant way during the 1982 crisis in Lebanon.[45] The value of the link to the USSR had again been drawn into question. The commitment of forces to Syria was a relatively non–confrontational way of avoiding the loss of Moscow's only significant remaining client in the region. In both of these cases, the deployment of Soviet forces was a means of underscoring the degree of Soviet interest in the region. In Afghanistan, the choice apparently facing the USSR was the collapse or defection of the Amin regime or invasion and the replacement of Amin. Soviet forces were the chosen instrument of policy, because they were the only one which provided some assurance of avoiding an unacceptable outcome in a regional conflict with direct security implications for the USSR.

The Syrian and Egyptian cases illustrate a further point. The USSR, in its decisions to deploy force in areas where it has considerable investments at stake, appears to be vulnerable to pressure from local allies to upgrade its commitment. In the Egyptian case, the USSR deployed its forces when Egypt threatened to sever its connection with the USSR. The Soviet provision of offensive weaponry to the Egyptians in 1973 occurred after Sadat had underlined his willingness to dispense with the tie to the Soviets if they failed to come up with the wherewithal for the Egyptians to mount offensive operations against the Israelis.[46]

In the Syrian case, Soviet prestige had plummeted in the aftermath of the Soviet failure to act in defense of Syria during the Lebanese crisis. The failure to do anything would have again drawn into question the value of the Soviet connection. In other words, Soviet involvement in Middle Eastern affairs and their reliance on local actors to provide them with an entry into regional politics create conditions where the Soviets can be coerced into actions which they might otherwise avoid.

This is related to a final point. Soviet use of force in the Third World, to judge from recent cases, is reactive and *ad hoc* in character. It is a response to local crises and generally to requests from local actors. (Afghanistan is again an exception to this last point).

To summarize, although it is clear that Soviet doctrine and behavior in the 1970s and early 1980s suggest a considerably more sanguine view of the utility of force in the attempt to influence the direction of regional politics in the Third World, the manner in which it has been used displays considerable caution. Soviet use of force has been defensive, reactive, and low risk. The only conspicuously offensive use of force was that in Afghanistan, and in that instance the other two generalizations hold. The Afghan case suggests that Soviet behavior vis–à–vis contiguous states where the West has no substantial presence and interest and in situations where Soviet policy–makers perceive Soviet security to be affected by peripheral instability may be considerably more aggressive than it is elsewhere. But these conditions are exceptional. The Afghan case tells us little about likely Soviet behavior in non–contiguous states or in contiguous states where superpower interests overlap.

Policy Implications and Prospects

The experience of the past decade and a half provides little support for the contention that the USSR is moving towards a policy of indiscriminate and aggressive use of force throughout the Third World. Soviet practice suggests, to the contrary, that Soviet policy–makers view the utility of force in the Third World to be limited and bounded in significant ways by the danger of confrontation with the other superpower and by the political costs associated with its indiscriminate use. This suggests that one should not overestimate the threat to Western interests stemming from what appears to be a growing Soviet willingness to use force in the Third World.

Nonetheless, it is apparent that the Soviet view of the utility of force *has grown* more sanguine over the past fifteen years. This shift may be accounted for partly in terms of the expansion in Soviet force projection capabilities, but the erosion of their fear of the escalation of Third World conflicts is also apparent and significant. This erosion is a result of their perception that the United States in the mid–1970s was both less willing and less able to use force in the Third World to defend its own interests. In a sense, therefore, Soviet perceptions of the utility of force are responsive to trends in American foreign policy. Although the Soviet view of the utility of force in Third World conflicts remains bounded in significant ways, in the absence of efforts to restore the credibility of Western conventional deterrence in the Third World, it may be expected that this process of erosion will continue, particularly as Soviet force projection capabilities continue to grow. Hence, to the extent that increased Soviet military activism in the Third World is a consequence of the reduced credibility of American conventional deterrence, efforts to re–establish this credibility make considerable sense. Moreover, whether or not Soviet military activity in the Third World displays restraint and avoids challenges to basic American commitments and interests, when it goes unchallenged, it may cause clients of the United States to question the utility of the American connection. In these senses, though it is possible to quarrel with specific aspects of the American program to modernize and expand U.S. force projection capabilities, to the extent that this investment underscores Washington's resolve to defend its interests in the Third World, it is commendable, as are exercises and prepositioning programs in areas where clear U.S. interests are at stake. These actions raise the perceived risk of confrontation and, thereby, that of escalation and serious East–West conflict stemming from Soviet power projection in the Third World.

Second, it is reasonably clear that one of the basic sources of more assertive Soviet behavior in the Third World is their desire to establish their claim to equal status in all spheres of international activity. One relatively effective way for Moscow to draw attention to this claim is to use their capacity to project force in order to establish a presence throughout the Third World and to carve out a role in Third World conflicts. To judge from Soviet procurement policy over the past decade, their capacity to use force in this fashion has grown considerably and is likely to continue to grow. That is to say, as time passes, the physical resources which back this claim will become steadily more impressive. While the intensity of Soviet military activity in the Third World may vary in the short run, they are not going to go away.[47] This raises the question of how long it is in our interest to ignore this claim and act as if Soviet involvement in Third World politics were somehow illegitimate. If the future is likely to be one of a continuing, persistent, and gradually growing Soviet effort to establish equal status, then a strategy of denial on our part is liable to be frustrating, potentially very costly, and difficult to sustain in the longer term. Perhaps we should be thinking instead about whether it is possible to channel these Soviet aspirations along more constructive paths.

In this context, it is worth remembering that although recent attempts to pursue regional security discussions with the Soviet Union have not been terribly encouraging (e.g., the Indian Ocean Force Limitation Talks and the Conventional Arms Transfer Talks), these failures cannot be ascribed solely to Soviet intransigence. Indeed, the evolution of American negotiating behavior in the latter set of talks casts considerable doubt on the *American* commitment to serious discussion of the issue.[48] Moreover, it should not be forgotten that there have in the past been constructive agreements with the USSR on problems of Third World security. The 1962 agreements on Cuba and Laos come to mind, and one might also include the 1954 negotiations on Indochina.

It is simply not true that there is no concrete basis for discussion of regional security with the Soviet Union. The Soviet commitment to anti–Western revolution in the Third World, its interest as a revisionist power in instability, and its striving through behaving like a global power to be recognized as one are now counter–balanced to some degree in a number of ways. First, the USSR now has interests of its own in the Third World which may be threatened by instability. Second, Soviet leaders have concrete experience with the fact that Soviet commitments in volatile regions such as the Middle East may be exploited by local actors in such a way as to force the USSR into a degree of involvement which it would rather avoid. The third point is related to the second. The USSR, in deliberating over the use of force in the Third World, and particularly in regions where major interests of both blocs overlap, must weigh the possible advantages of such use against the dangers of confrontation and uncontrolled escalation. Although this consideration may not have been particularly compelling during the Carter years, the intensely anti-Soviet policies and rhetoric of the Reagan Administration and the precipitous deterioration in Soviet-American relations since the invasion of Afghanistan render these dangers more pressing.[49] Fourth, it is quite plausible that the USSR now has considerable reason to doubt whether the gains made through the use of force are durable and of a value sufficient to justify the costs and the risks associated with force projection.[50] Fifth, recognition through dialogue addresses the Soviet concern to establish equal status.

In short, the effort to restore conventional deterrence should be supplemented by a willingness to recognize the Soviet right to a say on regional issues. As Dimitri Simes recently put it: "Vacillating enemies get nothing but contempt from the Russians. Yet an enemy who staunchly refuses to treat them with respect cannot expect to get much from them either."[51] It would be rash to expect such a dialogue to bring comprehensive agreements on major Third World security issues (e.g. a settlement of the Arab-Israeli dispute, a wide-ranging agreement on conventional arms transfers, or a comprehensive agreement on non-interference in internal and regional conflicts) if only because the superpowers do not possess sufficient control over the behavior of their regional clients and other actors in regional politics to be able to create and sustain this kind of order. But it might bring informal or formal agreements, for example, on crisis avoidance and limitation which would strengthen the existing tacit understanding and mutual restraint in such areas. Moreover, as long as the USSR is denied recognition as a party in Third World security issues, such as the conflicts in the Middle East, it has an interest in behaving as a spoiler, in sabotaging or impeding Western attempts to resolve regional disputes. Dialogue on regional security issues might in and of itself reduce this interest.

Finally, the fact that Soviet use of force in the Third World is largely reactive to opportunities which arise in the local environment suggests that one way to limit it is to reduce the number of such opportunities through preventive diplomacy. This could include prior agreement with the USSR on nonintervention in specific regions, support for efforts at conflict resolution by regional organizations, and direct sponsorship of negotiations between hostile regional actors (as currently in Southern Africa). Beyond this, given that it is often American support for one side in a regional dispute which forces the other side to seek assistance from the USSR and which places Soviet prestige on the line, one of the more promising forms of preventive diplomacy is perhaps neutrality and abstention from direct involvement in regional disputes where the USSR is not yet directly involved.

The prospect is, therefore, one of continued gradual growth in Soviet involvement in the Third World and its conflicts. What form this takes depends to a large extent on our own approach to the problem of Soviet expansion.

Notes

1. One could cite here Soviet intervention in Iranian affairs in support of the Gilan Soviet in 1920 and the Red Army's support of the Mongolian People's Party seizure of power in Outer Mongolia in 1921. Other salient episodes are Soviet assistance to the Kuomintang in the mid-1920s, Soviet military activity in Sinkiang in the late 1930s, and Soviet occupation of Northern Iran in the first year after World War II.

2. For a comprehensive account of Soviet naval policy in the Third World, see M. MccGwire, *et al.*, *Soviet Naval Policy: Objectives and Constraints* (New York: Praeger, 1975). For a discussion of Soviet arms transfer policy, see A. Pierre, *The Global Politics of Arms Sales*, (Princeton: Princeton University Press, 1982), pp. 73-82.

3. See D. Spechler's stimulating study of differences within the Soviet elite over the October 1973 war, in D. Spechler, *Domestic Influences on Soviet Foreign Policy*, (Washington, D.C.: University Press of America, 1978), in particular pp. 32-41.

4. Cf. G. Jukes, "Soviet Policy in the Indian Ocean," in MccGwire, *et al.*, *Soviet Naval Policy*, pp. 311-313.

5. Cf. A. Gromyko, "Rech' Tov. A. A. Gromyko," *Pravda*, April 4, 1971; and L. Brezhnev's speech in Minsk of March 1970, as cited in R. Kolkowicz, "The Military and Soviet Foreign Policy," in R. Kanet, ed., *Soviet Foreign Policy in the 1980s*, (New York: Praeger, 1982), p. 17.

6. R. Menon, "Military Power, Intervention, and Soviet Policy in the Third World," in *ibid*., pp. 268, 270.

7. J. Epstein, "Soviet Vulnerabilities in Iran and the RDF Deterrent," *International Security* VI 1981, No. 2, pp. 143, 144.

8. Although from the point of view of political philosophy and international relations theory, the concept of vital interest is somewhat

fluid and contentious, it is one which would appear to figure significantly in the perceptions and deliberations of policy–makers in both the USSR and the U.S.A. It would be difficult to deny, for example, that current American policy in Central America or Soviet policy in Eastern Europe is guided by some conception of the vital interests of these two actors shared by leading decision–makers and that recognition of this fact influences the behavior of each superpower in regions where the other's perceived vital interests are at stake.

9. Although Soviet writers have steadily denied the existence of any "linkage" between their support for anti–Western struggle in the Third World and the process of détente in East–West inter–state relations (Cf. *inter alia* G. Arbatov, "Manevry Protivnikov Razryadki," *Izvestia,* September 4, 1975; "Zayavlenie Sovetskogo Pravitel'stva," *Pravda,* May 22, 1976; L. Brezhnev, "Otchot Ts. K. KPSS," *Pravda,* February 25, 1976; L. Brezhnev, "Poseshchenie L.I. Brezhnevym Tikhoookeanskogo Flota," *Pravda,* April 8, 1978), their awareness of this point is to some extent suggested by their recognition that Soviet support for the "forces of progress" in the Third World may be used as a pretext by reactionary circles in the West to sabotage détente. For example see, L. Brezhnev, "Rech' na Plenume Ts. K. KPSS Oktyabrya 1976 Goda," *Pravda,* October 26, 1976; Brezhnev (1978), *op. cit.*; Yu. Andropov, "Edinstvo Naroda––Velikaya Sila," *Pravda,* February 12, 1980; M. Suslov, "Za Plodotvornyi Trud na Blago Naroda," *Pravda,* February 21, 1980.

10. *Marksizm–Leninizm o Voine i Armii* (Moscow: Voenizdat, 1965), pp. 69–115. Wars between socialist countries are deemed to be logically impossible.

11. This is ably chronicled in M. Katz, *The Third World in Soviet Military Thought* (London: Croom Helm, 1982), *passim.*

12. *Marksizm–Leninizm o Voine i Armii,* (1968 edition), p. 86; and *Sovetskaya Voennaya Entsyklopedia* (Moscow: Voenizdat, 1978), Volume 4, p. 200.

13. *Marksizm–Leninizm o Voine i Armii* (1968), p. 86. This innovation was only partially accepted. In the 1968 source, it was mentioned, but not numbered as a category in its own right. Discussion of the topic in the early and mid–1970s suggested considerable resistance to the concept, presumably because of the difficulty of generalizing about the social content of such conflicts. Contrary to Katz's inference (*op. cit.,* p. 98), wars between equal states were *not* included as a category of war in the contemporary epoch in the 1978 edition of the *Sovetskaya Voennaya Entsyklopedia.*

14. Cf. N. Khrushchev's speech in Obnova, Bulgaria (*Pravda,* May 19, 1962); L. Brezhnev's report to the 23rd CPSU Congress, in *23rd*

Congress of the CPSU, (Moscow: Novosti, 1966), p. 34; and his report to the 25th CPSU Congress (*Pravda*, February 25, 1976).

15. V. Sokolovskii, *et al.*, *Voennaya Strategia* (Moscow: Voenizdat, 1968), p. 222.

16. A.A. Grechko, "Rukovodyashchaya Rol' KPSS v Stroitel'stve Armii Razvitogo Sotsialisticheskogo Obshchestva," *Voprosy Istorii KPSS*, 1974, No. 5, p. 39. See also A. A. Grechko, *The Armed Forces of the Soviet Union* (Moscow: Progress Publishers, 1977), pp. 106–107.

17. Katz, *The Third World in Soviet Military Thought*, p. 21.

18. N.S. Khrushchev, "Za Novye Pobedy Mirovogo Kommunisticheskogo Dvizhenia," *Kommunist* 1961, No. 1, p. 18.

19. Cf. Katz, *The Third World in Soviet Military Thought*, pp. 39,67,97; and T. Wolfe, *Soviet Strategy at the Crossroads* (Cambridge: Harvard University Press, 1964), pp. 119–120.

20. V. Kulish, *Voennaya Sila i Mezhdunarodnye Otnoshenia* (Moscow: Izdatel'stvo Mezhdunarodnykh Otnoshenii, 1972), p. 47.

21. "Lokal'naya Voina," *Sovetskaya Voennaya Entsyklopedia*, Volume 5, p. 22.

22. For example, see the Central Committee Resolution, "Postanovlenie Plenuma Ts. K. KPSS ot 31 Yanvarya 1977 Goda: O 60–i Godovshchine Velikoi Oktyabr'skoi Sotsialisticheskoi Revolyutsii," *Pravda*, February 1, 1977.

23. S. Kaplan, *Diplomacy of Power* (Washington: Brookings, 1981), p. 167.

24. A. Yodfat, *The Soviet Union and the Arabian Peninsula* (New York: St. Martin's, 1983), pp. 3–4.

25. For an account of Soviet involvement in the War of Attrition and in the Sudanese counterinsurgency campaign against the Anyanya movement see A. Rubinstein, "Air Support in the Middle East," in S. Kaplan, ed., *Diplomacy of Power*, pp. 472–478, 493–494 and S. Kaplan, "The Third World," in *ibid.*, p. 170.

26. Soviet behavior in the October 1973 war is discussed in P. Jabber and R. Kolkowicz, "The Arab–Israeli Wars of 1967 and 1973," in *ibid.*, pp. 438–463.

27. See Rubinstein, "Air Support in the Middle East," p. 504.

28. C. Legum, "Angola and the Horn of Africa," in *ibid.*, pp. 583, 590, 593; Kaplan, "The Third World," *ibid.*, pp. 195–197.

29. C. Legum, "Angola and the Horn of Africa," *ibid.*, pp. 620–624.

30. For a very useful summary account of Soviet use of force in the Third World during the period under consideration, see S. Kaplan,

"The Third World," in *ibid.*, pp. 163–201.

31. R. Berman, *Soviet Air Power in Transition* (Washington: Brookings, 1978), p. 36.

32. *The Military Balance 1983–1984* (London: International Institute of Strategic Studies, 1983), p. 17.

33. See, for example, Col. E. Rybkin's comment on domestic opposition to interventionism making future American involvement in Third World conflict unlikely, in "Voiny Sovremennoi Epokhi i ikh Vlianie na Sotsial'nykh Protsessakh," *Kommunist Vooruzhonnykh Sil*, 1970, No. 11, p. 16.

34. The initial decisions for a buildup of strategic weapons were probably a response to massive American deployment of Minuteman and the consequent considerable ICBM superiority of the U.S. evident prior to the Cuban Missile Crisis. The deployment of missiles on Cuba was a short term fix while longer term programs gathered momentum.

35. For example, Brezhnev's report to the 25th Party Congress in 1976, proclaimed Soviet support for the national liberation movement, denied that détente (a matter concerning *inter-state* relations) meant abandoning the class struggle, and asserted that détente in fact created conditions in international relations which facilitated revolutionary struggle (*Pravda*, February 25, 1976).

36. One should not take this point too far. The characteristic shared by the East European and Afghan cases being underlined here is their proximity to the USSR and their direct relation to Soviet security interests. Historically, Soviet ties with the East European satellites were far more clearly established than were those with Afghanistan at the time of intervention.

37. I am indebted to Professor Robert Freedman for this observation.

38. Hence the relative quiescence of Soviet forces deployed in the Middle East in the 1967 and 1973 wars.

39. On the effect of Soviet reluctance to provide advanced offensive weaponry in large quantities to Egypt, and its effect on Soviet–Egyptian relations in 1970–1972, see R. Freedman, *Soviet Policy toward the Middle East since 1970*, 3rd edition, (New York: Praeger, 1982), pp. 51, 77, 84 and G. Breslauer, "Soviet Policy in the Middle East, 1967–1972: Unalterable Antagonism or Collaborative Competition?," in A. George, ed., *Managing U.S.-Soviet Rivalry: Problems of Crisis Prevention* (Boulder: Westview, 1983), p. 91.

40. *Ibid.*, pp. 77, 79; Rubinstein, *op. cit.*, pp. 471–472; Freedman, *Soviet Policy Toward the Middle East Since 1970*, p. 33.

41. P. Jabber and R. Kolkowicz, "The Arab–Israeli Wars of

1967 and 1973," in S. Kaplan, ed., *Diplomacy of Power*, p. 435.

42. *Ibid.*, p. 453. See also the statement of the Commander of U.S. naval forces in Europe to the effect that Soviet naval behavior in the Mediterranean was "restrained and considerate." Indeed, "it looked as though they were taking some care not to cause an incident." (*Ibid.*) Although some Soviet air defense crews were deployed in Latakia and Damascus after Israeli attacks on Soviet shipping and aircraft, the Soviet response to these attacks was largely verbal (*ibid.*, pp. 449–450).

43. Kaplan, "The Third World," pp. 196–197.

44. Breslauer, "Soviet Policy in the Middle East, 1967–1972," p. 81.

45. For a good discription of Soviet inaction during the 1982 Lebanese crisis, see D. Simes, "Moscow's Middle East," *New York Times*, November 10, 1982.

46. This willingness was evident in Sadat's decision to terminate the mission of Soviet military advisers and experts and resume control over Soviet bases in Egypt in July 1972. The Soviet response was to dramatically *increase* arms deliveries to Egypt by the end of the year. By September 1973, the Soviets had started to provide relatively large numbers of tanks and surface to air missiles, though they still refrained from providing fighter bombers and ground to ground missiles in numbers sufficient to constitute a serious strategic threat to Israel. The Soviets apparently did provide a small number of SCUD missiles to Egypt in the months before the war, perhaps as a deterrent against a sustained Israeli attack on the Egyptian homeland. This infusion of advanced weaponry was apparently sufficient for Egypt to take the final decision to go to war. This discussion follows that in Freedman, *Soviet Policy Toward the Middle East Since 1970*, pp. 87, 125–126, 135–136.

47. For an argument which suggests that in the short term there are good reasons to expect some moderation in Soviet behavior in the Third World, see N. MacFarlane, *Soviet Intervention in Third World Conflict*, Occasional Paper No. 2, (Geneva: Program for Strategic and International Security Studies, 1983), pp. 35–43.

48. See B. Blechman, *et al.*, "Negotiated Limits on Arms Transfers: First Steps towards Crisis Prevention?," in A. George, ed., *Managing U.S.-Soviet Rivalry*, pp. 267–268.

49. To judge from recent party literature, emphasis on the dangerous impact of "hotbeds of conflict" in the Third World on world peace appears to be enjoying a certain renaissance. See N. MacFarlane, "The Soviet Conception of Regional Security," an unpublished paper delivered at the March 1984 conference of the Western Section of the American Association for the Advancement of Slavic Studies, Stanford,

California.

    50. For an argument along these lines with respect to Angola, Ethiopia, and Afghanistan, see MacFarlane, *Soviet Intervention in Third World Conflict*, pp. 29–34.

    51. D. Simes, "What Are the Russians Up To?," *New York Times*, June 5, 1984.

2
Soviet Perspectives on Islam as a Third World Political Force

Carol R. Saivetz

Introduction

Islam as a potent political force is a relatively new item on the international agenda: Yet for the Soviet Union, Islam has long been an issue. As far back as 1917, Lenin addressed a special appeal to the "Toiling Muslim Peoples of the East" and in 1918 the new Soviet government established a Commissariat on Muslim Affairs. In the early 1920s, the new Soviet government became involved diplomatically with Iran, Turkey and Afghanistan, and since then, Moscow has maintained a consistent interest in the contiguous Muslim countries. In the post–World War II period, the Soviet Union established a very large stake in the Middle East–Persian Gulf region. Nonetheless, prior to the late seventies, the question of Islam as a factor in international relations was assiduously downplayed.

In 1979, events in Iran and Afghanistan thrust the Islamic question into the decision–making calculus of the Politburo. Suddenly, political problems with Islamic components could be found throughout the Middle East: the creation of an Islamic republic in Iran which turned out to be equally anti–Soviet and anti–American; the tribal and ethnic nature of the rebellion in Afghanistan which precipitated the introduction of Soviet troops; the outbreak of the Persian Gulf war between Shiite Iran and

------

The author would like to thank David E. Powell for his comments on an earlier draft of this article.

Sunni-led Iraq which undermined Soviet plans for a united anti-Israel, anti-American front; the assassination of Anwar Sadat by an Islamic group; and the activization of the Muslim Brotherhood in Syria which clearly threatened the regime of a pro-Soviet Middle East ally. And, this is by no means an exhaustive list.

Faced with a phenomenon which obviously affected foreign policy calculations (and perhaps domestic policy as well), Soviet officials and academics set out to investigate and explain the Islamic resurgence and to assess its political impact. Although Soviet Islamic studies, as conducted by anthropologists, historians and philosophers are not new, the resurgence of Islam as a political force since 1979 has galvanized the academic community. As early as 1980-1981, one can find, within the literature, calls for research on Islam. And, unlike earlier studies, this research was to be conducted by economists and political scientists with long-term Middle East experience and expertise. The Institute of Oriental Studies became the center of Islamic studies, sponsoring several working groups on ideological trends in the "East." According to a report detailing works in progress which appeared in *Narody Azii i Afriki*, events established the Islamic resurgence as the top research priority. Among the topics to be investigated are traditional religious ideologies, the doctrine of "Islamic economics," (especially as practiced in Pakistan) and the "Islamic state."[1]

Soviet analyses and perspectives on Islam may be found as well in official pronouncements, press reports and editorials. The official statements and academic works are linked by the close ties between the institutes and the policy-making world. First, academics not infrequently wear two hats. Not only are they researchers or professors within the institutes, but several are also members of the Central Committee's International Department. Second, while we cannot necessarily link the views of specific academics with those of the late Yuri Andropov, Konstantin Chernenko, or Mikhail Gorbachev, or their colleagues in the Politburo, we can infer that the debates occurring on the pages of scholarly journals or between institutes reflect unresolved political issues.

In the view of many Western observers, the general research areas are delineated by party higher-ups. Yet, other analysts argue that Soviet scholars do initiate a certain number of research projects themselves. It would seem probable that both assessments are accurate, to some extent. While some flexibility may exist in choosing topics, research within the social science institutes of the Academy of Sciences is responsive to party needs. In fact, the topics are frequently those on which policy-makers request assessments.[2] Whether to elaborate on Soviet foreign policy decisions or because the bureaucrats need specific information, the institutes dealing with contemporary issues are instructed to delve into timely research topics. Academics are called upon to do research, as the Soviets put it, "in light" of party congress decisions and there is evidence to indicate that internal working papers may be passed on to party officials. The new specialists on Islam openly acknowledged the link between their research projects and policy. One orientalist went so far as to admit that these presumably accurate assessments of political Islam would aid the Soviet propaganda effort.[3]

This paper will focus on Soviet perspectives on the international aspects of the Islamic question. The first section will explore how Soviet pronouncements and writings about political Islam fit into the general Soviet understanding of political processes in the Third World. In this section, we will also analyze earlier Soviet attitudes toward Third World Islamic ideologies. The next section will focus on the impact of the Iranian revolution. Although there are other manifestations of the Islamic revival, Iran has been the major focus of Soviet Islamic studies because it is the single case of a continuing self-proclaimed Islamic revolution. We will also look at overall Soviet assessments of the Islamic phenomenon. This analysis will include Soviet attempts to answer the following questions: Why has there been an Islamic "awakening?" And, how does it fit with the Soviet theories of "progressive" development? Finally, we will look at the implications for Soviet perspectives and policy posed by recent events: Can the USSR cultivate long-term relations with Islamic countries or will post-Khomeini Islam be a major obstacle to Soviet policy?

Soviet Third World Studies and Islam

Academic and official analyses and interpretations of the so-called Islamic revolution must be understood within the context of Soviet studies of Third World political processes. These studies, or *vostokovedenie*, were spurred by Moscow's increasing involvement in the Third World and reflect Soviet experiences there. In general, Soviet studies of the Third World reveal the analytical categories observers used to judge events and trends in this unstable terrain and which, therefore, underlie Soviet assessments of problems and prospects. The several analytical frameworks adopted by Soviet academics have proven to be a combination of Marxism-Leninist rhetoric and social science, and of increasingly sophisticated studies of the trends and dynamics of the Third World.

As the USSR's ties to the Third World countries proliferated, Moscow had to create a fit between its professed ideology and foreign policy. This process was complicated by the emergence in the 1960s of Third World leaders who espoused vehement anti–Westernism and proclaimed themselves socialist. Although the Soviets welcomed their anti–Westernism and even praised many of their domestic programs, these same leaders jailed, and sometimes executed, local communist party members. Thus, Soviet politicians and academics had to work out criteria to determine the "acceptability" of allies. The resulting criteria, in almost every case, were based upon a pro–Soviet foreign policy combined with radical domestic programs including an acceptable ideological base.

In the early sixties, scholars elaborated the Noncapitalist Path (NCP) which, as the name implies, was a "path" or direction from underdevelopment to socialism bypassing the capitalist stage of development. It included prescriptions intended to answer the problems of underdevelopment with programs designed to create pro–Soviet allies. As a measure of "acceptability," incremental steps along the NCP were considered "progressive." However, between 1965 and 1968 several pro–Soviet radicals who were said to be leading their states on the NCP were toppled by coups. These losses jolted the Kremlin leaders and Soviet academics into the realization that the noncapitalist construct was insufficient. It did not address the realities of Third World politics or provide an adequate measure of the reliability or longevity of Soviet friends. Under the guise of creative Marxism, scholars adopted newer constructs some of which were intended as models of developing societies and others which combined more realistic data collection with the never–abandoned socialist blueprint. Currently, academics and party officials alike refer to "States of Socialist Orientation." The new construct is a response to the advent of Third World radicals who proclaim themselves Marxist–Leninist. A socialist–oriented state is more orthodox than earlier noncapitalist states and the list of countries fitting the category is much shorter. (Among the socialist–oriented states are Angola, Ethiopia, Mozambique, and South Yemen.) Most of the programmatic recommendations remain, but new prescriptions are designed to institutionalize pro–Soviet orientations. Observers devoted additional attention to political institutions and methods which they hoped would ensure the tenure in power of pro–Soviet leaders.[4]

All of the modifications introduced into Soviet development literature over the last twenty–plus years seem designed to generate more accurate pictures of the politics and problems in the Third World countries. These included questions related to the political cultures and ideological development in those states in which the USSR has a military, economic and diplomatic stake. Many of these countries in which the Kremlin hopes to institutionalize a pro–Soviet foreign policy have significant

Muslim populations. In some, Islam is the proclaimed state religion, and in others, various brands of "progressive" quasi-socialist development strategies are infused with references to traditional Islamic culture.

In the 1960s, when optimism about Third World political change was greatest, Soviet scholars evidenced a striking ambivalence regarding Third World ideologies and socialism. They condemned African socialism as unscientific, un-"progressive" and in some cases dangerous. Simultaneously, the Middle Eastern varieties of Arab or Islamic socialism were handled differently. Ironically, the early Soviet development literature glossed over Islam. Although the emphasis on Islamic traditions in Egypt or Algeria, for example, was subjected to periodic criticism, the Soviets clearly recognized that Islam was useful in the then burgeoning anti-colonial struggle. (Islam became part of the nationalist rhetoric in many Middle Eastern and North African states and was, therefore, seen as anti-Western.) Hence, the criticisms were never as stinging as those reserved for African socialism.

The use of Egypt and Algeria as examples is no accident. Both at the time were portrayed as "progressive" states on the Noncapitalist Path. Moreover, Algeria, as we shall see below, is held up today as an example of an "acceptable" Islamic state. A history of Soviet evaluations of either Algerian or Egyptian political developments is beyond the scope of this paper, but several points need to be made. While Soviet orientalists took note of increasing nationalist fervor in Algeria prior to the outbreak of the Algerian war on November 1, 1954, they were definitely discomfited by the strength of Islamic elements within the nationalist movement. When open revolt against French authorities finally began, Soviet observers sided with the nationalists despite the Front de Liberation National's (FLN) declaration that its goal was the creation of a democratic and social government in agreement with the principles of Islam. Then, in 1962, when Algeria was declared independent, the FLN leadership drafted what came to be called the Tripoli program which outlined Algeria's socialist future. Again, several observers took exception to the emphasis placed on Algeria's Islamic heritage. By 1964 when Algerian President Ahmed Ben Bella seemed a secure Soviet ally, criticism of the Islamic factor softened. V. Kudriavtsev, *Izvestiia's* political commentator, stated that one must take into account the strength of the state's Islamic heritage in building a society based on socialist underpinnings.[5]

In the Egyptian case, ideological and religious issues surfaced briefly in 1962, but were glossed over in the generally positive appraisals of Nasser's Egypt. When in 1962 the Nasser government issued the Charter of National Action which was supposed to outline Egyptian socialist development, Soviet orientalists praised the document because it referred to scientific socialism. Yet, the charter also reaffirmed the religious nature of Egyptian society. In a *Pravda* interview given at approximately the same time, the Egyptian president underscored his view that Islam was the religion of socialism. The *Pravda* correspondent, V. Mayevskii, concluded that precisely because of its Islamic component, the charter reflected the "contradictions existing in the social development" of Egypt.[6]

This muted criticism of Islam did not interfere with Soviet relations with either country nor did it prevent positive if not glowing appraisals of both countries' "progressive" development. Fifteen years later, events in the Middle East, particularly the course of the Iranian revolution, indicated that Islam as a potent political factor could adversely affect Soviet foreign policy fortunes and, therefore, could no longer be downplayed.

The Impact of Iran

The Iranian revolution under the leadership of the Shiite clergy appears to have surprised the Soviet leadership as much as their Western counterparts. The USSR and Iran, their clear political differences notwithstanding, had developed mutually beneficial economic relations, including a joint pipeline venture. On the one hand, the Kremlin could not help but be pleased with the fall of the pro–American regime in Tehran; yet, on the other, the Soviet leadership watched uneasily as the several revolutionary factions fought for political position. Moreover, as the revolution unfolded, the key role of the clergy prompted in–depth analyses of the events and of Islam's revolutionary political potential. From the outset, most Soviet observers concluded that repressive conditions in Iran precluded the rise to leadership of groups other than the clergy. Calling Islam a "catalyst of nationalist attitudes," Soviet observers, at the time, went so far as to claim that the Iranian revolution was in no way a religious movement despite the active participation of the Shiite clergy.[7] In the period following the Shah's exit from Iran, Moscow was optimistic concerning the future of the Iranian revolution. *Pravda's* political commentator stressed that the collapse of the monarchy created the favorable preconditions for the end of imperialist domination and for the "democratization" of the country, *i.e.*, the participation of leftist (including communist) forces.[8]

Soviet optimism continued throughout 1979 despite the ethnic uprisings and intensifying political factionalism which complicated the process of regime consolidation. At this time, Moscow gave relatively high marks to the Iranian revolution. For example, as part of its May Day celebrations, the Soviet leadership sent "warm greetings to the Iranian people who have carried out an anti-imperialist national liberation revolution."[9] But, Soviet academics and journalists kept an eye on the consolidation process and presented detailed accounts of the problems confronting the Ayatollah Khomeini. Expressing concern about the lack of unity among the now victorious anti-Shah forces, several writers took note of the growing dispute between religious and secular revolutionary participants. While most writers were careful not to alienate the Khomeini forces, one did argue that the clergy "used" the peoples' movement.[10] In contrast, the majority argued at this time that socialism was not counterposed to Islam. The weekly, *New Times*, added in a prescriptive vein:

> If the revolution, which is not only Islamic but also national democratic, is to preserve its social content and progressive character . . . it must rely on a single front which besides the Islamic and democratic tendencies should contain an element of Marxism.[11]

It should come as no surprise that the tone of Soviet analyses changed significantly as Khomeini became increasingly anti-Soviet. Later assessments focused on the stages of the revolution, the class forces involved at particular stages, and the role of the clergy. It is the current consensus among Soviet experts that at each succeeding phase of the revolution, various groups opposed to the clergy were weeded out, ultimately including radicals and the Tudeh (communist) party. Moreover, the clergy seeking to protect their own interests, endeavored to institutionalize their Islamic principles and ideals.[12] By 1982, Soviet observers evidenced genuine contempt for Khomeini and his programs. Commentators claimed that Khomeini's social programs reminded them of the Middle Ages, while several journalists charged that the clergy gave priority to establishing their own monopoly on power rather than to the solution of pressing socio-economic problems.

With the arrest and trial of Tudeh party members in early 1983 and the expulsion of Soviet diplomats in May of that year, the Soviets resorted to outright name-calling. For example, Vladimir Volinskii, an Iranian specialist whose radio programs to Iran were initiated in 1982 to "clear up misconceptions," criticized Khomeini's drive to become the arbiter of all Middle East revolutions. He said: "Islam has been declared as the only and most revolutionary teaching and this propaganda has reached the point of buffoonery."[13] Still other observers claimed that Khomeini and the clergy had, in effect, perverted the course of the revolution. As one journalist said: "The tyranny under which Iranians are suffering has not been lessened yet . . . . In present day Iran those who want to cut short the hands of the exploiters and safeguard the Islamic revolution are branded as criminals . . . ."[14] Perhaps the final word has been given by R.A. Ul'ianovskii, a prominent orientalist and Deputy Director of the International Department. Claiming that religion is a primitive form of social awareness and that the Shiite clergy have instituted religious despotism, he added:

> [The clergy used only] that part of their traditions which was reflected in the conservative, and at times reactionary, dogmas of Islam struggling mainly to perpetuate the conditions of its existence and consolidate its political hegemony . . . . The clergy . . . did everything in its power to establish the *outdated* moral and ethical standards of the Koran and the Shari'a . . . .[15]

The apparent spread of political Islam prompted Soviet Third World specialists to develop more general explanations of the phenomenon and to evaluate its impact on the region. Extrapolating beyond the Iranian case, orientalists detailed the causes of what they saw as an Islamic awakening. In addition, within the parameters of existing Soviet development studies and concentrating on intra–state dynamics, scholars then attempted to determine Islam's political utility.

According to the general Soviet argument, the Islamic resurgence comprises an important element in the total liberation process. Soviet observers explained that the less developed countries are supposed to choose from competing development strategies. Yet, from the Soviet perspective, Iran demonstrated both that Western models are unsuited to transitional societies and that Iran and other states have rejected Western models of development. One leading scholar in the field of Islamic studies wrote that the Iranian revolution "proves that Western models of modernization are unacceptable for transitional multistructural societies [*i.e.* the LDC's]."[16] According to this line of reasoning it is precisely the penetration of alien Western models of modernization which trigger the politicization of the Islamic masses.[17] The authors of an important article which appeared in *Mirovaia ekonomika i mezhdunarodnye otnosheniia* went beyond the rejection of Western ideals to explain the Islamic revival. They listed: dissatisfaction with inflation; the ideological vacuum existing in the non–industrial states; and the consequent search for an Islamic alternative.[18]

One might conclude that the thrust of all these analyses is that Islam is a "useful" anti–Western force. And, there exists that element within Soviet assessments. As Brezhnev said in his speech at the twenty–sixth CPSU congress in 1981:

> Despite its [the Iranian revolution's] complex and contradictory nature, it is basically an anti–imperialist revolution although domestic and foreign reaction is seeking to alter this character . . . .
> The Iranian people are seeking their own path to freedom and prosperity. We sincerely wish them success and are prepared to develop good relations with Iran . . . .
> We communists respect the religious convictions of the people who profess Islam and any other religion . . . .
> The liberation struggle may develop under the banner of Islam.[19]

It is clear from Soviet writings about Third World Islamic movements that Moscow also sees Islam as a useful tool which complements the traditional communist emphasis on mass mobilization. As one Soviet writer put it: "the disillusionment of the politically active forces . . . in Western models of political struggle, the inclusion of the middle class in national liberation movements, the anti–Arab position of the West with regard to the Palestinian problem . . . led nationalists to [use] Islam as an instrument of the masses."[20] Moreover, scholars concluded that Islam becomes political all the more easily because the masses see in its dogma the rejection of inequality and injustice.[21]

But the example of Iran seems to haunt orientalists. Although initially seen as an opening, the Islamic revolution in Iran turned out to be equally anti–Soviet. The literature, reflecting Soviet experiences thus reveals a distinct ambivalence as to whether the Islamic resurgence is a right–wing or left–wing phenomenon. Despite its anti–Westernism which makes the Islamic revolution potentially "progressive," its "reactionary" elements are equally strong. According to a long analysis in *Nauka i religiia*, even so–called Islamic socialist ideals are in reality merely fronts for bourgeois forces. The author of this article charged further that "reactionary" (anti–Soviet) forces want to "ensure that the only thing remaining of Islam is religious zeal bordering on fanaticism which can be turned against the national liberation struggle."[22]

In their attempts to determine Islam's political thrust, scholars investigated traditional Islamic views on questions of justice and equality as well as on so–called Islamic economic models. International relations experts offered divided interpretations as to traditional Islam's pronouncements regarding these issues. Several orientalists claimed that it was anti–equalitarian; yet, these and other scholars also claimed that the masses were drawn to Islam's promise of social justice.

Because traditional Islamic society had very specific economic rules and because the Marxist–Leninist prism dictates a major concern with economics, it seems natural that a segment of the academic community devote its energies to studying proposals for Islamic economic systems in the Muslim Third World. A survey of the literature reveals an increasing number of articles detailing Islamic–style international economics and Islamic banks. Major differences of opinion exist on these issues as well. Certain scholars focused on the so–called Islamic economic system as implemented by President Zia al Haq of Pakistan. Indeed, they see the system as completely "reactionary" and condemn Zia for using Islam to further the cause of "reactionary" Muslim countries such as Saudi Arabia.[23] By the same token, other scholars see positive potential in these constructs––again, insofar as they are anti–Western. Evgenii Primakov, the Director of the Institute of Oriental Studies of the Soviet Academy of Sciences and a long–time Middle East hand, concluded that the "Islamic development strategy would work only insofar as it is based on leftist forces and the mobilization of the workers."[24] In the final analysis, the Soviet academic community concluded that Islamic economics is in all probability conservative. Yet, they were clearly unwilling to write it off completely.

The Implications for Policy

The Islamic revolution affects more than just the domestic politics of any given Muslim state; it has altered relations among Middle East and Persian Gulf states as well. Thus, the international aspects of the phenomenon may well have a significant impact on Soviet foreign policy in that not only Soviet bilateral relations are affected, but also regional objectives and calculations.

The record of Soviet involvement in the Third World suggests that Moscow's activities are guided by geopolitical considerations (*i.e.*, concern for ports and strategic access) and by the desire to counter Western (and Chinese) influence positions. Both motivations are of major consequence in the Middle East where the Soviets have sought a naval presence and acted to reinforce the anti–Western attitudes of many of the region's leaders. Another apparent Soviet goal in the Third World is the establishment of diplomatic relations with as many states as possible.

Moscow sees the proliferation of its state–to–state diplomatic ties as a symbol of its acceptance as an international actor and as a superpower. A corollary goal is to cultivate friends who will help achieve these aforementioned objectives. Cultivation, as a foreign policy goal, means convincing Third World elites that a genuine coincidence of interests exists between them and the USSR. Moreover, Soviet propagandists seem to feel that pro–Soviet orientations will thrive best where common issues dominate the political rhetoric. Observers expect their socialist heirs in the Third World to devote resources to political education and indoctrination. Yet, scholars also recognize that what one specialist called the "backwardness of the masses" will prevent the adoption of scientific socialism. The label "backward" seems to refer to ethnic and tribal identifications as well as to religious ideologies including Islam.

Interestingly, although the Soviets have exhibited some sensitivity to the potential contagion of political Islam, the very existence of a sizeable Muslim population within the USSR may facilitate the cultivation effort. Since the revolution in Iran and the near–collapse of the Marxist regime in Afghanistan, innumerable articles in Soviet journals and foreign language broadcasts have been devoted to Muslim life within the Soviet Union. The effort to depict Muslim life positively may be considered a significant part of the Soviet propaganda drive to allay fears among the Arab and Persian Gulf states of Moscow's hostility to Islamic principles. In fact, Soviet Muslim delegations frequently meet with co–religionists from the Arab world and the Soviet press contains references to the "international relations" of Soviet Muslims. However, the record of Soviet–Third World relations also illustrates that despite these efforts and despite Soviet attempts to achieve influence over Third World friends by distributing economic and military assistance, the best Moscow may be able to achieve is a coincidence of interests. With a small number of exceptions, formal alliances are few. Even in those cases in which friendship and cooperation treaties have been signed, serious policy disagreements have, on more than one occasion, disrupted relations. Therefore, the key question then becomes how strong and long–lived that congruence of interests may be.

For example, one current Soviet objective in the Middle East is the creation of a united anti–Israel, anti–American front composed of Persian Gulf and Middle East states under Soviet leadership. Thus far the Soviets have been unable to put together such a coalition, however. Islamic affiliations transcend left–right politics. Moreover, from the Soviet perspective Islamic ties may put Syria and Libya in the same camp as Saudi Arabia thus forming an exclusive club for which Moscow's membership credentials are not terribly strong, and its hopes for a leadership position are even weaker.

As with the question of the domestic uses of Islam, questions of Islamic solidarity and Islamic unity were downplayed until very recently. What little comment there was tended, in a prescriptive vein, to discourage unification schemes. Generally, the evidence indicates that Moscow is discomfited by calls for Islamic solidarity whether emanating from the Islamic Conference or from either Iran or Iraq as each pursues its military objectives in the Gulf War.

With the resurgence of political Islam, the Islamic Conference as an international governmental organization has acquired major significance. As a result, for the first time several articles detailing the workings of the organization and most importantly its international positions have appeared in the major Soviet foreign policy journals. As might be expected, Soviet observers approve of the organization insofar as its orientation is pro–Palestinian, anti–Israeli and anti–American. Nonetheless, these same commentators take issue with its composition. They accuse the conference of being unduly influenced by "rich conservative Muslim states" which permit the "reactionary uses of Islam" by imperialists. In particular, the Soviets are unhappy that the conference has discussed the situation of Muslims in the USSR and the fighting in Afghanistan. In fact, the Islamic Conference suspended Afghanistan's membership following the 1979 Soviet invasion. Thus, despite the conference's agreement with some Soviet policies, it is still distinctly anti–communist. Moreover, it would seem fair to conclude that Moscow's line would be even harsher were not several Soviet friends members of the conference.

The four year old Iran–Iraq war also illustrates how the Islamic factor may complicate Soviet foreign policy calculations. The war has divided the Middle East and pitted Soviet allies Syria and Libya, which back Iran, against friendly Iraq and against potential friends among the moderates, such as Jordan and Kuwait. A number of factors, beyond the scope of this paper, entered into Soviet attitudes toward the fighting in the Persian Gulf.[25] Although Moscow tried without success to use the hostilities to its advantage, as the war has continued, signs of the Kremlin's increasing dissatisfaction with the prolongation of the war are evident. The Soviets, with their claim of official neutrality, have seized upon its religious element to express their impatience with the confrontation. Moscow chose to attack the Shiite clergy without naming Khomeini directly. For example, the commentator on a domestic television program, "The World Today," noted:

Some circles in Tehran call today for the continuation of the war in order to punish the Iraqi leaders and to spread the Iranian type of Islam. Are these countries not paying too high a price in trying to clarify with the aid of military operations the point of who is better the Sunnis or the Shiites?[26]

Moscow has also encountered problems with an Islamic component in Afghanistan. Although Islam was not the major precipitating factor of the Christmas–time invasion, the tribal population's depth of Islamic feeling and resentment of the Kabul regime's policies continue to hamper Soviet efforts to stabilize the situation.

Over the years, the USSR maintained a strong interest in its mountainous neighbor including a 1921 treaty, military intervention in 1929 and economic and military agreements beginning in the early fifties. The Soviet stake in Afghanistan increased significantly in the period between the overthrow of the monarchy in 1973 and the April 1978 coup which brought the local communist party to power. Once a Marxist–Leninist regime came to power in Kabul, the Soviets intensified their involvement. By the fall of 1979, despite close ties with the Soviet Union (including a Friendship and Cooperation Treaty), the communist regime, threatened by political infighting and by intensifying attacks by Islamic tribal insurgents, was on the verge of collapse. The Soviet Union apparently decided that only armed intervention could save the regime to which its prestige was now linked. Five years later Soviet ground forces remain on Afghan territory and the insurgency continues.

To judge from public pronouncements regarding Afghanistan, the Soviets blame the Amin regime for much of their current difficulties. They accuse him of initiating ill–timed, radical reforms without regard to the Islamic sentiments of the local population. One report, for example, describes how a representative of the revolutionary committee would arrive in a village to redistribute land only to be followed by a local *mullah* who would proclaim that Allah did not permit seizing another's land. The report continued: "This is the reality of the situation. To be sure, it does not mean that land reform in Afghanistan is intrinsically unsuitable. But it did turn out that the initial land distribution was extremist, ill–conceived and unsuitable in specific conditions."[27]

As a result, the current propaganda effort stresses that the Karmal regime understands the Islamic underpinnings of Afghan society. An Afghan official, writing in *Partiinaia zhizn'* stated:

[Every effort is being made to] see that the ideals and goals of the April revolution would be correctly and deeply understood by faithful Muslims and by all laborers . . . . Considering that most of the country's population practices Islam, the [party] clearly and distinctly formulates its principled policy in relation to this religion. The revolution is a response to the aspirations and hopes of the laboring Muslims of the country.[28]

This theme has been echoed in broadcasts to Iran as well. A recent Farsi broadcast claimed that Islam would be taken into account when the Kabul government initiated new revolutionary programs. Moscow announced that the Karmal regime has created a Muslim affairs department, restored local mosques and permitted the celebration of Muslim holidays. But Radio Moscow in Farsi also underscored that tolerance did not include the active proselytizing of reactionary clergy who "eulogize" the Afghan monarchy.[29] Implicitly, the Kremlin is pointing out the possibility of a compromise between pro-Marxist programs and respect for the Islamic heritage of the many Middle East countries. In addition, a broadcast such as the one mentioned above has significant propaganda value. The USSR is clearly attempting not only to appease local Muslims and their counterparts in the rest of the region, but also to placate the Khomeini regime (which, it should be noted, has been arming the guerrillas).

It is apparent from Soviet official statements and from the works of Soviet academics, that there is a consensus that the strength of Islamic sentiment may indeed be an obstacle to Soviet Middle East-Persian Gulf objectives. That Kremlin policy-makers are unhappy with this turn of events is clear, but it is also clear that they recognize the need to come to terms with it. As was noted above, the thrust of current Soviet writings on the Third World is to suggest methods for consolidating power and maintaining pro-Soviet leaders in office. Consequently, the prescriptions now offered by Soviet Third World specialists include the need to blend tradition and modernity. Scholars and Kremlin politicians have come to the conclusion, albeit belatedly, that it is a mistake for local leadership to ignore the diverse religious, ethnic and historical traditions of the LDC's. Instead, they call for a compromise between the old (Islam) and the new (socialist orientation).

The journal *Nauka i religiia* argued, for example, that several states had achieved just such a compromise:

In countries of socialist orientation the governing revolutionary democrats take into account the religious character of the ideology of the masses . . . showing them that these reforms are not in conflict with the spirit of Islam. In the PDRY [South Yemen] for example, scientific socialism has become the official ideological platform of the national democratic revolution.[30]

Whether or not such a synthesis can succeed is still being debated within the foreign policy institutes. Although orientalists hope that the Islamic socialist ideologies of "progressive" leaders will evolve into full-fledged Marxism–Leninism, they also caution that bourgeois ideologues will use so–called Islamic socialism for their own ends.[31] And as was noted above, Evgenii Primakov argued that Islam could safely comprise part of a "progressive" ideology only if pro–Soviet, leftist elements are firmly in power. Nodari Simoniia, a Soviet expert on the Third World known for his cautious assessments, went even further. In a roundtable discussion he argued forcibly that the synthesis—that is of Islamic or other brands of socialism—alone will not ensure "progress." At some point, a "revolutionary shift" in power must take place. For Simoniia, pro–Soviet orientations can be achieved only by the accession to power of Marxist elements (if not a full–fledged vanguard party).[32]

These academic assessments reflect the Kremlin's desire to work with Islamic states and "progressive" Islamic forces, but most probably when Islam is not used as an end in itself. A Khomeini–type leader who seeks to implement an Iranian style revolution is not, therefore, a likely Soviet ally. But, an anti–Western "progressive" leader who nonetheless uses Islamic slogans would seem not only a target for cultivation, but also a potential Soviet friend. Moreover, the Kremlin appears to recognize that political Islam has acquired such momentum in the Middle East that no ruler can afford to ignore it. In the published proceedings of a conference of orientalists held in Tbilisi, it was noted that many contemporary Third World leaders see Islam as a "constituent part and key lever in the realization of their political and economic programs."[33] Given the emphasis on the consolidation of power and given the potency of political Islam, the prescription appears to be that a compromise must be worked out and that implicitly Islam should be used as a mobilizing and legitimating force wherever possible.

In this regard, it is interesting to note that Soviet Third World specialists are restudying the Algerian experience. The late President Houari Boumedienne and current Algerian leader Chadli Benjedid are lauded by experts for their use of Islam and for involving the clergy in their social programs. Ironically, when Boumedienne came to power in June 1965 through a coup which toppled pro–Soviet Ahmed Ben Bella, the Soviets were apprehensive about his promise to restore the primacy of Algeria's Islamic heritage. According to Middle East specialists, he made it clear that Islam did not preclude "progressive" reforms. His policy, it is said, illustrates that Islam "promotes the growing popularity of the revolutionary democrats and favorably influences the people's attitudes."[34] Algeria has thus become a model which Soviet authorities clearly hope other Middle East friends will follow.

Conclusion

Soviet diplomatic moves in the last few years make it clear that the Kremlin is not willing to rule out dealing cordially with the Islamic states. Relations with Syria, Algeria and others continue to flourish and attempts to cultivate other regional actors proceed. Yet, the proliferation of Soviet academic studies on Islam, the obvious concern about the course of the revolution in Iran, and the implicit concern regarding the spread of political Islam all indicate that Moscow is painfully aware of Islam's political potential. This helps to explain the sometimes tortured attempts to differentiate between "progressive" and "reactionary" aspects of the Islamic movement.

Islam continues to be a major research topic for the institutes and a significant concern for policy–makers. Evgenii Primakov, summarizing the tasks facing orientalists, announced the creation of a working section on "Islam in politics" which was to investigate the duality of Islamic political movements and the petty bourgeois nature of Islamic ideology. Moreover, Primakov proposed two related areas for study: 1. the influence and interrelationship between the religious factor and nationalism; and 2. class differentiation within the Islamic movement.[35] Nationalism, it should be noted, is anathema to the Soviets because it is the major obstacle to successful Soviet cultivation of these countries and the term class differentiation would seem to imply a reinvestigation of the "progressive/reactionary" question. In the final analysis, it seems clear that the USSR has yet to come up with a totally satisfactory assessment of the Islamic resurgence.

Notes

1. B.I. Ivanov and A.O. Tamazishvili, "Nauchnye issledovaniia instituta vostokovedeniia AN SSSR v svete reshenii XXVI s'ezda KPSS," *Narody Azii i Afriki*, No. 2, 1982, p. 121.

2. For an interesting analysis of the interrelationships between the institutes and policy–makers, see Oded Eran, *The Mezhdunarodniki*, (Ramat Gan, Israel: Turtle Dove Press, 1979).

3. L. Shaidullina, "Goodwill Mission," *Nauka i Religiia*, No. 3,

1981, pp. 23–34, abstracted in *Current Digest of the Soviet Press,* (hereafter *CDSP*) Vol. XXXIII, No. 18, (1981) p. 13.

4. For a detailed analysis of the several constructs adopted by Soviet Third World experts, see Carol R. Saivetz and Sylvia Woodby, *Soviet-Third World Relations,* (Boulder Colorado: Westview Press, 1985), especially chapter 1.

5. V. Kudriavtsev, "Algeria on the Advance," *Izvestiia,* April 25, 1964, p. 1.

6. "V. Mayevskii on ' Conversations in Cairo' ," in "Soviet and UAR Views on Socialism," *Mizan,* No. 8, September, 1962, pp. 7–12.

7. N. Prozhogin, "Stormy Time," *Pravda,* January 7, 1979, p. 4 in *CDSP,* Vol. XXXI, No. 1, January 31, 1979, p. 15.

8. V. Ovchinnikov, "Political Commentator's Notes," *Pravda,* February 13, 1979, p. 5 in *CDSP,* Vol. XXXI, No. 6, March 7, 1979, p. 15.

9. May Day Slogans––1979, *CDSP,* Vol. XXXI, No. 7, March 14, 1979, p. 5.

10. A.M. Aliev, "Antimonarkhicheskaia i anti-imperialisticheskaia revoliutsiia v Irane," *Narody Azii i Afriki,* No. 3, 1979, p. 53.

11. L. Medvedko, "Islam and Liberation Revolutions," *New Times,* No. 43, 1979, p. 21.

12. See the discussion in R.A. Ul'ianovskii, "Iranskaia Revoliutsiia i ee osobennosti, " *Kommunist,* No. 10, 1982, pp. 106–116.

13. In October, 1982, the Soviet Union initiated a new Persian radio series beamed at Iran. The editor/correspondent V. Volinskii was announced as a Persian specialist. This quotation is from a broadcast entitled "National Liberation Movements and Their Friends," October 31, 1983, in *Joint Publication Research Service* (Hereafter *JPRS),* 84861, December 2, 1983, p. 24.

14. Igor Sheftunov commentary: "What is Hidden Behind the Curtain of the Invitation to Export the Islamic Revolution." *JPRS,* 84861, December 2, 1983, p. 22.

15. R.A. Ul'ianovskii, "International Life: Moral Principles in Politics and Policy in the Sphere of Morals; Iran–––What Next?" *Literaturnaia Gazeta,* June 22, 1983, *Foreign Broadcast Information Service,* (hereafter *FBIS*) *SOV* 83–127, June 30, 1983, p. H–3. Italics added.

16. Liudmila Polonskaia, "Major Trends in the Ideological Struggle," *Asia and Africa Today,* (English) No. 3, (May–June) 1982, p. 2.

17. A. Ionova, "Islam and International Economic Cooperation," *Aziia i Afrika Segodnia,* No. 3, 1983, in *JPRS,* 84984, December 20, 1983, p. 17.

18. L. Polonskaia and A. Ionova, "Kontseptsii ' islamskoi

ekonomiki' : sotsialnaia sushchnost' i politicheskaia naplavlennost',"
Mirovaia ekonomika i mezhdunarodnye otnosheniia, No. 3, 1981, pp. 113,
116, 117.

19. *Pravda* and *Izvestiia,* February 24, 1981, in *CDSP,* Vol.
XXXIII, No. 8, March 25, 1981, pp. 7,8.

20. I.M. Smilianskaia, "Islam i problemy obshchestvennogo
razvitiia arabskikh stran," *Narody Azii i Afriki,* No. 1, 1984, p. 109.

21. See: "Vsesouznaia nauchnaia konferentsiia ' zakonomernosti
i spetsifika razvitiia revoliutsionnogo protsessa v osvobodivshikhsia
stranakh afriki i azii' ," *Narody Azii i Afriki,* No. 1, 1983, p. 128.

22. A. Germanovich and L. Medvedko, "A ' Revival of
Islam' or Awakening of the People," *Nauka i Religiia,* No. 7, July 1982,
JPRS, 82288, November 22, 1982, p. 8.

23. Irina Zhmuida, "Pakistan–Islamic Principles in the Country's
Economy," *Asia and Africa Today,* (English), No. 5, 1981, p. 40.

24. E. Primakov, "Islam i protsessy obshchestvennogo razvitiia
stran zarubezhnogo vostoka," *Voprosy Filosofii,* No. 8, 1980, pp. 61–62.

25. Relations between the two were tenuous at best. Even prior
to the fall of the Shah, territorial disputes and questions relating to the
Kurdish minority in Iraq prevented close ties. The Iranian revolution
exacerbated pre–existing ideological tensions between "progressive" Iraq
and monarchical and Shiite Iran. The Baghdad government of Saddam
Hussein felt threatened by Khomeini's appeals to the large Shiite
population of Iraq. By all indications, Hussein expected a quick victory
because of the turbulent conditions in Iran in September, 1980.

26. V. Zorin, "The World Today," August 5, 1982,
FBIS-SOV-82-152, August 6, 1982, p. H12.

27. Gabriel Hazak, "Afghanistan: The Nature of the Problem,"
Rahva Haal August 27, 1983, p. 3 in *JPRS,* 84740, November 14, 1983, p.
2.

28. Salekh Muhammed Zeray, "Afghanistan: Following the
Victorious Path of the April Revolution," *Partiinaia Zhizn',* No. 14, July,
1982, pp. 74–79 in *JPRS,* 81768, September 15, 1982, p. 20.

29. V. Volinskii, "Afghanistan's Popular Revolution and its
Opponents," in Farsi, November 12, 1983, *JPRS,* 84993, December 21,
1983, p. 6.

30. Germanovich and Medvedko, *op. cit.,* p. 6.

31. *Ibid.,* p. 7.

32. "Tradition and Contemporaneity in the Social Development
of Eastern Counties," *Asia and Africa Today,* (English), No. 6, 1983, pp. 2,
21.

33. "Vsesouznaia . . . ," p. 128.

34. Aleksandr Malshenko, "Algeria, Religious Tradition and the Policy of Revolutionary Democracy," *Asia and Africa Today*, No. 2, 1980 p. 38, and Germanovich and Medvedko, *op. cit.*

35. E. Primakov, "Aktualnye zadachi sovetskogo vostokovedeniia," *Narody Azii i Afriki*, No. 5, 1983.

3
Moscow's Perceptions of Recent American Involvement in the Middle East: Implications for Soviet Policy

Herbert L. Sawyer

Introduction

This essay on Moscow's perceptions of recent American involvement in the Middle East concerns itself with six issues. *First*, it describes Soviet perceptions of U.S. goals in the Middle East, narrowly defined as the eastern Mediterranean area, although there is also some discussion of the Persian Gulf.[1] *Second*, Moscow's assessment of the extent to which the United States is accomplishing its aims in the region is discussed. Particular attention is devoted to that period of the Lebanese crisis that began with the Israeli attack in June of 1982 and ended with the abrogation in 1984 of the agreement of May 17, 1983 between Israel and the Gemayel Government in Lebanon. The Soviet judgement is that America has suffered a substantial defeat in Lebanon that has negative implications for the United States throughout the region.[2] *Third*, one might expect that America's problems in the region would represent unadulterated gains for the Soviet Union, especially given the zero-sum game orientation of both superpowers regarding their relationship. This has not been the case. Moscow also has problems in the region, and interestingly some of these are closely related to those of Washington. These interconnections are explored at some length. *Fourth*, Moscow's assessment of problems and opportunities for Soviet policy towards the three key regional states of Israel, Egypt and Syria is discussed in the context of America's relations with those states. *Fifth*, some speculation is engaged in as to what policies the Soviets are likely to adopt towards those states in the foreseeable future. *Finally*, there is a brief analysis of the combined impact of recent developments in the region and the policies of the various actors on the prospects for a comprehensive peace.

I

Regarding Soviet views of American goals and interests, a few observations will be made about both the Persian Gulf and the Middle East. According to Soviet accounts, Washington sees the Gulf region as the most likely arena in which United States interests will be threatened in the immediate future.[3] This is a reasonable assessment of the American view, given both the importance of the region to the United States and the latter's limited capacity to influence events there. The United States' commitment to maintaining, and if possible increasing, American influence in the Gulf stems from that region's geostrategic significance and its oil. That there is currently a glut on the world oil market should not suggest that Persian Gulf oil is unimportant to the United States. The glut could disappear as a result of, for example, a spreading of the Iraqi–Iranian war, which in turn could reduce world oil supplies. The fact that American oil imports from the Gulf are now very much lower than they were at the end of the 1970s is often overemphasized. Oil, after all, is a fungible product. A sharp reduction in Gulf exports would reduce total world supplies, thereby increasing competition for non–Gulf supplies, which in turn would have a negative impact on United States imports. Also, the world oil price would increase. Thus, both in terms of supplies and prices, the United States could be affected directly. Moreover, even if that direct effect somehow were to be minimal, certainly the negative impact of decreased supplies and increased prices on the *global* economy would be substantial, a fact of considerable importance to the United States. Finally, if the effects of a major disruption in the world oil market were to be borne chiefly by Western Europe and Japan, such a development would have grave implications for the United States as the leader of the Western Alliance.[4] For these reasons, as well as America's assertedly hegemonistic aspirations, Soviet spokesmen claim that Washington seeks pretexts for increasing its permanent military presence in the Gulf region, and that currently the Iraqi–Iranian war is being exploited by Washington for that purpose. Therefore, it is observed, the war benefits only the imperialists and should be ended.[5]

Similarly, it is argued that the United States does not want a genuine peace in the Middle East, because such a peace would rob Washington of an "ace card" in its regional policy, that is, the advantages of the Arab–Israeli conflict. Israel, it is said, is the only reliable instrument for repressing the national liberation movement and for splitting the Arabs.[6] The idea that the United States opposes peace in the region is nonsense, of course, and decision–makers in the Kremlin are well aware of this. However, the problem from the Soviet perspective is that Washington wants peace *on its own terms*: a strong Israel; no independent Palestinian state; and, most importantly, minimal or no Soviet influence in the entire Middle East–Gulf region. Thus, although at one level the Soviet assertion that Washington opposes a Middle East peace can be dismissed as empty propaganda, the Soviets do correctly understand that Washington's approach to Soviet–American relations in the Middle East–Gulf region is a zero–sum one. That is, a Soviet loss is viewed as an equivalent American gain, and vice versa.[7]

To achieve its goal of bringing stability to the Middle East, while simultaneously excluding Moscow from the process, thereby decreasing Soviet influence in the region, the United States in recent years has undertaken five major initiatives: the Camp David process; the Carter Doctrine; the concept of an anti–Soviet "strategic consensus"; the Reagan Plan; and the May 17, 1983 agreement between Israel and the Gemayel Government.

The Soviet interpretation of the Camp David process argues that it was designed to remove the strongest Arab nation, Egypt, from "the anti–Israeli Arab Front," thereby greatly enhancing Israel's military position vis–à–vis the remaining Arab states. This was indeed accomplished by the May 26, 1979 Egyptian–Israeli Treaty. Since the signing of that treaty, moreover, the United States and Israel have been striving to keep the process going by attempting to get other Arab states to follow Egypt's example. Success in this endeavor would further enhance Israel's and, more importantly, America's position in the region, while at the same time precluding any significant role for Moscow in the peace process. To the extent that the Camp David process succeeds, then, American power and influence in the region increase, while those of the Soviet Union decline.

The Carter Doctrine went well beyond the Camp David process. That Doctrine was a reaction to the threat to American interests inherent in the recent turbulent developments in the Gulf region: the Iranian Revolution; the hostage crisis; the Soviet invasion of Afghanistan; and the Iraqi–Iranian war. Soviet policy in Afghanistan seemed to shock Washington more than did the other events.[8] Thus, it is important to remember that during its last year in office, the Carter Administration saw the Soviet threat to the Gulf region, not the Arab–Israeli conflict, as the much greater danger to American interests.

This was *a fortiori* the case with the Reagan Administration. The concept of an anti–Soviet strategic consensus followed logically from the the Carter Doctrine. It reflected the Reagan Administration's conviction that the key task, not only for the United States and the West, *but also for the states of the Middle East–Gulf region*, was the containment of Soviet power and influence. However, the Arab states reacted coolly, at least publicly, to the idea of an anti–Soviet strategic consensus. They argued that the Arab–Israeli conflict, not any Soviet threat, had to be placed first on the agenda.[9]

Indeed, Washington was forced by the tensions that arose in Lebanon during the summer of 1981 to give its attention to the Arab–Israeli struggle. One year later, during and after the Israeli attack in Lebanon, the Reagan Administration was much more deeply involved in that conflict. Nevertheless, in the early fall of 1982 Washington saw a resolution of the Arab–Israeli struggle as important not so much for its own sake, but rather as a necessary first step towards achieving the larger goal of containing Soviet power in the Middle East and the Gulf. Thus, developments in both regions were consciously linked. The Reagan Plan, which was to effect this linkage, was intended

> to assure both Israel and Jordan of United States opposition to the establishment of an independent Palestinian State. At the same time, it sought to assure Jordan that Washington would oppose Israeli annexation [of the West Bank]. According to the American 'script' these assurances were to prompt King Hussein to join the peace process and Israel to reciprocate.[10]

The resulting Arab–Israeli accommodation would then make feasible the anti–Soviet strategic consensus desired by Washington.

The Reagan Plan was rejected, however, and in the view of an authoritative Soviet source, K. N. Brutents, this led the Americans to concentrate on Lebanon.[11] In 1983, Washington urged the May 17th agreement upon the Gemayel Government and Israel.[12] That agreement, according to Brutents, became the cornerstone of Washington's policy, and seemed to have four aims: 1) to consolidate a pro–American regime in Lebanon, dependent on Israel and prepared to support a United States military presence in the country (in the form of a multinational force); 2) to detach a second country, Lebanon, from the anti–Israeli Arab front, thereby continuing the Camp David process; 3) to complicate the position of Syria, "the fundamental Arab link in the present situation opposing United States–Israeli plans"; and 4) on the basis of success in Lebanon "generally to consolidate United States positions in the Arab world and create . . . increasing pressure on the Palestinians . . . to embrace . . . Camp David and the Reagan Plan."[13] All of the above goals clearly are seen by Moscow as inimical to Soviet interests.

These interpretations of Camp David, the Carter Doctrine, the strategic consensus, the Reagan Plan and the May 17th agreement are consistent with the Soviet version of general United States policy in the Middle East–Gulf region. In that version, the main thrust of American policy is to forge an "anti–Soviet alliance," between the United States, Israel, Egypt, China, Pakistan and Saudi Arabia. While no such "alliance" exists, nor is one feasible in the foreseeable future, it is reasonable to think of these states, led by Washington, as constituting an anti–Soviet coalition, albeit a very loose, even brittle, one. These six countries frequently pursue, and sometimes coordinate, policies that are anti–Soviet in nature.[14] Hence, when one considers the five American initiatives discussed sketchily above in the context of Washington's general orientation towards Soviet–American relations in the Middle East–Gulf region, it is clear that Moscow has been reinforced in its conviction that Washington automatically views Soviet losses in the area as American gains.

II

Goals are one thing; realizing them is another. Therefore we must ascertain Moscow's perception of the extent to which Washington is accomplishing its aims, because that perception influences the formulation of Soviet foreign policy. This is especially so, in that Moscow, like Washington, basically views Soviet–American relations in the region as antithetical. An appropriate point of departure for judging Soviet perceptions is Moscow's assessment of the Lebanese crisis since the summer of 1982. Soviet sources have characterized U.S. policy in Lebanon as having been uninformed; lacking in foresight; insensitive to Arab pride; self–assured to the point of being smug; excessively reliant upon military power, which is not easily translated into political influence; and, in a single phrase, simplistic and unwise. Brutents, citing a West German Social Democratic leader, described Washington's policy as political dilettantism, because it ignored the fact that the agreement of May 17, 1983 was opposed by practically all Lebanese political factions.[15] Yet Washington forced it through, with disastrous results. According to another observer, the United States (and Israel) failed to foresee that Lebanon's humiliation resulting from the forcible imposition of the agreement would unify all factions opposed to it.[16] America's insensitivity, according to Brutents, was manifest in the cavalier way in which it treated Arab national interests and ignored Arab honor and dignity. U.S. self-assurance and smugness were reflected in the belief that the extraordinarily complicated Lebanese problem could be resolved by force. Washington, he said, relied too heavily on the Lebanese Army and perhaps even more on the multinational force.[17] Radio Moscow, for its part, noted that the United States was unable to influence the "political correlation of forces," even with the use of the battleship New Jersey.[18] Finally, Bovin argued that the United States underestimated the significance and capabilities of Syria, which emerged from the crisis with substantially enhanced prestige and authority.[19]

In the Soviet view, the results of Washington's recent policy in Lebanon represent a substantial and multi-faceted loss for the United States. It is argued that American credibility and influence in the region have decreased sharply. Washington's chief ally, Israel, has sustained serious losses.[20] Moreover, the U.S.-Israeli strategic alliance has proven to be less than invincible.[21] Other friends of the United States, who, like President Sadat of Egypt, had come to believe in America's omnipotence, have been weakened. Perhaps U.S.-Egyptian relations themselves have been strained, judging by President Mubarak's recent public statement in Washington that in effect castigated American policy in Lebanon.[22] U.S. ties with conservative Arab regimes are potentially weaker. Indeed, Brutents argued that the overwhelming majority of Arabs are hostile to America's "pouring lead" at Arabs on Arab soil thousands of miles from U.S. shores. He also argued that the positions of Syria, "the Lebanese national patriotic forces," and the anti-imperialist Palestinians have been strengthened. Henceforth, he continued, it will be more difficult for Washington to exploit differences within the Palestinian Liberation Organization (PLO). Most important of all, *the chances for a peace settlement on American terms have been weakened.*[23] All of these points represent positive developments for the Soviet Union, but this is especially true of the last assertion, because, as noted earlier, "American terms" involve precluding Soviet participation in the peace process, thereby reducing Soviet influence in the area.

The decline in America's credibility is sharply reflected in Washington's relations with President Gemayel, upon whom Washington imposed the May 17th agreement. As a result of that agreement, Gemayel found himself under great Syrian pressure, which the Americans were unable to eliminate. The subsequent abrogation of the agreement not only humiliated the United States, but also substantially increased Syria's influence over Beirut. A major effect of the American initiative, then, was the weakening, rather than strengthening, of the Gemayel

Government, hardly a development to engender confidence in Washington's ability to influence events or protect its friends in the region.

One of those friends, President Mubarak, has said that the withdrawal of the Marines from Beirut would be a catastrophe. That the Marines were in fact withdrawn in February 1984 will have a negative effect, although one difficult to measure with any precision, on Washington's ability to project military force into the Middle East–Persian Gulf region. This is an issue of central importance, because at the heart of Washington's policy towards the area is the commitment to maintain a permanent and direct United States military presence there.[24]

American decision–makers themselves are acutely aware of the credibility issue. Leading figures in the Reagan Administration have argued that the problem with the strategic consensus concept is U.S. credibility. If the Arabs have no faith in the ability of the United States to protect them, the argument goes, then why should they support the Camp David process or American initiatives in the Gulf.[25] This concern with American credibility is one of long–standing in Washington. Admiral Moorer, the former Chief of Naval Operations, wrote that the American military presence in the Middle East–Gulf region should have an official designation, which would symbolize the permanence of Washington's commitment to the area.[26] This is perhaps one reason that the Rapid Deployment Joint Task Force, the accelerated development of which was an American response to the Soviet invasion of Afghanistan, was redesignated as the Central Command, whose responsibilities are focused on the Middle East–Gulf region. A concrete example of the American commitment was reflected in the joint military maneuvers (Bright Star) conducted in the Middle East in 1981 and subsequent years by the United States, Egypt, and other countries. When Sadat was assassinated in October of 1980, the United States was concerned about the commitment of his successor, President Mubarak, to U.S.–Egyptian cooperation. Therefore, Washington offered to expand the Bright Star exercises that were planned for 1981, so as to demonstrate America's own commitment to the region in general and to Egypt in particular. Mubarak responded positively.[27]

Notwithstanding that particular positive response, any objective assessment of U.S. policy in the region leads to serious misgivings regarding America's credibility. This conclusion is unavoidable when one considers the fate of the major U.S. initiatives undertaken or continued since the Egyptian–Israeli Treaty of March, 1979: the Camp David process, while perhaps not completely dead, is certainly moribund. The Carter Doctrine, fortunately, some would argue has not yet been challenged fully. It is not clear that the United States has the capability to cope effectively with the broad range of crises (from terrorist activities against the oil fields to a Soviet invasion of Iran) that potentially could arise in the region. As for the strategic consensus and the Reagan Plan, they remain unrealized and their prospects are unpromising. Finally, the May 17th agreement was an unequivocal, costly failure. Given Moscow's zero–sum game approach to its relations with Washington, these American failures, especially the loss of credibility, must suggest to the Soviet leadership that there are great opportunities to be exploited in the region.

III

The tribulations of American foreign policy, however, are not unmitigated gains for Moscow. Even a cursory exploration of U.S.–Soviet relations in the Middle East–Gulf region demonstrates that although the superpowers themselves generally see their relations in the area as a zero–sum game, objectively this is not the case. I have discussed this assertion in detail elsewhere, but a brief summary of developments lending support to that view is in order.[28] Several events (the Yom Kippur War, the Camp David process, the Iranian Revolution, the hostage crisis, the Soviet invasion of Afghanistan and the Iraqi–Iranian war) contributed to the energy vulnerabilty of the West. This vulnerability elicited an American reaction that in turn had serious, negative consequences for Moscow. In addition to eliciting an American response, those same events had direct costs for the Soviets.

First, let us deal briefly with the developments, and then consider the U.S. reaction. The Yom Kippur War laid the groundwork for the Camp David process. The latter, in turn, brought about the Egyptian–Israeli Treaty of 1979, while simultaneously excluding Moscow from the peace process, thus reducing Soviet influence in the region. The Iranian Revolution, while initially welcomed by Moscow, brought major tensions to Soviet–Iranian relations.[29] The hostage crisis deeply reinforced Washington's conviction that it had to have an effective, direct and permanent military presence in the Persian Gulf region to protect American interests. The continuing implementation of that policy, notwithstanding difficulties facing the United States in this regard, is a matter of substantial concern to the Soviet Union.

The Soviet invasion of Afghanistan damaged Moscow's standing in the Muslim world. It reinforced still further the decision to deploy American military power in the region, and it brought about a strengthening of U.S.–Pakistani relations.[30] Also, the Iraqi–Iranian war has placed Moscow in a difficult position. If the Soviets support either side, their relations with the other will suffer. If they remain neutral, they risk alienating both sides, at least to some degree. Thus, although these developments (except for the Camp David process) had greater costs for the United States than for the Soviet Union, they nonetheless did create problems for Moscow as well.

Apart from the problems themselves, the most troubling development from the Soviet perspective has been Washington's reaction to them, the main thrust of which is the substantially increased direct U.S. military presence in the Middle East–Gulf region. Prior to his fall, the Shah of Iran had been viewed by Washington as its surrogate in the region, protecting U.S. interests. The Iranian Revolution demonstrated the danger of relying on such surrogates, and hence Washington's decision regarding a direct and permanent American military presence in the area. That decision was reinforced by the hostage crisis and the Soviet invasion of Afghanistan. Although the withdrawal of the Marines from Beirut did represent an American failure, it is important to note that this was only a single incident. More importantly, the withdrawal symbolized the failure of an essentially political policy, not a lack of American military capability in the region. While much has been written about the problems facing the U.S. Central Command, it has conducted extensive exercises in Egypt, and maintains an "over–the–horizon" naval presence in the Indian Ocean. To support that presence, the United States has access to military facilities in Oman, might be able to acquire naval and air facilities in Pakistan, and perhaps would be permitted to operate from Saudi Arabia in an emergency.[31] In the immediate periphery of the Gulf, it has access to the major staging base of Ras Banas in Egypt and military facilities in Somalia. It perhaps would have access to such facilities in the Sudan, and almost certainly in Israel, in an emergency. Further to the South, the United States has leasing arrangements in Kenya and is developing the British Island of Diego Garcia into a major military base.[32]

The seriousness of Washington's efforts to establish and develop a permanent and direct, albeit over–the–horizon, military presence in the region is demonstrated by substantial growth in the U.S. military budget under the Reagan Administration. A significant portion of that budget is allocated to the development of forces capable of operating in Southwest Asia, as well as to the network of bases just referred to.[33] Thus, the fact that Washington's Lebanese venture failed will by no means remove genuine Soviet concern regarding the American military presence in the Middle East–Gulf region. There are several specific reasons for this. For one thing, that presence, part of which consists of nuclear submarines, poses a strategic threat that the Soviets take seriously.[34] Also a permanent U.S. naval presence in the Indian Ocean poses problems for Moscow at the non–nuclear level. Given the Soviet Union's relatively underdeveloped land communications between the Asiatic and European parts of the country, the sea lanes of communications uniting these two regions take on great importance. Clearly, during any extended superpower crisis a substantial U.S. naval presence in the Indian Ocean would be a major threat to those sea lanes and therefore to Soviet interests. Even during non–crisis periods, an American naval presence negatively affects the regional balance–of–power from the Soviet perspective by inhibiting Soviet initiatives that otherwise might be taken.

In addition to a naval presence, the United States participates in the multinational peacekeeping force that was deployed in the Sinai after April 1982, when Israeli troops were withdrawn from the area in accord with the Egyptian–Israeli Treaty of 1979. Notwithstanding the small numbers involved, American troops are on the ground in the region. Also, in spite of the Marines' withdrawal from Lebanon, a Soviet source noted that whenever the Israelis undertake aggression, U.S. troops either replace the Israelis (the Sinai) or supplement them (Lebanon).[35] The notion of U.S.–Israeli cooperation regularly leading to an expansion of America's military presence in the region, however incrementally, cannot be welcomed in Moscow.

Yet another negative development for the Soviets is the institutionalization of military cooperation between the United States and some Persian Gulf states. Whereas in May of 1981, Oman's proposal that Washington play a major security role in the region was rejected by the other members of the Gulf Cooperation Council (Saudi Arabia, Kuwait, Qatar, Bahrein, and the United Arab Emirates),[36] by the late Spring of 1982, U.S.–Arab military cooperation for defense, motivated by the Iraqi–Iranian war, became institutionalized to a significant degree. This was especially so in connection with the emergence of a coordinated air–defense system based on U.S. AWACS (Airborne Warning and Control Systems) and carrier battle groups.[37]

Even if U.S. military power deployed in the region were totally passive, the potential for its use would be troublesome for the Soviets. When Washington *actually* employs force, the negative implications of America's military presence in the region for the Soviet Union are sharply underscored. The Reagan Administration's willingness to use military power has been demonstrated by the shooting down of two Libyan planes in the Gulf of Sidra in August 1981, the invasion of Grenada, and the Marine deployment in Lebanon. Inherent in the Lebanese crisis in late 1983 and early 1984 was the potential for an even greater use of U.S. military power than was actually brought to bear against Syria, the Soviet Union's principal "client" in the region. Had such force been employed,

Moscow would have been in the difficult position of choosing between unattractive alternatives: protecting Syria, which would have involved directly confronting the United States, or in effect abandoning Damascus, which would have seriously weakened Moscow's influence with Syria, and therefore Soviet influence in the region in general.

The Soviets had already been placed in an analogous position in 1982, when they remained inactive while the Israelis administered substantial defeats to Syrian forces and the PLO, Moscow's two chief sources of influence in the Middle East. The PLO must have seriously questioned the value of its relationship with Moscow when it had to turn to the Americans, not the Soviets, to extricate itself from the Israeli siege of Beirut. As for Soviet–Syrian relations, there were public, albeit indirect, recriminations. In replying to Arab critics who attributed the poor performance of the PLO and Syria to the inferior quality of Soviet weaponry, TASS reprinted portions of a Jordanian newspaper editorial, which noted that Soviet weapons had been good enough to enable the Vietnamese to defeat the Americans.[38]

To return to 1983, the situation was potentially much more threatening, because Moscow faced the possiblity of a direct confrontation, not with the Israelis, but with the United States itself. The extent to which the Soviets wanted to avoid such a confrontation is suggested by a Western report on Soviet–Syrian discussions in the Fall of 1983. On at least two occasions,

> Damascus . . . sought guarantees of Soviet military support. The first request was made, according to reliable sources, during the Druse–Lebanese army fighting in the Shuf Mountains in September 1983, when U.S. firepower directly supported Beirut's units. After the truck–bomb attack on the U.S. Marine Corps headquarters in Beirut one month later, the Syrians again asked the Soviets how Moscow would react if Syria countered American retaliatory attacks on Syrian targets by taking action against the U.S. fleet. Moscow told Syria to stay calm.[39]

That admonition must have raised questions in Damascus about Moscow's willingness to protect Syria from the other superpower. To raise questions about a relationship is to weaken it. Therefore, America's military presence in the region must sow doubt in Damascus about Soviet support, thereby creating problems for Moscow in its relations with Damascus. On the other hand, America's military presence increases Syria's need for Soviet support. Thus, the Syrians' attitude towards the Soviets must be that although we cannot do without you, you are not as valuable to us as you ought to be.

For their part, the Soviets evidently have different levels of commitment to Syria, depending upon the situation. The same Western source quoted above reports that

> . . . during private informal talks with Western visitors in Moscow, Soviet officials have said that they were not committed to defend Syrian forces against Israeli attacks in Lebanon. But the Soviets added that if Syria were attacked, the USSR would use its military power . . . .[40]

Moscow's major commitment to the defense of Syrian territory can be explained largely by the fact that currently it is through Syria that the Soviet Union can best retain some influence in the Middle East.[41] Therefore even the vaguest indication that Damascus might stray from the Soviet orbit must be viewed with sharp concern in Moscow. Relevant here is one Western analysis of Syrian policy in the summer and fall of 1982, which tentatively concluded that Damascus was making efforts "to broaden the dialogue with the United States." Evidence for this conclusion included the fact that Syria's Foreign Minister accompanied his Saudi counterpart on a visit to Washington in July. Also, Damascus was regularly accessible to Philip Habib, the U.S. mediator in the Lebanese crisis, and Syria was represented in the joint Arab delegation that met with President Reagan after the September Arab summit meeting in Fez.[42] Clearly Syria was demonstrating a willingness to negotiate with Washington. Indeed, in early 1984, Donald Rumsfeld, Habib's successor as America's mediator in the Lebanese crisis, did engage in talks with the Syrians.[43] While Damascus might have consulted with Moscow before undertaking these moves, it had in the past frequently acted independently of the Soviet Union and might have been doing so in 1982 and 1984. If this was the case, it was an unwelcome development for Moscow, in that it could have resulted in progress towards peace, with the Soviets again being excluded from participation in the process.

Progress in U.S.–Syrian affairs was not forthcoming, however, and soon it was clear that the May 17th agreement, Washington's major initiative after the rejection of the Reagan Plan, was also meeting resistance. A Soviet source observed that Washington had hoped Syria might be persuaded to improve relations with the United States and stop opposing the May 17th agreement in return for a vague American promise that a Syrian troop withdrawal from Lebanon could lead to discussions on the Golan. The Soviet source noted with satisfaction that Syria had rejected this.[44] Nonetheless, it is likely that Syria's flirtation with the

United States was unsettling for the Soviet Union.

There can be little doubt, then, that Washington's response to the salient events occurring in the region since 1978 has created substantial problems for Moscow. The major thrust of that response has been the establishment of a direct and permanent U.S. military presence in the Middle East–Gulf region. The negative implications of that presence for Moscow stem from an enhanced nuclear threat against the Soviet Union; the potential threat to Soviet sea lanes; a potential alteration of the regional balance–of–power; American troops, albeit in small numbers, on the ground in the area; the institutionalization of military cooperation between the United States and some Gulf states; the problems created by the use of American power, including the potential for a direct U.S.–Soviet confrontation, as well as the possibility of generating tensions in Soviet–Syrian relations; and finally, Syria's momentary flirtation with the United States in 1982. The length of this list by itself demonstrates that the deployment of a permanent U.S. military presence in the Middle East–Gulf region is a substantial negative development for the Soviet Union. The importance of the issues reinforces that conclusion.

IV

Three large issues have been addressed thus far: Soviet perceptions of America's goals in the region; Moscow's assessment of the limited degree to which Washington is realizing those aims; and yet a genuine Soviet concern elicited by events in the area and America's reaction to them, most especially Washington's commitment to a direct, permanent American military presence in the area. Those three issues, the Soviet Union's own goals, and the zero–sum–game orientation of both superpowers define the context within which Soviet Middle East policy is formulated. Moscow's goals include preventing the United States from decreasing Soviet influence in the area; preventing an increase, and, if possible, effecting a decrease, in American power in the region; and increasing its own influence there. Currently, the three key regional states to which the Soviets must address themselves in pursuit of these goals are Israel, Egypt and Syria.

Moscow analyzes Israel's foreign policy within the context of the U.S.–Israeli alliance. Although the Soviets perceive that alliance as basically strong, it has its strains. It became clear after the signing of the Egyptian–Israeli Treaty that Washington and Tel Aviv differed over how to resolve the Palestinian problem, a divergence that was reinforced by Israel's rejection of the Reagan Plan. More recently, the Israelis have been disillusioned by the May 17 agreement and its fate. A close advisor to Moshe Arens, then the Israeli Defense Minister, is reported to have described as "absolutely bizarre" a letter concerning that agreement from President Reagan to the Israelis. According to Aren's advisor:

> Reagan started out by saying he was strengthening the United States' . . . commitment in Lebanon . . . by retreating from Beirut. This means, of course, that we can never trust any written agreement between us and another Arab country that has been pushed by the Americans. The U.S. forced that May 17th agreement. Now it is like the U.S. abolishing its *own* contract.[45]

Clearly then, significant strains exist in U.S.-Israeli relations. The interests of Washington and Tel Aviv are not identical.

However, in spite of strains in the U.S.-Israeli relationship, Moscow sees Israel as the pivotal state in America's Middle East policy. This was reflected in an article by Bovin, who accurately attributed to the then Secretary of State, Alexander Haig, four key ideas regarding the Middle East-Gulf region: 1) the area is a single strategic entity; 2) the Soviet Union is the main threat to regional stability; 3) the Arabs have to move towards reconciliation with Israel and support for the Camp David process to foster the common goal of avoiding Soviet domination; and 4) the United States is prepared to guarantee regional security, but this requires an expanded American military presence in the region.[46] That the burden of reconciliation was placed on the Arabs, not the Israelis, demonstrated the latter's overriding importance to Washington's Middle East policy. Moscow, then, has to view Israel as an instrument of American policy that Washington can not afford to weaken in any basic way, notwithstanding some U.S.-Israeli tensions that have arisen both before and after Haig's tenure as Secretary of State.

Thus, it is not surprising that Moscow's Radio Peace and Progress, broadcasting in Hebrew to Israel, reacted with skepticism towards what it called leaks from official, but anonymous, Israeli sources suggesting that Israeli Prime Minister Shamir had twice appealed for contacts with the Soviet Union. We have the impression, Radio Peace and Progress said, that those leaks are motivated solely by a desire

> to divert public opinion from the promotion of strategic cooperation between Israel and the United States. But it is a well known fact that the U.S.-Israeli pact is directly aimed against the Soviet Union and the sovereignty and interests of the

Middle Eastern and African nations. It also conflicts with the vital interests of Israel, whose territory is becoming an arsenal for the United States.[47]

Indeed, the U.S.-Israeli allance *is* aimed against the Soviet Union. Among its goals is the deterrence of Soviet expansionism in the Middle East-Gulf region and a reduction of Soviet influence in the area by precluding Moscow from any meaningful role in the Middle East peace process. Hence the statement by Radio Peace and Progress, that "the U.S.-Israeli pact is aimed against the Soviet Union" focuses on an issue of substantial importance for Moscow. The statement also demonstrates the importance of identifying the interests of the Third World with those of the Soviet Union. Hence, the claim that "the sovereignty and interests of Middle Eastern and African nations" are also threatened by the same U.S.-Israeli pact that is aimed against the Soviet Union. Radio Peace and Progress, then, was reflecting two basic Soviet concerns: 1) Washington's continuing efforts to deny Moscow what the latter perceives to be its legitimate right, both as a superpower and as a nation bordering on the region, to exercise influence in the area; and 2) the long-standing effort by Moscow to inculcate in the minds of Third World peoples that the Soviet Union and Third World countries have common interests to which those of the United States are antithetical. Therefore, the U.S.-Israeli alliance, which is seen as the basic instrument for denying Moscow and the regional states their legitimate rights, is subjected to heavy and sustained Soviet attacks.

Radio Peace and Progress offered some advice implicitly aimed at the Israeli public. It suggested that "those who point to Shamir's proposals" regarding contacts with the Soviet Union should accept the fact that

it is impossible to get out of the political stalemate . . . by way of a military buildup . . . . A just peace . . . can be attained only if the IDF [Israeli Defense Forces] . . . withdraws from all . . . Arab territories conquered since 1967, and if the rights of all countries in the region, including Israel, . . . are secured in an independent, sovereign existence.

No separate deals could result in a comprehensive settlement . . . . The regional crisis can only be resolved through . . . an international conference with the participation of the Soviet Union, the United States, and all interested parties, including the PLO as the only legitimate representative of the Palestinian nation.[48]

Thus, the message of Radio Peace and Progress to Israeli public opinion was that if Israeli citizens want the Soviet Union to contribute to a solution of the Arab–Israeli conflict, then Tel Aviv must do four things: (1) draw back from its strategic alliance with Washington; (2) abandon the military option; (3) withdraw from all occupied Arab territories; and (4) seek a political solution through an international conference, which would enhance Soviet prestige, authority and influence in the region, through its participation on a par with the United States.

Given Israeli hostility towards and suspicion of the Soviet Union, there can be little expectation in Moscow that Tel Aviv would accept these conditions. Therefore, Israel will not be interested in any serious contacts or accommodation with the Soviet Union, notwithstanding any hints to the contrary. Indeed, in the Soviet view the basic soundness of the U.S.–Israeli alliance reinforces Tel Aviv's rigidity (including, paradoxically, Israel's rejection of the Reagan Plan).[49] Israel's rigidity is strengthened by a willingness to use force, which has been demonstrated several times. Moreover, that willingness might increase in the future. According to one Western analysis, Tel Aviv's withdrawal from the Sinai has increased the possibility of an Israeli pre–emptive strike against Egypt, if at some point it appears that the latter might attack Israel. The argument is that even before the withdrawal from the Sinai, "Israel felt after 1973 that it was not able to risk absorbing an Egyptian attack before moving to a counter offensive. The withdrawal . . . has reduced the margin of safety . . . and thereby lowered the threshold of Israeli preemption."[50]

The Soviet assessment of Israeli foreign policy as rigid and aggressive has important, conflicting, *practical* implications for the Soviet Union. On the one hand, Israeli rigidity and aggressiveness are positive factors from Moscow's perspective because they make the Soviet Union more valuable than it otherwise would be to the Arab states. On the other hand, Israeli policy creates serious problems for Moscow, an example of which is the strains elicited in Soviet–Syrian and Soviet–PLO relations as a result of the Israeli attack in Lebanon in 1982. Given this unpromising assessment of Tel Aviv's policies, especially within the context of what is perceived by Moscow to be a basically strong U.S.–Israeli alliance, it is unlikely that the Soviets see any opportunity for radical *demarches* in their own policy towards Israel.[51]

Although Moscow's assessment of Egypt must yield a substantially less clear picture than the above assessment of Israel——because from the Soviet perspective there are positive as well as negative aspects in the current Egyptian situation——Moscow's opportunities in its relations with Cairo are perhaps more modest than they appear. This is so in spite of the recent re-establishment of diplomatic relations between the Soviet Union and Egypt.[52] Nonetheless, there have been some positive developments from the Soviet perspective. Egypt's ties with the United States might have been placed in some jeopardy as a result of the Iraqi-Iranian war. An Iranian victory would have major negative consequences not only for Iraq, but for all Arab states. Therefore, as the potential for such a victory seemed to increase, those states saw the need to marshall all Arab forces, including the Arab world's strongest military power, Egypt. Thus, the war brought an end to Egypt's isolation in the Arab world. This, in turn, must be at the very least an irritant in Egyptian-Israeli affairs, because Israel's great gain from the Egyptian-Israeli Treaty of 1979 was precisely the detachment of Egypt from the anti-Israeli coalition of Arab states. Even though Cairo, upon its return to the Arab camp, did not repudiate its relations with Tel Aviv, improved relations between Egypt and other Arab states inevitably must raise Israeli concerns. If these concerns in any significant way heighten Egyptian-Israeli tensions, then Washington's relations with both Cairo and Tel Aviv will necessarily be placed under a strain. The thrust of America's Middle East policy is to increase Egyptian-Israeli cooperation as the core element in a regional framework designed to cope with the Soviet threat.

Whereas the Iraqi-Iranian war could conceivably weaken U.S.-Egyptian relations, the Lebanese crisis has in fact done so. American policy in Lebanon has eroded U.S. credibility, and Egypt's own standing in the Arab world must have suffered through a kind of guilt by association, given its close ties with the United States. Moreover, when visiting Washington in February 1984, President Mubarak is reported to have declared that a Marine withdrawal from Lebanon would be catastrophic. When that withdrawal subsequently took place it surely must have been interpreted in the Arab world, including within Egypt itself, as a sign that Mubarak's influence in Washington is slight, a costly perception for the Egyptian president. Finally, during the same visit Mubarak urged that all Israeli troops be withdrawn from Lebanon, that the United States negotiate directly with the PLO, and that it modify the May 17th agreement.[53] These propositions were unwelcome in Washington, especially given their public articulation, and, unless they were merely for public consumption, must have strained U.S.-Egyptian relations. Thus, as a result of American policy in Lebanon, U.S.-Egyptian relations have been weakened, and the Iraqi-Iranian war might have exacerbated the situation. As for Egypt's standing in the Arab world and Mubarak's position domestically, both have been strengthened by the war, but both have been weakened by American policy in Lebanon. Thus, these two developments might have cancelled each other out as far as their impact on Mubarak's position at home and Egypt's standing in the Arab world are concerned.

Given these developments, it could be argued that Cairo might be amenable to Soviet overtures. Indeed, *Pravda*, although not suggesting a cause and effect relationship, asserted that Egypt has recently expressed a desire for increasing economic cooperation with the Soviet Union.[54] Also, Butrus Ghali, the Egyptian Minister of State for Foreign Affairs, was quoted by a Soviet source to the effect that Egypt's strategic aim was the restoration of diplomatic relations with the Soviet Union,[55] a development that in fact subsequently occurred. Finally, one might speculate that the increased potential of an Israeli pre-emptive attack against Egypt might cause Cairo to seek closer relations with Moscow in the hope of deterring Tel Aviv.

On the other hand, it can be argued that the above developments could have the opposite effect. For example, the Iraqi-Iranian war might strengthen, rather than weaken, U.S.-Egyptian relations. Egypt's resumed participation in Arab affairs, which was elicited by the war, ultimately might have a moderating effect on Arab policies, at least marginally. This, in turn, would mitigate, if not eliminate, Israeli concerns about Cairo's return to the Arab fold, and such a development would tend to strengthen Egypt's relations with the United States. Also, as noted earlier, the war has already led conservative Arab states to increase their military cooperation with the United States. Thus, the overall impact of the Iraqi-Iranian war on U.S. relations with Egypt and the rest of the Arab world not closely tied to Moscow could be positive.

As to whether that positive effect would be sufficient to overcome the strains produced in U.S.-Arab relations by American policy in Lebanon, it is impossible to predict. However, specifically regarding Washington's relations with Cairo, those strains must be seen in the context of substantial mutual dependence between the two capitals. American aid to Egypt is very large. Also, U.S. military participation in the Sinai peace keeping force is important in helping to prevent Israeli-Egyptian tensions from getting out of control, a contribution that serves the interests of Israel, Egypt and the United States. Finally, the commitment of Egypt and the United States to the substantial military cooperation represented by the Bright Star exercises is a measure of the importance of each nation to the other. Regarding any weakening of Egypt's position because of its close association with the United States, that might have been mitigated by Mubarak's recent public distancing of himself from Washington's policies. Also, Washington and Cairo might be able to minimize Arab public attention to the cooperative aspects of their relationship, which would lessen the pressure on Mubarak from radical Arab elements.

Regarding the possibility of an improvement in Egyptian–Soviet relations reflected in increased economic activities, such an increase could occur without corresponding basic shifts in other areas, most especially military relations. The restoration of diplomatic relations, however, is an important change in regional affairs, although not necessarily a fundamental realignment of those affairs. Egyptian Prime Minister Kamal Hassan Ali has said that the decision to re–establish relations with the Soviet Union "would not affect ties to the United States and would not lead to greater Soviet influence in . . . [Egypt]." He stressed that Washington is, and will remain, Cairo's main source of weapons. Also, the state–controlled weekly publication, *News of the Day*, observed that "Egypt would never accept a ' repetition of our previous relationship with the Soviet Union,' which the newspaper described as ' bitter and restrictive to our freedom.' "⁵⁶

Finally, although the increased potential for an Israeli pre–emptive attack on Egypt was possibly one factor leading Cairo to seek closer relations with Moscow, it is unlikely that Egypt will rely heavily on the Soviet Union to deter such an attack. Close Soviet–Syrian and Soviet–PLO ties did not prevent Israel from attacking PLO and Syrian forces in Lebanon. Admittedly, the PLO is not a state. Also, the Israelis did not attack Syria itself, but rather Syrian troops in Lebanon. Nevertheless, the Israelis have sufficiently demonstrated their readiness to use military power when they perceive it as being in their interest to do so. It should be noted that during the war of attrition in 1970, the Israelis did not even shrink from deliberately ' baiting' Soviet fighters and shooting down four MIG–21s (*flown by Soviet pilots*) . . . ."⁵⁷

In light of the foregoing considerations, it is improbable that Moscow sees any possibility of restoring Soviet–Egyptian relations to what they were during the Nasser period. On the other hand, Egypt's policies vis–à–vis the superpowers could evolve *towards* "even–handedness," at least on the surface.

Whatever might develop in Soviet–Egyptian relations, the current focus of Soviet Middle East policy is on Syria. Although Soviet–Syrian interests are not identical, there certainly is a great coincidence between those interests, especially recently. The importance attributed by Moscow to Syria, through which the Soviets have been able to exercise some influence in the region, has increased significantly since the Lebanese crisis of 1982. There are some important reasons for this, which in turn have significant implications for the Soviet–Syrian relationship, and for Syria's role in regional affairs.

At various times during the last fifteen years or so, Soviet–Syrian relations have been characterized by both tension and shared interests. To mention only a few examples of tension, in 1970 the Soviet Union pressured Syria to withdraw from Jordan.[58] In the mid–1970s Moscow opposed Syria's entry into Lebanon during that country's civil war.[59] In late 1980, when Syria concentrated its troops on Jordan's border Damascus did not consult with Moscow. Nor did it do so in April of 1981, when it moved its surface–to–air missiles into Lebanon.[60] Finally, during Israel's attack in Lebanon in 1982, the Soviet Union, according to a well–informed observer, sent arms to Syria for transshipment to the PLO, but Damascus, because it wanted to bring pressure on the latter, "confiscated" the weapons.[61] If that report is correct, it is a striking example of Syrian independence. Nonetheless, the Soviet Union, although it did so only *after* the Syrian–Israeli clashes in Lebanon, massively resupplied Syria with arms and equipment, in spite of the indirect mutual recrimination, noted earlier, between Damascus and Moscow over the issue regarding the quality of Soviet weaponry. Against this background of mutual recrimination and substantial Syrian independence from Moscow, the latter's massive resupplying of Syria underscores the central importance of that country for Soviet Middle East policy. Given Syria's independent behavior and the mutual recrimination, it can be argued persuasively that if Moscow currently viewed Damascus as less than pivotal for Soviet interests in the region, then it might have acted with some restraint in rebuilding Syrian military capabilities.

The foregoing raises the question as to why Damascus is so important to Moscow. There are several reasons, but the chief one is that Syria currently is the main obstacle to the fulfillment of American plans in the Middle East. As has been observed frequently, the central thrust of those plans is to use U.S. military, economic and political influence to achieve a peace settlement, while simultaneously containing, and if possible reducing, Soviet influence in the region. Clearly, Moscow must attempt to frustrate this policy, and therefore the Soviets must destroy or weaken its framework: the Camp David process, the Reagan Plan and the May 17th agreement. Syria, at present, is the best instrument for Moscow's purposes, witness Damascus' success in bringing about the abrogation of the May 17th agreement. In discussing the latter, Brutents, it will be remembered, identified Syria as "the fundamental Arab link in the present situation in opposing U.S.–Israeli plans."[62]

Damascus is as opposed as Moscow to American policy. It was the Camp David process that brought about the Egyptian–Israeli Treaty of 1979, which "decoupled" Egypt from the Arab coalition against Israel. This occurred while Israel still occupied the Golan Heights, thereby leaving Damascus to confront Israel and the United States alone.[63] As for the Reagan Plan, although Syria did not publicly oppose it when it was first announced, Damascus was basically against it. Regarding the May 17th agreement, Damascus totally rejected it, because its implementation would have reduced, if not eliminated, Syrian influence in Lebanon. Also, the agreement might have been followed by successful U.S.–Israeli pressure on Jordan to join the peace process and ultimately sign a treaty with Israel. Such a series of victories for the U.S.–Israeli alliance would have precluded any possibility of Syria regaining the Golan, to say nothing of achieving its aspirations of a greater Syria, which would include portions of Lebanon and Jordan. Therefore, the May 17th agreement had to be abrogated, a result that in fact was effected by Syria's determined manipulation of Lebanon's domestic political–military forces.

The extent to which Moscow is currently committed to supporting Damascus in the latter's opposition to American policy is clearly demonstrated by the Soviet stand on recent Syrian–PLO relations. In the Spring of 1983, radical elements within the PLO were challenging Yasir Arafat's leadership. Bovin has recently analyzed that imbroglio. He suggests that the Palestinian defeat in Beirut brought to the surface two basic positions within the PLO. At one pole there was the "principled rejection of Israel as a state . . . , hence [the commitment to] war until final victory." At the other pole there emerged "a certain pessimism" regarding the establishment of an independent Palestinian state, especially among Arafat's associates. Therefore, "compromises of . . . the Camp David kind," that is, "interim solutions," had to be sought. "I think, [wrote Bovin] that Arafat's tactic was to get the United States to force Israel to return the West Bank to Jordan." Under such a circumstance the chances of the PLO gaining some degree of control over the West bank might be enhanced. The discussion of that prospect was possibly what motivated Arafat to engage in talks with King Hussein of Jordan and later with President Mubarak of Egypt.[64]

Apart from the details of Bovin's analysis, these events led Damascus to fear that the Arafat faction was indeed seeking an accord with Israel that would have been detrimental to Syrian interests. Therefore, Damascus began to mobilize the radicals within the PLO against Arafat,[65] and successfully frustrated any leanings within that organization towards an American approach to the Middle East settlement. As for Moscow, however much it might have regretted the splitting of the PLO, there can be no question but what it totally supported Damascus in the matter. To have done less would have alienated President Assad, who for Moscow is a far more important ally than Arafat. Moreover, Arafat was potentially moving in the direction of an American solution, an anathema to the

Soviet Union. Gromyko told a PLO delegation visiting Moscow in July of 1983 that cooperation is necessary between the PLO and "progressive Arab states," that is, between the PLO and Syria.[66] More recently, Bovin observed that an Israeli withdrawal from the West Bank is unimaginable, hence the only alternative is to strengthen Arab unity. This would increase pressure on Israel; resolve contradictions within the PLO; and improve relations between the PLO and all Arab states, especially those who resolutely oppose Israeli policy (again read Syria here). All of this will be difficult and will not occur immediately, Bovin acknowledged, but the PLO "must somehow restore relations with Syria . . . , adapt . . . to new conditions, and continue the struggle for . . . [Palestinian] national rights."[67] Brutents also strongly implied that Arafat's faction of the PLO will not enjoy Moscow's support, at the expense of Syria, at least in the immediate future. In discussing the result of the Lebanese crisis, he said that "there will be a weakening of those forces who have come to believe in America's omnipotence . . . ."[68] Although this assessment applied to President Gemayel and the conservative Arab states, its scope also included the Arafat faction of the PLO. The message was clear: anyone even inclining towards the U.S. approach to a Middle East settlement will be opposed by Moscow; conversely, those opposing the U.S. formula--and in the present circumstances this means Syria above all others--will enjoy Soviet support.

Evidence of this support for Syria goes well beyond choosing Assad over Arafat. The most conclusive development in this regard was the inclusion of Soviet SA-5 missiles in the massive rearming of Syria by the Soviet Union after the Beirut crisis. Moscow had never previously "transferred this system outside of the Soviet bloc, and, at least for some time to come . . . will have to man the system and its related air defenses . . . ."[69] This has raised Soviet stakes in Syria in a major way because "the SA-5s cover a significant amount of Israeli airspace--and could very directly limit Israeli options-- . . . , [thereby] increasing the likelihood of Israeli pre-emptive strikes against Soviet installations" in a crisis situation.[70] This was a bold Soviet step, and it demonstrates the extent of Moscow's determination to maintain a position in the Middle East through its support of Syria.

The willingness of the Soviet Union to take such a large risk is understandable. It will be recalled that the Soviets stood by while their two main sources of influence in the region--Syria and the PLO--absorbed major losses at the hands of the Israelis during the siege of Beirut. The PLO, practically speaking, was destroyed as a military organization and was dispersed throughout the region. Thus, if the

Soviets had abandoned Damascus *after*, as well as having remained passive during, the siege, Moscow would have completely alienated its other chief source of influence in the area, Syria, thereby suffering a further substantial loss.

Syria currently is the best instrument through which Moscow can maintain a position in the heart of the Middle East. Short of another war with Israel, it is unlikely that Egypt will permit itself to be drawn back fully into the Soviet orbit. Similarly, Jordan has little incentive to provide Moscow with a major base of operations, in spite of the recent tension in U.S.-Jordanian relations.[71] As for Iraq, although the Soviets are again supplying Baghdad with arms in its struggle against Iran, it is probable that Moscow will limit its support for Iraq. To do otherwise would destroy whatever remains of the Soviet-Iranian relationship (economic cooperation still exists) for the long-term.[72] Iran is far too important a potential prize for the Soviets to place at risk by supporting Iraq unreservedly. Moreover, the Iraqis themselves see their interests best served by maintaining relations with the West as well as with the East. This has been particularly so in economic affairs, especially since 1973 when the energy crisis brought many petro-dollars into Iraqi coffers, thereby enabling Baghdad to increase its trade with the West very much more rapidly than with the communist world.[73] Its possession of hard currency also enables Iraq to purchase arms from Western sources, thereby reducing its dependence on the Soviets in this area as well.[74] Therefore, there will be no striking improvement in Soviet-Iraqi affairs.

With Egypt, Jordan and Iraq being unlikely candidates, Syria is left as the major country in the geographic heart of the region through which Moscow can pursue its interests. This, in turn, cannot fail to have an impact on the nature of the Soviet-Syrian relationship. *Relatively* speaking, influence in this "senior partner-client" relationship has shifted in Syria's favor. This is not to say that prior to the Beirut crisis Syria had never exercised any independence from Moscow. It has already been noted that on more than one occasion Damascus has pursued its own interests, even though the actions involved sometimes were taken without consulting Moscow, sometimes were opposed by the Soviets, and on one occasion reportedly even frustrated Moscow's own policy (the confiscation by Syria of the Soviet arms intended for the PLO). However, because Syria has emerged from the Lebanese crisis with its authority in the region and its usefulness to Moscow greatly increased, there will be a tendency for the Syrians to be still more assertive vis-à-vis the Soviets. This is not an argument that suggests Syrian-Soviet equality, but Syria certainly has become "more equal" than before. It was not Moscow, but Damascus (as well as the terrorists who blew up the U.S. Marine compound in Beirut) who made a shambles of American policy in Lebanon by forcing the abrogation of the May 17th agreement. This not only frustrated Washington's policy in Lebanon, but also was a severe blow to American credibility throughout the region, a point discussed earlier.

The great importance publicly attributed by the Soviet Union to Syria's role in the region further supports the hypothesis that Damascus' leverage with Moscow has increased. This was reflected in a week-long visit to Moscow by a Syrian delegation in August of 1983. In the talks held during that visit, Soviet-Syrian opposition to the May 17th agreement was underscored.[75] Subsequent to the abrogation of the agreement, Moscow television gave credit to Syria for supporting the National Patriotic Forces in Lebanon, who resisted the agreement.[76] Moreover, *Izvestiia* wrote that Assad personally deserves credit for Syria's leadership in rallying the Arabs for an anti-imperialist "just and comprehensive solution to the Middle East conflict" and for "wrecking U.S.-Israeli hopes of imposing capitulationist solutions and separate deals on the Arabs."[77] Moscow's commitment to Damascus, then, was reflected in the choice of Assad over Arafat, the massive rearmament of Syria, including the deployment of the SA-5s in Syria, and the public praise lavished on Syria and its president.

Perhaps precisely because of the magnitude of that commitment (which underscores a degree of Soviet dependence on Syria) Damascus apparently continues to be an unruly "client." A strong hint of this came in a Radio Moscow broadcast to the Arab world. The commentator noted that the Soviet-Syrian Treaty of 1980 provides for regular consultations where "friendly and *frank* views are exchanged on questions between the two sides [and on] the Middle East."[78] In communist parlance, a reference to "frank" exchanges is a reference to conflicting views. That is, Damascus is arguing its positions with considerable vigor and perhaps with increasing effectiveness.

Hence, Syria's situation has dramatically improved since, say, 1980 when it signed a treaty with the Soviet Union. Among Syria's motivations for concluding that treaty was the extent to which Damascus was then isolated in the Arab world.[79] By the middle of 1984, Syria's stature had risen not only with its Arab neighbors, but also with the Soviet Union, for whom Damascus had become clearly the most important vehicle for pursuing Moscow's interests in the heart of the Middle East.

V

Given Moscow's assessment of Israel, Egypt and Syria, what policies towards these three key regional states are the Soviets likely to follow in the near future? Informed speculation about this question requires an appreciation of the context within which those policies will be formulated. Elements of that context include: 1) Moscow's assessment not only of the three states themselves, but also of U.S. goals, successes and failures in the region; 2) Moscow's conviction that Washington sees the Soviet–American relationship in the Middle East as a zero–sum game; 3) Moscow's own zero–sum orientation towards that relationship; and 4) Soviet goals in the region.

In light of the zero–sum orientation of both Washington and Moscow, the latter's most immediate goal is to prevent the United States from achieving its aim of decreasing Soviet influence in the Middle East. This requires the frustration of the Camp David process and other American initiatives.

Regarding potential Soviet policies towards Israel as ways of frustrating Washington's plans, a positive development for Moscow would be an improvement in Soviet–Israeli relations, which by definition would mitigate the threat posed by the U.S.–Israeli alliance. In an attempt to achieve such an improvement, the Soviets could offer to re–establish diplomatic relations with Israel, which were severed by Moscow after the 1967 War. However, this obviously would be detrimental to Soviet–Arab relations. Moreover, the prospects for a genuine improvement in Soviet–Israeli relations, even if formal diplomatic ties were to be restored, are minimal in the Soviet view, precisely because of the U.S.–Israeli alliance. That alliance is seen by Moscow as basically sound and inflexibly directed against the Soviet Union. This presents Moscow with a significant problem, because Israeli foreign policy in the past has placed the Soviets in the position of deciding to what extent they should support their "clients", when the latter are under Israeli military attack.

Because of this rather grim picture of Israeli policy, Moscow must see little or no opportunity for any basic Soviet initiative towards Israel. In fact, an American State Department official recently observed, although not for attribution, that the United States has been trying privately to engage the Soviets on the Middle East problem, but that Moscow will not even talk with the Israeli government.

Notwithstanding their unwillingness to talk with the Israelis, a major concern of the Soviets is to prevent a Syrian–Israeli conflict into which the Soviet Union could be drawn, especially given the deployment in Syria of Soviet–manned SA–5 missiles. Should such a conflict occur, the Soviet commitment to support Damascus in the defense of Syrian territory would be put to the test. The choice for the Soviets would be (a) to remain passive while their "client" *and Soviet missile crews* were under attack; (b) to provide unlimited arms supplies to the Syrians during the conflict and simultaneously threaten to intervene with their own forces; or (c) to actually engage the Israelis directly, thereby risking escalation to a superpower confrontation, given the U.S.-Israeli alliance. Option (a) would decrease Soviet influence, both in the region and generally. Option (b) could have the same effect, if the Soviets were to fail to follow through with their threat to intervene with their own forces. Option (c) is too dangerous. The Soviets have already demonstrated that they would much prefer to avoid having to make such a choice.

Therefore, one can expect that Soviet policy towards Israel will consist chiefly of hostile propaganda, interspersed with more measured pronouncements, such as the Radio Peace and Progress statement, designed to generate opposition within Israeli public opinion to aggressive Israeli policies.[80] Simultaneously, and more importantly, Moscow almost certainly will caution Syria against adopting high-risk policies vis-à-vis Israel.

Regarding Egypt, bringing that country back into the Soviet orbit would be a stunning victory for Soviet policy. Egypt would be a great prize for Moscow, for if it were to end its orientation to the West, that would mean a reversal, not merely a termination, of the Camp David process. On the other hand, a Soviet policy designed to entice and/or pressure Egypt to re-establish strong ties with Moscow (i.e., to go well beyond the re-establishing of formal diplomatic relations) could complicate Soviet-Syrian relations, given Egyptian-Syrian hostility. A major cause of that hostility is the desire of both Cairo and Damascus to be the preeminent regional power. Therefore, excessive Soviet attention, concessions or support for one of these states would almost certainly be seen by the other as detrimental to its own interests. Thus, the re-establishing of diplomatic relations between the Soviet Union and Egypt will have to be managed carefully by Moscow to avoid creating major problems with Damascus.

Improved Soviet-Egyptian relations could also exacerbate already existing Egyptian-Israeli tensions, thereby increasing regional instability. Much has been written about the advantages to the Soviet Union of such instability, but there is a threshold beyond which turbulence becomes a liability for Moscow. For one thing, turbulence has direct costs for Moscow, a fact demonstrated earlier.[81] Second, as turbulence increases, so too does unpredictability in a general way, a condition the Soviets are most uncomfortable with. Paradoxically, however, there is something that is reasonably predictable in the generally unpredictable Middle East-Gulf region. As regional turbulence increases, the probability of a continuing and possibly increasing U.S. military presence in the area also increases, a prospect harmful to Soviet interests.

Notwithstanding these serious potential difficulties, if Moscow were to see the "decoupling" of Egypt from the United States as feasible, it would be prepared to expend major efforts and resources to achieve this, given the magnitude of the potential gains. The problem from the Soviet perspective at this juncture and for the foreseeable future is that no rational Egyptian leader could choose a binding relationship with Moscow over a close relationship with Washington. Even considering Washington's decreased credibility in the region, the advantages of a close relationship with the United States over one with the USSR are considerable. Whatever military aid Moscow can offer, Washington can match and possibly exceed. The disparity is still greater in the economic sphere. Regarding the political dimension, Arab anti–Americanism, admittedly useful to Moscow, is offset by the fact that the Soviets have less capacity than the Americans to mitigate Israeli policy toward the Arabs. All that Moscow can provide in this regard is anti–Israeli propaganda, which it already produces in great quantities. Given these military, economic and political realities, Cairo will most likely follow a policy designed to improve relations with the Soviet Union only up to, but not beyond, the point where such an improvement would threaten in any basic way Egyptian–U.S. relations.

Thus, we come to Syria. The burden of what has been said in this essay about Soviet Middle East policy is that Damascus will be the main avenue along which Moscow will pursue its interests in the region for the foreseeable future. The reasons for this are three: Moscow and Damascus share the goals of frustrating present American policy in the region; Syria's current preeminence in the area; and the probability that Egypt will avoid being drawn back fully into the Soviet orbit. The foregoing has dictated two things: Moscow's unreserved support for Syria in the latter's opposition to Washington's policies and Moscow's strong commitment to defending Syrian territory, possibly even with Soviet military power. In effect, the Soviets are saying to the Syrians, we will protect your home territory, while you pursue our mutual interests in frustrating American policy, provided you do not drag us into a military imbroglio with Israel, which in turn could escalate to a superpower confrontation.

Two final points about Soviet policy in the Middle East ought to be kept firmly in mind. First, the Soviet commitment to being a major actor in the region will be maintained. This is clear from the fact that Moscow's very large, and relatively risky, investment in Syria has been made in the historical context of serious failures in Egypt in 1972 and Iraq in the mid–1970s, after similar large Soviet investments had been made in each country. Moscow persists! Second, the Soviets are flexible, witness what has just been said. That is, they will attempt to exercise their influence

through whatever vehicle is available at the given time. If radical changes
occur within Syria, or within the region in general, which substantially
reduce either Syria's own influence in the region or Moscow's influence
with Syria, then the Soviets will seek other instruments of policy. This is
implicit in Brutent's phrase that Syria is "the fundamental link *in the
present situation* in opposing U.S.–Israeli plans.[32]

VI

What does all of the foregoing portend for peace in the Middle East?
Peace is not an abstract phenomenon in international affairs. It does or
does not exist between particular nation states, and in the case of the
Middle East, the PLO, as well. Therefore, to assess the prospects for
peace in the region, the capabilities and desires of the actors have to be
identified. Regarding the superpowers, one would have to agree with the
Soviet assessment that Washington's ability to effect a solution of the
Middle East conflict has been diminished as a result of its loss of
credibility. As for Soviet influence in the region, it is essentially negative.
That is, Moscow has a significant, indirect capability to prevent a solution,
through supporting, for example, Syria whose demands evidently are
unacceptable to Washington and the regional states. The Soviets, on the
other hand, have little ability to bring about peace. To some extent this is
because of Washington's policy, which has been quite effective in
excluding Moscow from the peace process. However, even if it were not
excluded from that process, Moscow does not control the regional actors,
including, and maybe even especially, Syria. Hence it is not clear that the
Soviets could effect progress, even if they were committed to what the
Americans would consider a constructive contribution.

　　This brings us to a consideration of the regional states. No single one
of them is powerful enough to impose upon the region its solution to the
Palestinian problem, which itself is used in the struggle between the
regional states for military and political preeminence. The volatility of
this struggle brings about frequent realignments in the region. That
volatility and those realignments are but reflections of the region's
dominant characteristic: the demands of each of the regional states
vis–à–vis the others tend to be maximalist, which precludes meaningful
and lasting compromise. Without the latter, solutions will not be
forthcoming, unless they are imposed by force. But to reiterate, no
regional state has sufficient power to impose a comprehensive solution,
and it is far too dangerous, and in any event folly in the long run, for
either of the superpowers to do so.

The foregoing analysis suggests that no significant progress towards a comprehensive Middle East peace can be made until two key conditions are met. First, the key regional actors will have to see it as being more in their interests to reduce their maximalist demands than to permit the situation to remain unresolved, with all of the dangers attendant upon continuing outbreaks of violence, any one of which could lead to a superpower confrontation. Relevant here is the probability that the Israeli threshold for a pre–emptive attack against Egypt has been lowered. Also, relevant in the same regard is the deployment of the Soviet–manned SA–5 missiles in Syria. Second, the United States must permit the Soviet Union to play some kind of role in the peace process, because although Moscow does not have an absolute veto over the peace agreement, Syria for all practical purposes does. A substantial measure of Syria's strength, which gives it that veto, derives from the political and military support it receives from the Soviet Union. The latter certainly will not continue to provide such support, if Syria gives any real indication of adopting an American approach to a settlement. Such a settlement, incidentally, would require significant concessions from Israel, an unlikely development, considering the current policies of both Israel and the United States. Therefore, it is extremely unlikely that Syria will abandon its Moscow connection. This, in turn *does* provide the Soviets with an indirect veto over the peace process, as long as Syria has the capacity to frustrate that process.

Of the two prerequisites for peace, a moderation of the maximalist demands of the regional states is the substantially more important one. Unfortunately, there is little in recent developments to elicit optimism in this regard. As for the superpowers, the negative Soviet task of preventing agreement on American terms is far easier to achieve than the American one of bringing about peace. While the prospects of U.S.–Soviet cooperation in the interests of peace are slightly less grim than those of the regional states reducing their maximalist demands, those prospects certainly cannot be described as promising. This almost surely will be the case while the Reagan Administration remains in office. Moreover, even when the Carter Administration undertook a move in that direction, by publishing the Soviet–U.S. Joint Statement on the Middle East (October 1, 1977), pressures from both Israel and Egypt caused Washington to abandon the initiative almost immediately.[33]

Recent developments, then, have decreased the chances for peace and increased the dangers in the region. These developments include: America's decreased influence in the area; the Soviet Union's continuing determination to play an important role in the region, and its essentially negative power and orientation towards a peace settlement, which will continue as long as Washington is successful in excluding Moscow from the peace process; the negligible prospects for U.S.-Soviet cooperation, due to the zero-sum game orientation of both superpowers; the regional struggle for power, which has deep historical roots, and which can be, and is, exacerbated by the exploitation of the Palestinian problem; the insufficient power of any one of the regional states to impose a solution, combined with the maximalist demands of each of those states; and the increased fragility of the region because of (a) the possibly lower Israeli threshold for pre-emptive attack, and (b) the increased risk of a Soviet-Israeli, and possibly Soviet-U.S., confrontation, given the Soviet-manned SA-5s in Syria.

Hence, the outlook for the future is bleak, unless one or more of the actors prove to have sufficient vision, will and statesmanship to move the others towards a solution that will be less than totally satisfactory to all. Such genuine compromise will not occur until the increasing dangers inherent in rigid stances are perceived, both by the superpowers and the regional states, to outweigh the presumed advantages of pursuing maximalist demands.

Notes

1. The main reason for the "spillover" to the Gulf is that it and the Middle East are really sub-regions of a single, larger geostrategic area--the Middle East-Persian Gulf-Indian Ocean region--which comprises these two sub-regions plus Southwest Asia. Frequently, an event in one of the sub-regions influences developments in one, or both, of the other sub-regions. This "linkage" deserves systematic analysis that is not undertaken here, where the focus is on the Middle East, as the latter is narrowly defined in the text.

2. Use of the term "the Soviet judgement" is not meant to suggest an absence of debate in the formulation of Soviet policy. Indeed, my own view is that the Soviet political system is characterized by a kind of quasi-interest group politics, which, although different in substantial ways from Western group politics, is not totally dissimilar to the latter. Nonetheless, the Soviet political process does produce decisions, and the term "the Soviet judgement" is used in this essay simply as a shorthand device referring to those decisions, not the process through which they were arrived at.

3. G. M. Sturua, "The United States Reliance on 'Ocean Strategy'" *SShA*, No. 11, 1982, pp. 32-42, USSR Report, U.S.A.: Economics, Politics, Ideology, Foreign Broadcast Information Service,

4/4/83, p. 46.

4. I have discussed this point in my *Soviet Perceptions of the Oil Factor in U.S. Foreign Policy: The Middle East- Gulf Region* (Boulder, Colorado: Westview Press, 1983), pp. ix-x.

5. Vladimir Tsvetov, "The World Today" (Moscow Television Service), 2/28/84, reported in Daily Report, Foreign Broadcast Information Service, 2/29/84, p. H4. (Hereafter *FBIS*.)

6. V. Viktorov (review of Borisov, *U.S. Near East Policy in the 1970s*), *Mirovaia ekonimika i mezhdunarodnye otnosheniia*, No. 2, 1983, pp. 154-155. (Hereafter, *MEMO*).

7. See, for example, A. Bovin, "A Political Observer's Opinion: Meager Results," *Izvestiia* (morn. ed.), 4/15/81, p. 4, reported in *FBIS*, 4/22/81, p. A4.

8. Sawyer, *op. cit.*, p. 37.

9. Nimrod Novik, "The United States," in Mark Heller (ed.) with Dov Tamari and Zeev Eytan, *The Middle East Military Balance: 1983* (Tel Aviv: Tel Aviv University, Jaffee Center for Strategic Studies, 1983), p. 51.

Alfred L. Atherton, Jr., former Assistant Secretary of State for Near East and South Asia, has recently addressed this issue of conflicting priorities held by Washington and Arab States. He writes that Washington made efforts "to insulate the Middle East from Soviet inroads and preserve Western hegemony in the region. While work continued on aspects of the Arab-Israeli conflict, American policy focused increasingly on the role of the Middle East in U.S. global strategy vis-à-vis the Soviet Union . . . . Egypt and the other Arab countries, however, saw Israel as a greater threat than the Soviet Union." What is so striking about this passage in the context of our discussion is that Atherton was writing about the *early 1950s*. Admittedly, the parallel between the situation of thirty years ago with that of today can be overemphasized. For one thing, as Atherton points out, America's Middle East policy during those thirty years has fluctuated between a focus on "global strategy", on the one hand, and a regional approach, on the other. Nonetheless, the length of time over which Washington and the Arabs have held their conflicting views over which is the greater threat--the Soviet Union or Israel--is instructive, for it shows how deeply ingrained those perceptions are. (Alfred L. Atherton, Jr., "Arabs, Israelis--and Americans: a Reconsideration," *Foreign Affairs*, Summer 1984, pp. 1195-1196.)

10. Novik, *op. cit.*, p. 57.

11. V. S. Zorin, K. N. Brutents, A. Y. Bovin, "Studio 9" (Moscow Television Service), reported in *FBIS*, 2/27/84, p. CC12.

Brutents is a Deputy Chief of the International Department of the Central
Committee of the Communist Party of the Soviet Union.

12.   Lucinda Franks, "Israel after Lebanon," *The New York
Times Magazine*, 3/25/84, p. 38.

13.   Zorin, Brutents, Bovin, *op. cit.,* p. CC12.

14.   Sawyer, *op. cit.,* p. 60.

15.   Zorin, Brutents, Bovin, *op. cit.,* p. CC12.

16.   G. I. Gerasimov, N. I. Yefimov, V. S. Sobolev,
"International Observers Round Table," Radio Moscow, 2/26/84, reported
in *FBIS*, 2/27/84, p. CC7.

17.   Zorin, Brutents, Bovin, *op. cit.,* p. CC12.

18.   Radio Moscow, 3/4/84, reported in *FBIS*, 3/5/84, p. CC5.

19.   Zorin, Brutents, Bovin, *op. cit.,* p. CC13.

20.   *Ibid.,* p. CC10.

21.   Konstantin Gevandov, "Political Observers Opinion: In the
Front Line of Struggle," *Izvestiia*, 4/27/84, p. 5, reported in *FBIS*, 5/1/84,
p. H2.

22.   *Pravda*, through its Cairo correspondent, reported Mubarak's
demands that: 1) the United States guarantee PLO participation in
resolving the Palestinian problem; 2) Israel unconditionally withdraw its
troops from Lebanon; and 3) the May 17th agreement be modified.
These growing differences between the United States and Egypt, according
to *Pravda's* correspondent, stemmed from "Cairo's ' not entirely
Camp–David like' approach toward U.S.–Israeli policy in the Middle
East." (*Pravda*, 2/25/84, p. 5, reported in *FBIS*, 2/28/84, p. H.3.) On
the other hand, Brutents pointed out that when speaking privately with
Reagan, Mubarak said that a Marine withdrawal would be "catastrophic."
(Zorin, Brutents, Bovin, . . . , p. CC22.) This might suggest that his
"' not entirely Camp–David like' approach" was more for public
consumption than it was reflective of basic policy differences between
Washington and Cairo. Of course, Mubarak might have been sincerely
urging all four points: that 1) the Marines stay; 2) the Israelis leave
unconditionally; 3) the May 17th agreement be modified; and 4)
Washington guarantee public PLO participation in the peace process.

23.   Zorin, Brutents, Bovin, *op. cit.,* p. CC22.

24.   This point and its negative implications for the Soviet Union
are discussed below.

25.   Novick, *op. cit.,* p. 51.

26.   Alvin J. Cottrell (ed.), *Sea Power and Strategy in the Indian
Ocean* (Beverly Hills, Calif.: Alvin J. Cottrell and Associates, Published
in cooperation with the Center for Strategic and International Studies,
Georgetown University [by] Sage Publications, 1981), p. 122.

27. Novick, *op. cit.*, pp. 54–55.

28. Sawyer, *op. cit.*, Chapter 3.

29. For an excellent discussion of Soviet relations with the Khomeini regime see, Zalmay Khalilzad, "Islamic Iran: Soviet Dilemma," *Problems of Communism*, January–February, 1984, pp. 1–20.

30. Sawyer, *op. cit.*, pp. 37–38; 81–82; 92–95.

31. *Ibid.*, p. 57.

32. *Ibid.*

33. *Ibid.*, pp. 58–59.

34. Sturua, *op. cit.*, pp. 38–39; 42; 44–45. This article concerns the debate in the United States on an "ocean strategy." Sturua asserted that Washington is striving to acquire a first strike, counterforce capability that will paralyze the will of the Soviet Union, which must be made to fear escalation more than does the United States. The best weapons system for such a strategy, wrote Sturua, is the Trident II submarine. However, there is the alternative American strategy of a greater commitment to Western Europe. Sturua reported that in spite of the U.S. Navy's increased domestic political influence, the ocean strategy was rejected. Nevertheless, that rejection affords the Soviet Union little comfort. The result, according to Sturua, was not a choice between the Navy, on the one hand, and the Air Force and Army, on the other. Rather, there was a burgeoning of the military budget to accommodate a build–up of all the military services. Thus, it is reasonable to conclude that Sturua's article reflects genuine Soviet concern, not empty propaganda.

35. K. Gevandov, "Links in a Single Chain," *Izvestiia* (morn. ed.), 3/1/84, pp. 4–5, reported in *FBIS*, 3/6/84, p. H5.

36. Heller, *op. cit.*, p. 42.

37. Novik, *op. cit.*, pp. 53–54.

38. TASS, 6/29/82, reported in *FBIS*, 6/30/82, p. H1. See also report by KUNA, 10/21/82, reported in *FBIS*, 10/22/82, p. H4.

39. Zeev Schiff, "Dealing With Syria," *Foreign Policy*, No. 55, Summer, 1984, p. 94.

40. *Ibid.*

41. This assertion is discussed in some detail subsequently.

42. Heller and Novick, p. 49 (see note no. 9).

43. *The New York Times*, 1/12/84, p. 1; 1/14/84, p. 1.

44. "Tekushchie Problemy Mirovoi Politiki," *MEMO*, No. 10, 1983, p. 109.

45. Franks, *op. cit.*

46. A. Bovin, *op. cit.*

47. Moscow Radio Peace and Progress (broadcasting in Hebrew to Israel), 2/28/84, reported in *FBIS*, 3/2/84, p. H7.

48. *Ibid.*

49. Zorin, Brutents, Bovin, *op. cit.*, p. CC10. Israel was also described as expansionist, with its intention to occupy permanently southern Lebanon given as an example. Recently, it has become clear that Israel genuinely wants to withdraw from Lebanon. Thus, this example is perhaps not the best one for Soviet purposes. However, it could be argued that the desire to withdraw simply reflects the failure of the expansionist policy.

50. Heller, *op. cit.*, p. 28.

51. Likely Soviet policies towards Israel in the foreseeable future are discussed in the next section.

52. *The New York Times*, 7/29/84, p. 13.

53. See note no. 22. See also *The New York Times*, 2/15/84, pp. A1, A9; and *Newsweek*, 2/27/84, p. 23.

54. *Pravda*, 2/24/84, p. 4, reported in *FBIS* 3/1/84, p. H5.

55. Boris Kalygin, "The World Today" (Moscow Television Service), 4/26/84, reported in *FBIS*, 5/1/84, p. H4.

56. *The New York Times*, 7/29/84, p. 13. However, it should be noted that the *Times* also reported the following: "Earlier this month the West German newspaper *Die Welt* quoted sources as saying Egypt was interested in buying Soviet surface-to-air missiles. [Egyptian] Foreign Ministry sources said they knew nothing of the report."

57. Lawrence L. Whetten, "The Arab-Israeli Dispute: Great Power Behavior," in Gregory Treverton (ed.), *Crisis Management and the Super Powers in the Middle East* (Montclair, N.J.: Allanheld, Osmun & Co., 1981), p. 62.

58. *The New York Times*, 9/23/70, p. 1; 9/24/70, p. 18.

59. Adeed I. Dawisha, *Syria and the Lebanese Crisis* (New York: St. Martin's Press, 1980), pp. 136–137; *The New York Times*, 5/16/83, p. A6.

60. Heller, *op. cit.*, p. 49.

61. Eric Rouleau, "The Future of the PLO," *Foreign Affairs*, Fall, 1983, p. 146.

62. Zorin, Brutents, Bovin, *op. cit.*, p. CC12.

63. *Ibid.*, p. CC14.

64. *Ibid.*, pp. CC16–CC17.

65. *The New York Times*, 6/25/83, p. 1.

66. "Tekushchie problemy . . . ," p. 109.

67. Zorin, Brutents, Bovin, *op. cit.*, p. CC17.

68. *Ibid.*, p. CC21.

69. Dennis Ross, *The Soviet Union and the Persian Gulf* (Providence, R.I.: Brown University, The Center for Foreign Policy

Development, Working Paper, No. 4, June, 1983), p. 5.

70. *Ibid.*

71. *The New York Times,* 3/15/84, pp. 1, 10.

72. Moscow's desire to improve relations with Iran was evident in a recent Radio Moscow Persian language broadcast to Iran. The observation was made that because of the increasing two-way trade between Iran and Europe that passes through Soviet territory, Soviet-Iranian cooperation is of particular importance. This is especially true it was said, given the present difficulty of shipping Iranian goods through the Persian Gulf. The latter point underscored the importance of a recent agreement to continue planning Soviet-Iranian cooperation for the construction of a 175 kilometer railway in northeast Iran. When completed, this railway will link the Iranian and Soviet rail systems, thereby making it possible for Teheran to "transport its commodities to Japan through the shortest route by Soviet rail." (Radio Moscow, reported in *FBIS,* 5/2/84, pp. H4-H5).

73. Sawyer, *op. cit.,* pp. 16-18.

74. See *The Military Balance, 1975-76* (London: The International Institute for Strategic Studies, 1975), p. 90; *The Military Balance, 1977-78,* p. 97; *The Military Balance, 1978-79,* p. 105; *The Military Balance, 1979-80,* p. 104.

75. "Tekushchie problemy . . . ," p. 109.

76. Stanislav Kondrashov, "International Program" (Moscow television service), 2/26/84, reported in *FBIS,* 2/28/84, p. H4.

77. Konstantin Gevandov, "Political Observers Opinion: In the Front Line of the Struggle," *Izvestiia,* 4/27/84, p. 5, reported in *FBIS,* 5/1/84, pp. H1-H2.

78. Aleksandr Timoshkin, "Window on the Arab World" (Radio Moscow), 3/5/84, reported in *FBIS,* 3/6/84, p. H11. Emphasis added.

79. Heller, *op. cit.,* p. 48.

80. See section IV above.

81. See section III above.

82. See footnote 11.

83. Zbigniew Brzezinski, *Power and Principle: Memoirs of the National Security Advisor, 1977-1981* (New York: Farrar, Straus, Giroux, 1983), pp. 10, 121, cited in Sawyer, *op. cit.,* pp. 23, 148 (note no. 18).

4
Moscow, Damascus, and the Lebanese Crisis of 1982–1984

Robert O. Freedman

Introduction

One of the most interesting aspects of the Lebanese crisis of 1982–84 has been the interplay of Soviet and Syrian policy as the crisis developed. Moscow, with its global perspective, has had to juxtapose concerns about its relationship with the United States and Western Europe with its efforts to support its ally, Syria, and to exploit the Lebanese crisis to increase Soviet influence in the Middle East. Syria, by contrast, could concentrate on its regional goals during the crisis, all the while seeking to extract the maximum in Soviet support for Syrian objectives, especially the maintenance of Syrian hegemony in Lebanon. This study will examine the interplay of Soviet and Syrian policies in five specific periods of the crisis: (1) the period from the Israeli invasion of Lebanon in June 1982 until the death of Brezhnev in November 1982; (2) the period from the accession of Andropov through the May 1983 war scare; (3) the September 1983 period of fighting between the Gemayel government, backed by the U.S., and the Shii and Druze forces, backed by Syria; (4) the period from the destruction of U.S. Marine headquarters in October 1983 until the U.S. attack on Syrian anti–aircraft positions in December 1983; and (5) the period from the abrupt U.S. withdrawal from Lebanon in February 1984 until the abrogation of the Israeli–Lebanese treaty in March 1984.

Prior to beginning the analysis, however, it is first necessary to describe the overall policy goals of the Soviet Union and Syria in the Middle East in the period leading up to the Israeli invasion of Lebanon in

June 1982. Observers of Soviet policy in the oil rich and strategically located Middle East are generally divided into two schools of thought as to Soviet goals there. While both agree that the Soviet Union wants to be considered a major factor in Middle Eastern affairs, if only because of the USSR's propinquity to the region, they differ on the ultimate Soviet goals in the Middle East. One school of thought sees Soviet Middle East policy as being primarily defensive in nature; that is, as directed toward preventing the region from being used as a base for military attack or political subversion against the USSR. The other school of thought sees Soviet policy as primarily offensive in nature, as aimed at the limitation and ultimate exclusion of Western influence from the region and its replacement by Soviet influence. It is the opinion of the author of this paper that Soviet goals in the Middle East, at least since the mid–1960s, have been primarily offensive in nature; and in the Arab segment of the Middle East, the Soviet Union appears to have been engaged in a zero–sum game competition for influence with the United States. A brief discussion of the tactics and overall strategy employed by Moscow in its quest for Middle Eastern influence will serve as a background for the subsequent analysis of Soviet policy during the Lebanese crisis.[1]

In its efforts to weaken and ultimately eliminate Western influence from the Middle East, and particularly from the Arab world, while promoting Soviet influence, the Soviet leadership has employed a number of tactics. First and foremost has been the supply of military aid to its regional clients.[2] Next in importance comes economic aid; the Aswan Dam in Egypt and the Euphrates Dam in Syria are prominent examples of Soviet economic assistance, although each project has had serious problems. In recent years Moscow has also sought to solidify its influence through the conclusion of long term Friendship and Cooperation treaties such as the ones concluded with Egypt (1971); Iraq (1972); Somalia (1974); Ethiopia (1978); Afghanistan (1978); the People's Democratic Republic of Yemen (1979); and Syria (1980), although the repudiation of the treaties by Egypt (1976) and Somalia (1977) indicates that this has not always been a successful tactic. Moscow has also attempted to exploit both the lingering memories of Western colonialism, and Western threats against Arab oil producers. Another tactic has been the establishment of party–to–party relations between the CPSU (Communist Party of the Soviet Union) and the ruling parties in a number of the one–party states in the Middle East, and Moscow has also provided assistance in developing a security apparatus and other elements of political infrastructure to selected states in the region. In addition, the Russians have offered the Arabs diplomatic support at such international forums as the United Nations and the Geneva Conference on an Arab–Israeli peace settlement.

Finally, Moscow has offered the Arabs aid of a both military and diplomatic nature against Israel, although that aid has been limited in scope because Moscow continues to support Israel's right to exist both for fear of unduly alienating the United States with whom the Russians desire additional SALT agreements and improved trade relations, and because Israel serves as a convenient rallying point for potentially anti–Western forces in the Arab world.[3]

While the USSR has used all these tactics, to a greater or lesser degree of success over the last two decades, it has also run into serious problems in its quest for influence in the Middle East. The numerous inter–Arab and regional conflicts (Syria–Iraq; North Yemen–South Yemen; Ethiopia–Somalia; Algeria–Morocco; Iran–Iraq, etc.) have usually meant that when the USSR has favored one party, it has alienated the other, often driving it over to the West. Secondly, the existence of communist parties in the Middle East has proven to be a handicap for the USSR, as communist activities have, on occasion, caused a sharp deterioration in relations between Moscow and the country in which the communist party has operated.[4] The communist–supported coup d'etat in the Sudan in 1971, communist efforts to organize cells in the Iraqi army in the mid and late 1970s, and the activities of the Tudeh party in Iran against the Khomeini regime are recent examples of this problem. Third, the wealth which flowed to the Arab world (or at least to its major oil producers) since the quadrupling of oil prices in late 1973 has enabled the Arabs to buy quality technology from the West and Japan, and this has helped weaken the economic bond between the USSR and a number of Arab states such as Iraq. Fourth, since 1967 and particularly since the 1973 Arab–Israeli war, Islam has been resurgent throughout the Arab world, and the USSR, identified in the Arab world with atheism, has been hampered as a result.[5] Finally, the United States, and to a lesser extent, France and China, have actively opposed Soviet efforts to achieve predominant influence in the region and this has frequently enabled Middle Eastern states to play the extra–regional powers off against each other and thereby prevent any one of them from securing predominant influence.

To overcome these difficulties, Moscow has evolved one overall strategy—the development of an "anti–imperialist" bloc of states in the Arab world. In Moscow's view these states should bury their internecine rivalries, and join together along with such political organizations as the Arab Communist parties and the PLO, in a united front against what the USSR has called the "linchpin" of Western imperialism in the Middle East—Israel. Under such circumstances, it is the Soviet hope that the Arab states would then use their collective pressure against Israel's supporters, especially the United States. The ideal scenario for Moscow, and one which Soviet commentators have frequently referred to, was the situation during the 1973 Arab–Israeli war when virtually all the Arab states supported the war effort against Israel, while also imposing an oil embargo against the United States. As is well known, not only did the oil embargo create domestic difficulties for the United States, it caused serious problems in the NATO alliance, a development that was warmly welcomed by Moscow. Unfortunately for the USSR, however, this "anti–imperialist" Arab unity was created not by Soviet efforts, but by the diplomacy of Egyptian President Anwar Sadat and when Sadat changed his policies and turned toward the United States, the "anti–imperialist" Arab unity sought by the USSR fell apart. Nonetheless, so long as Soviet leaders think in terms of such Leninist categories of thought as "united fronts" ("anti–imperialist" Arab unity, in Soviet parlance, is merely another way of describing a united front of Arab governmental and non–governmental forces) and so long as there is a deep underlying psychological drive for unity in the Arab world, Moscow can be expected to continue to pursue this overall strategy as a long–term goal. It is in this context that Soviet policy during the Lebanese crisis can best be understood.

While Moscow has sought to rally the Arab world into an "anti–imperialist" front against the West, Syria has primarily viewed Moscow as a supplier of military equipment and diplomatic assistance both to enhance Syria's prestige in the Arab world and to aid Syria in its confrontation with its main regional enemy, Israel, with whom it engaged in war in 1948, 1967, 1973 and 1982, and who still occupies Syrian territory in the Golan Heights. Relations between the USSR and Syria became close for the first time in 1966 when a left–wing, Alawi–dominated, Ba'athist government seized power in Damascus. Relations remained close until 1970, although there was a disagreement within the Syrian regime between strongman Salah Jedid and then Defense Minister Hafiz Assad on how close to draw to Moscow. When Assad, who favored a more limited relationship, overthrew Jedid in November 1970, a marked cooling of Soviet–Syrian relations took place. Soviet support to Syria during the 1973 war helped to warm relations again, but the Syrian refusal to attend the Soviet–cosponsored Geneva Peace Conference in December 1973 and the successful shuttle diplomacy of Henry Kissinger, which led both to a separation–of–forces agreement on the Golan Heights between Israel and Syria and the re–establishment of Syrian–American diplomatic relations, again chilled Soviet–Syrian ties. Yet another change in relations occurred in 1975 when Syria again turned to the USSR after the Sinai II agreement, only to clash violently with Moscow the following year when the USSR both criticized Syria's military intervention in Lebanon and delayed promised shipments of arms.[6]

Interestingly enough, it was to be the Syrian intervention in Lebanon, coupled with Sadat's decision to sign a peace agreement with Israel, which was once again to turn Syria back to Moscow. Assad's decision to intervene in Lebanon on the side of the Christians in the Lebanese civil war was not popular in Syria where the majority Sunni Muslims had long suspected the Alawites, a Shii Muslim minority comprising only 11 percent of the population, of "deviationism." In addition, as Islamic fundamentalism began to rise in the Middle East in the aftermath of the 1973 war, the secular, Alawite–dominated Ba'athist regime, already noted for its widespread corruption, came in for increasing criticism. The end result was the development of a group which called itself the "Muslim Brotherhood" which sought to overthrow Assad. This group began terrorist attacks against Alawi officials in Syria.[7] Compounding this domestic problem for Syrian President Assad was a difficult foreign policy situation. On his eastern front was a hostile Iraq (Syria and Iraq had long charged each other with sabotage and attempts to overthrow each other's regimes). On the west, the Syrian army, although *ex post facto* under the mandate of the Arab League, was badly bogged down in Lebanon, and by the fall of 1978 had changed sides and was aiding the PLO and Muslim forces against the Christians. On the southwest lay an increasingly powerful Israel, now recovered militarily from the 1973 war, and led by hard–liner Menachem Begin. Only to the south was there an ally, Jordan, to which Syria had offered a military alliance in 1975 and with whom cooperation had reached the point of joint staff exercises in 1976.

As past history has shown, for Syria to have any hope in a confrontation with Israel, Egyptian participation on the side of Syria was a necessity. Yet Sadat's willingness to sign the Camp David agreement of September 1978 and a peace treaty with Israel in March 1979 appeared to take Egypt, the most militarily powerful Arab state, out of the Arab ranks. Consequently, Assad denounced the Camp David agreements, thereby taking a position coinciding with that of the USSR which also greeted Camp David with hostility, fearing it to be a major blow against the "anti–imperialist" Arab unity it had long sought. While Moscow was encouraged by the Arab unity in opposing Camp David, and especially by the rapprochement between Syria and Iraq which made possible the formation of a large anti–Egyptian bloc in the Arab world, the anti–Egyptian unity was to be very short lived. The renewal of the Syrian–Iraqi confrontation after the accession to power of Saddam Hussein in July 1979 (Jordan's decision to ally itself to Iraq in the renewed conflict further isolated Syria), the Soviet invasion of Afghanistan in

December 1979, and the Iraqi invasion of Iran in September 1980 served to split the Arab world once again.[s] Indeed, by the time of the Israeli invasion of Lebanon in June 1982, it appeared as if the Arab world had become divided into three major groupings. First there was what might be called the "Peace" camp of Egypt, the Sudan, Oman and Somalia, all of whom were pro–Western (to the point of providing facilities for the U.S. Rapid Deployment Force (RDF) and also to a greater or lesser degree committed to peace with Israel, while backing Iraq in the Iran–Iraq war. On the other extreme was the so–called Front of Steadfastness and Confrontation composed of Libya, the Peoples Democratic Republic of Yemen, Syria, Algeria and the PLO who were all, at least on paper, opposed to any kind of peace with Israel, and were also following a pro–Soviet line on such issues as the Soviet invasion of Afghanistan, while Syria and Libya were outspoken in their support of Iran in the Iran–Iraq war. Located between the "Peace" camp and the Front of Steadfastness and Confrontation was the rather amorphous group of Arab states which can be called, for want of a better term, the "Centrists." These states had indicated a willingness to live in peace with Israel (albeit under very stringent terms), had denounced both Camp David and the Soviet invasion of Afghanistan, and were backing Iraq in the Iran–Iraq war. These "Centrist" Arab states were composed of states that ran the spectrum from being mildly pro–Western, (such as Morocco, Saudi Arabia and the United Arab Emirates) to neutralists as in the cases of the Yemen Arab Republic (North Yemen) and Kuwait. Even Iraq, before 1978 among the most hostile Arab states to Israel, moderated its position to that country and could be considered part of the Centrist bloc for this reason as well as because of its improved relationship with the United States.

Given this situation, Moscow's goal was to try to move the Centrist Arab states back toward the Front of Steadfastness and Confrontation into an "anti–imperialist" bloc, much as had existed immediately after Camp David. On the other hand, however, the Soviet leadership had to be concerned about a rapprochement between the Egyptian camp and the Centrists, since this would leave the pro–Soviet Steadfastness Front in an isolated position in the Arab world with its individual components engaged in their own intra–Arab and regional confrontations (i.e. Algeria–Morocco; PDRY–Oman; Libya–Egypt; Syria–Iraq; Syria–Jordan; Syria–Israel; and PLO–Israel), a development that would also exacerbate some internal strains within the Steadfastness Front, especially the conflict between Syrian President Hafiz Assad and PLO leader Yasser Arafat.

Syria, because of its backing of Iran in the Iran–Iraq war, its renewed confrontation with Iraq, its continuing confrontation with Israel, its poor relations with Egypt, and its hostility to Jordan because of its support of

Iraq, was now extremely isolated in the Arab world. Given the fact that it could no longer count on Arab support for its confrontation with Israel, by 1980 it had begun to appeal to the USSR to give it the military assistance to, by itself, match Israel's power. In return, Assad became one of the few Arab leaders to support the Soviet invasion of Afghanistan, and, even more important, Assad agreed to sign a Friendship and Cooperation treaty with Moscow in October 1980, something he had been resisting for a decade.[9]

Yet, for Moscow, the signing of the Treaty with Assad and the provision of additional military aid posed a number of problems. In the first place, Moscow had to be concerned that Assad, beset by internal and external difficulties, might provoke an international crisis, either with Israel, or with one of his Arab enemies, and then drag in the USSR. Secondly, Assad, who had demonstrated his independence of Moscow on a number of occasions in the past, might do so again, thus complicating Soviet Middle Eastern policy at a time when, because of the Iran-Iraq war, Soviet policy was already in a state of disarray. Indeed, in the crisis with Jordan in late November 1980, and in the Syrian "missile crisis" with Israel which began in April 1981, Assad was to demonstrate just such an independent turn.[10]

In the year between the missile crisis of April–June 1981 and the Israeli invasion of Lebanon, there was evident strain in the Soviet-Syrian relationship. As Israel and the United States began to talk about "strategic cooperation", Syria redoubled its efforts to obtain increased military equipment from the USSR so as to increase its capability vis-à-vis Israel.[11] For its part, however, the USSR, perhaps remembering Syria's previous efforts to embroil Moscow in its adventures, appeared reluctant to meet Syrian requests. Thus a military delegation led by Syrian Defense Minister Mustafa Tlas which visited Moscow in September 1981 reportedly did not get all it wanted.[12] Even after Israel annexed the Golan Heights on December 13, 1981 (an event which led the U.S. to suspend the security agreement concluded with Israel two weeks earlier), Moscow did not move to step up its assistance to Damascus, although the USSR strongly denounced the Israeli move. One of the factors complicating Soviet-Syrian relations during this period was a clash between Assad and the Syrian communist party which attacked Assad's domestic policies in a front page article in the party newspaper.[13] In any case when Syrian Foreign Minister Khaddam journeyed to Moscow in January 1982, in an apparent effort to gain increased Soviet support following the Golan annexation, he did not have a great deal of success. In his luncheon speech welcoming Khaddam, Gromyko while debunking the U.S. suspension of the strategic cooperation agreement, pointedly avoided any specific commitment to Syria, and he reiterated the Soviet commitment to its three point peace plan which included Israel's right to exist.[14] While Khaddam, in his reply, stated that "we are convinced that the Soviet Union, the countries of the Socialist commonwealth, and all progressive forces" would support Syria in its struggle,[15] the joint communiqué released upon his departure noted only that "both sides reaffirmed their desire to continue to strengthen cooperation between the Soviet Union and Syria in all fields, including the military field."[16] The fact that the talks took place in what the communiqué described as "an atmosphere of friendship and mutual understanding" indicates that serious disagreements remained between the two countries.

In the aftermath of the Khaddam visit, both Moscow and Damascus were to encounter increasing problems in their Middle East policies. Moscow's hopes for Arab unity on an "anti–imperialist" basis deteriorated further as the Morocco–Algeria confrontation over the Spanish Sahara intensified and Morocco signed a major military agreement with the U.S. in which it provided transit facilities for the U.S. RDF, in an apparent quid pro quo for increased shipments of military equipment.[17] In addition, Morocco boycotted meetings of the Organization of African Unity, a pan–African organization which Moscow also wanted to see unified on an "anti–imperialist" basis, because some OAU members recognized the Algerian–backed Polisario rebels. In the case of Syria, there was an anti–regime uprising by the Muslim Brotherhood in the city of Hama in February in which as many as 12,000 people are reported to have been killed. Two months later, Syria blocked the Iraqi oil pipeline which ran through Syria, an event which, while weakening Iraq, exacerbated the Syrian–Iraqi conflict and made Moscow's hopes for an "anti–imperialist" Arab unity dim further. Meanwhile the Lebanese–based PLO, already under heavy Syrian pressure, found itself fighting against Shiite forces in southern Lebanon who were protesting PLO activities in their section of the country. This conflict was of particular worry to Moscow both because the Shiites, as the poorest element in the Lebanese population were a prime recruiting ground for the Lebanese communist party and other leftist Lebanese elements who were allied with the PLO, and also because the Shiite militia, AMAL, was now also fighting against leftist and Communist forces.[18] Perhaps the greatest problem for Moscow, however, was the gradual rapprochement between Egypt and the Centrist Arabs. Induced in part by the Israeli withdrawal from the last part of the Sinai on April 25, 1982, the rapprochement was accelerated by Iran's success in its war with Iraq as the Iranians took the offensive and threatened Iraqi territory in the late spring. The Iranian advance frightened the Gulf states who turned both to the United States and to Egypt for support. Soon after the outbreak of the Iran–Iraq war, Iraq had become a recipient of Egyptian military equipment and had moderated its position toward Egypt as a result,[19] and now other Gulf states moved in the same direction. In addition, the warm official greetings by Jordan and Morocco to Egypt after the final Israeli Sinai withdrawal also appeared to signal their interest in improved ties with Egypt.[20] Thus, by the time of the Israeli invasion of Lebanon, there was movement toward a rapprochement between Egypt and the Centrist Arabs. Indeed, a special meeting of the Steadfastness Front took place at the end of May 1982 to try to reverse this trend, as the Front proclaimed its opposition to any normalization of relations with Egypt until it renounced Camp David.[21]

In sum, it was a badly disunited Arab world, whose pro–Soviet members were isolated and whose Centrist states were gradually moving toward a reconciliation with Egypt, which faced Soviet policy–makers on the eve of the Israeli invasion of Lebanon.

The Crisis Period

1) From the Israeli Invasion until the Death of Brezhnev (June–November 1982)

Soviet inactivity during the period from the Israeli invasion of Lebanon until the exodus of the PLO from Beirut in August 1982 has already been discussed in detail elsewhere and need only be summarized here.[22] Suffice it to say that, contrary to its behavior during the Yom Kippur war of 1973, Moscow provided no military help during the course of the fighting, while its verbal warnings to Israel and to the United States were only of a very general nature––and very ineffectual––until the announcement of the possible deployment of U.S. troops to Beirut, and even then Brezhnev quickly backed down from his warning after it became clear that the U.S. was going ahead with the deployment. While Moscow did mount a resupply effort to Syria once the fighting had ended, as soon as it became clear that Israel was not going to invade Syria and was restricting its efforts to destroying the PLO infrastructure in Lebanon (although battering Syrian troops stationed in Lebanon in the process), Moscow took no substantive actions, thus demonstrating once again that the Soviet–Syrian treaty did not cover Syrian activities in Lebanon. To be sure, Moscow did appeal to the Arabs to unite to confront Israel and use their oil weapon against the United States, but the badly divided Arab world, threatened on the East by Iran, was to take neither action. Indeed, the Arab states were unable even to convene a summit conference until after the PLO left Beirut.

Interestingly enough, while there was a spate of Arab criticism of Moscow for its lack of assistance to the PLO and Syria (Libyan leader Muammar Kaddafi went so far as to berate a group of Soviet ambassadors, complaining that Arab friendship with the Socialist countries was almost "ready to go up in flames, the way Beirut is going up in flames"),[23] Syria held aloof from the cascade of public criticism against the Soviet Union. Instead, Syrian Information Minister Ahmad Iskander told a press conference in Damascus that the Soviet Union was a "sincere friend" of Syria which had "helped us defend our lands, wives and children", and he called for a strategic alliance with the Soviet Union.[24] While the Syrians appeared to be using their battle losses against Israel and the Iskander press conference in yet another effort to obtain the strategic alliance with the Soviet Union they had long wanted, Moscow utilized the press conference which was given prominent coverage by the Soviet news agency, TASS, to demonstrate its continuing importance in Arab affairs and the major role in aiding in Arab defense efforts it had already played.

Nonetheless, it was Washington, not Moscow, which controlled the pace of Middle Eastern events in the period leading up to the PLO exodus from Beirut, and the Soviet leadership could do little but sit on the diplomatic sidelines as the American–mediated exodus took place on August 20th. The U.S. moved to keep the diplomatic momentum in its favor. On September 1st President Reagan issued his plan for a Middle East settlement,[25] while the Arab states, finally convening their long–postponed summit in Fez, Morocco, issued their peace plan one week later.[26] With the U.S. and Arab peace plans now on the table, the USSR hastened to issue its plan, in a speech delivered by Brezhnev in mid–September. While a number of its points were repetitions of previous Soviet proposals, others seem to have been added to emphasize the similarity between the Fez and Soviet plans.[27] The elements of the Soviet peace plan which repeated earlier Soviet proposals were Moscow's call for the withdrawal of Israeli forces from the Golan Heights, the West Bank, the Gaza Strip and Lebanon to the lines which existed before the June 1967 war; the establishment of a Palestinian state on the West Bank and Gaza; the right of all states in the region to a secure and independent existence; and the termination of the state of war between Israel and the Arab states. While these points in many ways resembled the Fez plan, except for Moscow's more explicit call for Israel's right to exist and an end to the state of war between Israel and the Arab world, the new elements in the Brezhnev peace plan seemed to be virtually modeled on the Fez plan. Thus Moscow called for the Palestinian refugees to be given the right to return to their homes or receive compensation for their abandoned property, for the return of East Jerusalem to the Arabs and its incorporation into the Palestinian state, with freedom of access for believers to the sacred places of the three religions throughout Jerusalem, and for Security Council guarantees for the final settlement. Brezhnev also took the opportunity to repeat the long-standing Soviet call for an international conference on the Middle East, with all interested parties participating, including the PLO, which the Soviet leader again characterized as "the sole legitimate representative of the Arab people of Palestine."

In modeling the Soviet peace plan on Fez, Brezhnev evidently sought to prevent the Arabs from moving to embrace the Reagan plan. Nonetheless, with the United States clearly possessing the diplomatic initiative in the Middle East after the PLO pull-out from Beirut, and with both Jordan's King Hussein and PLO leader Arafat, along with other Arab leaders, expressing interest in the Reagan Plan, Moscow was on the diplomatic defensive. Given this situation, it is not surprising that Brezhnev seized upon the massacres in the Sabra and Shatilla refugee camps to point out to Arafat that "if anyone had any illusions that Washington was going to support the Arabs . . . these illusions have now been drowned in streams of blood in the Palestinian camps . . . ."[28]

Nonetheless, despite the massacres, Arafat evidently felt that there was value in pursuing the Reagan Plan, and he began to meet with his erstwhile enemy, King Hussein of Jordan, to work out a joint approach to the United States. Such maneuvering infuriated Syria, which sought to use pro-Syrian elements within the PLO to pressure Arafat into abandoning his new policy, a development which further exacerbated relations between Assad and Arafat. In addition, evidently fearing the weakening of the Steadfastness Front and the possibility of the PLO (or at least Arafat's followers) defecting from it, Moscow continued to warn the Arabs about what it called U.S. efforts to split the PLO and to draw Jordan and Saudi Arabia into supporting the Reagan plan, which the USSR termed a cover for Camp David.

It was at this point, in mid-November, that Brezhnev passed from the scene. His successor, Yuri Andropov, had the task of rebuilding the Soviet position in the Middle East which had suffered a major blow during the Israeli invasion of Lebanon.

2) Soviet Policy from Andropov's Accession to Power until the May 1983 War Scare

When Andropov took power in mid-November 1982, he had to face the fact that the Soviet Union's Middle East position had deteriorated in three major areas as a result of the Israeli invasion of Lebanon. In the first place, Soviet credibility had suffered a major blow because its frequent warnings to the United States and Israel during the course of the war had proven to be ineffectual. Second, the quality of Soviet military equipment and, to a lesser degree, the quality of Soviet training, had been called into question by the overwhelming victory of U.S.-supplied Israeli weaponry over the military equipment supplied by Moscow to Syria. Finally, Andropov had to deal with a situation where the United States had the diplomatic initiative in the Middle East. Not only was the Reagan Plan--and not the Soviet peace plan--the central factor in Middle East diplomatic discussions, but Arafat and King Hussein had begun to meet regularly, and the governments of Israel and Lebanon had begun talks on a Lebanese-Israeli peace accord. Under these circumstances, the new Soviet leader, although preoccupied with consolidating his power and trying to block the installation of U.S. Pershing II and cruise missiles in Western Europe, evidently felt that Moscow had to act before Soviet influence in the Middle East fell any further.

In an effort to rebuild the Soviet position in the Middle East, Andropov moved both militarily and diplomatically. On the military front in January 1983, he dispatched several batteries of SAM-5 missiles to Syria--along with the Soviet soldiers to operate and guard them.[29] This move went far beyond the Soviet resupply effort of tanks and planes to Syria which had been going on since the end of the Israeli-Syrian fighting in 1982. Indeed, by sending Syria a weapons system that had never been deployed outside the USSR itself, a system that had the capability of engaging Israel's EC-2 aircraft system which had proven so effective during the Israeli-Syrian air battles in the first week of the Israeli invasion of Lebanon in June, Moscow was demonstrating to the Arab world--and especially to Syria--that it was willing to stand by its allies.[30] Nonetheless, by manning the SAM-5 missiles with Soviet soldiers, Moscow was also signalling that it, and not Syria, would determine when the missiles would be fired. Given the fact that both in November 1980 and April 1981 Assad had tried to involve the USSR in his military adventures,[31] this was probably a sensible precaution--especially, as will be shown below, when Assad and other Syrian government officials began to issue bellicose statements several months later. Yet another cautionary element in the dispatch of the missiles was that Moscow never formally announced that its own troops were involved in guarding the missiles, thus enabling the USSR to avoid a direct confrontation with Israel (and possibly the United States) should Israel decide to attack the missile sites.

While Moscow was moving to enhance its political position in the Arab world by sending the SAM-5 missiles to Syria, it was also benefitting from developments in the PLO which challenged Arafat's opening to

Washington. Indeed, Moscow's interest in preventing a PLO turn to the United States was shared by both Syria and Libya which actively moved to undermine Arafat's position. The efforts of the anti-Arafat forces were to prove successful as the Palestine National Council which, after a number of postponements, finally convened in mid-February in Algiers, formally stated its refusal to consider the Reagan Plan "as a sound basis for a just and lasting solution to the Palestine problem and the Arab-Israeli conflict."[32] Needless to say, Moscow was very pleased with this development. *Pravda* correspondent Yuri Vladimirov praised the council's policy document as a reaffirmation of the organization's determination to continue the struggle against imperialism and Zionism.[33]

Meanwhile, as the Reagan Plan was faltering, thus weakening American influence in the Middle East, Moscow was seeking to underscore its improved position in the region by issuing a public warning to Israel not to attack Syria. The Soviet warning, issued on March 30th, came after a series of Syrian warnings, yet was limited in nature. Thus while Moscow warned that Israel was "playing with fire" by preparing to attack Syria, it made no mention of the Soviet-Syrian treaty. Indeed, in listing those on Syria's side in the confrontation with Israel, the Soviet statement merely noted "on the side of the Syrian people are Arab patriots, the Socialist countries, and all who cherish the cause of peace, justice and honor." The statement also emphasized the need to settle the Arab-Israeli conflict, politically, not through war.[34]

This rather curious Soviet warning can perhaps be understood if one assumes that Moscow did not seriously expect an Israeli attack on Syria. With the more cautious Moshe Arens as Israel's new Defence Minister, and with rising opposition to Israel's presence in Lebanon being felt in Israel's domestic political scene, it appeared unlikely that Israel would attack Syria, even to take out the newly-installed SAM-5 missiles. Indeed, even the hawkish Israeli Chief of Staff, General Eitan, in an interview on Israeli armed forces radio, stated that Israel had no intentions of starting a new war.[35] If Moscow, therefore, assumed that Israel would not go to war, then why the warning? Given the fact that Moscow's credibility in the Arab world had dropped precipitously as a result of the warnings it had issued during the Israeli invasion of Lebanon in the June/July 1982 period—warnings that had been ignored by both Israel and the United States—Moscow possibly saw a chance to increase its credibility in the region. Thus if Moscow, assuming Israel would not attack Syria, issued a warning to Israel not to attack Syria, and Israel then did not attack Syria, Moscow could take credit for the non-attack and could then demonstrate to the Arab world that Soviet diplomacy was effective vis-à-vis Israel, at least as a deterrent. If this, in fact, was

Moscow's thinking, not all the Arabs were to be convinced. Indeed, the Saudi paper *Ar-Riyad* expressed a lack of trust in the Soviet warning, noting that the limited value of Soviet statements had been proven during the Israeli invasion of Lebanon "which dealt a sharp and severe blow to the Kremlin when the Soviet missiles became no more than timber towers in the face of the sophisticated weapons the United States had unconditionally supplied to Israel."[36]

In any case, only three days after the Soviet warning to Israel, Soviet Foreign Minister Andrei Gromyko, who had recently been promoted to Deputy Prime Minister, held a major press conference in Moscow.[37] While the main emphasis of Gromyko's press conference was on strategic arms issues, he also took the opportunity to make two major points about the Middle East situation. In the first place, in response to a question from a correspondent of the Syrian newspaper *Al-Ba'ath*, Gromyko stated that "the Soviet Union is in favor of the withdrawal of all foreign troops from the territory of Lebanon, all of them. Syria is in favor of this." [38] Secondly, Gromyko noted once again that the USSR was in favor of Israel's existing as a state. "We do not share the point of view of extremist Arab circles that Israel should be eliminated. This is an unrealistic and unjust point of view."[39] The thrust of Gromyko's remarks were clear. The Soviet leader, by urging the withdrawal of all foreign troops from Lebanon--including Syrian troops--and by re-emphasizing the Soviet commitment to Israel's existence, seemed to be telling Syria that despite the provision of SAM-5 missiles, Moscow was not desirous of being dragged into a war in Lebanon on Syria's behalf. If this was indeed the message Gromyko was trying to get across, the rapid pace of Middle Eastern events was soon to pose additional problems for the Soviet strategy. Thus, one week after King Hussein had announced his refusal to enter into peace negotiations, the U.S. embassy in Beirut was blown up by a car bomb, with a massive loss of life. Reacting to both events, President Reagan dispatched his Secretary of State George Shultz, to salvage the stalled Israeli-Lebanese talks and regain the momentum for the United States in Middle East diplomacy. As Shultz toured the region, and shuttled back and forth between Beirut and Jerusalem, prospects for a Lebanese-Israeli agreement began to improve. Both Moscow and Damascus, for different reasons, wanted to see the Shultz mission fail. The USSR did not want to see any more Arab states following in Egypt's footsteps and agreeing to a U.S. plan for Middle East peace. Syria, for its part, had long sought the dominant position in Lebanon and feared that any Lebanese-Israeli agreement would strengthen the Israeli position in Lebanon at Syria's expense. In addition, Syria also did not wish to see any more Arab states moving to make peace with Israel, since this would leave

Syria increasingly isolated among the Arab confrontation states facing Israel. The end result was a rise in tension and yet another war scare in which Moscow was to play a role, albeit perhaps a somewhat unwilling one.

Less than a week after King Hussein refused to enter the peace talks, the Syrian government raised its price for a Lebanese troop withdrawal. While as late as March Syria had been willing to have a simultaneous withdrawal of Israeli, Syrian and PLO forces, on April 16th the Syrian government, strengthened both by its new Soviet weapons and by the Soviet warning to Israel, stated that Syria would not even discuss the withdrawal of its troops from Lebanon until all Israeli troops had left the country.[40] While the United States sought to assuage Syrian opposition in a letter from Reagan to Assad in which the U.S. President indicated that the United States was still pressing for Israeli withdrawal from the Golan Heights,[41] the U.S. ploy was not successful. Indeed, Syria appeared to step up tension by allowing guerrillas to infiltrate into Israeli lines to attack Israeli troops while simultaneously accusing the Israeli government of reinforcing its troops in Lebanon's Bekaa Valley and of staging "provocative" military exercises on the Golan Heights.[42] Meanwhile although Israeli Foreign Minister Shamir called the Syrian-induced tension "artificial",[43] Israeli Defense Minister Arens, concerned about Soviet and Syrian intentions, put Israeli troops on alert and indicated that Israel would not leave Lebanon until Syria did.[44] Syria then stepped up its pressure on April 26th when Syrian forces opened fire on an Israeli bulldozer near the cease fire line.[45]

Meanwhile, despite the rise in Syrian-Israeli tension, U.S. Secretary of State Shultz continued to work for an Israeli-Lebanese troop withdrawal agreement and on May 6th his efforts were crowned with success as the Israeli government accepted, in principle, a troop withdrawal agreement that had already been agreed to by Lebanon.[46] The next U.S. goal was to try to gain Arab support for the agreement so as to pressure Syria into also withdrawing its forces from Lebanon. As might be expected, neither Moscow nor Syria was in favor of a rapid Syrian withdrawal. Moscow, although interested in Syria ultimately withdrawing its troops from Lebanon, did not want any precipitate withdrawal in the aftermath of the Israeli-Lebanese agreement lest the United States reap the diplomatic benefit. Syria complained that Israel had gotten too much from the treaty and Damascus Radio asserted that Lebanon had "capitulated to the Israeli aggressor."[47] It was unclear at the time, however, whether Syria opposed the withdrawal of its own troops on principle, or whether President Assad was posturing so as to improve his bargaining position vis-à-vis Lebanon (so he could get a better deal than

Israel did); vis–à–vis the Arab world (Syria, long isolated because of its support of Iran in the Iran–Iraq war was now openly confronting Israel and should, thereby, merit Arab support); and vis–à–vis the United States (so as to get U.S. pressure on Israel for a withdrawal from the Golan Heights). Indeed, as the crisis was played out until the end of May, with military maneuvers and threats of war (almost all from the Syrians), it appeared as if Assad was enjoying the opportunity to play a major role once again in Middle East events.

As Syria was exploiting the Lebanese situation for its own ends, Moscow was cautiously supporting its Arab ally. Thus on May 9th, three days after Israel had agreed in principle to the accord, the Soviet Union issued an official statement denouncing the agreement, and in a gesture of support for Syria, demanded that "first and foremost" Israeli troops be withdrawn from Lebanon. The statement added, however, that "American and other foreign troops staying in Lebanon also must be withdrawn from it", an oblique reference to Moscow's continuing desire to see Syrian troops leave the country.[48] At the same time, perhaps to enhance the atmosphere of crisis, Soviet dependents were withdrawn from Beirut, although the Soviet ambassador to Lebanon stated that the departure of the dependents had occurred because of the beginning of summer camp in the USSR.[49] In helping to enhance the atmosphere of crisis, Moscow may also have seen that the situation could be used as a means of once again playing a role in the Middle East peace process after having been kept on the diplomatic sidelines since Sadat's trip to Jerusalem in 1977. Indeed, on May 10th, Shultz openly urged Moscow to use its influence to get Syria to withdraw its troops and stated he might meet Soviet Foreign Minister Gromyko to discuss the Middle East along with other international issues.[50] Shultz indicated, however, that the United States was not yet ready for an international conference on the Middle East, still a goal of Soviet diplomacy.[51]

Nonetheless, even in giving Syria a limited degree of support, Moscow had to be concerned as to the possibility of war erupting, especially as Syria began to issue increasingly bellicose threats––threats which involved Soviet support for Syria in case of war.[52] Thus on May 9th, Syrian Foreign Minister Khaddam, in an interview, noted that if war between Israel and Syria broke out, "We believe that the USSR will fulfill its commitments in accordance with the (Soviet–Syrian) treaty." The next day, Syrian Radio warned that any Israeli attack against Syrian forces anywhere, even in Lebanon, would mean an "unlimited war."[53] The Syrian bellicosity, however, may have overstepped the bounds of propriety insofar as Moscow was concerned. Thus in a broadcast over Beirut Radio, Soviet Ambassador to Lebanon Alexander Soldatov, when asked about

Khaddam's assertion that Moscow would fully support Syria if war with Israel broke out, replied that "the USSR does not reply to such hypothetical questions."[54] Soldatov added that the USSR continued to support the withdrawal of all foreign forces from Lebanon. These themes of caution were repeated during the visit of a Soviet delegation to Israel in mid–May to attend ceremonies marking the 38th anniversary of the defeat of Nazi Germany. One of the leaders of the delegation, the well–known Soviet journalist Igor Belayev took the opportunity to state upon arrival at Ben Gurion Airport that Syria's recent military moves in the Bekaa Valley were purely defensive and that Syria had no aggressive intent toward Israel.[55] Similarly, Karen Khachaturev, deputy director of the *Novosti* news agency, noted that the USSR favored a peace treaty between Israel and Lebanon––but only after all Israeli soldiers departed––and Khachaturev reiterated Moscow's support of Israel's right to live in peace and security.[56]

Meanwhile, Syria continued to escalate the political and military pressure to undermine the Israeli–Lebanese agreement. On the political front it formed an alignment with a group of Lebanese leaders opposed to the agreement including former Lebanese Premier Rashid Karami, former President Suleiman Franjieh, Druze leader Walid Jumblatt, and Lebanese Communist party first secretary George Hawi.[57]

While moving to strengthen his political position, Assad also stepped up the political and military pressure in the Bekaa. After refusing to see U.S. envoy Philip Habib, Assad, on May 23rd predicted a new war with Israel in which Syria would lose 20,000 men.[58] Two days later Syrian planes fired air–to–air missiles against Israeli jets flying over the Bekaa Valley––the first such encounter since the war in 1982.[59] Assad followed this up by conducting military exercises in the Golan and Bekaa, and the danger of war appeared to heighten.[60] Nonetheless, despite a limited countermobilization, Israel kept very cool during the crisis while for its part Moscow kept a very low profile (although it did send a new aircraft carrier into the Mediterranean), supporting Syria politically but issuing no threats against the United States or Israel and again appealing for a full withdrawal of all forces in Lebanon. In any case, by the end of May the crisis had subsided and the dangers of a Syrian–Israeli war in Lebanon had been replaced in the headlines by the growing revolt in the PLO against Arafat's leadership, a development engineered by Assad as the Syrian leader appeared to want to bring the PLO under Syrian control once and for all.[61]

The revolt against Arafat underlined the PLO leader's weakened position in the aftermath of the Israeli invasion of Lebanon which had eliminated his main base of operations. While he was supported by the bulk of Palestinians living outside Syria and Syrian–controlled regions in Lebanon, and while both Iraq and Algeria gave him support in the Arab world's diplomatic arena, he had no real power to resist Syria's crackdown against him. Thus, as the summer wore on, the positions of Arafat's supporters in the Bekaa Valley were overrun, and Arafat himself was expelled from Syria. In early August, the Palestinian Central Council, meeting in Tunis, called for an "immediate dialogue" to rebuild relations with Syria,[62] but this effort, along with others attempted during the summer, proved to no avail, and in early September Arafat, who had once again begun to meet with Jordanian officials, admitted that all attempts at negotiations with Syria had failed.[63]

As the revolt within Fatah developed, Moscow was again faced with the need to make a difficult choice. On the one hand, a victory for the Fatah hardliners would make it even more difficult for Moscow to succeed in promoting its Middle East peace plan. In addition, the split within Fatah and the fact that Iraq and Algeria, key Arab countries, were backing Arafat against the Syrian–supported opposition, further underlined the disunity in the Arab world. This was one more obstacle in the way of the "anti–imperialist" Arab unity Moscow had sought for so long. On the other hand, however, Moscow could not have been too unhappy with the fact that Arafat was being punished for his flirtation with the Reagan Plan. In any case, in a showdown between Assad and Arafat, *realpolitik* impelled Moscow to side with Assad, who in the aftermath of the Israeli invasion of Lebanon was the main Arab leader opposing U.S. diplomacy in the Middle East and who had granted to Moscow the use of Syrian naval and air force facilities as well.[64]

Meanwhile, in addition to bringing Arafat's forces in the Bekaa under his control, Assad was profiting from the growing war–weariness of Israel which was planning a unilateral withdrawal of its forces from the Chouf Mountains and seemed in no mood to go to war to throw the Syrians out of Lebanon. Indeed, on June 1st Prime Minister Begin had stated that Israel was not preparing to attack Syria,[65] and a week later Israel's Deputy Foreign Minister Yehuda Ben–Meir ruled out military action to remove Syrian forces from Lebanon.[66] One month later Shultz stated that U.S. Marines would not fill any vacuum created by a unilateral withdrawal by Israel in Lebanon.[67] Under these circumstances Assad was able to fill the vacuum with Syrian–backed forces, in large part because of mistakes by the Lebanese government. By July, the Lebanese government of Amin Gemayel had alienated two of the major forces within Lebanon, the Druze and the Shiites. In part because he had not established an equitable power sharing system, and in part because Phalangist policies in the Chouf Mountains and in Shiite areas of Beirut had angered the Druze and

Shiites, they entered into an alignment with Syria. Druze leader Walid Jumblatt did this explicitly by leading a newly proclaimed "National Salvation Front" (which also had as members Rashid Karami, a Sunni Muslim, and Suleiman Franjieh, a Christian opponent of Gemayel), while Shiite leader Nabih Berri gave tacit support to the organization.[68]

The strengthening of the Syrian position in Lebanon was, on balance, a plus for Moscow since by the end of August U.S. diplomatic efforts to secure a troop withdrawal agreement from Lebanon had all but collapsed and Moscow was again raising the possibility of a joint U.S.–Soviet effort to bring about a Middle East peace settlement.[69] Yet the situation also had its dangers for Moscow. As Israel stepped up its planning to withdraw its troops from the Chouf Mountains, the possibility that new fighting would erupt became increasingly strong, particularly since no agreement had been reached between the Druze and Gemayel about deploying the Lebanese army in the Chouf to replace the departing Israelis. Exacerbating the situation was the Syrian government statement on August 27 that it would defend its allies against the Lebanese army.[70] The danger for Moscow was that since the United States was backing the Gemayel government, a direct U.S.–Syrian confrontation could occur and then Moscow would again be faced with the problem of how to react to a military conflict in which its principle Arab ally was involved. This time, however, the opponent would most likely not be Israel, backed by the United States, but the United States itself. In short, Moscow faced the prospect of a superpower confrontation over Lebanon. But when the crisis did occur, the USSR adopted a very cautious policy so as to avoid any direct involvement.

3) The September 1983 Crisis

The crisis began at the end of August when warfare broke out between the Lebanese government and the Shiites of western and southern Beirut who resisted a Lebanese army push into their neighborhoods on August 30 and 31. The scale of fighting escalated sharply, however, after the Israeli redeployment of September 3 from the Chouf Mountains southward to the Awali River with Syrian–supported Druze forces clashing both with the Maronite (Phalange) militia and the Lebanese army. While the Phalangist forces were all but driven from the Chouf Mountains, the Lebanese army proved a tougher opponent for the Druze and a major battle was fought for the strategic mountain town of Souk el–Gharb which overlooked Beirut. While Israel held off from intervening both because of pressure from its Druze minority and because of assurances from Druze leader Walid Jumblatt that he would not permit the PLO to occupy positions in Druze–controlled areas, the United States decided to play an active role in the fighting in support of the Lebanese army which it was training. U.S. involvement in the conflict had actually begun before the Israeli withdrawal, as U.S. helicopters had fired on sniper and mortar positions that had harassed the Marines. The U.S. role escalated during the fighting in the Chouf Mountains as guns from U.S. warships in Beirut harbor were fired both in support of Lebanese army troops fighting in Souk el-Gharb[71] and against artillery positions that were firing on or near U.S. positions. After holding aloof from the fighting, France also got involved when its forces came under fire.[72] As the fighting escalated, Syria felt constrained to issue threats against the U.S. so as to back up its clients in the Chouf Mountains,[73] particularly as the U.S. battleship New Jersey, whose sixteen-inch guns had the capability of seriously damaging Syrian positions, neared Beirut.

As the crisis developed, Moscow reacted very cautiously. A TASS statement published in *Pravda* on September 1, merely noted that the Soviet Union was "deeply concerned" over the U.S. armed intervention in Lebanon. It also called for the end to U.S. intervention, the unconditional withdrawal of Israeli forces from Lebanon, and the withdrawal of U.S. troops and "the foreign troops that arrived with them." Interestingly enough there were no Soviet threats against the U.S., although Moscow may have balanced its lack of activity with the implicit support of Syria's right to remain in Lebanon, because there was no mention of any Syrian withdrawal in the TASS statement--a clear change from earlier Soviet policy.

The rapid escalation of the crisis, however, posed both problems and opportunities for the USSR. On the one hand, Moscow seized on the U.S. involvement in the fighting to discredit American policy in the Middle East by asserting that the U.S. was now directly fighting the Arabs. Vladimir Kudravtzev, one of *Izvestia's* more colorful commentators, emphasized this Soviet propaganda line with the statement, "By shedding the blood of Arab patriots, the United States had de facto declared war on the Arabs."[74] In addition, Soviet commentators also utilized the intervention to discredit the U.S. RDF, whose forces it claimed were fighting in Lebanon.[75] Moscow also sought to exploit the Lebanese fighting to divert attention from its shooting down of a Korean airliner in early September. Nonetheless, as American participation in the fighting grew, Moscow faced the dilemma of whether or not it should get directly involved, particularly as Syrian positions came under American fire. The Soviet press noted the escalation of the fighting, and also noted Syria's warning to the U.S. that it would fire back if fired upon, perhaps to prepare the Soviet public for a heightened crisis.[76]

Nonetheless, on September 20, the day after *Pravda* published the Syrian warning, the same Soviet newspaper published a TASS statement that carefully avoided any hint of Soviet involvement in the fighting. While it accused the U.S. of trying to intimidate Syria, and of seeking to establish its own hegemony in the Middle East, it issued no warning to the U.S. other than to state that Washington would not "evade responsibility" for the consequences of the escalated fighting.[77] To be sure, Moscow did not deny reports in the Kuwaiti press that the USSR had placed its forces in the southern part of the USSR on alert, and that a joint Soviet–Syrian operations room was monitoring the situation in Lebanon.[78] In addition, Moscow rejected a U.S. offer to cooperate in limiting Syrian participation in the conflict.[79] However, Moscow refused to formally offer military support to Syria; nor did it react to statements by Syrian officials that Damascus might turn to the USSR for help.[80] It also ignored the leftist Lebanese newspaper *As–Safir's* report that Assad had made a secret trip to Moscow in mid–September.[81] Perhaps most important of all, during the crisis Moscow failed to publicly mention the Soviet–Syrian treaty. In sum, Soviet behavior during the crisis was very cautious indeed, and it is not surprising that Moscow, which feared a superpower confrontation over Lebanon – an area of only tertiary interest to the USSR––warmly welcomed the ceasefire that ended the crisis.[82]

In looking at the September 1983 crisis, it is clear that it differed substantially from the one four months earlier. In May, Assad had been basically in control of the situation and he maneuvered accordingly. Since that crisis was essentially a *political* one, over the Israeli–Lebanese treaty, Syrian mobilizations and threats of war were essentially political acts, unlikely to get out of control. In September, the crisis was essentially a military one that escalated rapidly. Under these circumstances, it is not surprising that the USSR refrained from giving Syria overt support during the crisis; nor did Syria complain publicly about a lack of Soviet aid (thus repeating the strategy it followed during the Israeli invasion of June 1982), although Damascus could not have been too happy with the lack of Soviet support. Syria expressed its anger more openly against its fellow Arabs, intimating that whatever the position of the Arab governments, the Arab masses supported Syria.[83] The lack of Soviet and Arab support, coupled with the U.S. Congress' agreement to extend the stay of U.S. Marines in Beirut for an additional eighteen months, and the arrival near Beirut of the U.S. battleship New Jersey, seem to have persuaded Assad that at least a temporary compromise was in order, and he agreed to a Saudi–mediated cease fire plan that held out the possibility of a new distribution of power in Lebanon.[84] As soon as the cease fire had been achieved, however, Assad moved to strengthen Syria's position in Lebanon further by expelling the remaining troops loyal to Arafat from the Bekaa Valley, and forcing them to go over the mountains to Tripoli where Arafat had suddenly appeared in mid–September.

In the aftermath of the cease fire, the Soviet Union adopted what, on the surface, appeared to be a contradictory policy toward Syria. On the one hand, perhaps to assuage Syrian unhappiness at the lack of support during its confrontation with the U.S. in September, Moscow dispatched to Syria modern SS–21 ground–to–ground missiles with a range of 70 miles––long enough to strike deep into Israel, and with greater accuracy than the previously supplied SCUD or Frog missiles.[85] On the other hand, perhaps out of concern that if the Lebanese cease fire should break down, Syria might become involved in a major confrontation with the U.S., Moscow downplayed its military relationship to Syria. With Andropov ill, with a major Soviet campaign to prevent the deployment of U.S. Pershing II and cruise missiles underway in Western Europe, and with Moscow still trying to overcome the negative effects of the Korean airliner incident, the time was not opportune for the USSR to become involved in a Middle Eastern war. Thus Soviet treatment of the third anniversary of the Soviet–Syrian treaty was kept in very low key as far as Soviet military aid was concerned. A *New Times* article commemorating the treaty, for example, emphasized that Soviet aid had enabled Syria to enhance its defense potential and that the Syrian leaders had themselves repeatedly stressed that they possessed the means to repulse an aggressor.[86] Similarly, a *Pravda* commentary by Yuri Glukhov on October 8 cited the Syrian Prime Minister's statement that Syria relies on its own efforts first, and only then on the assistance of its friends. Perhaps to reinforce the point that the first friends Syria should look to for help were its fellow Arabs, an Arabic language broadcast commemorating the 10th anniversary of the 1973 Arab–Israeli war asserted that the effectiveness of aid from the Socialist countries is increased manyfold if the Arab states themselves united to fight the aggressor.[87]

4) The December 1983 Crisis

Moscow's low key approach to the simmering Lebanese conflict was jarred by the blowing up of the U.S. Marine headquarters in Beirut on October 24th and by subsequent American accusations that Syria was at least indirectly responsible. While *Pravda* senior Middle East correspondent Pavel Demchenko, attributed the explosion to the work of "Lebanese patriots", and asserted that it was the direct result of Reagan's "adventurist policy",[88] the deputy director of the CPSU International Department, Vadim Zagladin in a *Le Monde* interview on October 25, tried to play down the possibility of a Syrian–U.S. confrontation. He called the Beirut attack a "tragedy" and emphasized that Soviet aid to Syria was defensive and that Moscow had always told the Syrians that it was in favor of a peaceful solution to the Middle East conflict.[89] Zagladin, however, also utilized the interview to emphasize, in light of the explosion, that Soviet participation in a Middle East peace settlement would be useful.

Soviet commentary on U.S. policy in Lebanon became more shrill, however, after the U.S. invaded Grenada, with the Soviet media warning that even such moderate Arab states as Saudi Arabia, Morocco, and Oman might be next.[90] Meanwhile as threats of retaliation for the destruction of the Marine headquarters were repeated, and the U.S. began flying reconnaissance missions over Syrian lines in Lebanon, the possibility of a Syrian–U.S. clash grew stronger. At this point, as if to disassociate Moscow from the possibility of intervening, a major Arabic language broadcast minimized the Soviet military presence in Syria, repeating the now–familiar Soviet practice of citing Syrian statements that "Syria had enough means at its disposal to defend itself." In addition, the broadcast asserted that "there is no Soviet military presence in Syria at all, only experts helping Syria bolster its defense capability" and that Syria has "repeatedly replied vehemently to the lie of the alleged Soviet military presence on its soil."[91]

Nonetheless, as tension rose in Lebanon, Moscow evidently felt constrained to issue another warning to the U.S., if only to show its support of the "progressive" Lebanese forces which were backed by Syria. Thus on November 4th a Soviet government TASS statement, citing remarks by Reagan, Weinberger and Shultz that the U.S. was planning a "massive strike against Lebanese national patriotic forces," warned the U.S. "with all seriousness" about taking such action.[92] As in the case of the March 30th warning to Israel, the Soviet warning of November 4th was very limited. Not only was there no mention of Syria, let alone the Soviet–Syrian treaty, but there was not even the usual Soviet statement that the Middle East lay close to the southern borders of the USSR. While *Pravda* commentator Pavel Demchenko, two days later mentioned specifically that the U.S. was preparing "an act of retribution against Syria", he omitted any Soviet warning to the U.S. and also failed to mention the Soviet–Syrian treaty.[93]

While Moscow was seeking to limit its involvement during this period of rising tensions, Assad was exploiting the possibility of an escalated U.S.–Syrian confrontation to crack down on the last redoubt of Arafat's supporters, the refugee camps north of Tripoli. At the same time, it was announced that Syrian Foreign Minister Khaddam would shortly visit the Soviet Union.[94] It is not known whether the Khaddam visit was at the initiative of Moscow (which was unhappy at Assad's crackdown on Arafat's forces) or of Damascus. Whoever initiated it, it was clearly Damascus which was to exploit the atmosphere surrounding the visit. Thus despite American and Israeli statements that they were not going to attack Syria, Assad mobilized his army on November 8th.[95] While Moscow noted the Syrian mobilization in an Arabic language broadcast on November 9th, and also stated that Syria was exerting its additional defense efforts with the help of the USSR, on the basis of their bilateral treaty, the broadcast also stated that "the substance of this treaty is very well known."[96] The purpose of this qualification to the treaty may well have been to remind the Arabs that the treaty did not cover Syrian activities in Lebanon. Indeed, the latter part of the broadcast was devoted to a call for the Arabs to strengthen their unity and act collectively in the face of the U.S. threat. Interestingly, in a possible backhand slap at Syria, the broadcast also noted Soviet support "for the efforts of some Arab states aimed at healing the rift in the ranks of the Palestinian resistance movement and at consolidating the ranks of the Arabs."

While Moscow was urging the Arabs to unite on an "anti–imperialist" basis, Assad appeared to be painting his Soviet allies into a corner in which they had no choice but to support him, regardless of what he did to Arafat's forces. Thus on the eve of Khaddam's visit to the USSR, Syrian forces opened fire on four American reconnaissance planes.[97] At the same time the Syrian ambassador to Britain was stating during a television interview that a conflict caused by U.S. "aggression" against Syria would not be confined to one area, but would be "large scale" because of the help which we are supposed to get from our brothers and friends."[98]

Thus Syrian Foreign Minister Khaddam flew on to Moscow in the midst of a crisis which, like the one in May, seemed to have been orchestrated by Assad, who at this critical moment, however, suddenly became seriously ill. For its part, Moscow could not have been too pleased either with Syrian claims to Soviet aid in a widened conflict or to Syria's crackdown on Arafat's forces in the Tripoli area since Moscow still appeared to wish to see Arafat, and the PLO, as independent actors in the Middle East who would need Soviet support, rather than as a dependent element of the Syrian army. Gromyko's luncheon speech to Khaddam made this point very clear:

> We regard as highly important and urgent the need for overcoming strife and restoring unity within the ranks of the liberation movement of the Arab people of Palestine which must remain an active and effective factor of the anti–imperialist

struggle in the Middle East.[99]

Gromyko also pointedly called for increased Arab unity, stating "the fact is that the enemies of the Arabs seek, in no small measure, to rely in their aggressive policy precisely on their disunity." While Gromyko also condemned U.S. and Israeli threats against the Lebanese National Patriotic Forces and Syria, he pointedly refrained from mentioning the Soviet–Syrian treaty. Khaddam, in his return speech, totally ignored the Palestinian issue while pointedly mentioning, in a segment of his speech ignored by *Pravda* but reported by Damascus Radio, that Soviet support "helped Syria in its steadfastness" and "enabled it to confront aggression."[100] Khaddam did, however, state Syrian aims in Lebanon that seemed to coincide with those of the Soviet Union: the renunciation of the May 17th agreement; the full withdrawal of Israeli and multinational forces; and the achievement of national unity and the restoration of security in Lebanon. The joint communiqué issued at the conclusion of the talks reflected the clearly differing viewpoints of the two sides as it reported an exchange of opinions--the usual Soviet code words for disagreement--"regarding the U.S. and Israeli threats against Syria and the danger of aggression against Syria in this connection."[101] Moscow did, however, give a general statement of support for Syria against "the intrigues of imperialism and Zionism" and "confirmed its adherence" to its commitments under the Soviet–Syrian treaty.

If Moscow felt that it had succeeded in getting Syria to moderate its pressure on Arafat as a result of the Khaddam visit to Moscow, this proved not to be the case. Indeed soon after Khaddam's return to Damascus, Syrian–backed troops stepped up their attack on Arafat's forces and drove them out of the two Palestinian refugee camps north of Tripoli into the city itself. It is possible that Assad felt able to withstand Soviet pressure because at the same time his forces were fighting Arafat's followers near Tripoli, U.S. National Security Adviser, Robert McFarlane was warning Syria that the U.S. would retaliate if Syria continued to fire on U.S. reconnaissance planes (he specifically reminded Damascus of what the U.S. had done on Grenada),[102] and French and Israeli planes were attacking purported terrorist bases in parts of Lebanon under Syrian control.[103] Indeed, at the height of the fighting in Tripoli, Syrian Defense Minister Mustafa Tlas was threatening suicide attacks against U.S. warships and proclaiming that the USSR would never allow Syria to be defeated.[104] At the same time, Assad, in a Syrian TV broadcast of his interview with the American columnists Evans and Novak, was stressing the possibility of a Soviet–American confrontation if a new war broke out.[105]

As the twin Lebanese crises escalated, Moscow increased its rhetorical activity. An article by Demchenko in *Pravda* on November 17th, citing McFarlane's comments on Grenada, noted that the U.S. and Israel counted "on deriving the maximum advantage from the present situation in the region, which is complex enough as it is, with the senseless Iran–Iraq war continuing, inter–Arab discord exacerbated, and the PLO's internal differences having led to bloody clashes between rival groupings." He then appealed for cooperation among all "anti–imperialist" forces to counter the "dangerous development of events" and the U.S.–Israeli threats. Two days later, a *Pravda* editorial discussing the fighting in Tripoli made the point even more strongly:

> It is no accident that the inter–Palestinian discord is being exploited in the framework of the anti–Syrian campaign unleashed by imperialist circles. In these conditions, the senseless and perverse nature of the fratricidal clashes in northern Lebanon are particularly vivid.[106]

The editorial also repeated the section of Gromyko's luncheon address during Khaddam's visit in which the Soviet Foreign Minister had stressed that the PLO "had to continue to operate as an active and effective factor of the anti–imperialist struggle in the Near East." The editorial went on to say that Moscow was taking "active political steps to end the conflict."

As the Tripoli fighting escalated further, despite the Soviet pleas, Moscow stepped up the level of its public complaints with an appeal from the Soviet Afro–Asian Peoples Solidarity Organization. Reminiscent of similar pleas at the time of Syrian–PLO fighting during the Syrian intervention in Lebanon in 1976,[107] the AAPSO called for an end to the "senseless bloodshed" and for the restoration of unity in the ranks of the Palestinians, and the consolidation of all Arab anti–imperialist forces "in the face of the mounting military and political pressure on the part of the U.S.A., Israel and their Allies."[108]

Perhaps as a gesture to Arafat, Gromyko received Farouk Kadoumi, one of Arafat's closest allies in the PLO, on November 23rd. The fact that *Pravda* described the talks as having taken place in a "friendly, businesslike atmosphere", however, indicated that little agreement was reached--a probable indication that Kadoumi was told that Moscow would not take action against Syria--although Gromyko promised to help "in any way possible" to achieve a settlement among the Palestinian factions.[109] Fortunately for Moscow, however, an uneasy cease fire was achieved in Tripoli several days later, although to what degree Assad agreed to halt the fighting due to Saudi inducement, Soviet pressure, or the realization that Arafat continued to have widespread support in the Arab world and among Palestinians, is not yet clear. In any case, Moscow warmly praised the cease fire in an Arabic language broadcast on November 26th,[110] and three days later a joint Soviet party-government statement on the "international day of solidarity with the Palestinian people" saluted Arafat as the Chairman of the PLO executive committee.[111] At the same time it called for unity within the organization and its "close collaboration" with "those countries that are in the forefront of resistance to the U.S. and Israel", i.e. Syria, as Moscow continued to try to maintain good relations with both Arafat and Assad.

While Moscow was clearly relieved by the Tripoli cease fire, however tentative it may have been, it had to be concerned with the rise in U.S.-Syrian tensions. U.S. Defense Secretary Weinberger had asserted on November 11th that the attack on the Marine headquarters had been undertaken by Iranians with the "sponsorship and knowledge and authority of the Syrian government."[112] While Syria rejected the charge,[113] it also again asserted that its planes had driven off U.S. jets flying over Syrian-controlled areas.[114] At this point, with the cease fire holding in Tripoli, Moscow moved again to champion Syria. A *Novosti* article by Demchenko which was distributed to Western correspondents, warned that Syria was an ally of Moscow with whom it had a Treaty of Friendship and Cooperation and that aggression against Syria was an "extremely dangerous venture." This article also noted that the potential of forces opposing U.S. and Israeli policy in Syria and Lebanon did not compare "in any way with what the Pentagon faced on Grenada."[115] This was the strongest warning given by Moscow to the U.S. thus far in the Lebanese crisis, and was perhaps aimed at deterring the U.S. from any strike against Syria, although the fact that it took the form of a *Novosti* article, and not a TASS statement, indicated it was still low level. Nonetheless, such a warning again raised questions of Soviet credibility should a Syrian-American confrontation take place, either in the form of an American retaliation for the Marine headquarters explosion or an attack on Syrian positions in Lebanon in retaliation for the firing on U.S. reconnaissance planes. Syrian government statements such as the one broadcast on Syrian radio on November 29th that "Syria expresses its pride--before the Arab nation and the world--at the fact that it agitates a superpower" appeared to make some form of confrontation even more likely.[116]

The U.S. attack came on December 4th, following Syrian anti-aircraft fire on U.S. reconnaissance planes the previous day. The fact that the U.S. lost two planes, and had one of its pilots killed and another captured did not detract from the fact that the U.S. had openly attacked

Syria and that a major confrontation was underway. Under these circumstances Moscow was again faced with the dilemma of either supporting its client's policies in Lebanon--policies that the USSR did not thoroughly agree with--or else once again losing some of its diplomatic credibility, particularly since Reagan was threatening to strike Syrian positions again if U.S. forces continued to come under attack.[117] Once again Moscow was to take a cautious stand, although its diplomatic credibility was to suffer. Thus a TASS statement simply noted that the Soviet Union "declared its solidarity with the peoples of Lebanon, Syria, and other Arab countries in defending their independence" and that "the aggressive actions of the United States against Syria constitute a serious threat to peace not only in the Middle East region."[118] While the TASS statement also sought propaganda advantage by tying the U.S. attack to the strategic cooperation agreement concluded between Reagan and Israeli Prime Minister Yitzhak Shamir a week earlier, and claimed that by its attack the U.S. no longer qualified as an "honest broker" in the Middle East, the failure of the TASS statement to mention the Soviet–Syrian treaty indicated that Syria could not expect more than Soviet moral support against the U.S. so long as the confrontation was limited to Lebanon.

While Moscow was not willing to aid Syria militarily to confront the U.S., it did seek to utilize the American attack against Syria to undermine the U.S. position in the Middle East. Thus a *Pravda* editorial on December 10th, repeated the themes of the TASS statement that the U.S. no longer qualified as a mediator in the Arab–Israeli conflict and that the U.S. attack was the outgrowth of U.S.–Israeli strategic cooperation. The editorial went on to assert that the U.S. was now being opposed even in conservative Arab countries, and Moscow once again appealed for Arab unity on an "anti–imperialist" basis. An Arabic language broadcast on December 12th carried this theme further asserting that when the U.S. signed its "strategic alliance" with Israel, it challenged "all Arabs without exception, the progressives and the moderates alike."[119] Interestingly enough, however, the broadcast mentioned Soviet support for Syria only in passing and again called on the Arabs to unite and use their economic pressure against the U.S. It seems clear that Moscow, unwilling to use force to aid Syria, had gone back to the course of action it had pursued since the September crisis--an appeal to the Arabs to help Syria themselves. Unfortunately for the USSR, which hoped that the U.S. attack would force the Centrist Arabs to again rally around Syria and what was left of the Steadfastness Front, this was not to happen. With Syria's ally Iran again threatening to close the Straits of Hormuz, the Centrist Arabs, and particularly the members of the Gulf Cooperation Council, had no choice but to rely on the U.S. for help. Syria, to its apparent bitter disappointment, also realized this soon after the U.S. attack, as the Syrian media bewailed the lack of Arab support. As *Al Ba'ath* noted on December 8th:

> It is illogical to have Arab resources remain idle, waiting for the circle of aggression to reach them. It is also illogical to restrict the role of this or that Arab country to mere condemnation or denunciation of the aggressor.[120]

The end result was that Syria, without Soviet or Arab support against the U.S. and with its efforts to topple Arafat as leader of the PLO only moderately successful (the PLO leader, who continued to command widespread Palestinian support, left Tripoli under the UN flag), moved to de-escalate the tension. Thus it returned the body of the dead U.S. airman to the U.S., agreed to talk to U.S. mediator Donald Rumsfeld--despite the fact that the battleship New Jersey was firing on Syrian positions after U.S. reconnaissance planes were again fired upon--and finally, in a gesture which it said was aimed at "creating a circumstance conducive to the withdrawal of U.S. forces from Lebanon", released the captured U.S. airman, Lt. Goodman.[121] This was a major Syrian concession, given the fact that Syrian leaders had earlier said that he would not be released until after the "war" was over and U.S. forces had withdrawn from Lebanon.[122]

It is clearly possible that Assad, who had now recovered from his illness, was trying to exploit the rising tide of opposition in the United States to the Marine presence in Lebanon. Nonetheless, to release Lt. Goodman at a time when U.S. naval guns were still pounding positions held by Syria and its Lebanese allies indicated that the Syrian leader realized that his confrontation with the U.S. held the danger of getting out of control at a time when he could not count on either Soviet or Arab support. Fortunately for Assad, however, the ineptitude of the Gemayel government and war-weariness in both the United States and Israel, were soon to enable the Syrian leader to regain predominant influence in Lebanon, a development from which Moscow sought to profit.

5) Moscow and the Collapse of the U.S. Position in Lebanon.

The release of Lt. Goodman, coupled with the publication a few days earlier of the Long Commission report which analyzed the U.S. political-military mistakes in Lebanon in the period leading up to the destruction of the Marine headquarters,[123] increased the clamor in the U.S. for a pullout of the Marines, a clamor that was reflected in the U.S.

Congress.[124] At the same time the position of Amin Gemayel weakened considerably as negotiations for a disengagement plan among the various warring Lebanese factions broke down at the end of January. The diplomatic impasse was followed by heavy fighting in the Beirut area between the Lebanese army and Druze and Shiite forces, a development which led to the virtual collapse of the Lebanese army, the resignation of Prime Minister Wazzan and the seizure of West Beirut by Moslem militias. As chaos appeared to reign in Beirut, President Reagan suddenly announced the "redeployment" of U.S. Marines to Navy ships off the coast of Lebanon.[125] The U.S. redeployment, which was soon to be followed by the other members of the multinational force, was accompanied by American naval shelling of anti-government positions in the vicinity of Beirut, although the rationale for the shelling was never clearly explained by the Reagan Administration.[126] Indeed, the general course of U.S. policy during this period seemed confused at best, and whatever mistakes the U.S. had made in backing the Gemayel government up until this point, the hurried exodus of Marines from Beirut, coupled with what appeared to be indiscriminate artillery fire into the Lebanese mountains, could only hurt the U.S. image, not only in Lebanon, but in the Middle East as a whole. Naturally, such a weakening of the U.S. position was welcomed by Moscow which moved to coordinate policy directly with Syria following the Moslem takeover of West Beirut. On February 8, *Pravda* announced that Geydar Aliyev, the only Politburo member of Shii Moslem extraction, would be going to Syria for a "working visit." Just before Aliyev was to depart, however, Andropov died, the second Soviet leader to die during the Lebanese crisis. The succession of Konstantin Chernenko to power was quite rapid, and the new Soviet leader soon moved to exploit the U.S. defeat in Lebanon.

The first issue pertaining to the Lebanese crisis facing Chernenko was a French proposal to replace the multinational force in Beirut with a United Nations force. The Soviet leadership vetoed the French plan, ostensibly because it would not prevent the U.S. from shelling Syrian and pro-Syrian forces in Beirut behind the screen of the UN troops. It would appear, however, that the primary reason for the Soviet veto of the French proposal was to prevent the U.S. from using the insertion of the UN force as a cover for an American retreat from Lebanon, a development which might diminish the impact of the U.S. defeat.[127]

Moscow was to achieve another success for its Lebanese policy when Amin Gemayel, now virtually bereft of U.S. military support, could only turn to Syrian President Assad for help in staying in power. Assad, at least in the short term, proved willing to help--for a price. The price was the abrogation of the May 17 Israeli-Lebanese agreement, and Gemayel announced its abrogation on March 5. Yet even as Moscow was hailing this development (Soviet commentators were to call it a major blow to the entire Camp David process), and Aliyev was again getting ready to journey to Damascus, there were a number of problems which the new Soviet leadership had to face despite the collapse of the U.S. position in Lebanon. In the first place, a power struggle had erupted in Damascus over the succession to President Hafiz Assad who apparently had not fully recovered from his heart attack. Secondly, despite its victory in Lebanon, which the Syrian media was hailing as equivalent to Nasser's nationalization of the Suez Canal,[128] Syria remained in diplomatic isolation in the Arab world, while Egypt continued to improve its ties to Centrist Arab states. Egypt's rapprochement with the Centrist Arabs was reinforced by the surprise visit of Arafat to Cairo after his expulsion from Lebanon in December 1983 (Arafat later went to Jordan where he resumed discussions with King Hussein), and the rapprochement was highlighted by the decision of the Islamic Conference to re–admit Egypt to its ranks in mid–January, a development attributed by Moscow to the "pressure of conservative Moslem regimes."[129] Nonetheless the fact that Libya, Syria and South Yemen walked out of the conference indicated the continuing isolation of Moscow's closest Arab allies, while the USSR had to be concerned about the possible formation of a new Arab front that would move to reincorporate Egypt into the Arab League and possibly revive the Reagan Plan.[130] Soviet concern with such a development could only have increased with Mubarak's visit to King Hassan of Morocco––the first official visit to an Arab country by the head of the Egyptian state since the 1979 Peace Treaty, as Moscow TV unhappily noted[131] and by Mubarak's meeting with King Hussein in Washington in mid–February as the two Arab leaders prepared for talks with President Reagan.

Meanwhile, as Egypt's relations with Centrist Arab nations improved, Syria despite its victory in Lebanon, appeared to remain isolated. Thus not only was its influence insufficient to prevent the Islamic Conference from readmitting Egypt, it was again in isolation when the Arab League Foreign Ministers, in a meeting in mid–March which Syria and Libya boycotted, took a strongly anti–Iranian position, condemning Iran for its continuing "aggression against Iraq", and warning Iran that the continuation of the war would force the Arab states to reconsider their relations with it.[132] For its part, Moscow could only have been concerned with Syria's continued Arab isolation, not to mention that of Libya whose heavy–handed actions against the Sudan (the bombing of Omdurman) and Jordan (the storming of the Jordanian Embassy in Tripoli) served only to alienate two regimes Moscow was seeking to win over. Compounding

Moscow's difficulties in exploiting the U.S. failure in Lebanon was the situation in the Persian Gulf. Iran had again undertaken a major offensive against Iraq and was threatening the key southern Iraqi city of Basra, while at the same time repeating its threats to close the Straits of Hormuz if Iraq, using its newly-acquired Super-Entendard bombers interfered with Iranian oil exports. Moscow, at a time when its relations with Iran were at a low ebb in part because of the Khomeini regime's persecution of the Tudeh party, was clearly concerned that the United States, which had again pledged to keep the Straits open and which had increased the size of its fleet near the Gulf, would exploit the Iranian threats to reinforce its position in the Arab states of the Gulf, and thereby divert attention from its failure in Lebanon. As *Krasnaya Zvezda* noted on March 4, "Washington is trying [in the Persian Gulf] to compensate at least somehow for its political and military errors in Lebanon."[133] In a counter to the stepped up U.S. deployment near the Gulf, the Soviet government issued a statement on March 8 denouncing U.S. activity in the Gulf as a "grave threat to peace and international security", and stating that the USSR would not abide by any restrictions imposed by the U.S. in the Gulf region.[134]

Thus, when Geydar Aliyev came to Damascus, the overall Middle East picture was not as bright as Moscow would have wished, despite the failure of U.S. policy in Lebanon. In addition, the dinner speeches during Aliyev's visit reflected continued tension in Soviet-Syrian relations. Thus Khaddam, in hailing the defeat of American and Israeli policy in a dinner speech welcoming Aliyev, gave more credit to Syrian action than to Soviet aid, while also praising those Palestinian "patriotic forces who courageously opposed the policy of sliding, fragmentation, and departure from the decisions of the Palestine National Council, pursued by some Palestinian leaders to satisfy the Americans and Israelis."[135] In his speech in response, Aliyev first praised the Lebanese National Patriotic Forces for resisting U.S. pressure before mentioning the Syrian role, although he did have words of praise for the Soviet-Syrian treaty. He also called for the Arab people of Palestine, "under the leadership of the PLO, its sole legitimate representative, to be given an opportunity to establish its own state."[136]

The final communiqué issued after Aliyev's talks with Syrian leaders (Moscow made special mention of Aliyev's meeting with Rifat al-Assad who was "heartily congratulated" on his appointment as Vice-President, perhaps as a gesture to show that Moscow now had confidence in Rifat)[137] referred to a "spirit of friendship and mutual understanding", the usual Soviet code words for disagreement.[138] Thus while the two sides hailed the abrogation of the May 17 Israeli-Lebanese agreement as a great success and also expressed their aspirations to further strengthen Soviet–Syrian relations, the final communiqué noted "an exchange of opinions" regarding U.S. and Israeli threats against Syria, thereby, as in the visit of Khaddam to Moscow in November, 1983 probably indicating disagreement over the degree of Soviet support Syria might expect if it became involved in a war with the U.S. or Israel. An even more serious Soviet–Syrian disagreement was revealed over the Palestinian issue by the communiqué's notation that "a thorough exchange of opinions took place on questions relating to the state of affairs in the Palestinian Resistance movement." Nonetheless, perhaps reflecting Moscow's displeasure with the Arafat–Mubarak meeting, and the resumption of Arafat's talks with Hussein, the communiqué also noted:

> The Soviet Union and Syria are convinced of the need to preserve the unity of the Palestinian resistance movement and to overcome as speedily as possible the disagreement within the PLO, which is the sole legitimate representative of the Arab people of Palestine, on a *progressive–patriotic and anti–imperialist basis.*
>
> The sides believe that the implementation of the Palestinian national aspirations is impossible without observance of the Palestine National Council's decision aimed at countering the Israeli aggression and the Camp David policy of separate deals, including the "Reagan Plan" and without close cooperation by the PLO with Syria, all progressive Arab States, and patriotic forces of the Arab world.[139] (emphasis mine)

Another area of Soviet–Syrian disagreement was most probably Syria's continuing support for Iran at a time when Moscow was trying to end the Iran–Iraq war. While no mention of this dispute was made in the joint communiqué, the Kuwaiti periodical, *al–Qabas,* asserted that such differences had surfaced during the discussions.[140]

On balance, however, it appeared that Aliyev's visit helped to solidify Soviet–Syrian relations following the succession in Moscow and the power struggle in Damascus. As might be expected, Soviet broadcasts to the Arab world, highlighted the Aliyev visit, citing Syrian newspaper declarations of praise for Soviet–Syrian and Soviet–Arab relations.[141] Nonetheless, as far as Lebanon was concerned, Moscow did not appear ready to cede it to Syria as a satrapy. In the first place, despite the departure of the U.S. Marines and the abrogation of the May 17 agreement, Syria was not yet in a position to fully control events in Lebanon, as the failure of the Lausanne National Reconciliation

Conference, which was held under Syrian supervision, indicated. Indeed, while both Druze leader Walid Jumblatt and Shii leader Nabih Berri had cooperated with Syria against Amin Gemayel, neither was a Syrian stooge (according to most reports, Jumblatt's father had been killed by Syria) and both might act in an increasingly independent manner should a genuine power sharing system ever be worked out in Lebanon. Secondly, Israel continued to control the southern third of Lebanon and retained influence both with Lebanese Christians and with Lebanese Druze, although its relations with the Shiites in its area of control had deteriorated markedly. Under these circumstances Moscow evidently felt it was useful to develop its own ties with key Lebanese groups. Indeed, Walid Jumblatt, whose father had close ties to Moscow before his assassination, had been invited to visit the Soviet capital in January 1984.[142] There were frequent meetings between Soviet leaders and Lebanese Communist party officials, and at the end of March, Karen Brutents, deputy chief of the CPSU Central Committee's International Department, journeyed to Lebanon where he met Berri, Jumblatt, Lebanese Foreign Minister Elie Salim and Lebanese Communist party leader George Hawi, as well as Lebanese President Amin Gemayel. Moscow's goal in Lebanon at this time appeared to be to gain first-hand knowledge of the complex political situation there in order to help consolidate the victory of those Lebanese forces opposed to American influence so as to keep Lebanon out of the American-directed peace process. To be sure, at this time the United States was having more than its share of difficulties in its Middle East diplomacy. Not only had it suffered a near debacle in Lebanon, but the Reagan Plan suffered a major blow in mid-March when King Hussein of Jordan announced he would not enter into talks with Israel, even if the Israelis froze the construction of settlements in occupied territories, because the U.S. had lost its credibility and was no longer a "trusted mediator." Needless to say, Moscow was delighted with this development, with some Soviet commentators attributing the King's action to the failure of U.S. policy in Lebanon,[143] although Syrian commentators dismissed the King's speech as insignificant unless Hussein broke his ties with the United States.[144]

The Syrian commentators may well have been closer to the mark, given King Hussein's statement at a March 30 press conference expressing interest in a possible Labor Party victory in the forthcoming Israeli elections, a development that might once again breathe life into the Reagan Plan and the U.S.-mediated peace process.[145]

In any case, King Hussein's comments are a useful point of departure for analyzing the interplay of Soviet and Syrian policy during the Lebanese crisis of June 1982 – March 1984.

Conclusions

In evaluating Soviet policy during the Lebanese crisis of 1982–84 and the Soviet–Syrian relationship during this period, one can draw three general conclusions. First, in the aftermath of the Israeli invasion of Lebanon, where the Soviet role was essentially limited to issuing a series of ineffectual threats to Israel and the United States, Moscow sought to block U.S. policy in Lebanon, and throughout the Middle East as well, primarily by reinforcing Syrian opposition to Israeli and U.S. policy. Second, Moscow sought to exploit the continuing Lebanese crisis to demonstrate that without its participation, no settlement was possible for the Arab–Israeli conflict. Finally, while issuing periodic warnings to both Israel and the United States throughout the 1982–84 period, Moscow sought to avoid a military confrontation with them. Thus Moscow carefully limited the scope of its 1980 treaty with Syria to Syrian territory (excluding Lebanon), while at the same time urging the other Arab states to rally to the defense of Syria by using their economic and military resources to aid Syria in its confrontations with Israel and the United States.

Moscow's problem during this period was that while it was reinforcing Syria's ability to thwart U.S. diplomacy, whether in the form of U.S. efforts to expand the Camp David peace process, gain Arab acceptance for the Reagan Plan, or obtain approval for the May 17, 1983 Israeli–Lebanese accord, Damascus was exploiting Soviet support to achieve its own goals, both in Lebanon and in the Arab world as a whole, goals that were not always compatible with those of the Soviet Union. Thus Syria sought predominant, if not exclusive, influence in Lebanon, control over the PLO, and a leading role in the Arab world during this period. To be sure, Moscow was not adverse to Syria, a member of the pro–Soviet Steadfastness Front in the Arab world, obtaining a position of Arab leadership. This would mean that Syria would move out of the position of isolation in the Arab world caused by its backing for Iran in the Iran–Iraq war, and Moscow may have hoped that Syria could thereby win over some of the more important Centrist Arab states or at least keep them from a reconciliation with Egypt. Nonetheless, Syrian attempts to militarily confront first Israel in May 1983 and then the United States in the September–December 1983 period, confrontations which the Syrian leadership attempted to portray as Syrian "defense of the Arab nation against Zionism and imperialism", did not appear to meet with full Soviet approval. This was the case not only because most Arab states continued to remain cool to Syria but also because Syrian leaders threatened to drag in the Soviet Union to help Syria fight its Lebanese battles, especially by claiming that the Soviet–Syrian Treaty covered Syrian actions in Lebanon. Similarly, Assad's efforts to split Fatah and his subsequent crackdown on Arafat's supporters in the Bekaa Valley and in Tripoli appeared to be unpopular in Moscow. In the first place, it further splintered the already badly divided Arab world, with not only Iraq but also Steadfastness Front member Algeria supporting Arafat, thus making Moscow's long–sought "anti–imperialist" Arab unity even more difficult to achieve. Secondly, despite its unhappiness with Arafat's flirtation with the Reagan Plan, Moscow gave every appearance of wanting to keep the PLO as an independent actor in Arab politics—–one open to Soviet influence—–rather than having it become a mere appendage of Syrian policy. Finally, should the hard–liners in the anti–Arafat movement within Fatah win out, it would be far more difficult for Moscow to gain acceptance for its Middle East peace plan which called for the existence of a Palestinian state alongside of, not in place of, Israel.

In sum, the Soviet–Syrian relationship during the 1982–84 period was an uneasy one as each country sought to use the other to help further its goals. Nonetheless, if one asks which country profited more from the relationship, the answer would appear to be Syria. While Moscow benefitted from Syrian opposition to the U.S. diplomatic initiatives, the USSR also had to make important concessions to Damascus during this period. First, after initially demanding that all foreign forces, including Syrian, leave Lebanon by September 1983, the USSR, although realizing that the continued presence of Syrian troops in Lebanon carried with it the danger of a confrontation with the United States, no longer publicly called for a Syrian troop withdrawal. Secondly, after resisting a number of Syrian demands for more advanced weaponry so that it could have a degree of military power equivalent to that of Israel, Moscow agreed to send to Damascus two major weapons systems, the SAM–5 anti–aircraft system and the SS–21 surface–to–surface missile. Both systems had never before been deployed outside the Warsaw Pact area.

Interestingly, both weapons systems were sent after Moscow failed to give Syria support in a major military confrontation, the SAM–5 after Syria had been defeated by Israel during the Israeli invasion of Lebanon and the SS–21 after the September 1983 Syrian–American confrontation. By sending the two sophisticated weapons systems, Moscow may have tried to assuage Syrian unhappiness at the lack of Soviet support. It is, of course, quite possible that the weapons systems were sent to Syria with the primary purpose of aiding it in deterring an attack, thus making Soviet support in a crisis situation unnecessary. In addition, Moscow emphasized during the Syrian military build–up and the subsequent crisis that Syrian goals were defensive, another ploy aimed at averting the outbreak of war.

Nonetheless, the reason that Soviet troops manned the SAM-5s and appeared to control the SS-21s as well, may have been that Moscow was concerned that otherwise Syria would exploit the new weaponry to go to war in pursuit of its Lebanese or Middle Eastern goals. Indeed, by sending Assad such weapons, as well as by replenishing his 1982 losses to Israel, the USSR not only enhanced the Syrian leader's bargaining position vis-à-vis Israel, the United States and the other Arab states, but also gave him the means to more successfully wage war, should he so choose, as Syria approached its long-sought strategic equivalence with Israel. In taking such action, Moscow clearly ran a risk. On the one hand, its own credibility, and that of its weaponry, had come under strong attack by the Arabs during the Israeli invasion of Lebanon of 1982, and by providing such advanced weaponry to Syria, and also by issuing warnings to both Israel and the United States, Moscow evidently hoped to regain some of its lost credibility. The dilemma for the Soviet leadership was that Assad tended to exploit both the new weaponry and the Soviet warnings--limited as they may have been--to further his own ambitions in Lebanon and elsewhere in the Arab world. What made matters so dangerous for the Kremlin, particularly at a time when Andropov was ill, was that both in September 1983 and December 1983, Assad provoked the U.S. into a military confrontation, thus putting Moscow in the unenviable position of either backing its most important Arab ally, thereby risking a confrontation with the United States, or remaining silent and losing credibility as it had in 1982. Moscow was to choose the latter course, although it may have hoped that the U.S.-Syrian confrontation would so undermine the American position in the Arab world that the lack of direct Soviet support to Syria would be overlooked. Fortunately for Moscow the growing war-weariness in the United States which led Reagan to withdraw U.S. troops in February 1984, together with an increasingly broad consensus in Israel calling for another troop withdrawal, left Syria in the dominant position in Lebanon without having the need of direct Soviet support.

Nonetheless, the fact remained that Moscow's position in the Arab world, despite the victory of its client Syria, had to be somewhat shaky as a result of the Lebanese crisis. In the first place, the USSR did not provide any meaningful political or military assistance to the PLO or Syrian fighting forces in Lebanon during the 1982 war or to Syria during its confrontations with the United States, and Moscow's utility as an ally to Arab world clients must have become somewhat suspect as a result. While the USSR had continually appealed to the Arabs to unite during the invasion so that the Arab world as a whole could confront Israel and later had called on the Arabs to unite to confront the United States, the lack of

Arab unity did not, in the eyes of many Arabs, absolve Moscow of the responsibility of aiding its Arab allies. Secondly, the poor performance of Soviet weaponry in Syrian hands further lowered Soviet prestige. Middle Easterners with memories of the 1973 war could only remember how Soviet commentators had drawn positive comparisons between Soviet and American weaponry as operated by Arabs and Israelis in that conflict. In the Lebanese conflict of 1982, the only comparisons that could be drawn were negative ones, despite extensive Soviet efforts to show that Soviet weaponry had worked well. The supply of SAM–5 and SS–21 missiles to Syria really did not compensate for this. Indeed it remains a very open question as to whether Moscow's supply of the SAM–5 and SS–21 weapons systems to Syria––both taking place following, not during, a crisis period––and its very limited warnings to the U.S. and Israel will suffice to restore the decline in Soviet prestige caused by Moscow's inaction during the Israeli invasion.

In sum, while the United States has clearly suffered a major policy failure in Lebanon, as shown by its precipitous withdrawal and the subsequent abrogation of the May 17th Lebanese–Israeli agreement, it remains to be seen to what degree the Soviet Union will be able to profit from it.

Notes

1. For recent studies of Soviet policy in the Middle East, see Robert O. Freedman, *Soviet Policy Toward the Middle East Since 1970*, Third Edition, (New York: Praeger, 1982); Jon D. Glassman, *Arms for the Arabs: The Soviet Union and War in the Middle East* (Baltimore: Johns Hopkins, 1975); Galia Golan, *Yom Kippur and After: The Soviet Union and the Middle East Crisis* (London: Cambridge University Press, 1977); Yaacov Ro'i (ed.), *The Limits of Power: Soviet Policy in the Middle East* (London: Croom, Helm, 1979); and Adeed Dawisha and Karen Dawisha (eds.), *The Soviet Union in the Middle East: Policies and Perspectives* (New York: Holmes & Meier, 1982). For an Arab viewpoint, see Mohamed Heikal, *The Sphinx and the Commissar* (New York: Harper and Row, 1978). For a recent Soviet view, see E.M. Primakov, *Anatomiia Blizhnevostochnogo Konflikta* (Moscow: Mysl', 1978).

2. For studies of Soviet military aid, see Glassman, *op. cit.*, George Lenczowski, *Soviet Advances in the Middle East* (Washington: American Enterprise Institute, 1972), and Amnon Sella, "Changes in Soviet Political–Military Policy in the Middle East after 1973", in Ro'i, *The Limits to Power, op. cit.*, pp. 32–64.

3. For a view of the role of Israel in Soviet Middle East strategy, see Freedman, *Soviet Policy Toward the Middle East, op. cit.,* chapter 8.

4. For a study of Soviet policy toward the Communist parties of the Arab world, see Robert O. Freedman, "The Soviet Union and the Communist Parties of the Arab World: An Uncertain Relationship", in Roger E. Kanet and Donna Bahry (eds.), *Soviet Economic and Political Relations with the Developing World* (New York: Praeger, 1975), pp. 100–134, and John K. Cooley, "The Shifting Sands of Arab Communism", *Problems of Communism* vol. 24, no. 2 (1975), pp. 22–42.

5. For an analysis of the Islamic revival, see Daniel Pipes, "The World is Political!: The Islamic Revival of the Seventies", *Orbis,* vol. 24 no. 1 (Spring 1980), pp. 9–41.

6. For analyses of Soviet–Syrian relations up to Camp David, see Freedman, *op. cit.* and Galia Golan, "Syria and the Soviet Union Since the Yom Kippur War", *Orbis* vol. 21 no. 4 (Winter 1978), pp. 777–801. For an analysis sympathetic to the Syrian role in Lebanon, see Adeed I. Dawisha, *Syria and the Lebanese Crisis* (New York: St. Martin's Press, 1980).

For other analyses of Syrian politics and foreign policy, see John Devlin's study "Syria Since Camp David", in *The Middle East Since Camp David* (ed. Robert O. Freedman) (Boulder, Colorado: Westview Press, 1984). See also David Pryce–Jones, "Bloody Assad", *New Republic,* January 30, 1984, pp. 20–25.

7. For analyses of the domestic situation in Syria, see Nikolas Van Dam, *The Struggle for Power in Syria* (New York: St. Martin's Press, 1979); Stanley Reed III, "Dateline Syria: Fin De Regime?", *Foreign Policy* no. 39 (Summer 1980), pp. 176–190; and Chris Kutscheria, "Sticks and Carrots", *The Middle East* no. 80 (June 1981), pp. 8–9.

8. These events are discussed in Freedman, *Soviet Policy Toward the Middle East, op. cit.,* chapters 9 and 10.

9. *Ibid.,* pp. 395–396. See also Amiram Nir, *The Soviet–Syrian Friendship and Cooperation Treaty: Unfulfilled Expectations* (Tel Aviv: Jaffa Center for Strategic Studies, 1983).

10. These two crises are discussed in Robert O. Freedman, "Soviet Policy Toward Syria Since Camp David", *Middle East Review,* Fall–Winter 1982, pp. 31–42.

11. For a Soviet view of U.S.–Israeli strategic cooperation, see *Pravda,* September 15, 1981.

12. Nir, *op.cit.,* p. 19.

13. *Ibid.,* p. 20; interview with Hanna Batatu, Washington, D.C., December 19, 1983.

14. *Pravda,* January 16, 1982.

15. *Ibid.*

16. *Pravda*, January 17, 1982.

17. For Moscow's highly negative reaction to this development, see the Moscow Radio Arab language broadcast on May 28, 1982 (Foreign Broadcast Information Service Daily Report: The Soviet Union (hereafter *FBIS:USSR*), June 1, 1982, p. H–3).

18. For a description of the increasingly severe problems facing the PLO in Lebanon on the eve of the war, see David Butler, "In the Same Trench", *The Middle East*, June 1982, p. 6. See also his report, "Shiites in Beirut Clash", *The Middle East*, February 1982, p. 14.

19. Cf. remarks by Taha Ramadan, First Deputy Prime Minister of Iraq, Baghdad Radio, June 1, 1982 (*FBIS:ME*, June 2, 1981, p. E–2).

20. The Moroccan Foreign Minister, Mohammed Boucetta, paid a visit to Cairo on June 7, 1982 thus further ending Egypt's ostracism, as did Egyptian President Mubarak's attendance at the funeral of King Khalid of Saudi Arabia later that month.

21. Cf. *Pravda*, May 26, 1982.

22. The central reasons for Soviet inactivity during the Israeli invasion would appear to be: (1) the failure of the other Arab states to aid Syria and the PLO; (2) Israeli air supremacy in the region; and (3) uncertainty over the possible U.S. reaction to a Soviet intervention. The reasons for Soviet inactivity are discussed in Robert O. Freedman, "The Soviet Union and the Middle East: Failure to Match the United States as a Regional Power", *Middle East Contemporary Survey*, vol. 6, 1981–82 (ed. Colin Legum, Haim Shaked, and Daniel Dishon) (New York: Holmes & Meier, 1984), pp. 40–48 and Karen Dawisha, "The USSR in the Middle East: Superpower in Eclipse", *Foreign Affairs*, Winter 1982–83, pp. 438–452.

23. Tripoli, *Jana*, June 26, 1982, (*FBIS:ME*, June 26, 1982, pp. Q–2, Q–3).

24. TASS, June 1982 (*FBIS:USSR*, June 22, 1982, p. H–3).

25. For a description of the Reagan Plan, see Barry Rubin, "The United States and the Middle East From Camp David to the Reagan Plan", *Middle East Contemporary Survey 1981–82, op. cit.*, pp. 30–31.

26. For a description of the Fez Plan, see *The Middle East Journal*, vol. 37 no. 1 (Winter 1983), p. 71.

27. *Pravda*, September 16, 1982. For an analysis of the status of the Soviet Middle East peace plan on the eve of the Israeli invasion of Lebanon, see Robert O. Freedman, "Moscow, Washington and the Gulf", *American–Arab Affairs*, no. 1 (Summer 1982), pp. 132–134.

28. *Pravda*, September 11, 1982.

29. Cf. report by Edward Walsh, *Washington Post*, January 5,

1983 and Thomas L. Friedman, *New York Times*, March 21, 1983.

30. It is also possible that the Soviet move, in part, was a response to the emplacement of U.S. troops in Beirut, as well as a means of hampering U.S. air operations in the Eastern Mediterranean near Lebanon.

31. Freedman, "Soviet Policy Toward Syria Since Camp David", *loc. cit.*

32. Cited in report by Thomas L. Friedman, *New York Times*, February 23, 1983. The fact that PLO moderate Issam Sartawi, who publicly advocated a compromise between Israel and the PLO, was forbidden to speak at the meeting was a further indication of the erosion of Arafat's position. Sartawi was subsequently assassinated in April while attending the Socialist International Congress in Portugal. For general discussions of the PNC Council session, see Judith Perera, "Hammering Out a Compromise", *The Middle East*, no. 101 (March 1983), pp. 8–9 and Cheryl A. Rubenberg, "The PNC and the Reagan Initiative", *American– Arab Affairs*, vol. 4 (Spring 1983), pp. 53–69. For an analysis of trends within the PLO, see Aaron David Miller, "Palestinians in the 1980s", *Current History*, January 1984, pp. 17–20, 34–36 and "The PLO Since Camp David", in *The Middle East Since Camp David* (ed. Robert O. Freedman) (Boulder, Colorado: Westview Press, 1984).

33. *Pravda*, February 25, 1983.

34. *Pravda*, March 31, 1983.

35. Cited in *Christian Science Monitor*, March 30, 1983.

36. Riyadh *SPA*, April 2, 1983 (*FBIS:ME*, April 4, 1983, p. C–6).

37. The text of Gromyko's press conference may be found in *FBIS:USSR*, April 4, 1983, pp. AA–1 – AA–17.

38. *Ibid.*, p. AA–15.

39. *Ibid.*, p. AA–16.

40. Cited in Reuters report, *New York Times*, April 17, 1983.

41. Cf. report by David Landau, *Jerusalem Post*, April 20, 1983.

42. Cf. report by Herbert Denton, *Washington Post*, April 22, 1983.

43. Cited in *Jerusalem Post*, April 24, 1983.

44. Cited in *Jerusalem Post*, April 26, 1983.

45. Cf. *Jerusalem Post*, April 27, 1983.

46. For an analysis of the dynamics of the process leading to the Israeli–Lebanon agreement, see the report by Bernard Gwertzman, *New York Times*, May 10, 1983.

47. Cf. report by Herbert Denton, *Washington Post*, May 7, 1983.

48. TASS report, May 9, 1983 (*FBIS:USSR*, May 10, 1983, p. H-1).

49. Cf. reports by Thomas Friedman, *New York Times*, May 10, 1983 and Nora Bustany, *Washington Post*, May 10, 1983.

50. Cf. report by Bernard Gwertzman, *New York Times*, May 11, 1983.

51. Cf. report by John Goshko, *Washington Post*, May 11, 1983.

52. Damascus, *SANA*, May 9, 1983 (*FBIS:ME*, May 9, 1983, p. H-2).

53. Reuters report, *New York Times*, May 11, 1983.

54. Beirut Domestic Service in Arabic, May 10, 1983 (*FBIS:ME*, May 16, 1983, p. H-8).

55. Cited in *Jerusalem Post*, May 15, 1983.

56. *Ibid.*

57. Cf. report by Robin Wright, *Christian Science Monitor*, May 17, 1983.

58. Cf. report in *Jerusalem Post*, May 24, 1983.

59. Cf. report by William E. Farrell, *New York Times*, May 26, 1983.

60. Cf. report by Hirsh Goodman, *Jerusalem Post*, May 27, 1983.

61. For an analysis of Syrian-PLO relations at this time, see the article by Eric Rouleau, *Manchester Guardian Weekly*, May 15, 1983.

62. Cf. *CBIS:ME*, August 5, 1983, p. A-1.

63. Cf. *Al-Watan Al-Arabi*, cited by INA (*FBIS:ME*, September 2, 1983, p. A-1).

64. For a description of Soviet military facilities in Syria, see *Near East Report* vol. 27 no. 23 (June 10, 1983), p. 2.

65. Cited in report by David Shipler, *New York Times*, June 2, 1983.

66. Reuters report, *Baltimore Sun*, June 8, 1983.

67. Cited in report by Don Oberdorfer, *Washington Post*, July 8, 1983.

68. Cf. report by Nora Bustany, *Washington Post*, July 24, 1983.

69. *Novosti* article by Pavel Demchenko, cited in AP report in the *Jerusalem Post*, August 3, 1983. *Novosti* reports are often used as a direct means of trying to influence Western nations. See below.

70. *Tishrin* editorial, cited in Reuters report, *Washington Post*, August 28, 1983.

71. Cf. report by E.J. Donne, Jr., *New York Times*, September 20, 1983.

72. Cf. report by David Ottaway, *Washington Post*, September 18, 1983. Cf. report by Thomas L. Friedman, *New York Times*,

September 23, 1983.

73. Cf. report by Trudy Rubin, *Christian Science Monitor*, September 19, 1983.

74. *Izvestia,* September 4, 1983 (FBIS:USSR, September 7, 1983, p. H-4).

75. Editorial, *New Times*, no. 38, 1983, p. 1.

76. *Pravda,* September 19, 1983.

77. *Pravda,* September 20, 1983.

78. Cf. *Al-Quabas* (Kuwait), September 20, 1983 (*FBIS:USSR*, September 22, 1983, p. H-1).

79. Cited in report by Bernard Gwertzman, *New York Times,* September 23, 1983.

80. Cf. *Tishrin,* September 12, 1983, cited on Radio Monte Carlo (*FBIS:ME,* September 13, 1983, p. H-1).

81. Radio Monte Carlo, September 23, 1983 (*FBIS:ME,* September 23, 1983, p. H-1).

82. Andropov himself praised the cease fire (*Pravda,* September 30, 1983), in a page one report of his meeting with PDRY leader Ali Nasser Mohammed. A TASS statement published in *Pravda* on September 29 noted that the cease fire had been "favorably received" in the Soviet Union, and again opposed both the Israeli and American troop presence in Lebanon, and the May 17th Israeli-Lebanese agreement.

83. Cf. Damascus Domestic Service, September 15, 1983 (*FBIS:ME,* September 19, 1983, p. H-3), and September 14, 1983 (*FBIS:ME,* September 20, 1983, pp. H-1, H-2).

84. For the text of the cease fire agreement, see the AP report, *New York Times,* September 27, 1983.

85. Cf. report by Michael Getler, *Washington Post,* October 7, 1983. A report in the Arabic language *Al-Majallah* asserted that Moscow told Damascus that the missiles could only be used in self-defense (*FBIS:ME,* October 31, 1983, p. ii).

86. A. Stepanov, "Consistent Support", *New Times,* no. 42, 1983, p. 13.

87. Moscow Radio in Arabic, commentary by Alexander Timoshkin, October 6, 1983, (*FBIS:USSR,* October 7, 1983, pp. H-2, H-3).

88. *Pravda,* October 25, 1983.

89. Cited in *FBIS:USSR,* October 28, 1983, p. H-2.

90. Cf. Moscow Radio in Arabic, commentary by Aleksey Ziatorunsky, November 2, 1983, (*FBIS:USSR,* November 3, 1983, pp. H-1, H-2).

91. Moscow Radio in Arabic, Rafael Artonov commentary,

November 3, 1983 (*FBIS:USSR*, November 4, 1983, p. H-3).

92. *Pravda*, November 5, 1983.

93. *Pravda*, November 6, 1983.

94. TASS, November 4, 1983 (*FBIS:USSR*, November 8, 1983, p. H-2).

95. Cf. report by Bernard Gwertzman, *New York Times*, November 8, 1983.

96. *FBIS:USSR*, November 10, 1983, p. H-2.

97. Cf. report by Thomas Friedman, *New York Times*, November 11, 1983.

98. *FBIS:ME*, November 9, 1983, p. i.

99. *FBIS:USSR*, November 15, 1983, p. H-2.

100. *FBIS:ME*, November 14, 1983, p. H-2.

101. *Pravda*, November 13, 1983.

102. Cited in AP report, *New York Times*, November 14, 1983.

103. For Moscow's reaction, see *Pravda*, November 18 and 19, 1983.

104. Radio Free Lebanon, November 19, 1983 (*FBIS:ME*, November 21, 1983, p. H-1).

105. Damascus TV, November 15, 1983 (*FBIS:ME*, November 16, 1983, p. H-1).

106. *Pravda*, November 19, 1983.

107. Cf. Freedman, *Soviet Policy Toward the Middle East Since 1970*, pp. 255 and 261.

108. TASS, November, 20, 1983 (*FBIS:USSR*, November 21, 1983, p. H-2).

109. *Pravda*, November 24, 1983.

110. *FBIS:USSR*, November 29, 1983, p. H-8. There was some indication that Arafat was publicly angry with the lack of Soviet aid, but he moved quickly to deny the report published to that effect in the Egyptian newspaper *al-Akhbar* (Cf. Kuwait *KUNA*, November 29, 1983, (*FBIS:USSR*, November 29, 1983, p. H-1).

111. *Pravda*, November 29, 1983.

112. Cited in report by Richard Halloran, *New York Times*, November 23, 1983.

113. UPI report, *Washington Post*, November 24, 1983.

114. Cited in report by David Ottaway, *Washington Post*, November 27, 1983.

115. Cited in AP report, *New York Times*, November 27, 1983.

116. Damascus Domestic Service, November 29, 1983 (*FBIS:ME*, November 30, 1983, p. H-2).

117. Cited in *New York Times*, December 5, 1983.

118.   *FBIS:USSR*, December 6, 1983, p. H–1.

119.   *FBIS:USSR*, December 14, 1983, p. H–1.

120.   The article was read on Damascus Radio, December 8, 1983 (*FBIS:ME*, December 8, 1983, p. H–4).

121.   Damascus Domestic Service, January 3, 1984 (*FBIS:ME*, January 3, 1984, p. H–2).

122.   This point has been repeatedly emphasized by Defense Minister Mustapha Tlas, while Syrian Foreign Minister Khaddam only a few days earlier had linked the airman's release to the suspension of U.S. reconnaissance flights over Syrian positions (Radio Monte Carlo, January 1, 1984) (*FBIS:ME*, January 3, 1984, pp. H–1, H–2).

123.   Excerpts of the Long report were published in the *New York Times*, December 29, 1983.

124.   House Speaker Tip O'Neil was especially vocal. See the report by Phillip Taubman, *New York Times*, December 30, 1983.

125.   For an analysis of U.S. behavior at this time, see Thomas L. Friedman, "America's Failure in Lebanon", *New York Times Magazine*, April 8, 1984.

126.   Cf. reports by E.J. Dionne, *New York Times*, February 12, 1984, David Hoffman, *Washington Post*, February 12, 1984, and David Hoffman, *Washington Post*, February 15, 1984.

127.   For a Soviet explanation of the veto, see Moscow World Service in English, March 2, 1984 *(FBIS:USSR*, March 5, 1984, p. H–2).

128.   Damascus Domestic Service, February 29, 1984 (*FBIS:ME*, March 1, 1983, p. H–3).

129.   TASS, January 20, 1984 (*FBIS:USSR*, January 23, 1984, p. H–5).

130.   Cf. *Izvestia*, January 5, 1984 (*FBIS:USSR*, January 6, 1984, p. H–7).

131.   Moscow TV service February 8, 1984 (*FBIS:USSR*, February 9, 1984, p. H–6).

132.   Baghdad *INA* in Arabic, March 14, 1984 *(FBIS:ME*, March 15, 1984, p. A–2).

133.   Translated in *FBIS:USSR*, March 7, 1984, p. H–4.

134.   *Krasnaya Zvezda*, March 8, 1984 (*FBIS:USSR*, March 8, 1984, p. H–1).

135.   For a translation of the speeches, see *FBIS:USSR*, March 13, 1984, pp. H–3, H–4.

136.   *Ibid.*

137.   *Pravda*, March 15, 1984.

138.   *Pravda*, March 14, 1984 (translated in *FBIS:USSR*, March 14, 1984, pp. H–1 to H–2).

139. *Ibid.,* p. H–2 (emphasis added).

140. *Al Qabas* (Kuwait), March 19, 1984 (*FBIS:ME,* March 21, 1984, p. H–2). The article also asserted that the USSR had promised to "revolutionize" the Syrian air force to allow it to go on the offensive, as well as to improve the electronic defense system of Syria to compensate it for the reported Israeli link to the U.S. satellite system.

141. Cf. Moscow Radio in Arabic to the Arab world, March 14, 1984 (*FBIS:USSR,* March 15, 1984, p. H–2).

142. For the Soviet view of the Jumblatt visit, see *Pravda,* January 15, 1984.

143. Cf. *Izvestia,* March 28, 1984.

144. *Al Ba'ath,* Damascus, March 18, 1984 (*FBIS:ME,* March 22, 1984, p. H–1).

145. Cf. *FBIS:ME,* April 2, 1984, p. ii.

5
Soviet Policy in the Middle East: The Crucial Change

Dina Rome Spechler

Introduction

Western literature on Soviet policy in the Middle East is fraught with controversy over such crucial issues of substance as the chief objectives and major thrust of Soviet behavior. Some have argued that Soviet policy has been basically offensive, aimed at undermining the American and Western presence in the area and, by expanding Soviet influence, achieving control over the region's strategic assets. Others have maintained that Soviet policy has been fundamentally defensive, aimed primarily at preventing the area from being used to encircle, embottle, or attack the USSR.[1] Some claim that Soviet policy in the Middle East has been aggressive, provocative--even incendiary--and destabilizing, oriented toward the perpetuation of conflict and tension.[2] Others stress that the USSR has been notably cautious and restrained, deeply concerned to prevent a superpower collision in the region, and hence eager for the resolution or diminution of conflict and the elimination or reduction of tension.[3]

Despite these divergences on substance, however, Western literature on Soviet policy in the Middle East has been, for the most part, strikingly uniform in method or approach. Nearly all works on the subject, while occasionally speculating on the internal political debate which may have shaped policy outcomes, have adopted what has been described in a

----

The author wishes to thank the Political Science and Economics Departments of the University of Iowa, which generously provided support services for the preparation of this article.

133

seminal study of American foreign policy as a "strategic actor" or "rational actor" paradigm for the analysis of Soviet behavior.[4] The Soviet leadership is viewed as a single, unified entity, reaching decisions about what to do in the Middle East on the basis of a single set of goals and ordering of priorities, and rational calculation of the costs and benefits of the various options open to the USSR for achieving those goals.[5]

Focusing on the critical period 1967–1973, in which Soviet involvement in the Middle East steadily deepened, ultimately reaching massive proportions, this article will demonstrate the limitations of relying exclusively on a rational actor model. It will indicate the insights which may be gleaned from analysis of some of the diverse domestic influences on the formulation of Soviet Middle Eastern policy, and will suggest a methodology for ascertaining and analyzing those influences.[6] The article will show that both the "hawks" and the "doves" among Western students of Soviet behavior in the Middle East are right: the validity of each interpretation depends on the period or decision one examines and the internal forces which are most influential at the time.

Soviet Policy in the Middle East: The Crucial Change

There is a substantial body of evidence which suggests that Soviet policy in the Middle East––in particular Soviet policy toward the Arab–Israeli conflict––changed dramatically in the first months of 1973. This evidence suggests that while the major thrust of Soviet policy from the end of the Six–Day War onward had been to restrain the Arabs, to attempt to keep them from using force to "liberate" the territories occupied by Israel in that war, sometime early in 1973, probably in January, a decision was made to end that restraint and, in effect, to "unleash" the Arabs. After briefly summarizing this evidence, this article will address two questions: why was this restraint exercised in the first place, and more important, why was it ultimately lifted––why was a policy which had seemed to recommend itself highly for almost six years suddenly and dramatically reversed?

It would appear that while the Soviets proceeded with zeal and alacrity to rebuild the devastated war machines of Egypt and Syria in the months and years following the 1967 War, and while they reluctantly acceded to and ultimately came to Egypt's assistance in the War of Attrition, they also took great pains to see to it that the equipment they provided would not be used to launch an attack across the Suez Canal.[7]

In the first place, from June, 1967 on, the Soviets exerted very considerable diplomatic pressure on the leaders of the "confrontation" states to relinquish their ambition of recovering the territories by force and to accept instead a negotiated solution which the USSR would help arrange and guarantee.[8] What is more important, the USSR adopted a number of critical measures or rules of restraint to actually prevent Egypt and Syria from undertaking an offensive against Israel: 1) it denied Egypt and Syria permission to use the weapons it provided to recover the territories they had lost, enforcing this denial through the presence of Soviet advisors in every unit of the Egyptian armed forces down to the battalion level;[9] 2) it kept the majority of the most highly advanced weapons it supplied under Soviet operational control;[10] 3) it denied the Arabs what they, especially the Egyptians, considered a sufficient quantity of ammunition, spare parts, and crucial weapons to enable them to launch an attack on Israel; 4) it refused to provide its Middle Eastern allies with offensive weapons which could wreak significant damage upon the Israeli heartland.

The first two of these rules are self-explanatory. The latter two may be explained as follows. When Sadat came to power in September, 1970, he concluded, as Nasser had before him, that in order to launch a successful offensive action against Israel, his country must obtain a great deal more in the way of weapons than the Soviets had hitherto provided. Egypt's most pressing needs were for greatly strengthened air and coastal defense systems; a much larger supply of equipment and weapons for crossing the canal and engaging in combat in the Sinai, i.e., equipment and weapons for tactical offensive use (bridging equipment, modern tanks and combat aircraft, anti-tank and portable antiaircraft weapons); and offensive weapons of regional strategic significance, which would give Egypt the capability of retaliating in kind against Israeli bombing of Egypt's interior and would thus deter such bombing.[11] It was Soviet failure to supply these items that had forced Nasser to resort to a war of attrition, rather than the full-scale attack he would have preferred.[12] When Sadat assumed the presidency, he pressed the Soviets relentlessly to make good these deficiencies. Throughout 1971-1972, however, despite mounting evidence of an impending crisis in relations with Egypt, culminating in the expulsion of thousands of Russian advisors, the Soviet leaders failed to deliver the defensive and tactical offensive weapons in the quantities Egypt deemed necessary, and they provided no weapons at all with strategic offensive capability. While the Egyptians from time to time received assurances that some of the most critical items, including strategic weapons, would be forthcoming, these promises, with a few exceptions, were not kept.[13]

If Soviet behavior between mid-1967 and early 1973 seems to refute or at least seriously qualify the hawkish view of Soviet policy in the

Middle East, Soviet conduct from February through October, 1973 would seem, on the whole, to attest to the accuracy of that image. Although the Soviets continued during the second period to express a strong preference for a political solution to the Arab–Israeli conflict, and although they continued to try to persuade the Arabs to take this path, their policy seems to have undergone a very significant change by February, 1973.[14] Between February and October of that year they broke all four rules of restraint which had governed their behavior in previous years.

It was apparently in February, 1973 that the USSR for the first time gave the Egyptians (and thus indirectly the Syrians) to understand that it would not oppose an offensive aimed at reconquering the lost territories.[15] At the same time it promised, and shortly after began to deliver, the amounts of ammunition and parts and the numbers and types of weapons and equipment which the Arabs considered essential for going to war--weapons which met all three of Egypt's essential needs.[16] For defense the Egyptians received a very substantial increment of SAM-3 and mobile SAM-6 antiaircraft missiles (which offered them solid protection against the low–level attacks Israel had so successfully employed in the past to evade their defenses) and a sizable addition to their stock of coastal defense SAMLET surface–to–surface missiles. For tactical offense they were provided with large numbers of the most modern Soviet portable bridges, a very significant increase in their inventory of first–line T–62 tanks with infra–red ranging devices, huge quantities of portable antiaircraft and anti–tank weapons, including the powerful and deadly Sagger, and a few highly advanced SU–20 ground attack aircraft, not yet deployed in the Soviet armed forces. Most important, the Egyptians finally obtained what they considered a *sine qua non* for any offensive, weapons which would present a strategic threat to Israel. These were TU–16 medium bombers armed with Kelt stand–off missiles which, in contrast to the Kennel missiles previously supplied, had sufficient range that the bomber could launch them without being intercepted by Israeli fighters, and Scud high–explosive surface–to–surface missiles able to hit the coastal cities of Israel.[17] This was the first time the Soviets had provided surface–to–surface missiles of regionally strategic significance to a country outside the Warsaw Pact.[18] Even the most advanced of these weapons were placed under Arab operational control.[19]

In February, 1973, in other words, the Soviet Union gave Egypt and Syria the green light to go to war, and in the months between February and October, 1973, it proceeded to satisfy what they considered the necessary conditions for doing so. Equipment started pouring into Egyptian ports in vast quantities.[20] Sadat recalled that it seemed "as if all the taps had been turned on."[21] By the beginning of April, 1973, the

Egyptian President was able to assert, "The Russians are providing us with everything that's possible for them to supply. And I am now quite satisfied."[22] That the USSR's new policy played a critical role in precipitating the October War can be inferred from the fact that it was precisely in April, 1973, when Sadat became "quite satisfied" with the arsenal he was getting, that he definitively decided to go ahead with his previously tentative war plans.[23] Moreover, it was after receiving the first shipment of Scuds in the summer of 1973 that he set the date for the attack.[24]

Looking back, it is clear that the lifting of all four of the restraints previously imposed on the Arabs was a highly important step for the USSR, one which would have major consequences not only for the region regarding which it was taken, but also for the Soviet position in the Middle East and the future of Soviet–American relations. The war in whose initiation the Soviets were so instrumental would result in a marked increase in the United State's prestige in the Middle East at the expense of the USSR, setting back for at least a decade Moscow's efforts to expand its influence there. More significantly, perhaps, the Soviet role in facilitating the war, along with Soviet conduct during the hostilities, did a great deal to sour the American public and Congress on détente and thus greatly helped to doom it.[25]

Explaining the Change: The Rational Actor Paradigm

What explains this extraordinary and dramatic change in Soviet Middle Eastern Policy? To answer this question it is necessary to consider briefly why the policy of restraint was conceived and implemented in the first place, given its high costs for Soviet–Arab, especially Soviet–Egyptian, relations.

Nearly all who have dealt with this issue suggest that two reasons for restraint were the most salient: the Soviets wished both to avoid a military confrontation with the United States and, particulary from 1969 on, sought to develop and preserve détente with the West.[26] Other considerations may have played a supplemental role at various moments, but these would appear to have been either transient or of limited influence.[27] Only objectives which were arguably of central importance to Soviet global policy would seem adequate to explain why a course of action so detrimental to the realization of regional goals should have been adopted. Moreover, such "inside" evidence as is to be found regarding Soviet foreign policy aims and priorities in the late 1960s and early 1970s supports the view that prevention of confrontation and promotion of détente were, indeed, paramount.[28]

It is less clear, however, why these vital objectives should have ceased to govern Soviet Middle Eastern policy in the first months of 1973. The various interpretations of this change which can be gleaned from the work of Western scholars tend to fall into two schools, one explaining the decision in terms of Soviet global concerns, the other focusing on Soviet regional objectives and considering global issues only indirectly. What is common to both schools is that they rely exclusively on the rational actor paradigm, and for that reason, both are problematic. Some of the arguments offered by both schools are relevant to understanding this major shift in Soviet behavior, but only if they are used in conjunction with an alternative paradigm which takes into account internal influences on the formulation of Soviet foreign policy.

Consider first the explanation focusing on Soviet global policy:

1) Revealed preference

According to one interpretation of the change in Soviet behavior early in 1973, the Soviets had never really been serious about pursuing détente. That is, they had never really been prepared to sacrifice anything for it. They had never intended to forego for the sake of détente any foreign policy gain in the Third World. Despite their signature of two widely heralded agreements on the subject, they had never really been interested in cooperating with the United States to resolve conflicts and prevent the development of situations which could lead to confrontations between the superpowers.[29] It had always been their policy to exacerbate and exploit such conflicts whenever that promised to yield some advantage in their geostrategic competition with the U.S. However, the true nature of their attitude was revealed to the West only in 1973.[30]

The problem with this explanation of Soviet behavior is that it does not square with the restraint demonstrated by the USSR before February, 1973. By the time they made the decision which led to the October War, the Soviets had already sacrificed something very significant for détente; they had done a great deal to uphold their commitment to work to prevent a superpower confrontation. Their quest for a peaceful solution to the Arab–Israeli conflict had been undertaken and sustained with the awareness that this could well cost them their position in Egypt.[31]

2) Changed calculus

Another interpretation of Soviet behavior suggests that by early 1973 the perceived benefits of restraint for the USSR had become too low as compared with the perceived costs. By this time the Soviets had become disillusioned by and pessimistic about American behavior, especially in the Middle East. They were angered by American unilateralism, by U.S. efforts to resolve the Middle East crisis alone, without Soviet participation either in the process or in the ultimate arrangements for guaranteeing a settlement, and they were disappointed by American unwillingness to reciprocate Soviet pressure on the Arabs with similar pressure on Israel to make concessions for peace.[32] As a result of their experience with the United States in the Middle East, they no longer expected much from détente. Moreover, their felt need for détente was no longer so acute. The developing U.S.–Chinese relationship, which had emerged in the wake of repeated Chinese armed provocations and a massive military buildup on the border with the USSR, had been a major spur to the Soviet quest for détente. But by 1973 the Soviets had become confident of their ability to deter a major Chinese attack, and it had become clear that there were many obstacles to a Sino–American alliance.[33]

This interpretation, too, has its problems. If the Soviets were impatient with American policy in the Middle East, it is also probable that they understood that American efforts to induce Israel to make compromises were likely to be more successful after the election in that country, scheduled for October, 1973. It is likely that they were at least somewhat mollified by American assurances that the U.S. would undertake a major peace initiative after the new Israeli government had been chosen.[34] Moreover, even if the Soviets were unhappy with U.S. behavior in the Middle East, they were very pleased with the strong American support for the ratification of the German treaties, the access to the U.S. grain market they had obtained, the SALT I agreement signed at the Moscow summit in 1972, and apparent U.S. recognition at that time of the status of the USSR as a global power. There were many signs that they were very eager for the détente process to go forward–– for Brezhnev to be received in the United States, for an agreement barring nuclear war to be signed, and for Congress and the Administration to approve Most Favored Nation status and substantial credits for trade with the USSR.[35] There is no sign that by early 1973 they were generally disillusioned with détente or had ceased to expect it would bear highly valuable fruits.[36]

3) Misperception

According to this view, the Soviets misread the attitudes of the U.S. Administration and public and in so doing reached the mistaken conclusion that neither a war in the Middle East nor their role in bringing about such a war would affect détente. They were aware of impatience with Israel on the part of some Administration officials, growing scepticism in the U.S. about Israel's willingness to withdraw from the territories it occupied, and increasing American doubts about the justice of Israel's position. They therefore thought the United States would not regard as entirely unreasonable either Arab resort to force or Soviet facilitation of it.[37] At the same time, the Soviets thought Nixon's position had been so weakened by the Watergate scandal that he could not afford to jettison détente--regarded by many as one of his Administration's few successes--regardless of what the Soviets did.[38]

There are two major flaws in this argument. On the one hand, it is hard to see how the Soviets could have misinterpreted the Administration's position on Israel and the Middle East. It is true that a number of Arabists in the State Department had sometimes voiced sympathy for the Arabs' dilemma. However, Kissinger was viewed by the Soviets as the authoritative foreign policy spokesman for the Administration, and he had made clear to the Kremlin leadership how firmly the U.S. supported Israel and how much importance it attached to preserving peace in the Middle East.[39] He also emphasized to the Soviets on numerous occasions that détente "would not survive a foreign policy challenge."[40] The message, moreover, had gotten through. Even after the February, 1973 policy change, the Soviets apparently continued to tell the Egyptians that they must not go to war because that would jeopardize détente.[41] With regard to Nixon and Watergate, on the other hand, it is only later in the year that such considerations might have affected Soviet calculations. Watergate did not reach the proportions of a national scandal, with widespread assumption of presidential involvement in it, until mid–April, 1973.[42] At the beginning of the year, when they made their critical decision concerning the Middle East, they could not have known how deeply preoccupied with the affair Nixon really was.

The other set of explanations of the Soviet decision focuses on probable calculations by the leadership regarding the likely behavior of their Middle Eastern allies and its impact on Soviet interests in the Middle East:

1) Egyptian compromise

It has been argued that the Soviets waited to give Egypt the green light and sufficient means to go to war until they had received a firm commitment from Sadat that he would wage only limited, rather than total, war against Israel. Such a war, they assumed, would not require Soviet intervention and thus would carry no risk of a superpower confrontation.[43]

This explanation, too, is problematic. Lt. General Shazly writes in his memoirs that from the time he became Chief of Staff of the Egyptian armed forces in the spring of 1971, the Arabs had had only a limited offensive in mind and had made this clear to the Soviets long before the beginning of 1973.[44] Moreover, the weapons the Soviets supplied, even after February, 1973, were completely inadequate for the Arabs to attempt total war. Thus the USSR did not have to wait for an Egyptian pledge before supplying those weapons. Even if such a pledge was given, as it appears to have been, it is unlikely to have been a critical factor in the Soviet decision.[45] This is particularly the case because a commitment of this kind could have had very little value for the Soviets. The Kremlin leaders assumed to the very last that the Arabs would lose any war they began.[46] Thus the Soviets must have recognized that, whatever their allies' intentions, the USSR might well have to intervene to mount a rescue operation. They could not, therefore, rule out a confrontation with the United States on the basis of a promise from Sadat.

2) Miscalculation

It has been hypothesized that the Soviets assumed either that Sadat was bluffing and would not really go to war or that by cooperating with the Egyptians, they could exert more influence over them and ultimately prevent them from launching an offensive.[47]

It is true that Sadat had been threatening to go to war for some time without actually doing so. Yet it would appear that the Soviets had not taken these threats lightly, hence their restraint in supplying him with weapons. It is hard to see why they would suddenly have changed their assessment of the Egyptian leader's intentions and (if they wanted to prevent war) would have tempted him to carry out his program at last. As for the notion that they expected to be able to control the Egyptians, they had already failed to do this despite (or because of) their extensive arms aid in 1967 and 1969–1970. Now with their advisors gone, there is no reason why the Soviets would have expected to exert more influence over the Egyptians than they had in the past, especially inasmuch as they were relinquishing their most effective lever of control.

3) Egyptian blackmail

The third and final account of Soviet conduct which stresses the USSR's perceptions of the situation in the Middle East is the counterpart to the "changed calculus" argument outlined above. This explanation, however, focuses on the allegedly increased perceived costs, rather than diminished benefits, of restraint. The Soviets, it is asserted, were badly hit when Sadat, as part of the expulsion, ordered all the USSR's military facilities in the country to be turned over to Egyptian control. This move was followed by an Egyptian threat to sever all relations with the USSR, to abrogate the Treaty of Friendship between the two countries, and to deny the Soviets use of valuable port facilities unless they supplied the long–sought weapons. Fearing the loss of their entire political–military position in the Arab world, the Soviets caved in.[48]

As will be demonstrated later, there are some helpful insights to be found in this analysis of Soviet behavior in January–February, 1973. Yet, like the interpretation previously examined, it is by no means free of difficulties. There is an important piece of evidence which seems to support this explanation of the Soviet decision. On August 29, 1972 Sadat wrote to Brezhnev, informing him that he had set October 31, 1972, as "the target date for the settlement of relations between us." "We wish to have good relations with you," the Egyptian President averred, "but this will be determined by the extent to which our friends in the Soviet Union are prepared to assist us in the solution of our first and last problem, namely the liberation of our territory." If the Soviets failed to respond positively to the Egyptians' demands by the date he had set, Sadat declared, he would "take the decisions [he] deemed fit."[49]

Sadat claimed the Soviets understood very well what he meant by this vague threat, namely that "unless they changed their attitude, I would cancel the treaty of friendship between us and withdraw the facilities they enjoy in our ports, all of which would mean our relations would deteriorate further."[50] Shazly argues that the change in Soviet policy was a response to this ultimatum. Accordingly, he dates the change as having occurred just prior to or during the visit of Egyptian Prime Minister Sidky to Moscow October 16–18, 1972.[51]

In fact, however, it seems clear that Soviet policy did not change at that time. The Soviets may well have considered a new course in October, 1972. They may even have made some critical pledges of weapons in an effort to avert a precipitous move by Sadat.[52] But if such pledges were made, then by the time a high level Egyptian military mission arrived in Moscow a month later, these promises were withdrawn, and the mission was assured only that delivery of spare parts and replacements, suspended since the expulsion in July, would be resumed and some SAM-6's withdrawn in the wake of the expulsion would be returned.[53]

By the end of October, 1972, moreover, there were many signs that Sadat's position was weakening, his ability to stand up to the USSR diminishing. These signs mounted in subsequent weeks. Sadat had tried and failed to purchase the arms he needed in Western Europe. His National Security Advisor had been unable even to arrange a meeting with Kissinger. And there was growing domestic pressure on the Egyptian President to restore the alliance with the USSR.[54]

These developments must have reassured the Soviets that Sadat would be unable to carry out his threat. Any doubts they may have had on this score were surely dispelled in December, when Sadat, on his own initiative, renewed for a period of five years the Soviet–Egyptian agreement on use of Egyptian port facilities, which had been due to expire in March, 1973.[55] Without making any consessions, without altering their policy of restraint, the Soviets had secured the facilities they desired.

Even if Sadat had not yielded on this score, moreover, the Soviet position in the Arab world would have been far from desperate. In the previous two years they had succeeded in strengthening their political, economic and military ties to nearly all the "progressive" regimes in the area.[56] Most importantly, relations with Syria had in no way been damaged by the expulsion from Egypt, and in the fall of 1972, the USSR was granted bases there for reconnaissance operations against the Sixth Fleet. These replaced the bases it had lost in Egypt.[57]

In sum, while Sadat did use the threat of severing relations and withholding port facilities, and while his bold expulsion of Soviet military advisors gave that threat credibility, his ultimatum was withdrawn and the port facilities guaranteed to the USSR before it took the decision to change course. The Soviets were not faced with the likely loss of their political–military position in the Arab world. That position, in fact, was quite strong and did not have to be salvaged by a major policy reversal.

An Alternative Paradigm

Both the difficulty of explaining this critical decision using the rational actor paradigm and the puzzling inconsistencies in Soviet behavior prior to and after the decision (initial opposition to, yet eventual support for, the War of Attrition; repeated promises of weapons, but repeated failure to deliver them; authorization to go to war, followed by insistence on a peaceful solution) make it seem very likely that what changed early in 1973 was not a leadership consensus about the optimal means of pursuing global objectives or regional interests. Rather, what changed was very probably the balance of influence among competing conceptions of Soviet foreign policy held by competing political actors. Perhaps the decision to end the vital restraints imposed since 1967 reflected a shift in the relative power of various domestic forces with differing views on and priorities regarding U.S.–Soviet relations, Soviet Middle Eastern policy, and the relationship between the two. Perhaps, in other words, not only the American, but also the Soviet foreign policy process should be viewed as an ongoing conflict among elite actors, many of whose views are related to their differing functions or institutional allegiances.[58]

What kind of data would enable one to test the hypothesis that there is conflict over foreign policy among Soviet elites? If such conflict does exist, how can one determine the nature of the debate, the participants in it, and the influence of their respective positions at any given time? It is true that people in official positions in the USSR do not generally publish revealing memoirs or grant candid interviews on matters of foreign affairs. There is, however, a rich alternative data source: the principal organs of the national media. Not only do these contain discussions of foreign policy. The testimony of emigrants who have worked in the media suggests that each of these organs tends to be controlled by a powerful individual or group which speaks for a broad elite "constituency" and enjoys a major voice in policy.[59] Thus, taken together, these newspapers are likely to reflect the array of elite opinions which are represented in the top leadership.

One does not generally find explicit positions on specific foreign policy issues articulated in the press. However, one can find expression of the general outlooks which are the basis for specific policy positions, and these are in some ways even more helpful for understanding Soviet policy. Moreover, emigrant sources, official speeches, and the testimony of non-Soviet participant-observers can be useful for linking the organs examined and views expressed with identifiable individuals, groups, and institutions. Finally, analysis of authoritative resolutions, formal communiqués, and the timing of policy and personnel changes at or near the top can help to determine which set of views is dominant at a given time.[60]

An intensive study of six major Soviet newspapers in 1973 was undertaken by the author in an initial effort to determine whether the paradigm of elite conflict could be applied to the Soviet foreign policy process.[61] This study was supplemented by an examination of the other types of sources enumerated above and the findings were checked for relevance to the period 1967-1972. The results of this study are summarized below. These results are then used to explain the 1973 decision and the inconsistencies in Soviet behavior before and after that decision.

Elite Images of the United States and Positions on the Middle East

It was possible in the late 1960s and early 1970s to ascertain four distinct viewpoints or "tendencies of opinion" among Soviet leaders and political elites, with regard both to Soviet policy in the Middle East and to Soviet global policy. Of particular interest and importance is the finding that the views expressed by each media organ on the Middle East were related to and seemed to be derived from distinct images of and attitudes toward the United States and U.S.-Soviet relations. These images were cooperative, competitive, antagonistic, and a hybrid of cooperative and antagonistic. [62]

1) Cooperative image

This image was expressed in the Central Committee newspaper, *Pravda.* It was articulated by General Secretary Brezhnev and seems to have been representative of the view of an influential segment of the Central Party apparatus.[63] According to this image, the United States could be described as an *adverse partner.* While still an adversary, it was a potential partner of the USSR in solving key international problems. Those who held this image saw the possibility of "international relations of a new type," a situation in which adversaries recognized certain common interests and worked together to promote them. The holders of this image saw as the most acute problem facing the USSR the prevention of military confrontation with the United States. The Soviet Union should give the highest priority to solving this problem, working with the United States to reach agreements which would reduce the probability of such confrontations. A crucial objective, too, was the reduction of international tensions (which made confrontation more likely and cooperation more difficult).[64] This effort to construct a new relationship with the United States, in which possibilities for cooperation would be developed and residual conflicts of interest diminished as far as possible, was the meaning and purpose of détente.

The holders of the cooperative image were impressed by the inherent fragility of détente: they recognized that it was necessarily an effort to transcend--not eliminate--an underlying adversary relationship. They did not want events in the Middle East (or in any other region) to cause or deepen mistrust and hostility between the U.S. and the USSR. They wished to limit superpower involvement in and commitment to the Middle East and other Third World regions in order to prevent military confrontation.[65] They did not want the USSR to withdraw from the Middle East, but they did not want Soviet presence and activities there to cause needless alarm in the United States. They advocated an agreement between the superpowers specifying the activities permitted to each or establishing, in some other form, rules of the game governing their behavior in the Middle East and elsewhere.[66] They strongly desired to de-escalate conflicts between the regional allies of the U.S. and USSR throughout the world. Thus in the Middle East, they vigorously urged a political agreement between the Arabs and Israel.

2) Competitive image

This image was expressed in *Izvestia,* the organ of the Council of Ministers. Articulated by Prime Minister Kosygin, it apparently embodied the view of many officials involved in the consumer goods sector, technological development, and state administration. According to this image, the United States should be viewed as a *realistic competitor.* It was not a partner, but a rival in an economic contest. Soviet victory in that contest could be greatly facilitated if the USSR could induce the U.S. to provide technology and investment capital, as well as consumer goods, on favorable terms. This was, ironically, very much in America's interest, since its economy constantly required new markets and investment outlets.

For the holders of this image, the possibility of obtaining technology and capital was the chief rationale for the Soviet pursuit of détente. It was important to cultivate détente. However, major concessions were not necessary for this purpose, as the U.S. leaders and public realized how great was America's stake in economic exchange with the other superpower.[67]

It was desirable, from the standpoint of those who held this image, to find a political solution to the Arab–Israeli conflict. In the absence of a settlement, there would be periodic escalation of U.S.–Soviet tensions, and this would create a bad climate for developing an economic relationship. However, until a peace agreement had been signed––perhaps even after––the Arabs should be encouraged to maintain economic pressure on the West. There was no danger this would disrupt or prevent détente, and it might hasten Soviet victory in the economic contest, since such pressure could gravely weaken the West.

3) Antagonistic image

This image appeared in *Kransnaia zvezda, Komsomol'skaia pravda,* and *Trud,* the newspapers of the Ministry of Defense, the youth organization and the trade union organization, respectively. The speeches and writings of Defense Minister Grechko, Admiral Gorshkov, Party Secretary Suslov, KGB Chairman Andropov, and Trade Union head Shelepin contained this image, and it apparently reflected the ideas of influential factions in the military, substantial numbers of Party *apparatchiki* concerned with ideology and propaganda, and many officials who exercised functions of control and supervision of the Soviet population (police, trade union, and youth officials).[68]

According to this image, the United States was an *unalterable antagonist*, necessarily hostile and threatening to the USSR because of its economic and military power and aggressive intentions. The U.S. must be actively countered and contained, both militarily and politically. Highest priority should therefore be given to expansion of Soviet military power and political influence on a global scale. The USSR must acquire friends and military facilities wherever these would help contain or undermine American power. It must also maintain a high level of vigilance at home to counteract American efforts at political and ideological subversion. Détente was an American scheme to distract Soviet citizens and officials, to lure them into lowering their guard. Reduction of international tension was an illusory objective. Tensions would always persist because of America's inevitable enmity to the USSR.

It would not be tragic, indeed, it might be fortunate, if events in the Middle East were to disrupt or prevent détente. Should this happen, the inevitability of U.S.–Soviet antagonism could be more clearly demonstrated to Soviet citizens, and they could be better trained to cope with it. Necessary measures could also be taken to ward off U.S. subversion within the USSR. There was little reason to seek a peaceful resolution of the Arab–Israeli conflict. A settlement would be desirable only if it were likely to weaken American influence in the Middle East, e.g., a settlement which, by requiring Israel to accept millions of Palestinian returnees, would drastically alter its character and undermine its ties to the United States.[69]

4) Hybrid image

Sovetskaia Rossiia, the newspaper of the Council of Ministers of the Russian Republic, was linked in the late 1960s and early 1970s to First Deputy Premier, later Minister of Agriculture, Polianskii, to Premier of the Russian Republic, Solomentsev, and to a variety of Russian nationalist groups.[70] It presented an image of the United States as a *mitigable opponent.* That is, its stance vis-à-vis the U.S. and U.S.–Soviet relations was ambivalent. The U.S. was seen primarily as an antagonist, but one whose aggressive aspirations might be restrained by Soviet strength. Among the holders of this image there was, therefore, more interest in détente and less scepticism as to its attainability than among those who viewed the United States as an unalterable antagonist. Articulated along with this hybrid image was a fierce pride not only in Russia, but in the USSR as a whole, and in its achievements and status as a superpower. The interest in détente among those who subscribed to this image seemed to be based both on the hope that the new relationship with the United States would allow allocation of more resources to the development of Russian areas in the USSR and on the assumption that this relationship involved American recognition of the USSR as an equal partner in managing the international system.[71]

A key element in this tendency of opinion was fear and awe of, and intense animosity toward, the international Zionist movement.[72] The power of Zionism and Zionists (i.e., Jews) in American politics was viewed as the chief source of U.S. hostility to the USSR. It was Zionist influence on American foreign policy which made the United States potentially dangerous and threatening to the USSR. The holders of the hybrid image favored a de–escalation of the Arab–Israeli conflict to allow détente to develop, if possible, and above all, to reduce the influence of international Zionism on U.S. policy–makers and deflect Zionist enmity from the USSR. They supported a settlement, but with less ardor than the holders of the cooperative image, who were both more committed to and more convinced of the feasibility of détente.

Elite Images and Soviet Behavior in the Middle East

If one keeps in mind these four elite images of the United States and the four different elite attitudes toward the Middle East associated with and derived from them, one can better understand the important change in Soviet behavior which occurred early in 1973. Moreover, if one takes as a starting point competing elite images and conflict over policy, one can also explain the inconsistencies and contradictions in Soviet conduct prior to and after that change. It will be shown below that a variety of Arab and Soviet sources provide substantial evidence to support an explanation of this kind.

It may be argued that by the late 1960s, those who held the cooperative and competitive images of the United States had become the dominant force in the shaping of Soviet foreign policy. The quest for détente--reflected in the negotiations on the status of Berlin, the SALT talks, and the effort to obtain Most Favored Nation Status and U.S. trade credits--was undertaken at their insistence.[73] At no time were they completely in control, however, and in the formulation of regional policy, especially policy in the Middle East, their views sometimes did not prevail. Such instances include the decisions in 1969–70 first to allow Nasser to undertake the War of Attrition and later to commit thousands of Soviet personnel to direct combat roles in that war.[74] Yet until January, 1973, they were able both to determine the basic direction of and relationship between Soviet global and regional policies and to enforce their policy priorities by imposing critical limits on the nature of Soviet arms transfers.[75] After that they began to be less influential, especially in the formulation of Middle Eastern policy, although their views continued to have an impact and were reflected in important aspects of Soviet behavior during and after the October War.

In the years preceding the war, holders of the cooperative image, fearful of a U.S.–Soviet confrontation and anxious to preserve détente, were responsible for the extensive Soviet efforts to reach agreement with the United States on a formula for a Middle East peace settlement.[76] Those who held the cooperative and competitive images were likewise the chief source of the constant Soviet pressure on the Arabs to reach a peaceful solution.[77] As compared with the possibility of a superpower collision in the Middle East, the cooperativists were little concerned with the adverse effects of Soviet weapons restraint on Soviet–Egyptian and Soviet–Arab relations.[78] It was they who insisted that Egypt must not receive the advanced offensive weapons it repeatedly requested.[79]

The cooperative and competitive image holders were, however, continually criticized by those who subscribed to the antagonistic image, especially in the Party apparatus and the military.[80] Ideologues in the Party elite disliked the appearance of superpower condominium which any joint U.S.-Soviet peace plan would be sure to generate. They thought all efforts to arrive at a U.S.-Soviet agreement on the Middle East were futile, given the sharp contradiction between American and Soviet interests in the area, and they strongly opposed pursuing such efforts because of the unfavorable impression they created in the Third World.[81] Certain military officials may have pressed for fulfillment of the Arabs' requests because of what they saw as the need, largely unmet in Vietnam, to try out a wide range of Soviet weapons in combat. More important, influential military leaders saw Egypt and the Middle East as strategically vital. They wanted first priority to be given to the Soviet-Arab alliance, not to détente. They were ready to do whatever was necessary to maintain that alliance. Hence they advocated both a more sympathetic attitude toward Arab use of force and deeper Soviet military involvement in the Middle East.[82] They were ready, even eager, to "unleash" the Arabs and were not concerned by the possibility that this might lead to direct Soviet intervention and U.S.-Soviet confrontation.[83]

At no point were holders of the antagonistic image completely without influence on Soviet weapons transfer policy. Not only did they prevail with regard to the War of Attrition, it seems very likely that it was they who persuaded the Politburo to make or reiterate important new commitments of weapons to the Arabs on at least a half-dozen occasions in 1971-1972.[84] It was usually they who travelled to the Middle East to confirm these promises or make other concessions: they wished to make sure that the firmness of the USSR's friendship was fully and properly communicated to its vital Third World allies.[85] However, until February, 1973, cooperative image holders were sufficiently powerful to see to it that most of these promises were not kept.[86]

Pressure for a policy shift from holders of the antagonistic image became particularly intense after the July, 1972 expulsion of Soviet advisors from Egypt.[87] As they saw it, the expulsion had been a major blow to the USSR. It had deeply embarrassed and humiliated the Soviets, demonstrating to the entire world the fragility of the Soviet position in the Middle East. It had deprived the USSR of what some viewed as uniquely important strategic facilities, vital not only to the Soviet presence in the Mediterranean, but for operations in Africa and the Persian Gulf. It had created an image of the USSR as an unreliable ally for Third World countries and left the Soviets vulnerable to Chinese accusations of superpower collusion to obstruct the forces of national liberation. It would surely lead to the disintegration of the Soviet position in the Arab world--maybe even the Third World as a whole--unless Arab demands were met and Soviet willingness to support "progressive" forces demonstrated. At the very least, if the USSR failed to come through, Egypt and Syria would cut their ties to the Soviets and turn to the Americans to negotiate the return of their territories.[88]

It would appear that the expulsion greatly strengthened the hand of those who viewed the United States as an unalterable and dangerous antagonist. They were now able to argue more convincingly than before that too much was being sacrificed to détente. As might be expected, their arguments did not persuade the cooperativists. When Egyptian Premier Sidky visited Moscow in October, 1972, Brezhnev refused even to see him. Other holders of the cooperative image used the occasion to emphasize once again that Egypt must seek a peaceful solution.[89] But there were now signs that support for this approach in the Politburo was weakening, that holders of the antagonistic image had won some crucial allies. While Premier Kosygin referred to a peaceful settlement as a "feasible goal" in his speech honoring Sidky, he also affirmed that the Arabs had the right to use "any means" to liberate their territories.[90]

Those who subscribed to the competitive image of the United States had never been as strongly committed to a settlement as the cooperativists. There is evidence to suggest that they now agreed to support Arab use of force--and to provide the weapons needed for this--on condition that the Arabs would no longer be given easy credits, but would be required to pay cash for what they received.[91] Such payments would provide the hard currency which the competitivists eagerly sought to finance the purchase of Western technology and consumer goods.[92] Perhaps because of their shift, Sidky went home, as was noted earlier in the paper, with assurances that Sadat would be provided with what he most wanted: surface-to-surface missiles capable of striking Israeli cities.[93]

For one more time, the holders of the cooperative image were able to prevail. We have seen that the promises made in October were withdrawn in November, when an Egyptian military mission arrived in Moscow to discuss the details of the Soviet commitment.[94] But the position of those who gave first priority to avoiding confrontation and developing détente was now weaker than before the expulsion. It seems that in the eyes of many in the political elite, the July, 1972 events had discredited not only the policy of restraint, but even to some extent those who advocated that policy. Those events appear to have set in motion a gradual shift in the balance of power and influence among holders of the various images in favor of those who viewed the United States as an unalterable antagonist and the Third World as a crucial arena for combating this deadly foe. Developments in the United States itself may have reinforced this process. American failure to pressure Israel into making significant concessions, even after the November, 1972 elections in the U.S., made it harder for proponents of détente to argue that the new relationship would result in gains for "progressive" forces in the Third World. By the end of 1972, it would appear that holders of the antagonistic image had begun to wield more influence, and their views had begun to carry more weight in the Soviet political establishment.

A top–level reappraisal of Soviet–Egyptian relations was initiated in late December, 1972.[95] The outcome was not at the outset a foregone conclusion. Although less popular than previously, the policy of restraint apparently still had strong support within the Politburo.[96] But when a large amount of Saudi and Persian Gulf money was made available to Egypt for the purchase of arms at the end of December and beginning of January, it became virtually inevitable that at least some of those who held the competitive image would support the sale of the weapons requested.[97] Among holders of the hybrid image, more ambivalent about détente and less sure of its value of feasibility, there may well have been some who were convinced by the argument that the Soviet position in the Middle East and the Third World was at stake and must be preserved, even if U.S.–Soviet relations suffered. Very probably there were shifts, too, by individuals who had formerly supported the cooperativist position but who were now persuaded that the political and even economic costs of restraint had become too high. Given the growing influence of the holders of the antagonistic image, on grounds of political prudence alone there was now reason to change one's stand.

It was apparently sometime near the middle or end of January that a dramatic change of course was decided upon.[98] The decision did not meet with universal approval among the political elite.[99] Nor were key Politburo members ready to accept it.[100] Indeed, for a time it seemed as though some cooperativists had resolved to do all they could to confuse and antagonize the Egyptians and thereby obstruct the new policy. When the Egyptian Minister of War, Ismail Ali, came to Moscow in February, 1973, he found Grechko and other military leaders prepared to discuss a path–breaking military package. Brezhnev, however, pressed him to make peace and warned him that if Egypt went to war, it could not expect the Soviets to intervene to save it. [101]

In contrast to previous years, however, holders of the cooperative image were now unable to prevent the arms transfers they had steadfastly opposed. In the new circumstances which had emerged since the expulsion from Egypt, they could no longer maintain the priorities they wished to be accorded the various regional and global objectives of the USSR. For the first time since the inception of détente, therefore, U.S.-Soviet relations were given second place to preservation of the Soviet position in the Arab and the Third World.[102]

In the light of this analysis it becomes clear why Brezhnev was so disappointed when he failed to reach an agreement on the terms for a Middle East settlement with Kissinger in Moscow in May, 1973; why he tried so frantically to persuade Nixon to accept his proposal at San Clemente the next month; and why Gromyko at the United Nations and in Washington the following September made such urgent efforts to convey the seriousness of the situation in the Middle East.[103] By February, 1973, Brezhnev knew that war was inevitable in the absence of a major U.S. concession, and he deeply feared for the future of détente. When he himself failed to induce the United States to be more forthcoming, he sent his foreign minister to make one last try.[104] It also became clear why, after February, 1973, the Soviets were both giving Sadat the green light to go to war and telling him that he must not do so: the leadership really was of (at least) two minds on the matter.[105]

If one continues an analysis of Soviet behavior based on these findings of elite diversity and conflict, one may note that once war broke out, holders of the competitive image called loudly for the Arabs to use the oil weapon. They were not concerned about the impact that Soviet support for such measures would have on American public opinion and were delighted by the prospect of U.S. involvement in a "mad, mad fight for Arab oil."[106] Cooperative image holders were responsible for the immediate Soviet pressure on Egypt and Syria to accept a cease fire in order to avoid a U.S.-Soviet confrontation and the rupture of détente.[107] Even holders of the competitive image understood that détente would not survive direct Soviet intervention to bail out the Arabs--hence Kosygin's flight to Egypt to support this cease fire campaign after Israeli forces had begun to cross the canal and move toward Cairo.[108] Holders of the antagonistic image were, by contrast, notably uninterested in a cease fire.[109]

Those who subscribed to the antagonistic image were anxious to demonstrate to the Arabs, and to the rest of the world as well, the reliability of the USSR as an ally. As in the period before the war, they appeared to be less concerned about the dangers of escalation than about the possible negative consequences of excessive Soviet restraint. The air- and sealift appears to have been initiated at their insistence.[110] The cooperativists, on the other hand, apparently hoped to avoid the need for Soviet resupply of the Arabs, perhaps fearing that even indirect intervention might damage détente. This was probably the reason for

Brezhnev's private letters to Arab heads of state, urgently dispatched immediately after hostilities began, pressing them to do their utmost to aid Egypt and Syria.[111] Similarly, it was probably cooperativists who insisted on curbing the resupply effort, with the result that it was much less than the Arabs expected and felt they needed.[112] By limiting what was delivered, one may surmise, they sought both to demonstrate Soviet restraint to the United States and to put pressure on the Arabs to stop fighting.

Finally, the dualism of Soviet Middle Eastern policy after the war was likewise probably a reflection of competing influences, with holders of the antagonistic image urging massive, immediate rearming of the Syrians and holders of the cooperative image insisting that the Syrians participate in an international conference to negotiate a peace settlement under the co-sponsorship of the United States and the Soviet Union. As before the war, the cooperativists were particularly eager to arrange a settlement. They hoped to legitimize and secure the Soviet presence in the Middle East, thereby making it unnecessary to have to choose again between maintaining that presence and pursuing détente.

Conclusion

Looking back over the course of Soviet policy in the Middle East, it would appear that February, 1973 marked the end of a distinct period which began in the aftermath of the 1967 War. On the one hand, during this period the USSR became much more deeply involved in military support for the Arabs, not only massively rearming them, but assuming a much more direct role in the operation of their armed forces. In Egypt, Soviet advisors were placed in all combat units down to the battalion level; and thousands of Soviet personnel were sent to man advanced air defense systems, first in Egypt, then in smaller numbers in Syria. At the same time, however, Soviet policy was also characterized by extensive efforts to achieve a settlement of the Arab–Israeli conflict, including both repeated attempts at cooperation with the United States for this purpose and the bringing of considerable pressure to bear on the Arabs to negotiate, combined with notable restraint and caution in the transfer of arms. There were, moreover, many puzzling inconsistencies in Soviet policy in this period. These included concurrence in a limited war of attrition and assistance in the conduct of that war, accompanied by pressure to end it and measures to prevent its resumption; insistence on resolving the conflict with Israel peacefully, along with occasional hints that force might be acceptable; and many promises of weapons followed by repeated failure to provide them.

In February, 1973, Soviet policy underwent a major change. The Egyptians were informed that the Soviets would not oppose a war to liberate their territories, and between February and October, 1973, weapons essential to such an undertaking, hitherto carefully withheld, were delivered to Egypt and placed under Egyptian operational control. In this period, moreover, the contradictions in Soviet policy intensified, as the USSR both authorized a major war and made it possible, yet at the same time insisted that it must not be waged.

Soviet Middle Eastern policy in the period up to February, 1973 was shaped, first and foremost, by the requirements of Soviet global policy at the time, i.e., by the desire both to avoid a superpower military confrontation and to develop the new relationship of détente. The decision to end the policy of restraint vis-à-vis the Arabs appears to have been taken with full knowledge that both a confrontation and the rupture of détente could result. It is difficult to provide a satisfying explanation of this decision using the traditional "rational actor" paradigm. Use of a paradigm which assumes a diversity of views and conflict over policy priorities and objectives among the Soviet political elite greatly assists our effort to understand Soviet behavior. Both the February, 1973 change and the inconsistencies in Soviet policy which preceded it can best be explained if one focuses on (a) the diverse images of the other superpower held by various elites whose views were represented in the top leadership, (b) the conflicting priorities and objectives with regard to both global and regional policy, including Middle Eastern policy, derived from those different images, and (c) the gradual shift in power and influence among holders of those various images, brought on by what was widely perceived by Soviet elites as a major foreign policy setback. The inconsistency in Soviet policy which continued after February, 1973, can likewise be explained by the persistence of divergent elite images and policy positions and the enduring (although somewhat diminished) political influence of leaders and elites who had hitherto prevailed in policy debates.

What changed in February, 1973, in other words, was that the dominant voice in Soviet Middle Eastern policy, especially in arms transfer policy, ceased to be that of individuals and groups who gave high priority to confrontation avoidance and development of détente and became that of key elites who were concerned almost exclusively with expanding Soviet influence and building positions of strength in the Middle East and throughout the Third World.

What this case study suggests, in sum, is that if Soviet policy in the Middle East and other areas seems in different periods or even simultaneously to be cautious and adventurous, cooperative toward and antagonistic to U.S. interests, collaborative with and competitive vis-à-vis the United States, it is all of these. It embodies these contradictory strands at least in part because of the diverse images of the United States and conflicting views on global and regional policy held within the Soviet political elite and the changes over time in the relative power and influence of the individuals and groups which hold these competing views. Any attempt to understand Soviet international behavior will therefore be more fruitful if this diversity and conflict is examined, elucidated, and analyzed.

Notes

1. See Robert O. Freedman, *Soviet Policy Toward the Middle East Since 1970*, 3rd ed. (New York: Praeger, 1982), p. 1.

2. This perspective is articulated in Freedman, *Soviet Policy Toward the Middle East Since 1970*; Robert O. Freedman, "Détente and U.S.-Soviet Relations in the Middle East During the Nixon Years (1969–1974)," in Della W. Sheldon, ed., *Dimensions of Détente* (New York: Praeger, 1978); Alvin Z. Rubinstein, *Red Star on the Nile* (Princeton: Princeton University Press, 1977); John C. Campbell, "The Communist Powers and the Middle East: Moscow's Purposes," *Problems of Communism* 21, no. 5 (September–October, 1972); Abraham S. Becker, "The Superpowers in the Arab–Israeli Conflict," in Abraham S. Becker, Bert Hanson, and Malcolm Kerr, eds., *The Economics and Politics of the Middle East* (New York: American Elsevier Publishing Co., 1975).

3. This argument is made in Jon D. Glassman, *Arms for the Arabs* (Baltimore: Johns Hopkins University Press, 1975); Lawrence L. Whetten, *The Canal War: Four Power Conflict in the Middle East* (Cambridge: The MIT Press, 1974); Galia Golan, *Yom Kippur and After* (Cambridge: Cambridge University Press, 1977); Karen Dawisha, *Soviet Foreign Policy Toward Egypt* (London: Macmillan Press Ltd., 1979); George W. Breslauer, "Soviet Policy in the Middle East, 1967–1972," in Alexander L. George, ed., *Managing U.S.-Soviet Rivalry* (Boulder: Westview Press, 1983).

4. The strategic or rational actor paradigm is described in Graham Allison, *Essence of Decision* (Boston: Little, Brown, 1971).

5. This is essentially the paradigm employed in all the works cited in notes 2 and 3, with the exception of Dawisha, *Soviet Foreign Policy Towards Egypt*. Dawisha discusses the possibility of leadership conflict over objectives and priorities in the formulation of Soviet policy toward the Middle East. This discussion (on pp. 142–150) relies almost entirely

on an article by Ilana Dimant-Kass, "The Soviet Military and Soviet Policy in the Middle East 1970-73," *Soviet Studies* 26, no. 4 (1974). This article, along with Kass's later work, *Soviet Involvement in the Middle East: Policy Formulation, 1966-1973* (Boulder: Westview, 1978), and Dina Rome Spechler, *Domestic Influences on Soviet Foreign Policy* (Washington, D.C.: University Press of America, 1978), are the only published studies of Soviet policy in the Middle East which systematically examine internal debate and its impact on decisions taken.

6. This methodology and other findings based on its application are presented in detail in Spechler, *Domestic Influences on Soviet Foreign Policy.*

7. It is questionable whether the Soviets ever really agreed to the War of Attrition. One well-placed Arab source claims they did, but notes that they subsequently begged Nasser to halt the war. (Mohamed Heikal, *The Sphinx and the Commissar* [New York: Harper and Row, 1978], pp. 193-194.) Sadat maintained they never gave their agreement, and indeed, never forgave the Egyptians for starting and continuing the war against Soviet wishes, even "punishing" them by withholding critical weapons and failing to make good Egypt's loss of ammunition in the war until the 1973 airlift. (Anwar el-Sadat, *In Search of Identity: An Autobiography* [New York: Harper and Row, 1977], pp. 196-197.) This account of Soviet opposition to the war does not seem to square with the fact that the USSR markedly increased Egypt's tactical offensive capabilities during the war (Glassman, *Arms for the Arabs*, p. 109) and provided air defense not only for the Egyptian interior, but for Egyptian positions along the canal. Breslauer, however, makes a persuasive case that these steps were taken to strengthen Egypt's bargaining position and thereby make possible not only a cease fire, but a negotiated settlement of the conflict. ("Soviet Policy in the Middle East," pp. 82-83, 86.) Glassman points out, moreover, that the Soviets never provided enough weapons to assure the success of the War of Attrition, much less of a cross-canal offensive. (*Arms for the Arabs* , p. 196.) The hypothesis that the USSR opposed the war is supported, too, by the fact that once a cease fire had been declared, the Soviets told the Egyptians they would not support them should they resume a war of attrition and, to demonstrate their seriousness, removed their missile crews, aircraft, and air-defense equipment from the vital Aswan Dam area. (See Whetten, *The Canal War*, p. 154; Rubinstein, *Red Star*, p. 163.)

8. See Heikal, *The Sphinx and the Commissar*, pp. 186, 187, 193, 195, 216, 217, 222; Mohamed Hassanein Heikal, *Al Ahram*, July 10, 1968 (quoted in *Middle East Journal*, Autumn, 1968, p. 439); Cairo Radio, July 24, 1972 (Sadat Speech); Sadat, *In Search of Identity*, p. 249; "The Soviet

Attitude to the Palestine Problem: From the Records of the Syrian Communist Party, 1971-1972," *Journal of Palestine Studies* 2, no. 1 (Autumn, 1972), 188-189; Alexander Prlja, "A Reappraisal in Soviet-Egyptian Relations," *International Affairs* (Yugoslavia) 23, nos. 542-543 (November 5-20, 1972), p. 29; Henry A. Kissinger, *Years of Upheaval* (Boston: Little, Brown & Co., 1982), p. 204; Breslauer, "Soviet Policy in the Middle East," pp. 71, 72, 74, 82-87, 91, 94.

9. Cairo Radio, April 3, 1974 (Sadat speech); Glassman, *Arms for the Arabs*, p. 84. Only after expelling the Soviets did Sadat feel free to go to war. (Sadat, *In Search of Identity*, p. 232.)

10. These included many of the MIG-21 interceptors and SAM-6's; many, if not all, of the SAM-3's; all of the SU-11 and MIG-23 interceptors, MIG-25 interceptors (used for reconnaissance), and TU-16 electronic reconnaissance aircraft. (Mohamed Heikal, *The Road to Ramadan* [New York: Quadrangle/The New York Times Book Co., 1975], pp. 161-163; Glassman, *Arms for the Arabs*, pp. 105, 111.)

11. Heikal, *The Sphinx and the Commissar*, pp. 220, 249-250; Sadat, *In Search of Identity*, p. 198; Lt. General Saad el Shazly, *The Crossing of the Suez* (San Francisco: American Mideast Research, 1980), p. 159; Glassman, *Arms for the Arabs*, pp. 96, 104-107.

12. Glassman, *Arms for the Arabs*, pp. 108-110.

13. Cairo Radio, July 24, 1972 (Sadat speech); *Newsweek*, August 7, 1972 (Sadat interview); Cairo Radio, April 3, 1974 (Sadat speech); Sadat, *In Search of Identity*, pp. 187, 198, 212, 219-221, 225-228; Heikal, *The Sphinx and the Commissar*, pp. 249-251; Shazly, *The Crossing of the Suez*, pp. 28-29, 102, 106, 141, 157-158, 160-162. See also Glassman, *Arms for the Arabs*, pp. 90-94, 102, 111-112. The Soviets did supply in this period some MIG-21 interceptors (which were no match for the Phantom fighter-bombers Israel possessed), a limited number of mobile SAM-6 antiaircraft missiles, a small quantity of Sagger antitank missiles, and a handful of T-62 tanks. (Glassman, *Arms for the Arabs*, pp. 105-106, 218 n. 90.)

14. With regard to Soviet behavior between February and October, 1973, Sadat complained that the Soviets never abandoned their preference for a negotiated solution and never ceased to put pressure on the Egyptians to "rule out" military means. (Cairo Radio, May 1, 1973, May 14, 1973, April 3, 1974 [Sadat speeches]; *Time Magazine*, March 25, 1974 [interview with Sadat].) See also Golan, *Yom Kippur and After*, pp. 47-55.

15. The Soviets apparently promised aid and diplomatic support in the event of war, so long as the objective of the offensive was solely to regain the territories yielded in 1967, not to destroy the Jewish state. This,

at any rate, is the way Sadat understood the assurances given to his National Security Adviser, Hafez Ismail, and his Minister of War, General Ahmed Ismail Ali, who visited Moscow February 6–10, 1973 and February 26–March 2, 1973 respectively. (Cairo Radio, April 3, 1974 [Sadat speech]; Kissinger, *Years of Upheaval*, p. 469.) The Soviets had on three previous occasions, in April, July and October, 1972, issued joint communiqués with visiting Egyptians which affirmed the right of the Arabs to use "any" or "diverse" means to liberate their territories (*Pravda*, April 30, 1972, July 14, 1972, October 19, 1972) but apparently no such authorization had been made in actual discussions with Arab leaders or officials, nor was the crucial commitment to provide wartime support made until February, 1973.

16. These promises were apparently made during the Hafez Ismail and Ismail Ali visits mentioned in note 15 above, and the arms began to arrive within days of Ismail Ali's return. (Shazly, *The Crossing of the Suez*, pp. 197–198; *Newsweek*, April 9, 1973 [Sadat interview]; Cairo Radio, July 23, 1973, April 3, 1974 [Sadat speeches].)

17. Shazly, *The Crossing of the Suez*, pp. 197–198; Heikal, *The Sphinx and the Commissar*, pp. 253–254; Glassman, *Arms for the Arabs*, pp. 105–107, 112–114.

18. Glassman, *Arms for the Arabs*, p. 5.

19. *Ibid.*, p. 114.

20. Shazly, *The Crossing of the Suez*, p. 199. See also Heikal, *The Sphinx and the Commissar*, pp. 253–254.

21. Heikal, *The Sphinx and the Commissar*, p. 254.

22. *Newsweek*, April 9, 1973 (Sadat interview).

23. *Ibid.*; Cairo Radio, April 3, 1974 (Sadat Speech).

24. Glassman, *Arms for the Arabs*, pp. 102, 113; Golan, *Yom Kippur and After*, p. 66.

25. Soviet behavior before and during the war, writes Alexander George, "called into question within the U.S. the entire détente relationship." "Although it would be going too far to say that détente was dealt a mortal blow by the October War, the relationship between the two sides was never the same thereafter." (Alexander L. George, "The Arab–Israeli War of October 1973: Origins and Impact," in Alexander L. George, ed., *Managing U.S.–Soviet Rivalry: Problems of Crisis Prevention* [Boulder: Westview, 1983], pp. 148, 150.) See also Glassman, *Arms for the Arabs*, p. 2.

26. See, for example, Glassman, *Arms for the Arabs*, pp. 3–4, 93, 103–104; Golan, *Yom Kippur and After*, p. 21; George, "The Arab–Israeli War of October, 1973," p. 140. This is also the analysis of most Arab observers. Cf., for example, *Cairo Radio*, August 29, 1967 (comments by

Heikal).

27.   Glassman argues, for example, that at various moments the Soviets sought to punish Sadat for domestic and foreign policy moves they did not like, such as his removal of their protégé Aly Sabry from the vice-presidency, accompanied by his arrest in 1971 of 110 of Sabry's associates, and his support for the anti-Communist counter-coup in the Sudan, also in 1971. (*Arms for the Arabs*, pp. 3–4, 89–93, 104–105.) However, the USSR's restraint both antedated and substantially postdated both these events, suggesting that they were not of paramount significance in determining Soviet policy. Similarly, the Soviets may have been unable or unwilling to deliver substantial quantities of arms to the Arabs during the Indo-Pakistani War at the end of 1971 because they desired or felt committed to give India the military backing it needed. (Cf. Glassman, *Arms for the Arabs*, pp. 92–93, 103.) This, too, was a brief episode, however, and the Soviets' vast resupply of Egypt and Syria, not only during the October War, but in the months following the June War, clearly demonstrated that they did not lack the capacity to deliver arms in great quantities to the Middle East. Finally, the Soviet desire to keep highly advanced weapons, or data about their performance out of Western hands may have inhibited them from placing certain items, such as the MIG-25 interceptor or crucial components of their electronic counter-measure systems, in Arab hands, but this cannot account for the entire pattern of Soviet restraint, which extended to many far less sensitive items.

28.   When Nasser visited the USSR in July, 1968, the Soviets told him bluntly that they did not wish to risk "a confrontation with the United States." (Heikal in *Al Ahram*, July 10, 1968, quoted in *Middle East Journal*, Autumn, 1968, p. 439.) In a long discussion between high Soviet officials and leading Syrian Communists in Moscow in May, 1971, the Syrians were told that the Arabs must seek a political solution to the conflict with Israel because war would lead to a confrontation between the U.S. and USSR. ("The Soviet Attitude to the Palestine Problem," 188.)

29.   The two documents were "Basic Principles of U.S.-Soviet Relations," signed on May 29, 1972 (*Department of State Bulletin*, June 26, 1972, pp. 898–899) and "Agreement on Prevention of Nuclear War," signed June 22, 1973 (*United States Treaties and Other International Agreements*, Vol. 24, part 2, 1973, pp. 1479–1485).

30.   This is the thrust of the argument in Freedman, "Détente and U.S.-Soviet Relations in the Middle East."

31.   Particularly after Sadat came to power, Egypt's constant demands for weapons and repeated reproaches for the USSR's failure to deliver them created substantial tension between the two countries. For

this reason the Soviets made a major effort in 1971–1972 to diversify their bases of influence in the Middle East, strengthening their ties to Syria, Iraq, Libya, Algeria, Morocco and South Yemen, and even making overtures to the conservative monarchies in the region. (Glassman, *Arms for the Arabs*, pp. 96–97; Whetten, *The Canal War*, p. 216; Freedman, *Soviet Policy Since 1970*, pp. 51–84; Breslauer, "Soviet Policy in the Middle East," p. 90.) By 1972, Sadat was already issuing thinly veiled warnings that if the Soviets were not more forthcoming, he would "have to act—a decision [would] have to be taken." (Sadat, *In Search of Identity*, p. 228.) That the Soviets understood what he had in mind is indicated by Brezhnev's rejoinder: "the presence of Soviet advisors in Egypt [is] an international necessity." (Shazly, *The Crossing of the Suez*, pp. 161–162.) Mohamed Heikal, editor of the influential Egyptian newspaper *Al Ahram*, notes on the basis of his contacts with high Soviet officials in Egypt that the Soviets were not surprised by the expulsion and, indeed, "had prepared themselves in advance for something of the sort." (*Road to Ramadan*, p. 175.) Even Kissinger acknowledges that the Soviets had been prepared to sacrifice their relationship with Egypt in order to promote détente. (Henry A. Kissinger, *White House Years* [Boston: Little, Brown and Co., 1979], p. 1297; *Years of Upheaval*, p. 204.) Cf. Glassman, *Arms for the Arabs*, p. 3. Kissinger similarly notes that the Soviets had also sacrificed the goodwill of their Vietnamese allies and would make significant compromises in domestic policy, rescinding the exit tax on Soviet Jews, for the sake of their developing relationship with the United States. (*Years of Upheaval*, pp. 252–253, 287.)

32. This is Breslauer's characterization of the Soviet outlook by mid–1972. ("Soviet Policy in the Middle East," pp. 89–95.)

33. See Freedman, "Détente and U.S.–Soviet Relations in the Middle East," p. 102.

34. See Kissinger, *Years of Upheaval*, p. 460.

35. Kissinger, *White House Years*, pp. 1141–1142; Kissinger, *Years of Upheaval*, pp. 231, 247, 268, 274–276, 986.

36. Only in the autumn of 1973, well after the January decision, did this begin to be the case, i.e., after the fall of Allende in Chile and the passage of the Jackson–Vanik Amendment to the trade bill by the House Ways and Means Committee. On the issue of trade, moreover, the Soviets never really gave up hope until Congress imposed a flat ceiling of only $300 million on all loans to the USSR, and this did not occur until June 30, 1974. (Kissinger, *Years of Upheaval* , pp. 990–998.) On the impact of Allende's fall on the Soviet attitude to détente see Glassman, *Arms for the Arabs*, pp. 118–119.

37. Glassman, p. 119.

38. Freedman, *Soviet Policy Toward the Middle East Since 1970*, p. 137; Freedman, "Détente and U.S.-Soviet Relations in the Middle East," p. 102.

39. At the 1972 Moscow summit, for example, Soviet Foreign Minister Gromyko tried for four solid hours to win Kissinger's agreement to a set of general principles regarding the Middle East which would have been palatable to at least some of the Arab moderates. Kissinger stubbornly stood his ground until the Soviets eventually signed a document which, by alluding to the possibility of border rectifications, made an important concession to Israel. Also on American insistence, the U.S.-Soviet communiqué issued at the close of the summit emphasized the need for military relaxation in the Middle East. The communiqué and the declaration of principles seemed to Sadat to go so far in support of the Israeli position that he regarded them as a sellout. (Kissinger, *White House Years*, pp. 1246–1248 1493–1494 notes 3–4.)

40. Kissinger, *Years of Upheaval*, p. 247.

41. *Middle East Journal*, Autumn, 1973, p. 489.

42. Kissinger, *Years of Upheaval*, pp. 72–81, 122–123.

43. Glassman, *Arms for the Arabs*, p. 98.

44. Shazly, *The Crossing of the Suez*, pp. 28–29.

45. Sadat claimed he assured the Soviets that he did not need a single Soviet soldier and did not intend to provoke a confrontation between the superpowers. (*Newsweek*, April 9, 1973 [Sadat interview].)

46. Heikal, *The Sphinx and the Commissar*, pp. 256–257.

47. Freedman, *Soviet Policy Toward the Middle East Since 1970*, p. 136; Rubinstein, *Red Star on the Nile*, p. 235; Golan, *Yom Kippur and After*, p. 41.

48. Rubinstein, *Red Star on the Nile*, p. 246; George, "The Arab-Israeli War of October, 1973," p. 145.

49. Sadat, *In Search of Identity*, pp. 233–234; Heikal, *The Sphinx and the Commissar*, pp. 251–252.

50. Shazly, *The Crossing of the Suez*, p. 175.

51. *Ibid.*, p. 172.

52. Shazly claims a squadron of highly advanced interceptors (MIG-23's) and a brigade of Scuds were promised to Sidky. (*Ibid.*, p. 172).

53. Golan, *Yom Kippur and After*, pp. 35, 268, n. 84.

54. On arms purchases in Western Europe see Rubinstein, *Red Star on the Nile*, pp. 212, 224; on the Kissinger meeting, Kissinger, *White House Years*, p. 1300; on domestic pressure, especially from the military, Radio Amman, October 23, 1972 and *Al-Nahar* (Beirut), October 31,

1972, both quoted in *The USSR and the Third World* 11, no. 10 (1972).

55.   Cairo Radio, April 3, 1974 (Sadat speech); Sadat, *In Search of Identity*, pp. 237–238.

56.   See note 31.

57.   Glassman, *Arms for the Arabs*, p. 97.

58.   It is not being suggested here that identical paradigms should be employed for the analysis of elite conflict in the U.S. and the USSR. For a discussion of some of the problems encountered in using paradigms derived from the American experience to analyze the Soviet foreign policy process, see Karen Dawisha, "The Limits of the Bureaucratic Politics Model: Observations on the Soviet Case," *Studies in Comparative Communism* 13, no. 4 (Winter, 1980), pp. 300–346.

59.   Interviews with Soviet emigres conducted by the author in 1975–1982. Subjects were journal and newspaper editors, journalists, writers, literary critics, and other individuals who had had close or frequent contact with journal editors or Party officials responsible for supervising the media. A similar interview project, designed to ascertain the role of the media as a vehicle for the expression of elite views in the USSR was conducted by Lilita Dzirkals, Thane Gustafson, and A. Ross Johnson (see *The Media and Intra-Elite Communication in the USSR* [Santa Monica: The Rand Corporation, September, 1982]). Like the respondents in the Rand study, the emigrants interviewed by the author stressed that many Politburo leaders and other high officials, by virtue of their official functions, are responsible for overseeing individual media organs and can therefore exert considerable influence on them. Unlike the Rand interviewees, mine were intentionally selected so as to include, as far as possible, individuals who had worked in or with the media during the Khrushchev, as well as the Brezhnev, period. This may account for the fact that they seemed to emphasize far more than did the Rand respondents the importance of the media as an outlet for elite debate. The results of my research confirm the finding of the Rand study that the frequency and amount, as well as the significance, of media divergence declined sharply under Brezhnev. Since the Khrushchev period, there has been far less opportunity for a media organ to publish dissent against the central values or institutions of the Soviet system or even against established policies. (See Dina Rome Spechler, *Permitted Dissent in the USSR* [New York: Praeger, 1982].) However, there have been, both under Brezhnev and under his successors, a number of occasions on which media divergence on highly important issues was extremely marked. (See Dina Rome Spechler, *Russian Nationalism and Political Stability in the USSR* [Cambridge, Mass.: Center for International Affairs, Harvard University, and Center for International Studies, Massachusetts Institute of

Technology, 1983]; Jiri Valenta, *Soviet Intervention in Czechoslovakia, 1968: Anatomy of a Decision* [Baltimore: Johns Hopkins University Press, 1979]; Kass, *Soviet Involvement in the Middle East*; Dan L. Strode and Rebecca V. Strode, "Diplomacy and Defense in Soviet National Security Policy," *International Security*, 8, no. 2 [Fall, 1983], 112–113.)

60. Some of the problems with this methodology, reasons why those problems should not ultimately deter one from undertaking this sort of analysis, and additional assumptions about the Soviet foreign policy process which underlie this approach are discussed in Spechler, *Domestic Influences on Soviet Foreign Policy.*

61. *Ibid.* The six papers were *Pravda, Izvestiia, Komsomol'skaia pravda, Trud, Krasnaia zvezda* and *Sovetskaia Rosiia.*

62. See *ibid.*, pp. 63–70, and the evidence for the existence of these images on pp. 17–61. The author began the analysis of the six newpapers with the intention of ascertaining only the array of views expressed on the Arab–Israeli conflict and the Soviet role in that conflict. It quickly became apparent, however, that there was a connection between the positions taken by a given newspaper on this subject and the position it expressed on Soviet global policy, particularly policy toward the United States. When this was discovered, the research was broadened to include a systematic survey both of opinions expressed about American international behavior and U.S.–Soviet relations, and of the linkages made by each paper between these subjects and the Middle East.

63. Cf. Alexander Yanov, *Détente After Brezhnev: The Domestic Roots of Soviet Foreign Policy* (Berkeley: Institute of International Studies, University of California, 1977), pp. 1–42, and Kass, *Soviet Involvement in the Middle East*, pp. 162, 217–218.

64. Cf. Kissinger, *Years of Upheaval*, p. 234. Brezhnev told Kissinger he wished to devote his tenure to bringing about a condition in which war between the U.S. and the USSR was unthinkable. Kissinger believed Brezhnev was sincere in saying this. The assessment of Nixon's National Security Adviser was that on the one hand Brezhnev was as likely as any other Soviet leader to take advantage of opportunities to alter the power balance in favor of the USSR. On the other hand, however, he was genuinely devoted to peace and for its sake ready "to explore the requirements of genuine coexistence." (It is argued here that Brezhnev's willingness to refrain from exploiting certain opportunities to enhance Soviet power in order to ensure the preservation of peace was in fact greater than that of other Soviet leaders.)

65. Cf. Kass, *Soviet Involvement in the Middle East*, pp. 159, 198, and Dimant–Kass, "The Soviet Military and Soviet Policy in the Middle East," 502–521. Kass found that in the early 1970s *Pravda* downplayed

American involvement in the Middle East and attached relatively little importance to the area for the USSR. This was probably part of an effort to justify a limited or decreased Soviet commitment.

66. Cf. Joanne Gowa and Nils H. Wessell, *Ground Rules: Soviet and American Involvement in Regional Conflicts,* (Philadelphia: Foreign Policy Research Institute, 1982), p. 2.

67. Cf. Kissinger's recollection that in his meetings with the Soviet leaders in Moscow in May, 1972, Kosygin spoke eloquently about the advantages of increased commerce to the U.S." . . . [H]e never failed to claim that he was doing us the greater favor by opening up the Soviet market to our exports." He was so ardent in his interest in trade that he "even inspired Commerce Secretary Maurice Stans to dream that the two of them might join as hard-headed businessmen to settle the world's ills by economic exchange; innumerable other American business leaders came away from meeting him salivating at the prospect of huge contracts . . . ." (*White House Years,* pp. 1214–1215.) *Izvestiia* espoused a rather different line, more antagonistic to détente, in 1969–1970. Probably at that time the newspaper was controlled by a different group of state officials from the defense and producer goods sectors. (Cf. Kass, *Soviet Involvement in the Middle East,* pp. 160–162, 223–226.) The pro-détente group may have become more influential as the possibilities of and need for a highly profitable economic relationship with the West began to loom larger in the early 1970s. Kass reports a change in *Izvestiia's* line by 1972. (*Ibid.,* pp. 208–209.)

68. Cf. Kass, *Soviet Involvement in the Middle East,* pp. 219–222.

69. Cf. Kass's finding, that in the period 1969–1972 *Krasnaia zvezda* consistently argued that the USSR should support Arab use of force to regain the conquered territories. (*Soviet Involvement in the Middle East,* pp. 159, 163–164, 207–208; Dimant-Kass, "The Soviet Military and Soviet Policy in the Middle East," 502–521.) See also Heikal, *Road to Ramadan,* p. 67; *The Sphinx and the Commissar,* p. 29. Heikal portrays Shelepin as an enthusiastic advocate of arming the Egyptians, and claims that his political decline in the late 1960s and early 1970s partly explains Soviet restraint at that time. For a very different reading of the position of Shelepin and *Trud,* see Kass, *Soviet Involvement in the Middle East,* pp. 196–199, 203.

70. See Spechler, *Russian Nationalism and Political Stability in the USSR.*

71. The ambivalent character of the image of the United States and the different grounds for interest in détente conveyed by *Sovetskaia Rossiia* may reflect the two different, often contradictory, strands in the Russian nationalist movement. One is more spiritual, concerned with the

preservation of Russian culture and tradition, the other more statist, concerned with the preservation and expansion of Russian and Soviet power. See Spechler, *Russian Nationalism and Political Stability in the USSR.*

72. Cf. Golan, *Yom Kippur and After*, pp. 27, 266 n. 40.

73. Cf. Breslauer, "Soviet Policy in the Middle East," p. 88. Breslauer points to 1969 as the year Brezhnev "pushed to the fore," forging a dominant coalition based on his priorities in domestic and foreign policy. These included his emphasis on détente.

74. The Soviets could have prevented or quickly halted the War of Attrition by withholding ammunition. That there was deep disagreement in the leadership over Soviet policy toward that war is suggested both by the heated public debate in the USSR at the time over the proper Soviet role in the Arab–Israeli conflict and by the apparent contradictions in Soviet behavior regarding the war––promises of new types of weapons to be used in the war and subsequent failure to provide them; intense pressure to end the war followed by decisive support for the conduct of it (air defense not only of the interior, but of Egyptian positions along the Canal). (Kass, *Soviet Involvement in the Middle East*, pp. 157–163; Heikal, *The Road to Ramadan*, p. 67; Sadat, *In Search of Identity*, p. 197; Heikal, *The Sphinx and the Commissar*, p. 193; Glassman, *Arms for the Arabs* , pp. 78–79.) That the cooperativists were overruled on the matter of sending Soviet personnel to man Egypt's air defenses is indicated by *Pravda's* opposition to greater Soviet involvement in the conflict, which continued almost to the day the soldiers were dispatched. (Kass, *Soviet Involvement in the Middle East*, pp. 162–163.) Further evidence of unsuccessful cooperativist opposition to the decision is provided in the account by Nasser's close confidant, *Al Ahram* editor Mohamed Heikal, of the Egyptian President's meeting with the Soviet leaders in January, 1970. When Nasser begged the Soviets to assume responsibility for the air defense of Egypt, Heikal writes, Brezhnev put up stiff resistance, declaring that " . . . this would be a step with serious international implications. It would provide all the makings of a crisis between the Soviet Union and the United States." (Heikal, *Road to Ramadan*, p. 86.)

75. Cf. Kass, *Soviet Involvement in the Middle East*, pp. 208–209.

76. Heikal, who participated in many high–level talks between the Egyptians and the Soviets, writes, for example, that the Politburo was split on the question of whether Kosygin should meet President Johnson after the June 1967 War to attempt to reach agreement on the terms of a settlement. Brezhnev's defense of the plan was decisive, Heikal avers. (*The Sphinx and the Commissar*, pp. 188–189.)

77. Heikal recalls that almost as soon as the guns stopped firing in the 1967 War, the Soviets began pressuring the Arabs to come to terms with Israel, even if this required diplomatic recognition. The two Politburo figures most involved in this effort, Heikal notes, were Brezhnev and Kosygin. (*The Sphinx and the Commissar*, pp. 186–187, 194.) It was apparently Kosygin who had initially taken the lead in this area. Even before the June War, he had tried to bring the Arabs to the bargaining table with Israel, suggesting to Nasser in 1966 that he consider an "Arab–Israeli Tashkent" to resolve the conflict. (*Ibid.*, p. 280.) But Brezhnev appears to have been equally, if not more eager for a peaceful solution. When Presidents Aref of Iraq and Boumedienne of Algeria went to Moscow shortly after the June War to plead for greater assistance to the Arab cause, Brezhnev was unforthcoming. He reportedly told his guests that he spent sleepless nights worrying about a new war in the Middle East. Such a war, the General Secretary declared, "would bring the whole world to the brink of catastrophe." (Heikal, *The Road to Ramadan*, p. 48.) When the Commander–in–Chief of the Egyptian armed forces, Mohamed Sadek, visited Moscow for the same purpose in June, 1972, Brezhnev's response was similar but more pointed. Sadek was told that Egypt and the USSR must work together within the framework of U.N. Resolution 242. If the Egyptians did not cooperate in this effort and tried war, the Soviet Party Chief warned, they could not expect the USSR to intervene to rescue them. (Shazly, *The Crossing of the Suez*, pp. 161–162.)

78. Brezhnev made no attempt to disguise his impatience with the Egyptians over their repeated requests for more and better arms. He told Sadat more than once that he was "sick and tired of being asked for new aircraft and refused to discuss it anymore." (Heikal, *The Road to Ramadan*, p. 158.)

79. Brezhnev reportedly told Sadat that it was he personally, "and nobody else," who decided to delay the delivery of the strategic weapons promised on several occasions prior to February, 1973. (*Ibid.*, pp. 158–159.)

80. Less is known about specific efforts on the part of "controllers" (police and trade union officials and youth leaders) to change Soviet policy in the Middle East between 1967 and 1973. This may be partly because such individuals had no official mandate to speak out on foreign policy matters and thus had to be more circumspect in doing so. Also, figures like Andropov and Shelepin, with no official responsibility for formulating, implementing, justifying or explaining Soviet policy abroad, were not usually included in meetings with Arab leaders, and foreign participants in such meetings were thus generally unable to observe them

in action. (As a Central Committee Secretary from 1961–1967, Shelepin appears to have had a considerable foreign policy role, and often travelled abroad. However, after his January, 1969 visit to the Middle East, an effort was apparently made to exclude him from this arena.)

81.   Nasser learned, for example, that Party Secretary Suslov had vigorously attacked the proposed Kosygin–Johnson meeting in 1967, declaring that no good could come of it. (Heikal, *The Sphinx and the Commissar*, pp. 188–189.)

82.   On the occasion of the visit to Moscow of Egyptian Commander–in–Chief Mohamed Sadek in June, 1972, Soviet Defense Minister Grechko took the extraordinary step of telling the Politburo in Sadek's presence that the policy of restraint must be abandoned. The Egyptians should prepare for war, Grechko declared, and "Egypt must be supplied with the weapons to insure victory." (Shazly, *The Crossing of the Suez*, pp. 161–162.)

83.   Grechko made this clear on at least two occasions. When the Egyptian Minister of War was about to leave Moscow just prior to the June 1967 War, his Soviet counterpart admonished him, "Stand up to them! The moment they attack you, or if the Americans make any move, you will find our troops on your side." Two years later, after the Israeli September 9 raid on the Egyptian military post at Ras Zafarana on the Red Sea, Grechko complained to members of the Egyptian mission in Moscow, "You should be more daring. You should have stopped them . . . . Why are you afraid? The Soviet navy in the Mediterranean is following the American Sixth Fleet like a shadow. They can't do anything. If the Americans put their marines into Israel, we are ready to land our troops on your territories." (Heikal, *The Sphinx and the Commissar*, pp. 28, 194.)

84.   These occasions were in March, May, July and October, 1971 and February and October, 1972. (Sadat, *In Search of Identity*, p. 220; Heikal, *The Road to Ramadan*, pp. 158–159; Shazly, *The Crossing of the Suez*, pp. 113, 137, 172.)

85.   Shelepin in January, 1969; Grechko in February and May, 1972. (Heikal, *The Road to Ramadan*, p. 67; Kass, *Soviet Involvement in the Middle East*, pp. 208–209; Shazly, *The Crossing of the Suez*, pp. 156–157.)

86.   See note 79 above.

87.   *Krasnaia zvezda* initiated a campaign at that time to convince the leadership of the importance of the Soviet–Arab alliance. (Kass, *Soviet Involvement in the Middle East*, pp. 210–211.)

88.   Both Grechko and Admiral Gorshkov, the head of the Soviet navy, travelled to Egypt in May, 1972 to inspect Soviet facilities there.

Gorshkov emphasized that the Soviet navy could not properly operate without even more naval facilities in Egypt, not only in the Mediterranean, but on the Red Sea Coast. (Heikal, *Road to Ramadan*, p. 164.) Heikal reports that after the expulsion, there were

> plenty of those in the [Soviet] leadership, especially among the military, who . . . felt that the position in the Middle East must be maintained at all costs, because of its military significance, the importance of the sea routes, and possibly of the oil supplies, as well as, of course, for reasons of political prestige . . . . The military, and in particular Marshal Grechko, argued repeatedly in the Politburo that . . . the flow of military aid to the Arabs must be stepped up. They feared that the Arabs were contemplating abandonment of their alliance with the Soviet Union and were in favor of direct talks with the Americans. Let the Arabs have sufficient arms to enable them to risk a battle, the argument continued. Should this happen, and should the Arabs win, their victory would have been achieved thanks to Soviet arms. Should they be defeated, or the fighting reach a stalemate, it is still to the Soviet Union that they will have to look for rescue in the aftermath of the battle. (*The Sphinx and the Commissar*, p. 253.)

89. Prlja, "A Reappraisal in Soviet–Egyptian Relations," p. 29.

90. *TASS*, October 16, 1972.

91. Reports that such a demand had been made of the Egyptians circulated in the West in September, 1972. (*Le Monde*, September 2–3, 1972, cited in Golan, *Yom Kippur and After*, p. 40.) According to Shazly, such a demand had been made earlier (in March, 1972) but was quickly withdrawn, apparently on Grechko's insistence. (*The Crossing of the Suez*, pp. 142–143, 156–157.) By October, 1972, Grechko was apparently prepared to assure Kosygin and other competitivists that the demand would be sustained.

92. Gur Ofer suggests that the economic burden of Soviet arms transfers to the Arabs may have generated opposition to such transfers among many Soviet economic experts. ("The Economic Burden of Soviet Involvement in the Middle East," *Soviet Studies* 24, no. 3 [1972], 329–48.) One may surmise that if the burden were transformed into an asset, opposition in such quarters would probably be changed to support.

93. See note 52 and the discussion in the text preceding it.

94. See note 53 and the discussion in the text preceding it.

95. *New York Times*, December 20, 1972.

96. Knowledgeable East European diplomats concluded at the time that the USSR had decided not to resume an active role in Egypt. (*Ibid.*)

97. On the money made available in December–January and its impact on Soviet decision–making, see *ibid.* and Rubinstein, *Red Star on the Nile*, p. 242. That Kosygin was among those who supported the sale is suggested by his assertion in Stockholm a few weeks later that, "We consider that Egypt is entitled to have a strong army at the present time in order to . . . liberate its own lands." (*New Times*, no. 15 [April, 1973]). That Kosygin's "defection" was decisive is indicated by Kissinger's analysis based on his observations of the Soviet leadership in action in May, 1972. Although Brezhnev was "clearly the top man," Kissinger noted, he "appeared to need the support of Kosygin and Podgorny to carry the Politburo with him." (*White House Years*, p. 1214.)

98. Although Sadat had begun making serious preparations for war as early as August, 1972, it was only in January, 1973, evidently on the basis of reports of Moscow's changed position, that he became satisfied he could go through with his plans. (*Ahbar al Yom*, August 3, 1972 [Sadat interview]; Middle East News Agency, October 8, 1974 [Sadat Interview]; both cited in Golan, *Yom Kippur and After*, p. 37.) At the end of January, 1973, moreover, the Soviet propaganda apparatus began to issue militant statements about the Middle East which justified and affirmed the new policy. The propaganda weekly *New Times* accused Israel of planning and preparing for war against the Arabs, and Moscow Radio, commenting on the visit of a Vietnamese delegation to the USSR, suggested that Vietnamese use of "resolute military action, together with different forms of political and diplomatic struggle," should be a model for the Arabs. (*New Times*, January 26 and February 16, 1973; Moscow Radio [in Arabic], January 27, 29, 31, 1973, both cited in Golan, *Yom Kippur and After*, pp. 38–39.)

99. That even some holders of the competitive image were not persuaded of the merits of the new course is suggested by a very different analogy between the Middle East and Vietnam drawn by *Izvestia*. This news organ maintained that U.S. experience in Vietnam had demonstrated that "arms were irrelevant for obtaining solutions, and even the most difficult conflicts could be resolved." (March 8, 1973, cited in Golan, *Yom Kippur and After*, p. 39.)

100. Brezhnev's speech to the Vietnamese reiterated his longstanding fear of a superpower confrontation in the Middle East and stressed that U.S.–Soviet cooperation would make possible a peaceful settlement of the crisis there. (*TASS*, January 30, 1973, cited in Golan, *Yom Kippur and After*, p. 39.)

101. Cairo Radio, April 3, 1974 (Sadat speech). When Egyptian National Security Adviser Hafez Ismail visited Moscow in July, 1973,

Brezhnev likewise apparently stressed to him that the USSR did not want Egypt to go to war because this would jeopardize détente. (*Middle East Journal* [Autumn, 1973], p. 489.)

102. That the reversal of Soviet policy in January–February, 1973 was the result of a gradual increase in the power and influence of holders of the antagonistic image who opposed détente is confirmed by several developments in the months following the decision: a) In April, 1973, Minister of Defense Grechko and KGB head Andropov, both leading subscribers to the antagonistic image who had expressed serious reservations about détente, were elevated to the Politburo––indicating a major political victory on their part. (Cf. Dawisha, *Soviet Foreign Policy Toward Egypt*, p. 147.) (It does not appear that the appointment of Foreign Minister Gromyko to that body at this time represented a gain for the proponents of détente. Gromyko was known not so much for his support for any particular line or set of priorities as for his technical expertise on a wide range of subjects, especially those relating to the United States. [Cf. Kissinger, *Years of Upheaval*, p. 230.] He was probably placed on the Politburo to make it possible to exploit more fully his expertise in the formulation and implementation of global policy.) b) Also in April, 1973, resolutions issued by the Party Central Committee began expressing similar reservations about détente, stressing "the need for constant vigilance and readiness to rebuff any provocations of the aggressive reactionary imperialist circles." (*Pravda*, April 28, 1973.) c) At the beginning of August, 1973, for the first time since the mid-1960s, the Politburo issued a public statement echoing those sentiments: "in contemporary international conditions, as before, vigilance is necessary against the intrigues of the reactionary forces." (*Izvestiia*, August 5, 1973.) d) Soon after, Brezhnev's speeches on détente began to take on a defensive tone, as if he now felt it necessary to contend with the arguments of a powerful opposition:

. . . one can sometimes hear statements that the agreements concluded are unsatisfactory as they do not solve the real problems . . . once and for all . . . . [It is said] that what has been done are half measures. One can only be amazed at the naivete of such an approach . . . . The principle of all or nothing is in no way suitable in international politics. (*Pravda*, September 25, 1973.)

103. Kissinger, *Years of Upheaval*, pp. 230, 296–298, 463; Richard M. Nixon, *Memoirs* (New York: Grosset and Dunlap, 1978), pp. 885, 1031; *Pravda*, September 26, 1973 (Gromyko's speech to the United Nations).

104. Even Kosygin appears to have reconsidered his sanguine position at this time. (See the joint Soviet-Yugoslav communiqué issued at the close of Kosygin's visit with Tito, September 24–October 1, 1973. [*Pravda,* October 2, 1973.])

105. On the ambivalence about Arab use of force reflected in Soviet public statements between February and October, 1973, see Golan, *Yom Kippur and After,* pp. 42–55.

106. *Izvestiia,* October 20, 1973. See Spechler, *Domestic Influences on Soviet Foreign Policy,* pp. 28–30.

107. Almost as soon as the war started, while the Egyptians were scoring tremendous successes in crossing the canal, Brezhnev sent a personal message to Sadat, pleading with him to agree to a cease fire. (Heikal, *The Road to Ramadan,* p. 209.) When Sadat refused, Brezhnev contacted Tito, appealing to him to try to persuade Sadat. He told the Yugoslav President that by being so stubborn Sadat would "precipitate disaster," not only for the Arabs, but "for the world at large." (Sadat, *In Search of Identity*, p. 254.)

108. Spechler, *Domestic Influences on Soviet Foreign Policy,* p. 28.

109. *Ibid.,* pp. 32–33.

110. *Ibid.,* pp. 32–35, 48.

111. *Ibid.,* p. 20; Golan, *Yom Kippur and After,* p. 81.

112. Sadat, *In Search of Identity,* pp. 258–259, 263, 267.

Part 2

The View from Washington

Part 2

The View from Washington

6
Oil as a Factor in U.S. Policy Toward the Middle East

David G. Haglund

The recent extension of fighting in the Iran–Iraq war to include attacks on oil tankers and other vessels in the Persian Gulf has once again focused attention on the issue of the Western world's dependence on Middle Eastern crude oil, especially that coming––as does most Middle East crude––from suppliers in the Gulf region. For the first time since the onset of the war in 1980 policy–makers and policy analysts are beginning to give serious thought to whether the economic, political, and even military security of the Western states might be adversely––some say gravely––affected by the possible spread of combat throughout the Persian Gulf littoral. To some, there is the impending menace of a third oil "shock"; while to others, there looms the far more ominous spectre of a potential clash between the superpowers.

The student of international oil politics might be forgiven if he imagines himself now living, in Ortega y Gasset's phrase, at "the height of the times." No doubt much excitement attends the thinking and writing about momentous events; but scholarship on the precipice also has its drawbacks, perhaps the greatest of which is the temptation that crisis situations offer those who should know better to take speculative leaps, during which they unburden themselves of their "knowledge" of what, in calmer moments, they would concede to be fundamentally unknowable, namely the future. In what follows, I will try to avoid succumbing to the temptation of punditry and will refrain from pronouncing judgment on events yet to unfold; instead, I will direct my efforts to the more modest goal of gauging what "interests" the United States might be said to have in Middle Eastern oil, and what can be done to protect those interests.

What I will not be discussing is what I suspect many first think of (and some *only* think of) when the subject of oil and U.S. Middle Eastern policy arises: the extent to which American policy towards Israel has, over the past decade or so, been affected by a recognition in the United States that certain of the country's economic interests might be better served if Washington were seen as being less supportive of Israel and more eager to promote closer relations with certain Arab states. There is a spirited, if not a vast, literature on this subject--a literature that more than adequately conveys the full dimensions of the debate over whether the U.S. is, or should be, tilting toward Saudi Arabia or any other Arab state. [1] Although I will touch tangentially on this question, the issues addressed directly in this paper will be of a different and less provocative kind, and will be above all embedded in the explication of such concepts as "national interest," "interdependence," and "strategic minerals," each of which is pregnant in significance for an analysis of the oil "factor" in U.S. Middle Eastern policy. In addition to being significant in its own right, each concept leads in turn to consideration of other terms that have both theoretical and practical salience.

There are at least two ways to go about identifying factors as important foreign-policy interests of states, as "national interests." This problem of identifying something (in this case, a raw material) as a national interest has been skillfully handled by Stephen Krasner in his seminal work, *Defending the National Interest*, and it is Krasner's approach that has guided my own attempt to demonstrate that Middle Eastern oil has been and is, an important, some say "vital," interest to the United States. [2] The first way to make the identification is through a logical-deductive exposition that seeks to show, in this instance by means of an analysis of the concepts "strategic mineral" and "interdependence," that states have legitimate interests in access to oil (and other minerals), among other reasons because they regard themselves as vulnerable to supply disruptions of minerals in which they have some degree of import dependence.

The second way is to follow an empirical-inductive path. In this approach, what one looks for is evidence, in the form of statements and behavior of those involved in the policy process, that Middle Eastern oil is indeed considered a national interest of the United States. As I shall argue below, such evidence is not difficult to come by. Thus, if one conceives national interest broadly as the goals sought by a state, a convincing case can be made that access to Middle Eastern oil has widely been acknowledged as a "vital" interest of the United States over the past few years. Whether it still remains a "vital" interest is a question I will leave for the concluding pages of this paper, where I discuss ways in which states can respond to the related issues of insuring access to minerals and reducing vulnerability to mineral-supply disruptions.

Let us begin by saying what can be deduced about Middle Eastern oil and U.S. foreign-policy interests from an examination of strategic minerals and interdependence.

Since the First World War, states, especially those with pretensions to greatness, have been acutely aware of the relevance of minerals to economic strength and therefore to military potential and power. Mineral production and processing need not, and usually do not, make up a very large part of the national income of modern industrialized societies, but it is difficult to deny that minerals constitute the foundation on which such societies rest.[3] Minerals, however, are not evenly distributed among states; indeed they are scattered "haphazardly and whimsically over the world."[4] Because they are so inequitably distributed, no country--not even the largest--can attain anything approaching self-sufficiency in all the minerals needed to sustain modern industry. The words of C. K. Leith, a leading minerals analyst of the interwar period, remain in this regard as relevant today as they were a half-century ago: "It is a costly and, in the long run, a futile effort to create by enactment something which was not created by nature."[5]

Not only will every state lack some important mineral needed by its industries, but many have lacked, and will continue to lack, a wide range of such industrial inputs. (One thinks in this context of Japan, which has been aptly termed a "minerals museum," because it contains most mineral deposits in amounts sufficient for museum exhibition only.)[6] Lacking domestic sources of needed minerals, states have sought and will continue to seek foreign sources of supply. Thus, for minerals as for no other class of commodity, the most salient international political concerns center on the question of *access*, about which I will have much more to say below.

Minerals analysts, especially those in the United States, often employ the label "strategic minerals" to cover those minerals that are held to be both essential to a state's economic and military well-being and sufficiently problematical in terms of origin to occasion reasonable doubts about the reliability of future supply.[7] Because of its obvious and powerful influence on national economies, oil has for some decades been regarded as the single most "strategic" mineral in international trade. Although as recently as World War I iron ore and coal were justifiably considered to be the minerals most essential for the attainment of world-power status, oil soon supplanted them.[8] It was only with slight exaggeration that, in the middle of the 1920s, French statesman Aristide Briand observed that "international politics today are oil politics."[9] Since then, oil has remained, as Robert Lieber notes, "a resource . . . nearly as essential as food or water"--only unlike food and water, oil is a resource in which most OECD countries do not find themselves in the fortunate position of being self-sufficient.[10]

It may legitimately be asked why Western industrialized states (or any other states, for that matter) should worry about not being self-sufficient in oil. In a strictly economic context, does it not make sense for consumers to buy their goods from the most efficient producer, irrespective of location, and thereby contribute to the maximization of their own, as well as global, economic welfare? As one oil analyst has suggestively put it, "in and of itself, dependence on foreign oil is no worse than dependence on any other imported commodity."[11] But dependence on imported oil does concern states in a way that dependence upon, say, imported tomatoes does not; and in order to address this issue of concern over oil dependence, I should like to introduce the second of the three concepts adverted to above, "interdependence."

Hardly an unambiguous concept, interdependence has been a touchstone for a great deal of discussion in the realm of international political economy since the latter part of the 1960s. The international political system is argued by many to be increasingly characterized by interdependence, often loosely interpreted to mean nothing more than increased interconnectedness among national economies.[12] Some have carried empirical hypotheses into the realm of normative theory, and have claimed not only that states are growing more "dependent" upon one another, but that it is good that they should do so, as this lessens the dangers of conflict thought to inhere in systems where states are relatively more autarchic (the "lessons" of the 1930s often being cited as proof of this contention).[13]

The reason why considerations of economic efficiency cannot suffice for policy-makers when strategic minerals such as oil are at issue must be sought in the character of the international political system. Theorists of international politics argue (persuasively, in my opinion) that the international political system is most fruitfully conceptualized as an "anarchy," in which the security--indeed, the very survival--of states rests ultimately upon their ability to look to their own protection, or in other words, to practice self-help. Interdependence, according to this conceptualization, can lead to enhanced economic welfare for all, but it can also challenge the security of all, for a necessary corollary of high interdependence is heightened *dependence*. As Kenneth Waltz explains: "Like other organizations, states seek to control what they depend on or to lessen the extent of their dependency. This simple thought explains quite a bit of the behavior of states: their imperial thrusts to widen the scope of their control, and their autarchic stirrings toward greater self-sufficiency."[14]

To say that self-help systems subordinate economic gain to security considerations is only part of the explanation for the current concern about U.S. mineral supply, in this case Persian Gulf oil supply. Also of relevance is the particular relationship between oil (and other forms of energy) and the power of states. Ian Smart has observed that indigenous sources of energy supply can constitute a valuable power asset for states; that is to say, all other things being equal, a state will be stronger to the extent that it is self-sufficient (or otherwise enjoys "security of supply") in oil and other energy commodities. Power in this context can be of the "positive" sort that stems from the ability of exporting countries to exploit their control over a valued resource to achieve economic or non-economic foreign-policy ends (e.g. OAPEC wielding its "oil weapon" in 1973-74); alternatively, it can be "negative" power in that it endows states with the ability to withstand attempts by resource exporters to practice economic coercion (or "resource diplomacy").[15]

Now, in one sense there is nothing novel about oil being deemed a "power asset"; Albert Hirschman brilliantly showed, nearly four decades ago, that many commercial items have the potential to become elements of national power. International trade, argued Hirschman in his classic study of the commercial offensive embarked upon by Nazi Germany in 1934, is necessarily a "political act," because it can and does affect the power ranking of states. The effect is twofold: because trade can enhance a state's economic and military potential through the creation of wealth and the supply of essential inputs (usually minerals), it possesses a property known as the "supply effect"; and because it can serve as a direct source of influence over others, it possesses an "influence effect." Insofar as this second effect is concerned, Hirschman observed that "the power to interrupt commercial or financial relations with any country . . . is the root cause of the influence or power position which a country acquires in other countries, just as it is the root cause of the ' dependence on trade.' "[16]

What makes oil so important is that, while it is like many other traded commodities (in that it can serve as a power asset), it has a far greater role in today's industrial economies than any other mineral. A glance at recent U.S. mineral-trade balances illustrates this point: in 1980, the United States had a net energy import bill (most of which consisted of crude oil and products) of $74.9 billion, compared with $2.9 billion worth of net imports of nonfuel minerals. The year before, aggregate world exports of metallic ores, concentrates, and scrap amounted to slightly more than 1 percent of total world exports. "Looked at in a more graphic way," writes Hans Landsberg apropos of U.S. mineral-trade balances, "one day's petroleum imports costs the same as importing two years' supply of tungsten, six months' supply of cobalt or three of platinum."[17]

Interdependence in oil (or, properly speaking, "dependence" in oil) can confer advantages on consumers, but it can also impose economic and political costs, as the Western world discovered twice in the 1970s. Economic costs are readily identifiable: a stimulation of inflation, coupled with a reduction in economic growth, resulted in the "stagflation" of the 1970s that most observers hold to be largely (though not entirely) a function of massive transfers of purchasing power to OPEC, through what has been termed the "OPEC tax." Daniel Yergin has put the cost borne by the "big seven" industrialized nations (the United States, Japan, West Germany, Britain, France, Italy, and Canada) as a result of the oil shocks of the 1970s at $1.2 trillion. And, he hastens to add, most developing countries were relatively much more seriously affected.[18] Political costs were reflected in the severe stresses put on democratic polities throughout the West, as well as in an increase in friction between the OECD states, as various countries adopted policy responses to the oil shocks that put them at odds with each other. (Included in this context would be divergent Western policies toward the Arab–Israeli issue.)[19]

If one word could sum up the dilemma in which American and other Western analysts saw their countries enmeshed as a result of their dependence on foreign oil, it would be "vulnerability." Probably no other concept associated with discussions of interdependence is as appropriate to an analysis of the oil–access issue as is vulnerability. It is important to stress that vulnerability is not synonymous with dependence, though it is clearly related to it. Dependence suggests a relatively objective depiction of a country's trade position in respect of a particular commodity (or set of commodities), and can be reasonably accurately expressed through the use of net import statistics. Vulnerability, on the other hand, is largely a subjective condition; that is to say that states "feel" themselves to be vulnerable, if certain conditions in addition to dependence are associated with their import position with regard to any given commodity. Obviously, the more essential that commodity, the more pointed will be the sense of vulnerability connected with it.

Besides essentiality, the conditions that bear on whether states consider themselves vulnerable to supply disruptions include: a) the degree of concentration of production of the commodity in question; b) the identity of the supplying countries; c) whether there are alternative supply prospects (including domestic production possibilities); d) the opportunities for substitution; e) the opportunities for recycling and conservation; and f) the presence of stockpiles in the consuming countries.[20]

An examination of the above conditions should clarify why dependence--even near-total dependence--need not translate into vulnerability. The American experience with nickel is instructive here, for although the United States has limited nickel reserves of its own and has to rely largely, and sometimes exclusively, on imports, very few analysts have considered the country to have a vulnerability problem in this strategic mineral. This is because the principal supplier of nickel to the United States has always been Canada, and because of contiguity and the particular historical circumstances of the Canadian-American relationship, American policy-makers and analysts have tended to regard Canadian supply as, in the words of one analyst, "equivalent to a domestic source."[21] T. S. Lovering accurately captured conventional U.S. wisdom on this matter when he noted during World War II that "the possibility that Canada would sever diplomatic relations with the United States and cut off our nickel supply seems no more likely than the possibility of a revolt in northern Minnesota and the consequent cessation of the iron ore supply from that region."[22]

Nickel sheds some useful light on the current oil-vulnerability issue, for it points up that while high oil-import dependence might be discomfiting, it does not in and of itself constitute prima facie grounds for concluding that one's future oil supply is *likely* to be disrupted. That such supply *can* be disrupted by other countries is, of course, a proper conclusion to draw from the fact of high import dependence; but more important to a determination of vulnerability is the probability of disruption, and this is a function more of the identity of the oil suppliers than it is of simple import levels. For a decade now the countries of the OECD have talked of, as well as experienced, an "energy crisis." For most of these countries what has changed in the past ten years has not only been the magnitude of their dependence on imported oil, but their assessment of the wisdom of continuing reliance upon Middle Eastern suppliers.

Their long-established practice of regarding oil as a strategic mineral may have led oil-importing states to adopt a certain hypothetical and general attitude toward access issues (namely, to regard them as important); but it has taken the presence of conditions other than dependence to transmute these diffuse access worries into the specific vulnerability fears of the present. It is hard to escape the conclusion that, as far as the OECD states are concerned, the single most disturbing feature of their oil supply situation is the extent to which so much of it comes from one region, the Middle East. In 1982, more than a quarter of total global oil production of some 53 million barrels a day (MBD) originated in the Middle East. And given the relative paucity of exports from the world's two largest oil producers--the Soviet Union and the United States--oil from the Middle East figured more prominently in total world oil trade than it did in world oil production. By this measure, approximately 40 percent of the oil in world trade originates in the Middle East.[23]

Perhaps even more important than the mere fact of concentrated production is the specific identity of the main oil exporters. By this I mean that if we could imagine that North America, or the "Pacific Basin," or just about any other geographical region, were to have as great a share of global oil production as does the Middle East, then we might reasonably expect a much reduced degree of anxiety about the likelihood of oil-supply disruption.[24] Concentration matters, to be sure; but location seems to matter more.

Students of geopolitics sometimes employ the term "gray areas" to refer to those ordinarily peripheral regions that, for reasons usually related to resource endowment, take on disproportionate importance in international politics.[25] And when these peripheral regions are also thought to be "political vacuums," the way becomes open for major powers to enter into competition, if not conflict, with each other.[26] By most reckonings, the Middle East--and, in particular, the part of it comprising the Persian Gulf, through which 90 percent of Middle Eastern oil exports pass--is by far the most important "gray area" in the world today. It is also highly unstable. In the well-chosen words of one student of the region, "the Gulf today is very much as it has always been--turbulent, backward, intrinsically unstable--and it is this instability which poses the greatest threat to Western interests in the region."[27]

One hardly knows where to begin in assessing the source of instability, whether in the narrower region of the Gulf, or the broader one of the Middle East. It may be, as Nazli Choucri suggests, that there is no one cause of instability, but that rather there are five "robust, persistent, and interdependent political conflicts," each of which has potential negative implications for Western oil supply: 1) the spread of superpower rivalry into the region; 2) the Arab-Israeli conflict; 3) strife among oil-producing states in the region; 4) ethnic and religious enmity among Moslem countries; and 5) the clash of interests between oil producers and oil consumers.[28] Whatever the cause or causes of Middle Eastern instability, it bears stressing that what most troubles Western consumers of the region's oil is not the element of supply concentration, but rather the fact of location.

It will be observed that this section, which began as an attempt to adduce a U.S. interest in Middle Eastern oil, has melded into a discussion of something called "Western" interests in the Middle East, and especially in the Gulf. The reason that many analysts (particularly in the United States) have tended recently to link the U.S. interest in Gulf oil with the question of other states' access to oil from the region is that, without the linkage, it would be more difficult today than it was five years ago to claim that America has a "vital" interest in oil supply from the Middle East. I will return to this point presently, when I examine some of the options available to the United States either to attempt to gain access to oil, or to reduce its vulnerability to supply disruptions. For the moment, let us pursue this matter of an empirical–inductive identification of oil as a national interest of the United States.

As noted above, one of the bases for claiming that the national interest of the United States is somehow connected to crude–oil production of Middle Eastern countries would be the existence of evidence that, over time, U.S. policy–makers have spoken and acted as if they believed important interests to be at issue in the Middle East––interests not derived exclusively from either the Arab–Israeli dispute, or from the desire to contain the spread of Soviet influence in the area.[29] As early as the 1920s, one can see clear evidence of a felt need on the part of the U.S. for access to overseas oil supply, including oil from the Middle East. It may seem somewhat curious that there should have been such a concern about continued access to oil, given that by the 1930s the United States' principal problem with oil seemed to be overproduction and not shortage, but the concern was present nonetheless. It inspired, as Krasner details, a quite vigorous oil–diplomacy designed to gain entry for American companies into the oil–rich Middle Eastern provinces.[30] It was commonly assumed during the early 1920s that American oil reserves would not last beyond another decade, and some minerals analysts were daring to predict that "our children will in all probability see the end of the petroleum industry."[31]

The immediate post–World War II period was also a time of worry in the United States about continued oil supply, and again the Middle East took on enlarged importance to U.S. minerals analysts and policy–makers. This concern for oil–supply was in part based on the broader fear that the United States had so depleted its mineral reserves in World War II that it could not avoid becoming dangerously dependent in a wide range of minerals. Alfred Eckes has observed of American perceptions in the late 1940s: "The U.S., it seemed, was becoming a ' have–not' power, like Germany, Italy, and Japan, the three aggressive nations who sparked the global conflict."[32] But it was the strain that combat had put on U.S. oil reserves that proved most troubling in Washington. From the time of the Pearl Harbor attack until the defeat of Japan, Allied forces consumed nearly 7 billion barrels of oil, of which some 6 billion were supplied by the

United States alone. As early as 1943, officials in the executive departments and the armed services had begun seeking ways to extend the life–span of American reserves, and as Michael Stoff writes, "their search brought them to the Middle East. War made the region prominent, oil made it vital. Through rationalized development, planners hoped to transform the Persian Gulf into a wellhead for Europe after the war."[33]

The Gulf did become a wellhead in the post–World War II decades, not only for Europe, but for Japan and, by the early 1970s, North America as well. Although the United States changed from being a net exporter of oil to a net importer in 1946, its import–dependence was so slight that it remained nearly self–sufficient throughout the 1950s and 1960s; and what oil it did import came from secure sources in the Western Hemisphere, Venezuela and Canada.[34] But the growth in American demand for oil, coupled with a decline in domestic reserves and an increasing inability (and unwillingness) of Venezuela and Canada to supply the American market led the United States to become more dependent upon Middle Eastern oil by the early 1970s. By the time of the first oil shock, the United States was getting 15 percent of its total imports of crude oil and products from the Persian Gulf producers, and 36 percent of its overall consumption was being supplied by imported oil; in 1977, at the height of its dependence on imported oil, the United States was acquiring 36 percent of its imports from suppliers in the Middle East, and was dependent on imports for 47 percent of consumption.[35]

The entire West, it seemed, was becoming dangerously dependent upon Middle Eastern oil as the 1970s drew to a close, and even a traditional exporter such as Canada was relying on Persian Gulf suppliers to meet half of its fast–growing import requirements by the start of the 1980s.[36] The implications of collective Western dependence upon the Middle East appeared ominous indeed. In one of the more somber articles ever published by *Foreign Affairs*, oil analyst Walter J. Levy predicted in 1980 that it would take the West at least 30 years to overcome its dependence on imported oil, and that until it did, "at best, it would appear that a series of future emergencies centering around world oil will set back world progress for many, many years. And the world, as we know it now, will probably not be able to maintain its cohesion, or be able to provide for the continued economic progress of its people against the onslaught of future oil shocks––with all that this might imply for the political stability of the West, its free institutions, and its internal and external security."[37]

If access to Middle Eastern oil first emerged as a national interest of the United States in the post–World War I years, and re–emerged after World War II, then by the early 1980s many in the U.S. were speaking and writing of it as a truly "vital" interest, one even worth committing American military force to defend.[38] This evident determination to inject force into the oil–access issue was clearly demonstrated in January 1980, when President Carter enunciated what has become known as the "Carter Doctrine" in which the president promised that "an attempt by any outside force to gain control of the Persian Gulf region will be regarded as an assault on the vital interests of the United States of America, and such assault will be repelled by any means necessary, including military force."[39] To lend credibility to his words, the president ordered the creation of a Rapid Deployment Force (renamed, in January 1983, the Central Command). In discussing U.S. interests in the region, a once–secret Defense Department report of 1982 stated: "Our principal objectives are to assure continued access to Persian Gulf oil, and to prevent the Soviets from acquiring political–military control of the oil directly or through proxies."[40]

Few would question the importance that access to foreign, including Middle Eastern, oil has had to the United States. But whether the American national interest in access to Gulf oil is important enough to deserve the modifier "vital" is a matter that requires more discussion than it has had to date; for the United States is not now, unlike five years ago, very dependent upon Middle Eastern oil. In 1983, the United States imported slightly fewer than 5 MBD of crude oil and products—an amount representing a 44 percent reduction from U.S. crude and product imports in the record year 1977, when 8.8 MBD entered the domestic market. Significantly, only 390,000 barrels a day were purchased from producers in the Gulf in 1983; this amount constituted but 8 percent of U.S. crude and product imports, or only 2 1/2 percent of the total domestic consumption of 15.2 MBD.[41] As a gauge of either dependence or vulnerability, these figures hardly suggest a "vital" American interest in access to Middle Eastern oil.

But, say some, the U.S. interest cannot be considered apart from the interests of America's NATO allies and Japan. According to these analysts, "it is precisely the dependence of the Western allies, with whose fate that of the United States is so deeply intertwined, that occasions the urgency of U.S. strategy. Soviet strategy today is *inter alia* precisely to divide America from Europe by capitalizing on the differential of dependence on imported oil . . . . It is difficult to understand the depth of the present crisis in the Western alliance without taking into account this discriminating Soviet strategy."[42]

Whether the Soviets have such a "discriminating" strategy to exploit dependence differentials and split NATO is a matter of doubt to many (but perhaps the wisest thing to note here is that the only thing harder to prove than that the Soviets do have such a strategy is that they do not). What is less difficult to state is that for some decades there have been those analysts who have argued, and perhaps believed, that as part of a "masterplan" for victory over the West, the Soviets would resort to economic warfare (or economic "cannibalism"),[43] most recently by taking control of Persian Gulf oil, and "quickly bring[ing] the industrial democracies to their knees. Short of absolute control, clear predominance in the area would afford the USSR the opportunity to manipulate and hold hostage the various Western countries who depend on the region's oil."[44] For a while, arguments of this nature were buttressed by apparent evidence (in the form of a 1977 CIA report entitled *Prospects for Soviet Oil Production*) that the USSR itself would, by the mid–1980s, become a net importer of oil, and, lacking foreign exchange, might have to seize Persian Gulf oil; it now appears, however, that the Soviets will continue to enjoy self–sufficiency for some time to come, though for how long is obviously impossible to determine.[45]

Perhaps the one thing that can be stated with some certainty in regard to a Soviet threat to the Gulf is that only in this connection can one speak of a "vital" U.S. interest in the region's oil––and even then it needs to be shown that the allies would be incapable of overcoming their dependence upon Middle Eastern oil. Recalling Voltaire's epigram about God, I would argue of those who do propound a vital U.S. interest in Persian Gulf oil that if the Soviet Union did not exist, it would be necessary for them to invent it. The Soviets do have interests in the Persian Gulf, just as the United States has interests in Central America; what is at issue is the degree to which *oil* is the crucial element in the calculation of U.S. interests vis–à–vis the Soviet Union.

I have been arguing that, on its own, the United States cannot now be said to have a vital interest in Persian Gulf oil, that only by bringing in both American allies and the USSR can the claim to a vital interest be kept alive. What is the extent of the import dependence and vulnerability of the allies? It is common to speak of the "allies" as an undifferentiated and highly dependent bloc, but in reality the term disguises a variety of oil situations, ranging from self–sufficiency or near self–sufficiency of the United Kingdom, Canada, and Norway, to the high dependence of Japan, West Germany, and France. But even West Germany has managed to reduce its dependence on Persian Gulf oil to only 13 percent. Japan, at 56 percent, and France, at 36 per cent, remain uncomfortably reliant on Gulf oil, it is true, but their dependence has declined over the course of the past decade––and in the case of France, declined quite substantially.[46] Gulf oil still remains an important interest to the allies, but the reduction in their dependence that has taken place should not be overlooked. Indeed, some have gone so far as to write that "Europe's ' battle for oil' could thus be all over bar the shouting, except for the continued period of uncertainty up to 1985 or thereabouts, until when the alternatives to imported oil cannot be available in large enough quantities to enable the system to be effectively controlled."[47]

If Europe's oil problems are not yet over, they are far nearer solution than Japan's. In a real sense, Japan is the one country that most contributes to the West's vulnerability. Although the Japanese have been extremely reluctant to countenance the use of force to secure access to oil (perhaps as a result of their previous experience with using force to secure access to oil in 1941),[48] they stand to lose the most if supplies of Persian Gulf oil are seriously disrupted. The Japanese buy one out of every two barrels of oil sold by Gulf producers, and rely on this oil to supply some 56 percent of total oil consumption--and 75 percent of Japan's primary energy demand is supplied by oil.[49] But even Japan's situation is not as tenuous as it appears since Japan has been successfully reducing its dependence on Middle Eastern oil. Moreover, Japan possesses, after the United States, the largest oil stocks of all OECD countries, some 280 million barrels as of the end of 1982.[50] And the Japanese should be able to avail themselves of idle capacity in world oil production, estimated at more than 3 MBD for non-Gulf OPEC producers (a group that does not include Mexico and other important producers).[51]

Whether the West's need for Middle Eastern oil necessitates the use of force to secure access is, to say the least, a contentious issue. Ever since the publication in January 1975 of Robert W. Tucker's controversial *Commentary* article on intervention and oil, policy analysts and policy-makers have weighed the pros and cons of the utilization of American (or largely American) military units to somehow keep the oil flowing.[52] Though there may have been a time when the need to secure access could have justified intervention it would appear that insofar as the United States by itself is concerned, that time is past. Nor is it clear that the United States would be applauded by the very allies its intervention was presumably designed to aid if it did move into the Gulf militarily. Japanese diffidence in this regard has already been cited; as for the other allies, it is difficult to detect a crescendo of support for intervention. Enoch Powell recently ridiculed the idea of any British participation in a U.S.-sponsored intervention, on the grounds that Persian Gulf oil not only is *not* a vital British interest, but as a major producer of oil, Britain would stand to benefit economically from any price rise effected by a major disruption of Gulf supplies.[53] Even *New York Times* columnist William Safire, no shrinking violet when it comes to the question of intervention in Central America (and elsewhere), is against using U.S. forces in the Gulf except to repel a Soviet move in the region: "The notion that we should treat the Arab regional interests, and the European and Japanese customer interests, as an American vital interest is muddle–headed."[54]

What has been obscured by all the attention given to the issue of intervention is that there are other options open to the United States (and the allies) to reduce vulnerability to supply disruption––options that do not necessarily oblige these nations to address the problem of securing access. Insofar as securing access is concerned, force and diplomacy are the two most often–cited prescriptions. Neither is without its drawbacks, and it is not clear, despite years of discussion on the merits of a "dialogue" between producers and consumers, whether such an activity can ever be worthwhile, given the unfortunate realities of international politics.[55] Perhaps there has been an oil–supply disruption where some sort of "dialogue" might have been appropriate, (the 1973–1974 situation comes to mind) but the record of those countries that did try to "bargain diplomatically" (i.e. that agreed to change their policy toward Israel) to secure their oil does not inspire confidence in "dialogue" as a means to achieve anything other than loss of face. Certainly there seems to be very little opportunity for talk to bring about security of supply in the present Gulf situation.

Rather than concentrate on access, consuming nations would do better (and indeed, most have been doing better) by focusing on the reduction of vulnerability. There are five principal kinds of vulnerability–reducing strategies open to consumers: 1) *stockpiles* can be amassed to lessen the costs of short–term supply disruptions (and even to serve as a deterrent in some circumstances); 2) *import diversification* away from unstable and toward more stable producers can be pursued; 3) *domestic production* can be increased by a variety of methods; 4) *substitution* of some other mineral for crude oil can be adopted by those countries with an adequate resource endowment; and 5) *conservation* measures can be applied more vigorously.[56]

The United States has, to a greater or lesser degree, pursued all of these interrelated options in its successful bid to minimize its vulnerability to Persian Gulf supply disruptions. I should briefly like to review American policy starting with *stockpiling*. Stockpiling has been a preferred policy for reducing vulnerability to supply disruption in the entire range of strategic minerals for decades, at least in the United States.[57] Though not a problem–free option, stockpiling has attracted support even from those liberal economists, such as Hans Landsberg, who wish to see market distortions minimized by whatever policies governments adopt in responding to vulnerability concerns. Stockpiling, it is argued, theoretically has the potential to be nearly self–financing, and it is in any event less costly to consumers than would be a policy of creating domestic productive capacity through subsidization of high-cost producers.[58] The United States started stockpiling various commodities in World War II, and now has a Strategic Stockpile of some 93 materials (83 of which are metals or nonfuel minerals), valued at some $12 billion.[59]

The most strategic of all minerals, oil, has not been included in the strategic stockpile. To remedy this anomalous situation, the United States created in 1975 the Strategic Petroleum Reserve (SPR), a stockpile of crude oil that is planned to hold, in salt caverns and mines in Texas and Louisiana, 750 million barrels of oil, at an estimated cost of at least $40 billion--by far the most ambitious and expensive stockpile in history.[60] Plagued with problems in its early years, the SPR contained (as of April 1, 1984) 392 million barrels of oil, and was being filled at a rate of 140,000 barrels a day.[61] The SPR is now more than half-filled, and when it is full, it is expected to have a drawdown capacity of between 4 and 5 MBD--roughly the extent of total American crude-oil imports at present. While it is not known for certain what the maximum drawdown capability of the SPR now is, tests in 1981 indicated that the system could draw and ship 1 MBD with no great difficulty. That is an amount of oil more than twice current U.S. imports from the Persian Gulf.

Import diversification is another option the United States has pursued in reducing its vulnerability to Gulf supply disruptions. That the United States and other countries have been able to shift their purchases of oil toward other producers is a reflection of the degree of "oil proliferation" the world has experienced in the last ten years.[62] As a result of significant new production of oil from countries that, at the start of the 1970s, were either minor exporters or net importers, the relative importance of both OPEC and the Gulf oil-producing states has diminished markedly. Whereas ten years ago OPEC accounted for half the world production of 60 MBD, today its share of global production is approximately a third. Gulf producers alone in 1973 accounted for 21 MBD; in January 1984, these same countries produced only 11 MBD of crude oil.[63]

Indicative of the shift of U.S. imports away from the Persian Gulf is the fact that in 1983 the United Kingdom supplied more oil to the American market than did Saudi Arabia! But the central element in the U.S. diversification strategy has been Mexico, now far and away the country's principal foreign supplier of oil, responsible for sending 822,000 barrels a day to the American market in 1983.[64] What many in the United States had been advocating since the mid-1970s (and what not a few in Mexico have feared) seems to be happening: the United States is overcoming its dependence on Middle Eastern oil with Mexican "help."[65]

In addition to stockpiling and import-diversification, the United States has been able to minimize its vulnerability to oil-supply disruption by relying on *domestic production*. With domestic production of 8.6 MBD in 1983, the United States is second only to the USSR in the production of crude oil.[66] There is no reason to expect major additions to reserves and increased production over the short term, but on the other hand most analysts remain fairly confident about the country's ability to sustain current production levels. Assuming major increases in world oil prices, the United States would have the option to *substitute* for crude oil by switching to coal- and shale-based oil production. One casualty of the oil glut in the early 1980s has been the ambitious synthetic fuel programs mandated by the Energy Security Act of 1980: $88 billion was to be lavished on substitutes for conventional crude oil, and in 1987 the U.S. was supposed to be producing 500,000 barrels of oil a day from coal and shale. But in 1983, only two synthetic fuel plants were still under construction, with a combined planned capacity of only 32,000 barrels a day.[67]

Finally, there is *conservation*. Although it is less easy to substantiate statistically the degree of vulnerability reduction provided by this option, many analysts are convinced that it has been the real success story of the past few years, insofar as weaning the West from Persian Gulf oil is concerned. Writes Daniel Yergin: "[B]y far the most important and powerful form of adjustment has been on the demand side, in terms of greater energy efficiency. Indeed, it has proved much more potent than most analysts would have expected even in the middle 1970s."[68] A useful way to gauge conservation is the "coefficient of energy use," which measures the rate of increase in energy use and the rate of increase in the level of economic activities. During the heady days of cheap oil and rapid growth, it was not uncommon for advanced industrial economies to have a coefficient greater than 1, which meant that energy (usually oil) consumption was increasing at a rate greater than the rate of growth of the Gross Domestic Product.[69] By the end of the 1970s, most OECD countries had reduced their energy-use coefficients to between .6 and .9, and by the early 1980s the average OECD coefficient had declined to .34.[70] The United States has benefited more, in absolute terms, from this trend than any other OECD country, given its large consumption of oil--particularly in the transportation sector, where substantial fuel savings have been made in the past few years as a result of the shift toward more energy-efficient vehicles.

In conclusion, it can be said that the U.S. "interest" in imported oil has been diminished in the past five years, and that inasmuch as the proportion of American imported oil that originates in the Middle East has declined dramatically, it is more difficult than formerly to substantiate the claim that the United States (as distinct from the NATO alliance, or the OECD) has a "vital" interest in Middle Eastern oil. The United States does, to be sure, have important, perhaps even "vital," interests in the Middle East distinct from access to oil, but the lesson of the past five years seems clear; oil as a "factor" in U.S. policy toward the Middle East can no longer be deemed of overriding importance--unless, of course, one insists on equating the "national interest" of the United States with the oil-supply prospects of the allies.

The equation is, to be sure, made regularly by U.S. policy-makers. To a certain extent, there is validity in equating the allies' need for access to Middle Eastern oil with U.S. "vital" interests, but only, as I indicated above, if the principal threat to Japanese and Western European oil supply stems from Soviet activity. *If* the Soviets decided to attempt the economic crippling of certain NATO countries and Japan by depriving them of a vitally needed industrial input, then it would be difficult indeed to deny that such an act of economic warfare constituted a profound challenge to American interests. But in the absence of an actual Soviet menace to Gulf oil supply, the equation between Western access to oil and U.S. vital interests becomes tenuous, at best. It becomes tenuous because in the absence of East-West rivalry as the source of oil-supply disruption, such disruption ceases to be an overtly military and political challenge to the Western alliance as a whole, and becomes instead a selective economic challenge to certain countries.

What is being claimed by those who insist on the vital-interest equation in the absence of a clear and actual (as opposed to ambiguous and potential) Soviet threat is nothing other than that the American public has a duty to safeguard the economic well-being of those countries that much of that same public (as well as some branches of the American government) have considered and continue to consider to be America's premier economic rivals, and to some the major source of American economic misfortune.

I do not wish to enter the debate over whether the Japanese or Western European "challenge" is responsible for most or any of the malaise affecting the industrial heartland of the United States. Suffice it to note that there is no shortage of proponents of the view that "unfair" foreign competition is putting Americans out of jobs. But I do wish to draw attention to a certain illogicality in the position of the American executive branch, which insists that the economic well-being of America's military allies (and, to varying degrees, economic competitors) is an abiding concern of U.S. public policy. If it *is* such a concern, and it may well be, then at the very least one would expect that prior to contemplating potentially costly and dangerous strategies aimed at securing access to Gulf oil, the United States would take such measures that are easily within its power for the purpose of safeguarding and strengthening the economies of Japan and Western Europe. Among the first of these measures that come to mind would be the lifting of protectionist measures against Japanese automobile imports, and the refraining from imposing protectionist measures against European steel imports.

Notes

1. For a worried assessment of what one scholar regards as America's "growing subordination to Saudi Arabia," see Steven L. Spiegel, "The Middle East: A Consensus of Error," *Commentary* 73 (March 1982): 15–24.

2. Stephen D. Krasner, *Defending the National Interest: Raw Materials Investments and U.S. Foreign Policy* (Princeton: Princeton University Press, 1978).

3. John E. Tilton, *The Future of Nonfuel Minerals* (Washington: Brookings Institute, 1977), p. 91.

4. Charles F. Park, *Earthbound: Minerals, Energy and Man's Future* (San Francisco: Freeman, Cooper, 1975), p. 27.

5. C.K. Leith, *World Minerals and World Politics: A Factual Study of Minerals in their Political and International Relations* (New York: Whittlesey House, McGraw–Hill, 1931), p. 104.

6. International Economic Studies Institute, *Raw Materials and Foreign Policy* (Washington: IESI, 1976), p. 15.

7. The evolution and contemporary usage of this concept are discussed in David G. Haglund, "Strategic Minerals: A Conceptual Analysis," *Resources Policy* 10 (September 1984): 146–52.

8. Edwin C. Eckel, *Coal, Iron, and War: A Study in Industrialism Past and Future* (New York: Henry Holt, 1920).

9. Quoted in P.H. Frankel, *Essentials of Petroleum: A Key to Oil Economics,* new ed. (London: Frank Cass, 1969), p. 3.

10. Robert J. Lieber, "Cohesion and Disruption in the Western Alliance," in *Global Insecurity: A Strategy for Energy and Economic Renewal,* ed. Daniel Yergin and Martin Hillenbrand (Harmondsworth, Middlesex: Penguin Books, 1983), p. 347.

11. David Leo Weimer, *The Strategic Petroleum Reserve: Planning, Implementation, and Analysis* (Westport, Conn.: Greenwood Press, 1982), p. 190.

12. There is a large corpus of scholarly writing on interdependence. Useful starting points are Robert O. Keohane and Joseph S. Nye, Jr., *Power and Interdependence: World Politics in Transition* (Boston: Little, Brown, 1977); David A. Baldwin, "Interdependence and Power: A Conceptual Analysis," *International Organization* 34 (Autumn 1980): 471–506; and Kenneth N. Waltz, "The Myth of National Interdependence," in *Globalism versus Realism: International Relations' Third Debate,* ed. Ray Maghroori and Bennett Ramberg (Boulder, Colo.: Westview Press, 1982), pp. 81–96.

13. The assumed relationship between autarchy and conflict, and liberalism and peace, is critically examined in Barry Buzan, *People, States and Fear: The National Security Problem in International Relations* (Brighton, Sussex: Wheatsheaf Books, 1983), pp. 137–50.

14. Kenneth N. Waltz, *Theory of International Politics* (Reading, Mass.: Addison–Wesley, 1979), p. 106.

15. Ian Smart, "Energy and the Power of Nations," in Yergin and Hillenbrand, *Global Insecurity*, pp. 350–54.

16. Albert O. Hirschman, *National Power and the Structure of Foreign Trade* (Berkeley: University of California Press, 1944), pp. 14–16.

17. Hans H. Landsberg, *Minerals in the Eighties: Issues and Policies* (Oak Ridge, Tenn.: Oak Ridge National Laboratory, Program Planning and Analysis, 1982), pp. 19–20.

18. Daniel Yergin, "Crisis and Adjustment: An Overview," in Yergin and Hillenbrand, *Global Insecurity* , pp. 4–6. Also see, for a discussion of the economic effects of the oil shocks, Milton Russell, with Mary Beth Zimmerman, "Energy Is an International Good," in *U.S. Interests and Global Natural Resources: Energy, Minerals, Food,* ed., Emery N. Castle and Kent A. Price (Washington: Resources for the Future, 1983), pp. 10–47.

19. Robert Pfaltzgraff, *Energy Issues and Alliance Relationships: The United States, Western Europe and Japan* (Cambridge, Mass.: Institute for Foreign Policy Analysis, 1980); Garret FitzGerald, *et al., The Middle East and the Trilateral Countries,* Triangle Papers: 22 (New York: Trilateral Commission, 1981).

20. Amos A. Jordan and Robert A. Kilmarx, *Strategic Mineral Dependence: The Stockpile Dilemma,* The Washington Papers, vol. 7, no. 70 (Washington: Center for Strategic and International Studies, Georgetown University, 1979), pp. 18–19; Hans H. Landsberg and John E. Tilton, with Ruth B. Haas, "Nonfuel Minerals," in *Current Issues in Natural Resource Policy,* ed. Paul R. Portney (Washington: Resources for the Future, 1983), p. 106.

21.   John M. Dunn, "American Dependence on Materials Imports: The World–Wide Resource Base," *Journal of Conflict Resolution* 4 (March 1960): 118. For Canadian–American nickel trade, see John I. Cameron, "Nickel," in *Natural Resources in U.S.–Canadian Relations,* vol. 2: *Patterns and Trends in Resource Supplies and Policies,* ed. Carl E. Beigie and Alfred O. Hero, Jr. (Boulder, Colo.: Westview Press, 1980), pp. 45–92; and U.S. Bureau of Mines, *Mineral Commodity Summaries, 1983* (Washington: Department of the Interior, 1983), p. 106.

22.   T.S.   Lovering,   *Minerals   in   World   Affairs*   (New   York: Prentice–Hall, 1943), p. 237.

23.   U.S.   Energy   Information   Administration,   *Monthly   Energy Review: December 1983* (Washington: United States Government Printing Office, February 1984), pp. 100–1.

24.   Middle Eastern producers of crude oil are Bahrain, Iran, Iraq, Kuwait, Oman, Qatar, Saudi Arabia, Syria, and the United Arab Emirates. Not included in the category of "Middle Eastern" producers are these Arab countries: Algeria, Egypt, Libya, and Tunisia. U.S.   Energy Information   Administration,   *1982   International   Energy   Annual* (Washington: United States Government Printing Office, September 1983), p. 29.

25.   Klaus Knorr, *The War Potential of Nations* (Princeton: Princeton University Press, 1956), p. 6.

26.   Ruth W. Arad and Uzi B. Arad, "Scarce Natural Resources and Potential Conflict," in *Sharing Global Resources,* ed. Ruth W. Arad *et al.* (New York: McGraw–Hill/Council on Foreign Relations, 1979), pp. 74–75.

27.   J.B.   Kelly, *Arabia, the Gulf, and the West* (London: Weidenfeld and Nicolson, 1980), pp. vii–viii.

28.   Nazli Choucri, "Power and Politics in World Oil," *Technology Review* (October 1982): 27–28. Also see, for assessments of causes of Gulf instability: Gary Samore, "The Persian Gulf," in *Energy and Security,* ed. David A. Deese and Joseph S. Nye, Jr., A Report of Harvard's Energy and Security Research Project (Cambridge, Mass.: Ballinger, 1981), pp. 49–110; Richard D.   Erb, ed., "The Arab Oil–Producing States of the Gulf: Political and Economic Developments," *AEI Foreign Policy and Defense Review* (Washington: American Enterprise Institute for Public Policy Research, 1980); Shahram Chubin, "U.S. Security Interests in the Persian Gulf in the 1980s," *Daedalus* 247 (Fall 1980): 31–62; and Fredric S. Feer, "Problems of Oil–Supply Disruptions in the Persian Gulf," in *Policies for Coping with Oil–Supply Disruptions,* ed. George Horwich and Edward J. Mitchell (Washington: American Enterprise Institute for Public Policy Research, 1982), pp.

11-30.

29. For an analysis of the three major U.S. interests in the Middle East, see Jerome Slater, "The United States and the Middle East," in *American Foreign Policy Since Détente*, ed. Robert C. Gray and Stanley J. Michalak, Jr. (New York: Harper & Row, 1984), pp. 54-84.

30. Krasner, *Defending the National Interest*, pp. 110-18. For a contemporary journalistic account of Anglo-American oil rivalry in the 1920s, see Ludwell Denny, *We Fight for Oil* (New York: Alfred A. Knopf, 1928).

31. Eckel, *Coal, Iron, and War*, p. 118.

32. Alfred E. Eckes, Jr., *The United States and the Global Struggle for Minerals* (Austin: University of Texas Press, 1979), p. 121.

33. Michael B. Stoff, *Oil, War, and American Security: The Search for a National Policy on Foreign Oil, 1941-1947* (New Haven: Yale University Press, 1980), p. 209. The 6 billion barrels supplied by American producers during the time the U.S. was an active combatant represented nearly 4 1/2 million barrels a day (MBD).

34. Percy W. Bidwell, *Raw Materials: A Study of American Policy* (New York: Harper & Bros./Council on Foreign Relations, 1958), p. 316; U.S. Congress, Joint Economic Committee, *Outlook on Venezuela's Petroleum Policy*, 96th Cong., 2nd session (Washington: United States Government Printing Office, February 1980); Ted Greenwood, "Canadian-American Trade in Energy Resources," in *Canada and the United States: Transnational and Transgovernmental Relations*, ed. Annette Baker Fox, Alfred O. Hero, Jr., and Joseph S. Nye, Jr. (New York: Columbia University Press, 1976), pp. 97-118; Helmut J. Frank and John J. Schanz, Jr., *U.S.-Canadian Energy Trade: A Study of Changing Relationships* (Boulder, Colo.: Westview Press, 1978).

35. *Monthly Energy Review: December 1983*, pp. 36-37; Richard R. Fagen and Henry R. Nau, "Mexican Gas: The Northern Connection," in Richard R. Fagen, ed., *Capitalism and the State in U.S.-Latin American Relations* (Stanford: Stanford University Press, 1979), p. 387.

36. David G. Haglund, "Canada and the International Politics of Oil: Latin American Source of Supply and Import Vulnerability in the 1980s," *Canadian Journal of Political Science* 15 (June 1982): 281-82.

37. Walter J. Levy, "Oil and the Decline of the West," *Foreign Affairs* 58 (Summer 1980): 1015.

38. See, for example, Robert W. Tucker, *The Purposes of American Power: An Essay on National Security* (New York: Praeger, 1981).

39. Quoted in FitzGerald, *The Middle East and the Trilateral Countries*, p. 41.

40. Quoted in Richard Halloran, "Poised for the Persian Gulf," *New York Times Magazine*, April 1, 1984, p. 39. For critical assessments of the (then) Rapid Deployment Force, see Kenneth N. Waltz, "A Strategy for the Rapid Deployment Force," *International Security* 5 (Spring 1981): 49–73; and Christopher van Hollen, "Don't Engulf the Gulf," *Foreign Affairs* 59 (Summer 1981): 1064–78.

41. *Monthly Energy Review: December 1983*, pp. 32–33, 38–39.

42. W. Scott Thompson, "The Persian Gulf and the Correlation of Forces," *International Security* 7 (Summer 1982): 160. Also see James L. Plummer, "Conclusions: Analytical Results, Directions for Policy, and Important Unanswered Questions," in *Energy Vulnerability*, ed. James L. Plummer (Cambridge, Mass.: Ballinger, 1982), p. 342.

43. The "cannibalism" phrase appeared in a lecture that Harvard's Charles C. Abbott gave at the Naval War College in November 1948, and referred to presumed Soviet designs to interdict raw–material supplies to the Western European countries. See Eckes, *United States and the Global Struggle for Minerals*, p. 149. The notion of a Soviet "master–plan" is discussed in Dennis Ross, "Considering Soviet Threats to the Persian Gulf," *International Security* 6 (Fall 1981): 159–180.

44. Amos A. Jordan, "Energy and National Security: Sizing Up the Risks," *Washington Quarterly* 3 (Summer 1980): 156. Also see Robert Moss, "Reaching for Oil: The Soviets' Bold Mideast Strategy," *Saturday Review*, April 4, 1980, pp. 14–22; and Edward Friedland, Paul Seabury and Aaron Wildavsky, *The Great Détente Disaster: Oil and the Decline of American Foreign Policy* (New York: Basic Books, 1975), p. 50.

45. Thane Gustafson, "Energy and the Soviet Bloc," *International Security* 6 (Winter 1981/82): 65–89; Arthur A. Meyerhoff, "Energy Base of the Communist–Socialist Countries," *American Scientist* 69 (November/December 1981): 624–31.

46. *New York Times*, May 27, 1984, 4:1. For comparative dependencies in the 1970s, see the Rockefeller Foundation, *Working Paper on International Energy Supply: A Perspective from the Industrial World* (London: Institute of Petroleum, 1978); as well as the relevant country sections in *The Energy Decade, 1970–1980: A Statistical and Graphic Chronicle,* ed. William L. Kiscom (Cambridge, Mass.: Ballinger, 1982).

47. Peter R. Odell, *Oil and World Power*, 7th ed. (Harmondsworth, Middlesex: Penguin Books, 1983), p. 137. For a discussion of the European Community's oil–import situation, see Dennis Swann, *The Economics of the Common Market*, 4th ed. (Harmondsworth,

Middlesex: Penguin Books, 1981), pp. 205–22.

48. On the relationship between Japanese "have–not" status in oil (and other minerals) and peace, see C.K. Leith, "Mineral Resources and Peace," *Foreign Affairs* 16 (April 1938): 521; and Robert C. North, "Toward a Framework for the Analysis of Scarcity and Conflict," *International Studies Quarterly* 21 (December 1977): 584.

49. *1982 International Energy Annual,* pp. 37, 40; Teruyasu Murakami, "The Remarkable Adaptation of Japan's Economy," in Yergin and Hillenbrand, *Global Insecurity,* p. 138.

50. *1982 International Energy Annual,* p. 38.

51. Edward J. Frydl and William A. Dellalfar, "The Shifting Balance in the World Oil Market," *Federal Reserve Bank of New York Quarterly Review* (Autumn 1982): 43.

52. Robert W. Tucker, "Oil: The Issue of American Intervention," *Commentary* 59 (January 1975): 21–31. Also relevant is Geoffrey Kemp, "Military Force and Middle East Oil," in Deese and Nye, *Energy and Security,* pp. 365–85.

53. Enoch Powell, "Oceans Apart in the Gulf," *Manchester Guardian Weekly,* March 18, 1984, p. 6. Also see, for a Canadian perspective, John Gellner, "Persian Gulf Dilemma: Force Can't Resolve it," *Globe and Mail* (Toronto), May 24, 1984, p. 7.

54. Quoted in the *Whig–Standard* (Kingston), May 29, 1984, p. 10.

55. An advocacy of such a "dialogue" can be found in Øystein Noreng, *Oil Politics in the 1980s: Patterns of International Cooperation* (New York: McGraw Hill/Council on Foreign Relations, 1978), chap. 7.

56. Any of these options can be pursued unilaterally, and some are amenable to collective action, either through the International Energy Agency or some other organizational forum.

57. The classic work on stockpiling remains Glenn H. Snyder, *Stockpiling Strategic Minerals: Politics and National Defense* (San Francisco: Chandler, 1966).

58. Hans H. Landsberg, "What Next for U.S. Minerals Policy?", *Resources,* no. 71 (October 1982): 9–10. Whether stockpiles do become self–financing, or nearly so, depends of course on whether they are sold at some future date, and also on the price level of alternative future supplies on the world market. In this instance, "self–financing" becomes a matter of having one's cake *only* if one is prepared to eat it, for unconsumed stockpiles clearly cannot be made self–financing.

59. U.S. Federal Emergency Management Agency, *Stockpile Report to the Congress: October 1981–1982* (Washington: September 1982); V. Anthony Cammarota, "America's Dependence on Strategic Minerals," a paper presented to the Conference on Strategic Minerals and

International Economic Assistance, Wilmington, Delaware, December 9, 1982.

60. Ruth M. Davis, "National Strategic Petroleum Reserve," *Science* 213 (August 1981): 618–22.

61. U.S. General Accounting Office, *Status of Strategic Petroleum Reserve Activities as of March 31, 1984* (Washington: GAO, April 1984).

62. I have borrowed the phrase "oil proliferation" from U.S. Congress, Joint Economic Committee, Subcommittee on Energy, *A Strategy of Oil Proliferation*, 96th Cong., 2nd session (Washington: United States Government Printing Office, June 1980).

63. *Energy Decade*, p. 429; Venezuelan Ministry of Energy and Mines, *Boletin Mensual* 13 (April/May 1984): 27.

64. *Monthly Energy Review: December 1983*, pp. 38–39.

65. American views on the desirability of Mexican oil imports can be found in Richard B. Mancke, *Mexican Oil and Natural Gas: Political, Strategic, and Economic Implications* (New York: Praeger, 1979); David Ronfeldt, Richard Hehring, and Arturo Gándara, *Mexico's Petroleum and U.S. Policy: Implications for the 1980s*, Executive Summary for the U.S. Department of Energy (Santa Monica, Cal.: Rand Corporation, June 1980); Edward J. Williams, *The Rebirth of the Mexican Petroleum Industry: Development Directions and Policy Implications* (Lexington, Mass.: D.C. Heath, 1979); and Richard R. Fagen, "Mexican Petroleum and U.S. National Security," *International Security* 4 (Summer 1979): 39–53. For Mexican nationalist concerns over increased exports to the United States, see John Saxe–Fernández, *Petróleo y Estrategia: México y Estados Unidos en el Contexto de la Politica Global* (Mexico City: Siglo Veintiuno, 1980).

66. *Monthly Energy Review: December 1983*, p. 32.

67. Andy Plattner, "Energy Issues Shoved Onto Back Burner," *Congressional Quarterly*, May 29, 1982, pp. 1249–52; Hans H. Landsberg and Michael J. Coda, "Synfuels––Back to Basics," *Resources* (February 1983): 12–14.

68. Yergin, "Crisis and Adjustment," in Yergin and Hillenbrand, *Global Insecurity*, pp. 8–9.

69. Arnold E. Safer, *International Oil Policy* (Lexington, Mass.: D.C. Heath, 1979), p. 16.

70. Robert Stobaugh and Daniel Yergin, "Energy: An Emergency Telescoped," *Foreign Affairs: America and the World 1979* 58 (1980): 584; Odell, *Oil and World Power*, p. 247.

7
Faulty Assumptions, Failed Policy: The Arabists and the PLO During the First Reagan Administration

Martin Indyk

Introduction

The professional bureaucrats in the Near East and South Asia Bureau (NEA) of the State Department and their counterparts in the CIA and the Pentagon have come to be known as Arabists. These are the experts who have responsibility for recommending and implementing America's Middle East diplomacy. Over the three decades since the creation of the state of Israel, the Arabists have consistently espoused a particular approach to the Arab–Israeli conflict, characterized by a basic assumption about the source of the conflict and the core of instability in the volatile Middle East, i.e., that they are both caused by the failure to solve the Palestinian problem. Since the 1973 Yom Kippur War, the Arabists have also assumed that this problem can be solved by the creation of a Palestinian entity in the West Bank and Gaza. In their view this is to be achieved through American–sponsored negotiations between Israel and representatives of the Palestinians. It is a common Arabist assumption that the Palestine Liberation Organization represents the Palestinians and that it is therefore the "wisdom of diplomacy" to have the PLO included in the peace negotiations.

During the Nixon and Ford Administrations, Secretary of State Kissinger did not share these assumptions, preferring to avoid dealing with what he understood to be an intractable problem in favor of negotiating step–by–step agreements that would serve to reduce the risk of war and build trust between Israel and its Arab neighbors. It was in this context that Kissinger gave a written commitment to Israel, in September 1975, that the United States would not "recognize or negotiate with the PLO so long as the PLO does not recognize Israel's right to exist and does not accept Security Council Resolutions 242 and 338."

In the era of the Carter Administration, however, the Arabists found sympathetic ears both on the Seventh Floor of the State Department and in the Oval Office in the White House. President Jimmy Carter and Secretary of State Cyrus Vance undertook a series of efforts in 1977 to bring the PLO to the negotiating table and tried again in 1979 after they had negotiated the peace treaty between Israel and Egypt.

When Ronald Reagan and Alexander Haig assumed responsibility for America's foreign policy, it was widely assumed that they would eschew Arabist advice when it came to dealing with the PLO. Ronald Reagan referred to the PLO as a "terrorist organization" and made combatting terrorism a priority item on his foreign policy agenda.[1] Alexander Haig was on record as sharing the views of Henry Kissinger towards PLO involvement in the peace process.[2] Their common worldview emphasized the East-West conflict and the paramount need to combat the Soviet Union. In this context, the PLO was perceived to be a Soviet proxy helping to promote revolution not only in the Middle East but also in Central America.

Moreover, until September 1982, Reagan and Haig demonstrated little apparent interest in promoting the peace process, on the assumption that it could be placed on the "backburner" while they concentrated on generating a "strategic consensus" between Israel and pro-American Arab states aimed at preventing Soviet encroachment on the Middle East. Even when the President came to address the Arab-Israeli conflict--in the form of the September 1982 Reagan Plan--he specifically excluded the possibility of establishing an independent Palestinian state in favor of an association of the West Bank with Jordan. The Reagan Plan focused on bringing King Hussein to the negotiating table, not the PLO. Thus it has been widely assumed that Arabist advice on the PLO was generally ignored by the Reagan Administration's decision-makers in favor of allowing Israel to deal with the PLO by military means. The reality, however, is more complex.

While Ronald Reagan's attitude towards the PLO appears to have undergone little change, the Arabists were able to exploit various opportunities created by circumstances in the Middle East to promote a two-phase strategy towards the PLO. In the first phase, which lasted from August 1981 to June 1982, the Arabists sought to entice the PLO into direct negotiations with Israel under a formula which came very close to the Carter Administration's design for dealing with the PLO. In the second phase, which lasted from September 1982 to April 1984, the Arabists sought to bring the PLO into negotiations with Israel through the "back door" of Jordanian participation.

The purpose of this paper is first to show how the Arabists promoted this two–phase strategy and then to analyze why such a policy, predicated on the simplistic assumption of PLO "moderation," is bound to fail.

The Influence of Saudi Arabia and Israel

The Arabists' opportunity to promote their policy came surprisingly early, primarily because of the influence of Saudi Arabia. Within the President's entourage there was a strong corporate pro–Saudi element which manifested itself in the appointment of Caspar Weinberger as Secretary of Defense and the early announcement that the administration would proceed with the controversial sale of AWACS to Saudi Arabia. The Saudis were expected to play a key role in Reagan's policy of strategic consensus, particularly as it applied to defense of the Persian Gulf. As a consequence, Saudi Arabia came to exert considerable influence over the policies pursued by the Reagan Administration. The Arabists were able to exploit this influence since the Saudis shared their assumption that the PLO had to be recognized by the U.S. and included in the negotiations. And in the process, the Arabists were able to persuade Reagan and Haig to proceed on the basis of another of their assumptions––that the Saudis were capable of exercising considerable influence in the region in favor of American interests.

The Saudis were quick to weigh in on the side of the Arabists. When Haig travelled to Riyadh in April 1981, he was disabused of the notion that the Saudis would put aside their concern for a resolution of the Palestinian problem in favor of strategic consensus. Instead, as they had done with Carter four years earlier, they argued forcefully that the U.S. should enter into a dialogue with the PLO to resolve what they claimed was the real threat to their existence.

Haig's private response to this entreaty is not known, but the public record shows a shift in his approach. Haig now argued that the peace process was "high on our agenda" and that "talking about strategic consensus is not placing our emphasis on the peace process in a lower priority. We feel progress with one contributes to progress with the other."[3] As for the PLO's role in this process, Haig now listed only one condition for its inclusion, that it accept UN Resolution 242. And instead of reiterating the President's dismissal of the PLO as a terrorist organization, Haig reverted to the State Department's formulation that there were terrorist elements *within* the PLO.[4]

In subsequent months, events in Lebanon would reinforce the Arabists' arguments about the importance of the PLO and the influence of the Saudis. The escalating violence there enabled the Arabists to argue that the PLO would have to be taken into account were the situation to be stabilized. Consequently, when fighting broke out between Israel and the PLO in southern Lebanon in July, Reagan dispatched Special Envoy Philip Habib to negotiate a ceasefire with the PLO. The negotiations were conducted indirectly using the Saudis as intermediaries. As a result of this experience, the Arabists could claim that the PLO was willing to abide by agreements and that the Saudis were capable of persuading them to do so.

On the other side, the Arabists were also able to exploit Israel's actions to cast doubt on Reagan's perception of the Jewish state as a "strategic asset." Israel's use of American aircraft to destroy Iraq's nuclear reactor in June and to attack the PLO's Beirut headquarters in July, could well have been perceived by Ronald Reagan and Alexander Haig as serving American interests. Instead, they were interpreted as a nuisance and an embarrassment and, in response, Reagan suspended the delivery to Israel of already contracted F–15s and F–16s. Moreover, the President's personal irritation with Israel grew as he became involved in the fight to gain Congressional approval for the AWACS sale to Saudi Arabia in the face of opposition from Israel and its supporters in Congress. Conversely, the AWACS battle served to reinforce the perception of Saudi Arabia's moderating influence, not so much because of any particular action by the Saudis but rather because of the administration's need to constantly reiterate Saudi Arabia's helpfulness and commitment to the peace process as a means of justifying the sale.

By the end of July 1981 then, the Reagan Administration was less willing to respect the constraints of its relationship with Israel and more willing to depend upon Saudi influence to ameliorate the Arab–Israeli conflict. In these circumstances, the Arabists were able to initiate phase one of their policy towards the PLO.

Phase One – The Mroz Mission[5]

An opportunity for the Arabists arose when Khaled el–Hassan, a Fatah Central Committee member and a key adviser to Yasir Arafat, secretly visited Washington and conveyed to State Department officials a PLO five–point plan to gain U.S. recognition. Because of the 1975 commitment to Israel not to negotiate with the PLO, an intermediary was required. John Mroz, President of the Institute for East-West Security Studies in New York, was chosen to act as a go-between.[6] He was well-known to Arafat and for some time had promoted U.S. recognition of the PLO. In August, Mroz brought a seven-point revised plan from Arafat to the Arabists. On the basis of this plan, which apparently contained an explicit reference to Israel's right to exist, Assistant Secretary of State for Near East Affairs, Nicholas Veliotes, his deputy Watt Cluverius, and the CIA's National Intelligence Officer for the Middle East, Robert Ames, prepared an Action Memorandum for Haig which argued that an effort to entice the PLO into recognizing Israel could have real benefits for the administration's wider strategy of combatting the Soviet Union. If successful, they argued, such a strategy could split the PLO, taking the PLO "moderates" out of the Soviet camp and delivering them to the negotiating table with Israel. This, they asserted would represent a victory for U.S. influence in the Middle East, a blow to the Soviet Union, and might well loosen the logjam in the Camp David autonomy negotiations. It would also placate the Saudis. The memorandum suggested that Mroz should be authorized to "feel Arafat out," and that he should be able to demonstrate the Reagan Administration's genuine interest by conveying to Arafat a decision to grant visas to two senior PLO officials.

Haig apparently discussed the memorandum with the President and then sent it back to Veliotes with an authorization to proceed provided that nothing were done that would go beyond the U.S. commitment to Israel. Although Haig was skeptical, Veliotes and Mroz were apparently optimistic that Arafat would be prepared to recognize Israel in return for the promise of U.S. recognition. They expected that this would be followed by direct negotiations between Israel, Arafat, Jordan and Egypt under America's auspices.

From August 1981 to June 1982, Mroz and Arafat engaged in four hundred hours of negotiations. Mroz reported to Cluverius and Veliotes; Ames was used as a back-channel to the PLO; and a senior non-Arabist State Department official acted as control officer. In the process, all the formalities were apparently worked out, including what both sides would say, when Arafat would be received in Washington, and who he would meet with there.

The Saudis became involved in the process on September 12, 1981 when Haig met Crown Prince Fahd in southern Spain. Fahd apparently gave Haig the same message that Mroz transmitted in early August--that the PLO was ready to recognize Israel. In return, Haig is reported to have asked Fahd to use his influence with Arafat and to promise the PLO leader his Kingdom's support in the event that the PLO split over the plan to recognize Israel. President Reagan confirmed the Saudi role in this effort two months later. He was asked by an interviewer whether the U.S. would talk to the PLO:

> A: I think this is part of what's at stake here. I think Saudi Arabia could be an element in this.
> Q: You mean to bring in the PLO?
> A: Yes.
> Q: And will you bring in the PLO through quiet diplomacy?
> A: I think a solution has to be found for their problem.
> Q: So it means talking to them eventually even if it means through quiet diplomacy.
> A: Providing they are willing to recognize Israel's right to exist.[7]

By the end of November, however, Arafat had still not mouthed the words of recognition of Israel, and it was not at all clear, either to Veliotes or to Arafat, whether the Saudis were willing to fulfill their part of the bargain. Then in December, the initiative became side–tracked by an inter–Arab dispute over the Fahd Plan. Although Arafat had initially approved of this plan, he came under heavy pressure from Syria as well as key advisers within Fatah to repudiate it. The Saudis were upset by Arafat's prevarication and, as Arafat told the *Washington Post*, the U.S. "should not count on its close relationship with Saudi Arabia to provide a moderating conduit to the PLO."[8]

Thus by January 1982, having heard nothing back from Veliotes, Haig began to lose interest in the Mroz mission. It had at least become clear to him that Arafat and the Saudis could not deliver and that there would be no quick breakthrough. Moreover, American interests now demanded greater sensitivity to Israel's concerns for two major reasons: first, Israel was set to complete its final withdrawal from Sinai in April and the Israelis were now intent upon nailing down an agreement on autonomy before their departure; second, Haig had been informed that, if provoked by PLO actions, Israel would invade Lebanon and put an end to the PLO threat there.

But while Haig concentrated on the Sinai withdrawal and restrained Israel from entering Lebanon, Veliotes, Cluverius and Ames took advantage of Haig's original authorization to pursue their strategy of wooing the PLO. First, Veliotes tried to persuade Haig in January that the U.S. should respond to any Israeli invasion of Lebanon by recognizing the PLO. When he received no response from Haig, he apparently tried to generate a PLO response by drafting a "notional text" of what the U.S. and the PLO would say to achieve their mutual recognition.[9] This text, written on plain paper, was presented by Mroz to Arafat on April 29, 1982. Arafat apparently replied that he would present the text to a meeting of the PLO's Executive Committee with a view to responding by mid–June.

The Executive Committee, however, never met. Instead, by mid–June Arafat found himself besieged in Beirut by Israeli forces. This offensive by Israel against the PLO's infrastructure in Lebanon ended the Mroz Mission. But it did not end Phase One of the Arabists' policy toward the PLO. Haig may have reverted to treating the PLO as a terrorist organization but the Arabists, now backed by the Joint Chiefs of Staff and other elements in the Pentagon, apparently saw in this new crisis an opportunity to advance the policy promoted by Veliotes in January, the thwarting of Israel by recognizing the PLO. As Haig noted in his memoirs: "The foreign policy bureaucracy, overwhelmingly Arabist in its approach to the Middle East and in its sympathies, saw the crisis as an opportunity to open direct negotiations between the U.S. and the PLO." And as Arafat subsequently confirmed, "the discussions were continuing at that time."[10]

The efforts of the Arabists were now given a boost by the return of the Saudis to their side. Unwilling to take any action to assist the PLO in Lebanon, the Saudis insisted instead that the United States do something. And those elements in the Reagan Administration who were responsive to Saudi entreaties now promised them that the United States would not allow Israel to enter Beirut and that a change in U.S. policy was coming.[11] Accordingly, in mid–July, the PLO announced that U.S. recognition was now the price for its departure from Beirut. Arafat dispatched Khaled el–Hassan to accompany the Saudi Foreign Minister, Saud al–Faisal, to Washington to consummate this effort to convert military defeat into political victory. Meanwhile, in Washington, U.S. officials let it be known that they were leaning towards direct contact with the PLO as the best method for securing its withdrawal from Beirut.[12]

This time, however, Ronald Reagan––true to his instincts––resisted the entreaties of his Arabist advisers and the Saudis. Instead, the President told the Saudi Foreign Minister that the PLO were terrorists. Reagan, nevertheless, did promise him that once the PLO had evacuated Beirut, the U.S. would address the Palestinian problem through a new initiative. Both in his private meeting and then publicly a week later, the President reiterated that the U.S. would not recognize the PLO until it accepted both Israel's right to exist as well as UN Resolutions 242 and 338.

This statement effectively put an end to Phase One. The effort to get Arafat to sit down with Israel had failed. True to form, Arafat had not agreed to recognize Israel and the Saudis had not used their influence to persuade him to do so. In the wake of Israel's offensive, the PLO had been seriously weakened and, in these circumstances, the President saw a new opportunity to pursue his preferred policy for solving the Palestinian problem--the Jordanian option. Nevertheless, the fact that the United States prevented Israel from launching a final assault on the PLO's forces, negotiated the terms of their departure from Beirut, sent in Marines to protect them, and even put up the money for the ships to take them away (subsequently repaid by Saudi Arabia), reflected the influence of the Arabists and their desire to preserve a role for the PLO in America's Middle East diplomacy.

Phase Two: The Reagan Plan

Just what role the PLO was to play in the President's September 1 "fresh start" was not clear at the outset. In his plan, Reagan explicitly ruled out both self-determination for the Palestinians and the establishment of an independent Palestinian state as the outcome of negotiations. Since these were the PLO's minimum requirements, and since the President made it clear that his preferred solution was that the occupied territories should be ruled "in association with Jordan," it appeared that the PLO was to be ignored. However, Henry Kissinger, one of the original architects of the Reagan Plan, was not so sure. He felt that the language of the Plan was too ambiguous, leaving room for different interpretations:

> [The] danger is that the Reagan Plan will turn into a subterfuge for rehabilitating the PLO, establishing it with essentially unchanged composition and program on the West Bank, threatening simultaneously Israel and Jordan . . . . That is the key strategic question we must all be clear about. The Reagan Plan must not turn into a device for introducing the PLO in its present form and with its present concepts on the West Bank. Jordan would thereby become not so much the principal negotiating partner as a cover for PLO domination of the West Bank.[13]

Kissinger's concern was a public reflection of the fact that the Reagan Plan was by no means designed as a "pure Jordanian option" in which Hussein would be encouraged to replace the PLO as spokesman for the Palestinians. Although this had been Kissinger's intention, he had been opposed by Veliotes and Ames who had sought to make the Reagan Plan part of their "PLO option" by arguing that it should include a reference to self-determination for the Palestinians--thereby, they argued, making it possible for Arafat to endorse the Reagan Plan. The new Secretary of State, George Shultz, rejected their suggested language but apparently accepted the argument that Hussein would have to gain PLO approval before entering negotiations with Israel. In other words, the Reagan Plan was in fact a "Jordan-PLO option," hence Kissinger's fear that it could turn Hussein into a proxy for the PLO.

Thus Phase Two of the Arabist approach to the PLO had been put in place. It involved securing PLO approval for King Hussein to negotiate with Israel on behalf of the Palestinians. In effect, the PLO was to be given a veto over the Reagan Plan. Accordingly, Secretary of State Shultz dispatched John Mroz to Athens on September 1, 1982 where he apparently briefed Arafat on the Reagan Plan before the President announced it on television. Subsequently, Shultz sent Mroz to Tunis in mid-September to propose to Arafat that he "accept American conditions for recognition and facilitate diplomatic steps then under-way . . . ."[14]

Arafat refused to see Mroz on that occasion but the U.S. intermediary did meet with senior PLO officials in October 1982, again at Shultz's request. Although this appears to have been the last time that Mroz was used as an intermediary, further communication between the Reagan Administration and the PLO may have taken place in December 1982 when General Vernon Walters, the President's roving ambassador, is reported to have met with a senior PLO official in Morocco to urge the PLO to endorse the Reagan Plan.

For his part, Arafat indicated his willingness to play along with the Reagan Administration when he announced in Amman on October 12 that he saw positive elements in the Reagan Plan. To further associate the PLO with this American initiative, Khaled el-Hassan was sent back to Washington on October 22, this time to accompany an Arab League delegation that visited Reagan to discuss the Fez plan. Arafat returned to Amman in mid-December where he reached agreement with King Hussein "to pursue political moves together on all fronts." Then Hussein journeyed to Washington, again accompanied by the PLO's Khaled el-Hassan.

All of these maneuvers did much to convince the Arabists that Hussein would gain Arafat's approval and the PLO would be brought into the negotiations through the "back door." But they did nothing to change the attitude of the PLO. When the Palestinian National Council met in Algiers in February 1983, it denounced the Reagan Plan as "inadequate as a valid basis for a fair and lasting settlement," insisted that the PLO remain the *sole* legitimate spokesman for the Palestinians, and demanded the right to a sovereign and independent state.[15]

This setback, however, provided the Arabists in the Reagan Administration with fuel for their argument that the Reagan Plan had not provided sufficient inducement for the PLO because of its exclusion of an independent Palestinian state. Moreover, the Saudis made clear that they wanted a better deal for the PLO. Accordingly, when Saudi Arabia's ambassador, Prince Bandar, came calling on the President in early March, he was sent away with a document from Reagan which stated that "confederation" was one of the possible outcomes envisaged by the Reagan Plan.[16] Under international law, a "confederation" is defined as a federation between *independent* states.[17]

This hint that the Reagan Plan did not exclude the PLO's minimum requirement, duly passed onto Arafat by the Saudis, seems to have been designed to provide further encouragement to Arafat to give Hussein the green light. Yet all this was to no avail. Although Arafat reached a tentative agreement with Hussein in early April 1983 for the King to negotiate on the basis of the Reagan Plan together with a delegation of PLO–approved Palestinians, the PLO chairman declined to sign the document. Instead, he flew to Kuwait where the agreement was repudiated by the PLO Executive Committee and then by the Central Committee of Fatah, Arafat's own organization.[18] In turn, King Hussein declared on April 10, 1983, that he would not enter peace negotiations "separately or in lieu of anybody."

For the time being this spelled the end of the Reagan Plan. But it did not spell the end of the Arabists' efforts to woo the PLO. On the contrary, the administration's Arabists explained to the President, who explained to the public, that "some radical elements of the PLO" had prevented the moderates from modifying the PLO's position.[19]

In this way, the Arabists laid the groundwork for a new round of wishful thinking about the PLO. For in the next six months, Arafat faced a Syrian–backed rebellion not only in the PLO but also within his own organization, Fatah. In Washington, this revolt was interpreted as the very split in the PLO which the Arabists had been trying to encourage since 1981. Moreover, in place of the Saudis, the Egyptians now came calling on the President to offer their services in support of PLO "moderation." Egypt's Foreign Minister, Kamal Hassan Ali, visited Washington in December 1983 bringing with him the news that Arafat intended to visit Cairo if he could escape the siege in Tripoli. To the Arabists this meant that Arafat had finally decided to break with his Syrian–backed opponents in the PLO and throw in his lot with Egypt, the one Arab country to have made peace with Israel.

Accordingly, following the discussions with Kamal Hassan Ali, a decision was made in Washington to protect Arafat by providing safe passage for him from Tripoli to Cairo--in particular by pressuring Israel not to interfere. And when Arafat turned up in Cairo to be embraced by Egypt's President Mubarak, both the White House and the State Department hailed the meeting as "an encouraging development" because--they claimed--it held out the prospect of reviving the Reagan Plan.[20]

In background briefings, administration officials explained that the split in the PLO enabled Arafat to pursue diplomacy without the hinderance of the "extremists." Egypt's support, according to their calculations, provided a counter-balance to Syrian influence and a replacement for the Saudi support that the Arabists had originally sought when they launched their strategy in 1981. In public, President Reagan expressed the wishful thinking of his advisers by arguing that a "breakthrough" in the peace process was now possible. He noted that before the PLO split, Arafat had been talking to King Hussein about participating in the peace process. Now, he said, President Mubarak was trying to persuade Arafat to begin the process again, and he added: "we are optimistic."[21]

The optimism, however, was unfounded. Arafat had travelled to Cairo to demonstrate that he retained his independence from the Syrians. He had not gone there to talk about peace with Israel. For their part, the Egyptians were even less capable than the Saudis of extending support and protection to Arafat if he chose to moderate his position because they were isolated in the Arab world as a result of the peace treaty with Israel. Welcoming Arafat enabled the Egyptians to claim that they were helping the Palestinians and therefore serving pan-Arab interests, but it did nothing to advance the peace process.

Indeed, just as Arafat's earlier diplomatic excursions to Amman had been rejected by the PLO's policy-making bodies, so now did his Cairo initiative bring down a hail of criticism and condemnation on his head from his supposedly "moderate" supporters. The Fatah Central Committee, following a meeting in which ten of the fourteen members condemned Arafat's action, announced that the Cairo rendezvous was a "personal initiative" and an "organizational violation."[22]

Accordingly, when Arafat returned to Amman in February 1984 to resume his negotiations with King Hussein, the great expectations of the Arabists were quickly disappointed. This meeting produced a typically vague communiqué calling for joint action on the basis of the 1982 Fez Plan (which called for a separate Palestinian state on the West Bank). The communiqué did not mention the Reagan Plan. In fact, the negotiations had gone badly because Arafat's position among his own supporters had become so precarious that he could no longer afford the luxury of hinting at the idea of negotiations with the United States, let alone Israel. The final blow to the Reagan Plan, however, was left to King Hussein to deliver. In mid–March 1984, Hussein announced that he had ruled out negotiations with Israel and had barred any American role in the process.[23]

For Secretary of State Shultz, this latest episode, coming on the heels of so many other failed initiatives towards the PLO provided a lesson for U.S. policy: "The problem is not with the communications system, the problem is with the content. I feel myself that before discussions with the PLO should take place, the content should change, as we have specified."[24]

While the statements of Hussein and Shultz mark the end of Phase Two of the Arabists' policy towards the PLO, it would be wrong to assume that the story will end there. For despite the manifest failure of this two–stage strategy of PLO enticement, Arabists still harbor the belief that Arafat must be brought into the peace negotiations. And they draw new hope from the fact that Syria's refusal to reconcile with Arafat has left the PLO chairman with the hard choice of maintaining a paralyzed organization or throwing in his lot with Hussein and Mubarak. As long as such hopes exist, the Arabists are likely to continue to advocate policies designed to woo the PLO and entice Arafat into negotiations.

In short, during his second Administration, President Reagan and his Secretary of State can expect to come under continued pressure from the Arabists to adopt some variant of the two strategies of PLO enticement which they have advocated for the past four years.

Faulty Assumptions

Why is it that Alexander Haig, George Shultz and Ronald Reagan––people whose worldview would predispose them to see the PLO as an opponent of American interests in the Middle East––should have been prepared to accept Arabist prescriptions for involving the PLO in the American–sponsored peace process? How is it that they were persuaded to give the PLO veto power over the American–sponsored peace process? And why is it that, despite the manifest failure of an eight–year effort to bring the PLO into negotiations, the Arabists have not altered the nature of their policy recommendations? The answer lies in the unchallenged assumptions on which this failed policy has been based.

The key assumption is that the PLO is an umbrella organization comprised of a mainstream of "moderates" and a periphery of "extremists." These "moderates" may not be "sole" representatives of the Palestinians but in view of the proponents of this policy, they are a "legitimate" representative because the PLO in general, and Arafat in particular, enjoy widespread support among the Palestinians. Since the Palestinian problem is believed to be the core of the Arab-Israeli conflict, and since that conflict is believed to be the real source of instability in the Middle East, and since the PLO represents the Palestinians, it therefore follows that the PLO must be involved in the American-sponsored peace process. Failure to do so, they argue, will foredoom the peace process.

This chain of reasoning breaks down, however, if the PLO is taken at its word. After all, its Charter, which has never been amended and has constantly been reaffirmed, calls explicitly for the destruction of Israel, and the PLO remains committed to "armed struggle" (i.e. terrorism) as the means for achieving this objective. Moreover, the PLO consistently refuses to recognize Israel's right to exist and rejects all the American formulas for a resolution of the conflict--from UN Resolutions 242 and 338 to the Camp David Accords and the Reagan Plan. On the face of it then, the PLO does not have the appearance of a "moderate" organization ready to make peace with Israel.[25]

The assumption of PLO "moderation," therefore, is in essence an assumption that the PLO is willing to change its attitude towards Israel. In other words, the wish is father of the thought. Because the PLO, according to this logic, must be a partner to the peace negotiations, it must therefore be willing to participate in making peace. Its failure to indicate this willingness in an unequivocal way is then explained by a number of subordinate assumptions:

i) that the "extremists" are able to exercise a veto over the "moderates" when it comes to recognizing Israel;

ii) that the "moderates" have managed to shift the PLO's position to acceptance of a mini-state on the West Bank and Gaza, which constitutes evidence of their true moderation;

iii) that the PLO cannot accept Resolution 242 or other peace formulas because they do not recognize Palestinian national rights;

iv) that acceptance of Israel is the PLO's "last card" to be played only after it has acquired recognition of these national rights.

Once this reasoning is accepted, the prescription for U.S. policy follows rather logically. The "moderates" must be encouraged to split with the "extremists" by American inducements. Specifically, the "moderates" should be offered U.S. recognition of their leadership and their people's national rights in return for their recognition of Israel. Moreover, the U.S. should secure moderate Arab support for the PLO "moderates" to facilitate their shift in attitude towards Israel and to withstand the opposition of the "extremists" who enjoy the support of radical Arab states. In essence, these were the policies adopted by the Arabists during the Carter Administration. By the time Reagan took office, they had developed a more sophisticated version, cloaked in anti–Soviet rhetoric to suit their new masters.

Given George Shultz's experience with the PLO, it is unlikely that he would be prepared to act again on these Arabist assumptions. But the fact that the Arabists were able to get their way in the first Reagan Administration should indicate the attractiveness and plausibility of the thesis of PLO "moderation."

What should deter them is the simple reality that the strategy of enticing the PLO has been tried in all its variants over eight years and has never produced the expected outcome of PLO recognition of Israel. Throughout this period, the PLO has taken no concrete action to revise its avowed objective of destroying Israel, has failed to endorse any of the American formulas for peace, and has never abandoned its promotion of terrorism. This has been a consistent pattern regardless of the PLO's circumstances. When it was riding high in Lebanon and enjoyed the recognition of most of the world, the PLO maintained its rejectionist position; when the PLO lost its stronghold in Lebanon but retained the sympathy of most of the world, it refused to modify its approach; and when the organization split, its "moderate" branch was still incapable of mouthing the words of recognition of Israel.

Yet the naive optimism of the Washington environment provides fertile ground for Arabists and their assumptions. Thus experience will never be enough, and the assumptions themselves must be challenged and refuted to demonstrate why wooing the PLO is bound to fail.

1) PLO "moderation"

As an organization, the PLO is structurally incapable of moderation. The PLO is an umbrella grouping of eight terrorist organizations, all of whom remain steadfastly committed to the destruction of Israel. Armed struggle against the Jewish state is the very *raison d'etre* for these organizations. Their purpose is to liberate Palestine. Israel, for them, is Palestine. This is as true for the Fatah mainstream as it is for the Popular Front for the Liberation of Palestine (PFLP). Thus Khaled el–Hassan, the strongest exponent in Fatah of seeking U.S. recognition, argues publicly that "there will be no existence for either the Palestinian people or for Israel unless one of them disappears . . . there will be no peaceful coexistence with Israel. The PLO has no right to discuss recognition of the enemy Zionist state."[26] His brother, Hani el–Hassan, a member of Fatah's Central Committee and another exponent of U.S.

recognition, argues that an abiding principle of PLO policy is that "we will not recognize Israel [and] should not become involved in a formula that leads to the recognition of Israel . . . . A revolution that stops half way is doomed to die."[27]

The fact that this core ideological commitment to Israel's destruction has remained unaffected by the PLO's fortunes or by its actual ability to achieve such an objective should tell us something about the nature of the organization and its real potential for moderation. Yet the Arabists continue to base their policy advice on the belief that change for the better in the PLO is not only possible but actually underway.

To be sure, there are historical examples of revolutionary movements adjusting their ideology when confronted by reality. But in the case of the PLO such an adjustment is impossible because of the structural constraints--both external and internal--which determine the political dynamics of the organization. To understand this, it is necessary to place the PLO in the context of inter-Arab politics. The organization was established in 1964, not by popular demand of the Palestinian people, but rather by a joint decision of Arab governments (at the Arab Summit Conference in Cairo in January 1964). Consequently each Arab government has established or backed a particular terrorist group within the PLO with their patronage sometimes shifting from one to the other.[28]

This incestuous relationship between Arab regimes and the various terrorist organizations which make up the PLO is an abiding reality. First, since the creation of Israel "liberating Palestine" has always been the core issue of inter-Arab politics. To establish their pan-Arab credentials and thereby bolster their internal legitimacy, Arab regimes have found it necessary to engage in a contest in which each tries to outbid the other in order to demonstrate fidelity to the cause. Once the PLO had been established, support for the organization became the most tangible expression of this commitment. It also became an excuse for ignoring the problem of the Palestinian refugees. And, for the shaky conservative Arab monarchies, it served as an insurance policy by focussing Arab revolutionary impulses on Israel rather than on themselves. Second, the PLO could not survive without the succor of these Arab regimes because it lacks an independent base of operations and independent sources of finance. Thus sponsorship of the PLO provides the Arab regimes with legitimacy as well as a means for exercising guardianship over the pan-Arab cause that the PLO has come to represent. In turn, as Daniel Pipes has observed, "the PLO flourished by becoming an organization answerable to rulers rather than refugees."[29]

The net effect of this relationship is that the PLO has become a microcosm of the inter-Arab conflict. And, as is the case with the attitudes of Arab states towards Israel, the PLO's attitude is determined by the "weighted average" of Arab opinion. This means the PLO cannot afford to step outside the minimum Arab consensus of deeply divided Arab states. And that minimum consensus has always translated into hostility towards the Jewish state. Any Arab leader that steps beyond that consensus is rewarded by assassination (as happened to King Abdullah of Jordan, President Sadat of Egypt and President–Elect Beshir Gemayel of Lebanon).

As a reflection of this dynamic, the PLO has consistently broken with those Arab leaders willing to recognize or negotiate with Israel. In 1970, for example, when President Nasser of Egypt accepted a U.S.–sponsored ceasefire with Israel and an accompanying peace initiative, the PLO condemned the man who had represented the embodiment of pan–Arabism. When Sadat announced his decision to travel to Jerusalem, he too was roundly condemned by the PLO. The fear of PLO opposition to Hussein's entering negotiations with Israel is a major factor behind his refusal to support the Reagan Plan.

In short, the PLO is so constrained by its dependence on Arab regimes and the Arab regimes are in such a strong position to influence the PLO's decisions that the PLO will only be capable of moderating its attitude to Israel when the minimum consensus of Arab rejectionism changes.[30] However, should the PLO ever acquire such a capability, it would still have to alter its own core ideological commitment to the destruction of Israel, and that will depend upon the internal political dynamics of the PLO.

2) "Extremists" vs. "moderates"

In analyzing the internal dynamics of the PLO, the Arabists are quick to argue that here there is a basic division between "moderates" and "extremists" and that if the "extremists" could be outflanked, the PLO's true "moderation" would be revealed.

Certainly, there is considerable divergence amongst the views and ideologies of the various groups that comprise the PLO but to term some "moderate" and others "extreme" is to misunderstand the nature of the debate within the PLO. There is no argument in the PLO about the right of Israel to exist––all groups within the PLO reject it outright. Any individual within its ranks who suggests such a modification is repudiated. Thus, in February 1983, Issam Sartawi, the man who eight months earlier had announced to the Western press that the PLO was ready to recognize Israel's right to exist, was refused even an opportunity to put his case to the Palestine National Council meeting in Algiers. More significantly, Yasir Arafat's efforts to achieve U.S. recognition by offering some vague formulas which could be interpreted as hinting at Israel's right to exist, have been consistently repudiated by the PLO's policy-making committees--with some of his closest "moderate" advisers voting against him. Moreover, any member of the PLO who remains outside this rejectionist consensus is eliminated (as happened to Issam Sartawi, Said Hammami and more than a dozen West Bank leaders who did not immediately reject the Camp David Accords). The argument within the PLO is about strategy and tactics, not about the strategic objective.

Consequently, there has never been a move to amend the fifteen clauses (out of a total of 33) of the PLO's Covenant which refer to the PLO's objectives of destroying the "Zionist entity." Nor has any move been made within the PNC to alter political resolutions adopted in 1968 and reaffirmed in 1977, which clearly and unequivocally reject UN Resolution 242 as well as any negotiations based on this resolution. Nor has any PLO leader argued for the renunciation of "armed struggle" as "the only way to liberate Palestine." As Khaled el-Hassan, one of the PLO "moderates" who frequently visits Washington, argues: "Recognition of Israel means in the first instance annulment of the Palestinians' right of return."[31]

The argument within the PLO is rather one between what we can call "ideological extremists" and "pragmatic extremists." The pragmatists argue that "armed struggle" should be combined with a "political struggle" to gain world-wide recognition for the PLO. The ideologues argue that recognition is worthless and that what counts is revolutionary activism, not only directed against Israel, but also against "reactionary" regimes in the Arab world. No one in the PLO argues that armed struggle should be renounced in favor of negotiations with Israel. Thus, on the pragmatic side, Arafat's deputy, Khalil al-Wazir (alias Abu Jihad) recently explained:

> The Palestinian revolution has never renounced the military option. It is wrong to say that the Palestinian revolution has stopped its armed struggle and has chosen to drown in political activities instead . . . . Our struggle has never stopped . . . . The Palestinian revolution has both military and political wings. Political moves do not mean renouncing the military struggle and its escalation.[32]

Similarly, Hani el-Hassan, a member of the Fatah Central Committee, recently stated:

> We believe that political success and the right of

self-determination can be achieved only with the gun. Just as
political action is the PLO's lifeline, armed struggle is the way to
reap political gains. He who does not sow, does not
reap . . . .[33]

But it is left to Salah Khalaf (alias Abu Iyad), another member of the
Fatah Central Committee, to explicitly reject the Arabist notion of PLO
"moderation":

Let us not attach titles like 'moderates' or 'non-moderates'
to the Palestinian leadership . . . . Any Palestinian leader
who would forego his gun during this pre-liberation period is
not worthy of being called a representative [of the Palestinians].
His entire worth depends on his gun and on the battle. That is
why Haig's appellations are of no interest to us . . . in
giving out titles of 'moderates' and 'non-moderates,' the
aim is to break our ranks. The Americans are fools and so is
their policy, because they busy themselves with marginal matters
which provide no grounds for decision-making. The people
who will make the decisions are the people with the gun.[34]

3) The "West Bank" Solution

In overlooking the true nature of the debate within the PLO, the
Arabists point to the PLO's willingness to accept an independent state in
the West Bank and Gaza as proof positive of the Organization's move in a
"moderate" direction and of the ability of the "moderates" to overcome
the negativism of the "extremists." This argument avoids a careful
analysis of what the relevant PNC resolutions actually say. The oft-cited
resolution of the 13th Palestine National Council held in Cairo in
February 1977 states:

The PNC has decided to continue to struggle to regain the
national rights of our people, in particular their rights of return,
self-determination and establishing an independent national
state on their national soil.[35]

This resolution does not declare the territorial boundaries of the
"independent national state." Rather, the PNC purposely avoided a
territorial definition to ensure consistency with the PLO's strategic
objective of the total liberation of Palestine. Far from declaring that the
establishment of a West Bank/Gaza state would resolve Palestinian
grievances and lead to peace with Israel, the PLO explained that such a

move would represent the first step in a "phased strategy" of total liberation. The second envisaged step would be Israel's compression to the boundaries set by the 1947 Partition Plan, followed by the eventual establishment of a Palestinian state in all of historical Palestine.[36] The Political Statement accompanying the resolution of the 13th PNC explicitly calls for the establishment of a Palestinian state in all of Palestine. Moreover, Article 9 of the resolution calls for the "liberation of all occupied Arab areas . . . without any conciliation or recognition [of Israel]."[37]

When the vagueness of the West Bank resolution is combined with the explicitly declared strategy of *marhaliyya* (the liberation of Palestine in stages) and the commitment not to make peace with Israel, it becomes evident that the PLO has simply managed to develop a formula which could accommodate the differing approaches of the pragmatists and ideologues. Thus the pragmatists could argue to their interlocutors in the United States that they were empowered to negotiate for an independent state in the West Bank and Gaza while covering their flanks by pointing out to the ideologues that this would only be the first step towards total liberation. Similarly, the ideologues could accept the logic of the phased strategy because it did not require them to abandon their commitment to "regaining all our rights, not just some of them."[38] The lowest common denominator between the two approaches remained the refusal to recognize or make peace with Israel and the insistence on retaining the Covenant's objective of destroying the "Zionist entity."

4) Resolution 242

The PLO orchestrated a similar process of obfuscation on the key issue of UN Resolution 242. Since its acceptance by the Security Council in November 1977 this resolution has formed the basis for all negotiations aimed at settling the Arab–Israeli conflict. In fact the only precondition for such negotiations has been the acceptance of UN Resolution 242—a position, however, that the PLO has consistently refused to adopt. Indeed Article 1 of the Political Resolution of the 13th PNC explicitly rejects Resolution 242:

> The PNC affirms that the Palestinian issue is the essence and the root of the Arab–Zionist conflict. Security Council Resolution 242 ignores the Palestinian people and their firm rights. The PNC therefore confirms its rejection of this resolution, and rejects negotiations at the Arab and international levels based on this resolution.[39]

On the basis of this Article, however, Arabists were able to explain that the reason for the PLO's rejection of Resolution 242 lay in its treatment of the Palestinians as a "refugee problem." This overlooked the PLO's other objection to 242: the fact that it only referred to territories occupied by Israel in 1967 (i.e. the West Bank and Gaza) and the fact that it recognized Israel's right to exist within secure and recognized boundaries. That these objections were at least as important as 242's supposedly inadequate reference to Palestinian rights, should have become evident in 1977 when the Carter Administration offered to amend UN Resolution 242's language on the Palestinians to make it acceptable to the PLO. The PLO's Executive Committee and its Central Council voted overwhelmingly to reject such a formula.[40]

Again, in July 1982, the PLO's real attitude to Resolution 242 was revealed. Besieged in Beirut, Arafat signed a piece of paper proffered by U.S. Congressman Paul McCloskey, which stated that the Chairman of the PLO accepted "all UN resolutions relevant to the Palestinian question." This was quickly interpreted as proof that Arafat had accepted UN Resolution 242 in the context of other General Assembly resolutions, particularly UNGA Resolution 3236 which recognized Palestinian "inalienable rights" to self–determination.[41] However, the PLO's representative at the United Nations was quick to point out the PLO's real position of continued rejection of Resolution 242. As he explained it, Arafat had only accepted "relevant" UN resolutions "and 242 is not relevant."[42]

The PLO's real position on Resolution 242 is best expressed by Abu Iyad:

> The Palestinian revolution will continue in its unswerving political position––and will forcefully say No to Camp David, No to Resolutions 242 and 338 and No to recognition of Israel.[43]

5) The "Last Card"

The final argument in the effort to portray the PLO as "moderate" focuses on the reasons underlying its refusal to recognize Israel. According to the Arabists, the PLO cannot recognize Israel because this is the PLO's "last card," to be played at the end of the negotiations after Israel has agreed to the establishment of an independent Palestinian state. They argue that the PLO is too weak to make the first concession and it is Israel which must agree to the PLO's minimum requirements before the PLO can be expected to respond.

If this argument were to be accepted, however, it would follow that the PLO's recognition of Israel's right to exist is the principal *quid pro quo* for Israeli concessions. This would be totally unprecedented. No state will accept that its existence should be made the subject of negotiations. In any negotiations, mutual recognition is assumed from the outset. Recognition cannot therefore be the "last card." It must rather be the "first card," the card that the PLO must play to get itself into the negotiations with Israel, the one thing that would indicate that the PLO is genuinely interested in reconciliation and peaceful coexistence. In short, if the PLO is not prepared to recognize Israel's right to exist, there is nothing to negotiate about. Certainly, Israel cannot be expected to bargain for its existence. As Henry Kissinger points out:

> Recognition of Israel is the beginning of a process, not the end; it does not meet--by itself--the needs of the situation. It is not, when all is said, much of a concession for the PLO to make.[44]

It is especially not much of a concession when one considers for a moment the likely consequences of Arafat's mouthing the words of recognition of Israel. First, the United States would no longer be bound by its 1975 commitment to Israel and would immediately recognize the PLO and enter into negotiations with it, precipitating a crisis in U.S.–Israeli relations. Similarly, though of lesser importance, the member states of the European Community could be expected to hail the PLO's moderation and pressure Israel to respond. Israel's international isolation would be complete. Moreover, such a move--if it were not repudiated by the PLO--would also divide the Israeli polity, with many influential voices calling upon the government not to miss an opportunity to negotiate peace, in much the same way as happened when Sadat indicated his willingness to make peace by visiting Jerusalem.

Given these clear advantages involved in turning the "last card" into the "first card," Arafat's refusal to mouth the words must be determined by other more significant factors. First, the PLO may actually mean what it says when it calls for the destruction of Israel. Although it contradicts Arabist thinking, it is at least possible that the PLO refuses to mouth the words because it simply does not accept Israel's right to exist. Second, while Arafat himself may recognize the advantages that would flow from such a rhetorical gesture it is entirely possible that his advisers and followers and the Arab governments which back him remain unreconciled to Israel's existence and would therefore turn on him and denounce him as a traitor.

The evidence to support such contentions is much stronger than the evidence that the PLO is really ready for peace but will only say so later. Every hint at recognition of Israel made by a PLO spokesman is immediately denied or contradicted by another equally authoritative spokesman. Every modification of the PLO's political program is couched in terms which maintain the PLO's adherence to its ultimate objective. Every effort by the United States and others to meet the PLO's requirements, either by offering to modify Resolution 242 or by redefining Palestinian rights, has been rejected.

Some Arabists concede that the PLO is not ready to recognize Israel and argue that before Arafat can persuade his followers of that necessity he must be guaranteed recognition of Palestinian rights. This argument, however, overlooks the fact that President Carter offered Arafat just such an inducement and it was rejected. First, Carter publicly advocated a "homeland" for the Palestinians and he then offered to change the wording of UN Resolution 242 to accommodate the PLO's concerns. In response, Arafat made no effort to persuade his constituency that they should modify their attitude to Israel. Instead, he put it to a vote and it was rejected out of hand.

Similarly, this argument overlooks the fact that the Camp David Accords recognized the "legitimate rights" of the Palestinians, provided for the Palestinians to "participate in the determination of their own future," and made room for them to sit at the negotiating table where the ultimate status of the West Bank and Gaza was to be decided. Had they done so, negotiations would now be taking place about the final disposition of the West Bank. As Carter's National Security Adviser, Zbigniew Brzezinski, recently argued, if the PLO had accepted the Camp David Accords "today there would be Arab political institutions on the West Bank and that would be a giant step towards some eventual resolution."[45] Or as Henry Kissinger has observed:

> Once there was an elected self-governing authority on the West
> Bank an irreversible political fact would be created . . . .
> However limited this authority it would soon turn into the
> nucleus of something like a Palestinian state, probably under
> PLO control.[46]

Yet the PLO rejected the Camp David Accords out of hand and did so long before the Israeli government sought to restrict the definition of Palestinian autonomy provided for in these documents.

Third, this argument ignores the fact that the Reagan Plan also provides an opportunity for the Palestinians to achieve the rights they claim. Although the President explicitly excluded the option of self-determination for the Palestinians and ruled out PLO participation in the negotiating process until it recognized Israel's right to exist, the Reagan Plan also excluded Israeli sovereignty over the West Bank and Gaza and clearly indicated that these territories should be under Arab sovereignty. Moreover, the territories were to be ruled by Palestinians "in association with Jordan," and in February 1983 President Reagan committed himself on paper to the concept of "confederation" as one of the possible means for achieving this association. As already noted, "confederation" has a precise definition--it means a federation between independent states. Although Arafat spent a good deal of time negotiating with Hussein about the Reagan Plan, the Palestine National Council, the PLO's Executive Committee and Fatah's Central Committee all rejected it.

It is true that the United States has not recognized a Palestinian right to an independent state, but the Camp David Accords and the Reagan Plan taken together hold out the potential of achieving that in practice. As Henry Kissinger, one of the architects of the Reagan Plan, has noted, there is a danger that this plan "will turn into a subterfuge for rehabilitating the PLO, establishing it with essentially unchanged composition and programme on the West Bank, threatening simultaneously Israel and Jordan."[47] But Kissinger's "danger" should have been seen as a clear and distinct advantage from the PLO's perspective if the Arabists were right and the PLO was only waiting for a U.S. commitment to Palestinian rights before it moderated its position.

And yet the PLO has rejected the Reagan Plan and has rejected any approval for Hussein to negotiate on that basis. The manifest failure of the PLO to make the slightest move in the direction of "moderation," despite America's willingness to consider Palestinian rights to sovereignty over the West Bank and Gaza and to a "confederation" with Jordan, provides sufficient evidence to refute the Arabist argument. In these circumstances there is no reason to believe that going one step further and recognizing Palestinian "national rights" will provide the magic formula that will transform the PLO. Arafat has had plenty to work with if he genuinely wanted to moderate the PLO but he has never attempted to do so. Instead he has presented various formulas to the PLO's decision-making bodies and then has accepted their rejection. As Arafat told journalist Eric Rouleau in April 1983, to do otherwise--to actually recognize Israel--"would assuredly result in the fragmentation of the PLO, a split within Fatah, and his own denunciation as a traitor."[48]

These were prophetic words. Within months, Fatah had indeed split, Arafat had been denounced as a traitor by the PFLP and DFLP, and had only just managed to escape a siege by Syrian-backed Palestinians in

Tripoli. But these events had not been precipitated by any Arafat announcement that he was prepared to recognize Israel. On the contrary, Arafat had again refused to do so. Rather, they were precipitated by Arafat's negotiations with King Hussein about a Jordanian negotiation with Israel and by Arafat's decision to visit Egypt, the one Arab country to make peace with Israel. The very thought that Arafat might take a small step towards those in the Arab world who believe in negotiating with Israel was enough to jeopardize his tenure as chairman of the PLO. Clearly, were Arafat actually to mouth the words of recognition of Israel, he would cease to represent the PLO and would place his own life at even greater risk.

In short, the "last card" assumption is nothing more than a rationalization for the PLO's refusal to recognize Israel, and Arafat's unwillingness and inability to change this reality. Faced with a choice between recognizing Israel or maintaining the unity of the PLO, Arafat has consistently chosen the latter.

6) The Damaging Consequences

If, as I have argued, the PLO is incapable of moderation, will not renounce its objective of destroying Israel through "armed struggle," will only accept a West Bank state as the "interim" stage in a strategy of phases, will not accept Resolution 242, and is not waiting for some magic U.S. formula to which it can respond, it necessarily follows that an American strategy designed to entice the PLO into changing its stripes cannot succeed. This explains why eight years of continuous efforts to persuade the PLO to moderate its position have failed. Nevertheless, given the abiding assumption in Washington that the Palestinian problem can and must be solved, policy–makers continue to adhere to the maxim "if at first you don't succeed, try, try again."

Moreover, many who accept that the PLO is incapable of genuine moderation will nevertheless argue that these efforts to woo the PLO are basically harmless because they are bound to fail. They argue that as long as the U.S. abides by its commitment to Israel and refuses to recognize the PLO until it unequivocally recognizes Israel, it matters little whether intermediaries waste their time talking to the PLO.

What both these skeptics and the Arabists overlook, however, are the damaging consequences of pursuing a policy of enticement of the PLO. First, this policy undermines King Hussein's longstanding efforts to replace the PLO as spokesman for the Palestinians. If the United States, through this policy, signals that it considers it necessary for the PLO to be involved in the peace negotiations, there is no reason for the Palestinians to turn to Hussein to represent them. Moreover, there is little incentive for Hussein to challenge the PLO's claim to be sole spokesman if he believes that even the United States does not support him in this effort.

Second, attempts to woo the PLO undermines Israel's faith in the fidelity of the United States to its written commitments. This does nothing to encourage Israeli confidence in the American-sponsored peace process. Moreover, every Israeli government has made it abundantly clear that it will not negotiate with the PLO even if the PLO recognizes Israel's right to exist. In these circumstances, if the United States were actually to succeed in getting Arafat to the table, Israel would not be there.

Third, efforts to entice the PLO give the PLO no incentive to alter its rejectionist position. On the contrary, these efforts encourage the PLO to believe that if it will just hang on long enough, the United States will eventually come around to recognizing it without any change in its attitude. Indeed, that is precisely why the PLO tries to entice the U.S. into negotiations by holding out the promise of moderation while never actually delivering on this promise. The U.S. response serves to stimulate PLO hopes that America's refusal to recognize the PLO is not absolute and that change in the PLO's position is unnecessary.

Finally, policy-makers should consider what interest would actually be served by including the PLO in the peace process. The minimum requirement of the PLO is an independent state; but such a state would be a threat to America's fundamental interest in stability in the Middle East. Henry Kissinger understood this well when he was Secretary of State:

> The PLO was overtly anti-American as well as dedicated to the destruction of two important friends of the United States: Israel and the Hashemite Kingdom of Jordan. In these circumstances we did not have a high incentive to advance the "dialogue" with the PLO . . . not because of Israeli pressure but because of our perception of the American national interest.[49]

Kissinger was not beguiled by Arabist arguments about PLO "moderation." He understood that the creation of a PLO state would undermine American interests:

> A Palestinian state run by the PLO was certain to be irredentist. Even should it change its professed aims, it would not likely remain moderate for long; its many extremist factions would see to that. Its Soviet ties would lead it in the direction of becoming a radical state like Libya or South Yemen. Any Palestinian structure on the West Bank had every incentive to turn on Jordan--if only to gain a secure base for later operations against

Israel and to avoid the provisions of a peace accord that would inevitably demilitarize the West Bank . . . . To them a West Bank mini–state could be only an interim step toward their final aims.[50]

Conclusion

U.S. policy–makers face a strategic decision in their efforts to resolve the Arab–Israeli conflict. They must decide whether American interests are better served by pursuing a Jordanian or a PLO solution to the Palestinian problem. There is no middle road available because Jordan and the PLO are at heart competitors for control over the Palestinians in the West Bank and Gaza. For eight years the United States has been ambivalent in its approach to this issue. On the one hand, it has sought a solution which would return the West Bank to Jordan. On the other hand, it has sought to involve the PLO in the peace process with the unstated objective of establishing a Palestinian state in the West Bank. In the process, the United States has failed to solve the Palestinian problem.

It may well have been wiser for the United States to recognize that the Palestinian problem was insoluble and to have left well enough alone. But the Arab–Israeli conflict impacts on so many American interests that it seems impossible for the United States to avoid trying to solve the problem. In these circumstances, the least the United States can do is to avoid making matters worse. Eight years of wooing the PLO has indeed made matters worse. The United States has unwittingly weakened Hussein's efforts to undermine both PLO influence over the Palestinians and its claim to be their "sole" representative. And, at the same time, it has demonstrably failed to alter the PLO's rejectionist attitude.

Now, with the PLO split and paralyzed, and with a new Israeli government interested in building an independent leadership in the West Bank and Gaza, King Hussein has a unique opportunity to re–establish his legitimacy and influence among Palestinians in the territories. But this will be a slow and fragile process, easily disrupted by any American effort to resuscitate the PLO by seeking to involve it, either directly or indirectly, in the peace process. At the outset of its second term, the Reagan Administration should eschew Arabist policy advice in this regard and instead make a clear strategic choice in favor of a Jordanian–Israeli solution to the Palestinian problem.

Notes

1. See Abraham Ben-Zvi, *The Reagan Presidency and the Palestinian Predicament*, Center for Strategic Studies, Tel Aviv University, Paper no. 16, September 1982, pp. 10–11.

2. *Ibid.*, p. 13.

3. *New York Times*, April 11, 1981.

4. *Ibid.*, Ben-Zvi, p. 14.

5. Unless otherwise noted, material in this section is based on the following sources: author's interviews with key people involved in the State Department and the Mroz Mission; and Bernard Gwertzman, "U.S. Reportedly had Contact with the PLO for 9 Months," *New York Times*, February 19, 1984.

6. Whether President Reagan actually approved the Mroz mission is unclear. Gwertzman reports that Haig told Reagan in a private meeting in California and subsequently told his aides that Reagan had approved the idea. This is confirmed in Sol Sanders, "Washington is Secretly Wooing Yasir Arafat," *Business Week*, November 30, 1981. However, after Gwertzman's account was published, National Security Adviser Robert C. McFarlane stated that neither he nor the President had been aware of the affair. See Bernard Gwertzman, "Reagan Reported in Dark on Talks," *New York Times*, February 20, 1984.

7. Trude Feldman, "I Do Too Have a Middle East Policy," *Washington Post*, November 1, 1981.

8. *Ibid.*, December 13, 1981.

9. According to the Gwertzman account, the "notional text" stated that "if the PLO agreed to language accepting Israel's right to exist and Resolutions 242 and 338, the United States would agree with it that the Palestinian question involved territorial and political problems as well as refugee ones." The document also stated that the United States, "through its traditional principles, favors the 'principle of self-determination.' "

10. See Alexander Haig, *Caveat: Realism, Reagan and Foreign Policy* (New York: Macmillan, 1984). Flora Lewis, "The Irrepressible Arafat," *New York Times*, March 8, 1984.

11. Haig says that Weinberger and Bush conveyed this message to the Saudis when they attended King Khaled's funeral in Riyadh. *Ibid.*

12. *Washington Post*, July 20, 1982.

13. "After Lebanon: A Conversation," *The Economist*, November 13, 1982, pp. 28–29.

14. Bernard Gwertzman, *New York Times*, February 19, 1984.

15. *Washington Post*, February 15, 1983, p. A12.

16. Karen Elliott House, "Reagan Plan's Failure Began at Home," *Wall Street Journal*, April 20, 1983.

17. According to John Mroz, "International lawyers define a confederation as a number of independent states linked by a treaty in a union with a central government. The central government has specific powers over the confederation's member states but not over its citizens. This confederation brings states together for a specific purpose but leaves each member state sovereign and independent in other respects." Mroz, *Beyond Security, Private Perceptions Among Arabs and Israelis* (New York: International Peace Academy, 1980), p. 165.

18. See Eric Rouleau, "The Future of the PLO," *Foreign Affairs*, 62(1), Fall 1983, p. 151.

19. John Goshko, "Reagan Still Hopeful of Further Progress," *Washington Post*, April 11, 1983.

20. *New York Times*, December 23, 1983.

21. Bernard Gwertzman, "Reagan Sees Hope for a Resumption of Mideast Talks," *Ibid.*, December 25, 1983. As John Goshko reported, "Now, with the PLO fragmented and Arafat forced to abandon his last stronghold in Lebanon, U.S. officials believe there is a chance that he might try to salvage his authority by moving into close alliance with moderate Arab states like Egypt and Jordan that favor negotiations on the occupied territories." *Washington Post*, December 23, 1983.

22. See Foreign Broadcast Information Service, *Daily Report*, Middle East and Africa, January 5, 1984, p. 1 A1.

23. See Judith Miller interview, *New York Times*, March 15, 1984.

24. *Ibid.*, February 23, 1984.

25. See Aaron David Miller, "Whither the PLO?," *Middle East Review*, 16(3), Spring, 1984, pp. 40–43.

26. Interview in *Sada el-Usbu*, cited in UAE News Agency, January 12, 1982.

27. Interview in *Al-Hawadith*, October 1, 1982.

28. See Aaron David Miller, *The PLO and the Politics of Survival*, The Washington Papers, No. 99, Georgetown Center for Strategic and International Studies, Washington, 1983, ch. 4.

29. Daniel Pipes, "How Important is the PLO?," *Commentary*, April 1983.

30. The ill-fated Fahd Plan provides a good example of this consensus at work. Arafat at first endorsed the Plan. But Syria––and its PLO arm, *As-Saiqa*––strongly opposed it, as did Libya and South Yemen. This opposition, combined with a series of car bomb explosions outside Arafat's Beirut headquarters, persuaded Arafat to change his mind.

When the Arab League convened a summit in Fez to consider the Fahd Plan, these rejectionist states boycotted the meeting. Consequently, the PLO did not attend either.

31. *Al-Hawadith*, August 31, 1981.

32. *Ad-Dustur*, April 14, 1984.

33. *Ash-Sharq al-Awsat*, February 29, 1984.

34. *Al-Watan*, January, 18–19, 1981.

35. Cited in Y. Harkabi, *The Palestinian Covenant and its Meaning* (New Jersey: Valentine Mitchell, 1979), p. 157.

36. See interview with Faruq Qaddumi in *Newsweek*, March 7, 1977; I. Altman, "The PLO," in C. Legum ed., *Middle East Contemporary Survey*, (London: Holmes and Meier, 1979), Vol. I, p. 187.

37. Harkabi, p. 157.

38. *Al-Talak*, November 1, 1982. (*As-Saiqa's*, newspaper).

39. Harkabi, p. 151.

40. Helena Cobban, *The Palestinian Liberation Organization--People, Power and Politics* (Cambridge: Cambridge University Press, 1984), pp. 88–89.

41. UN General Assembly Resolution 3236, November 22, 1974.

42. *New York Times*, July 26, 1982.

43. *Radio Monte Carlo*, August 21, 1982.

44. *The Economist*, November 13, 1982.

45. *Los Angeles Times*, May 3, 1984.

46. *The Economist*, November 13, 1982.

47. *Ibid.*

48. Rouleau, p. 149.

49. Henry Kissinger, *Years of Upheaval* (Boston: Little, Brown, 1982), p. 625.

50. *Ibid.*, p. 626.

8
American Perceptions of the Israeli-Palestinian Conflict and the Iranian-Iraqi War: The Need for a New Look

James R. Kurth

U.S. Policy Seen in the Light of Lebanon and the Persian Gulf

Recent events have provided both an opportunity and the need to reexamine some of the basic perceptions and assumptions underlying the policies of the United States toward the Middle East. The collapse of the Reagan Administration's policy in Lebanon revealed grave errors in the way U.S. policy-makers perceived the politics of that hapless Middle Eastern country, just as the collapse of the Carter Administration's policy in Iran earlier revealed similar errors about the politics of that apparently solid Middle Eastern ally.[1] And the increasing involvement of U.S. naval vessels and military aircraft in the spreading Persian Gulf war carries with it the probability that comparable errors in perceiving the Middle East will lead to even more costly failures in the region.

The repercussions from the advance of Syria and the retreat of Israel in Lebanon in turn raise anew the question of U.S. policy toward the disputed territories of the West Bank (Judea and Samaria), East Jerusalem, the Golan Heights, and the Gaza District. Similarly, the repercussions from the growth of Shiite power in Lebanon and the growth of U.S. involvement in the Persian Gulf raise anew the question of U.S. policy toward the Iranian-Iraqi war and particularly toward the spread of the Shiite revolution from Iran into other countries of the Gulf and to the west. This essay accordingly will examine the need to reconstruct U.S. policies toward (1) the Israeli-Palestinian conflict and (2) the

Iranian–Iraqi war, upon new and truer perceptions and assumptions about
the realities of politics in the Middle East.

U.S. Policy toward the Israeli–Palestinian Conflict:
The Centrality of the Disputed Territories

The United States and Israel each held national elections in 1984
which will set the course of their countries for several years to come. The
period after these elections, particularly 1985, might provide an opportune
time to reconstruct U.S.–Israeli relations on a foundation that accords with
new conditions, on a basis that will be more mature and realistic than has
been the case in recent years.

The essential commonality of interests between the United States and
Israel is well known, and the fundamental basis of U.S.–Israeli relations is
quite sound. The U.S. values Israel as a strategic asset, one that provides a
wide range of military and intelligence benefits for the U.S. policy of
containing the military expansion of the Soviet Union in the Middle East.[2]
The U.S. also values Israel as a political democracy, one with which
Americans share political, cultural, and religious norms and practices.
From time to time, of course, there have been disputes about a variety of
issues, such as sales of U.S. advanced weapons to Arab countries, the
amount of U.S. aid to Israel, and the Israeli invasion of Lebanon. But
these disputes have generally been temporary, and after the issue has been
decided, the fundamental equilibrium of U.S.–Israeli cooperation has been
restored.

There is indeed only one major and continuing issue of dispute in
U.S.–Israeli relations, and this concerns the territories that Israel acquired
as a result of the 1967 Arab–Israeli War, that is, the West Bank (Judea
and Samaria), East Jerusalem, the Golan Heights, and the Gaza District.
It is the argument of this essay that the position of the United States on
this issue rests upon assumptions which no longer correspond to the
realities of the Middle East, and that the time and the opportunity have
come to bring this dispute to an end.

The new realities of the disputed territories. It has now been a
generation since Israel entered into these territories. Israel has now ruled
the West Bank and East Jerusalem almost as long as did Jordan, and the
Gaza District almost as long as did Egypt. And it is usually forgotten that
the Jordanian occupation, like the Israeli one, was never recognized by
other Arab states. Indeed, the only states that recognized Jordanian rule
in these territories were Britain and Pakistan.[3]

It has also been almost a generation that U.S. administrations have been fruitlessly objecting to the continuing, expanding, and maturing Israeli presence within the territories. This presence now comprises a dense network of many strands--economic integration, political administration, military security, and permanent Jewish settlements--and it is now highly institutionalized. Indeed, in the view of many sober and responsible analysts of this presence--including both those who support it and those who criticize it--it is now irreversible.[4]

The territory most in dispute, and the one for which U.S. policy–makers have had the greatest expectations for Israeli reversal, is of course the West Bank, i.e., Judea and Samaria. And of the strands of the Israeli presence in the disputed territories, it is the permanent Jewish settlements on the West Bank that have been especially objectionable from the perspective of the U.S. But as we shall see below, these settlements have now also become especially important in establishing the irreversibility of the Israeli presence in the West Bank.

The realities of West Bank geography. The West Bank comprises an area of 2165 square miles, or about the size of the state of Delaware or twice the size of the country of Luxembourg. It contains a population of 750,000, of which more than 93 percent are Arab.[5] These basic statistics seem to suggest that an independent Palestinian state on the West Bank, while admittedly small, would nevertheless be large enough, and homogeneous enough, to be in the same class as many members of the United Nations.

Other features of the political and economic geography of the West Bank, however, lead to a less formalistic and more realistic conclusion. Almost all of the Arab population of the West Bank lives in the western two–thirds of the territory. The eastern one–third, rising from the Jordan River Valley, is very arid and therefore largely uninhabited, except for a string of Jewish settlements, established for the purposes of military security under the Allon Plan, and the Arab town of Jericho, which is built around an oasis (and is one of the most ancient towns in the world).[6] The Arab population of the West Bank, therefore, is bounded on the west by large centers of Jewish populations, such as Tel Aviv, which comprise the core of Israeli society; and it is bounded on the east by a string of Jewish settlements, which comprise the shield of Israeli security. The Arab land is a sliver in a Jewish sandwich. And this area that the Arab population resides in is relatively poor both in natural resources and in industrial establishments, those normal bases of a healthy economy.

These features of the political and economic geography of the West Bank do not represent a very promising foundation for a viable, independent Palestinian state. Rather, they suggest that any Palestinian state on the West Bank would have to rely upon some larger Arab state or combination of states (e.g., Jordan or Syria) in order to survive. Or it would be led to expand further into Israel itself. In any event, it is easy to see why Israel cannot look with serenity upon the establishment of a Palestinian state on the West Bank. Conversely, since geography condemns the West Bank to be heavily influenced by some larger state, it is natural that Israel would choose to be the one.

The realities of West Bank settlements. The permanent Jewish settlements on the West Bank now compose an ensemble of considerable variety and great extent: (1) towns and settlements surrounding Jerusalem; (2) settlements on the Western ridges of the Samarian mountains overlooking the coastal plain; (3) settlements in the Jordan River Valley; and (4) settlements in the heartlands of Judea and Samaria adjacent to Arab cities, such as Nablus, Ramallah, and Hebron.[7]

Of these categories of settlements, the first three are overwhelmingly supported by all major groups and parties in Israel, including both the Likud and the Labor coalitions. And even the fourth category is supported by groups with substantial political strength and effectiveness.

The towns and settlements surrounding Jerusalem and on the Samarian ridges are natural extensions, indeed extended suburbs, of the cities of Jerusalem and Tel Aviv. Many of these settlements are bedroom communities that are within a thirty-minute commute from their city. These settlements rest upon a solid base of economic and social realities. It is precisely their suburban quality, their very ordinariness, which will make them an enduring presence, whatever the ebbs and flows of Israeli party politics. Indeed, they will become a solid mass that will help guide that ebb and flow; in the multiparty Israeli political system, even a small group, if it represents a concentrated and consistent interest, can acquire substantial leverage, or at least a veto power, as an indispensable element of the governing coalition in the Knesset. The suburban voters on the West Bank are likely to become such an interest.[8]

Some of these towns and settlements stretch north-west from Jerusalem where they merge with others stretching south-east from Tel Aviv. Still others stretch south from Jerusalem and include the cluster known as the Etzion Block. Also in this area south of Jerusalem is Bethlehem, the major Christian Arab city on the West Bank, along with two other Christian Arab towns. Together, the Jewish and Christian towns and settlements around Jerusalem encompass about 10 percent of the total area of the West Bank.

The settlements in the Jordan River Valley grow out of the Allon Plan of Labor and also the supporting policies of the Likud. Lying between the Jordan River itself and the hills rising to the west, they result from the recognition that the most, indeed the only, viable eastern strategic frontier for Israel is the river and its hills. These frontier settlements form a line reaching from the Red Sea to the Sea of Galilee; two–thirds of this distance lies in the West Bank territory acquired in 1967. Without the settlements in the Jordan River Valley and on the western ridges of the Samarian mountains, central Israel around Tel Aviv is only nine to thirteen miles wide. With them, the width of central Israel quadruples to about forty–five miles. These settlements rest upon a solid base of military necessity. The strategic reasoning has been summed up well in the following analysis by Brigadier General Ariel Shalev, a retired senior officer in the Israeli Defense Forces:

> Against an enemy with offensive capabilities, Israel lacks sufficient strategic depth to defend the Coastal Plain, because Judea and Samaria are much higher and overlook the Coastal Plain. The width of the State of Israel in those regions is between 14 and 20 kilometers. According to Soviet estimates, that is the depth of a defensive division and, according to the American estimate, it is of a brigade . . . . Thus, the defense of that area so vital to Israel from within the Green Line [the pre–1967 boundary] . . . is possible merely on a tactical level because of the narrowness of the area . . . . It is very doubtful whether it would be possible . . . to succeed in the task of defending that vital area, where 67 percent of the inhabitants of Israel live and to prevent a high number of losses, unless the depth is increased and the potential threat is removed to the other side of the Jordan. Moreover, an enemy that knows that, in a single tactical maneuver, he might be able to achieve the strategic goal of dividing Israel in its vital territory, would be strongly tempted to try it. That knowledge alone would be enough to make the beginning of a war more likely.[9]

Thus, in Israel the only controversial category of settlements is the fourth, those in the heartland of Judea and Samaria adjacent to Arab cities. But even these settlements are now supported by such powerful and committed political constituencies that even a new Labor government would be most unlikely to abandon them, and certainly not the present government composed of a coalition of Labor and Likud.

The current position of the two main parties on the territories has been described well by Gershom Shocken, the publisher and editor of *Ha'aretz* in his account of the 1984 Israeli election:

As to the occupied territories on the West Bank of the Jordan and the Gaza Strip, Likud stressed its commitment to keep the whole of the Land of Israel. Labor did not disavow its readiness for a territorial compromise with Jordan as a partner, but neither did they make a strong stand of the issue. They stressed the portions they intend to retain rather than those they would give up. After 17 years of Israeli occupation, talk of readiness to abandon territory does not help win votes.[10]

Given these new realities about the disputed territories, particularly the West Bank, why have U.S. policy-makers persisted in their increasingly sterile and counterproductive opposition to the Israeli presence?

The American conception of the disputed territories. At one level, the motives behind the U.S. position have been to maintain good ties with the "moderate Arab states," to appear "even-handed" in the Arab-Israeli conflict. This has especially been the case in regard to Saudi Arabia, with its obvious oil wealth; Jordan, with its presumed strategic potential (for example, a possible strike force for use in the Persian Gulf); and even Syria, which U.S. State Department officials have perennially hoped to wean away from the Soviet Union.

This view of the importance of the Arab-Israeli conflict for U.S. relations with the moderate Arabs might have been a plausible enough approach in the first few years after 1967. But today, it is now clear that the policies of different Arab states will vary over time for a host of reasons completely unrelated to the issue of the territories.[11] Does anyone really think that any Arab state gives high priority to the PLO, given the fate of the PLO in Arab politics in the past two years? Or that the Jordanian monarchy would be any less rickety and its policy any less vascillating if it had the responsibility to govern the West Bank or had an independent Palestinian state as a neighbour? Or that the Syrian regime would be any less a Soviet client if the Golan Heights were returned to it?

There is another, more fundamental level of perception, however, which better explains the persistence of the U.S. opposition. Here, the motive behind the U.S. position on the territories has been the idea or premise that the Israeli presence in them is somehow unnatural, that the occupation of the territory of one people by the state of another is not feasible in the contemporary world, that "nationalism" is the relevant issue and the inevitable reality. This premise behind the U.S. opposition to Israeli policy in the territories rests upon the misapplication of European and American conceptions of politics to Middle Eastern realities.

People in the West view the Middle East through the prisms of their own political experiences. For Europeans, this is especially the prism of the nation–state; for Americans, it is especially the prism of the pluralist democracy (although by now, most U.S. policy–makers have recognized that this idea is wildly irrelevant to the Middle East, and they have retreated to the European notion). But in the real Middle East, there are no nation–states (other than Turkey), and there are no pluralist democracies (other than Israel itself).

It is true that for about two generations––from about 1945 to about 1975––there was among some Arabs a hope, and among most Europeans and Americans an expectation, that there would soon be real nation–states in the Middle East, perhaps even one great, unified Arab nation–state. But this idea largely faded away in the 1970s, with the death of President Gamal Abdel Nasser of Egypt, with the failure of every attempt at unity between Arab states, and with the Islamic revolution in Iran.[12] And the fading of this idea allows us to see what was always the real political structure of the Middle East, which had been operating there all the time beneath the fog of Arab nationalism.

The Middle Eastern reality of millet societies. The reality of the Middle East always has been a series of political and military *centers*, or cores, constructed by peoples who are more organized and more militant than their neighbors. Each center, or core, is surrounded by a series of other peoples or ethnic communities who are less organized, less militant, or perhaps merely less numerous than those in the core. Together, the core and the associated peoples form a society. The core people organize the state structure and the military security which in turn surrounds and provides the framework for the entire ensemble of disparate peoples. The associated peoples and their leaders, however, assume many of the other political and administrative tasks involving their own ethnic community. For example, the daily life of the associated peoples will be largely governed by the traditions and customary laws of their particular ethnic community.[13]

The rulers of the wider society, who are also the leaders of the core people, normally do not administer directly the individuals in an associated ethnic community. Rather, the rulers deal directly with the leaders of the community (e.g., the traditional religious hierarchy or the patrons of the most prominent families); they thus administer the community indirectly and as a group. It is a pattern of indirect rule and patron–client relations.[14]

At its best, this is a system of shared authority and communal autonomy (e.g., Lebanon in its "Golden Age" from 1946 to about 1970). More commonly, it is a system of bureaucratic authoritarianism and precarious autonomy (e.g., Egypt under Sadat). And at its worst, it is a system of secret police and state terror (e.g., contemporary Syria and Iraq).

In Ottoman times, this Middle Eastern reality could be called by rather accurate terms; there was what was known as the "Ottoman ruling institution," which ordered a complex society of ethnic communities, known as "millets."[15] In modern times, however, Westerners have given this reality their own misleading terms; they try to see in the Middle East a series of actual and potential nation–states.

It would be impossible, however, to redraw the map of the Middle East or of any particular state within it so that all or even most ethnic communities have their own states, as in much of contemporary Europe. The ethnic communities of the Middle East are, and always have been, condemned to live several of them together in a wider society and under a "ruling institution," that is, in a state structure organized primarily by one of them.

It would also be impossible, of course, to redesign the societies of the Middle East so that this ensemble of communities could live together in a pluralist political system, as in the United States. This arrangement can work in a society in which religion and politics, church and state have been largely separated since nearly the origin of the society. However, in the Middle East, nothing like this separation, this "secularization," exists.

There is today, however, one major political system whose ethnic components are organized very much in the way of the Ottoman Empire (and of the Byzantine Empire before it). That is the Soviet Union (like the Russian Empire before it). In the Soviet Union, the Russians (more precisely, the Great Russians as distinct from the Little Russians or Ukrainians and the White Russians or Byelorussians), who have always been more organized and more militant than their neighbors, have organized the state structure and the military security which, in turn, has surrounded the ensemble of disparate peoples, ranging from Estonians to Kazakhs. In regard to this particular multi–ethnic system, of course, one would not say that the associated peoples and their leaders assume many of the other political and administrative tasks involving their own ethnic community. Rather, in the Soviet Union, we have something of a worst–case analysis, i.e., secret police and state terror.[16]

It is, however, this very way of organizing an ensemble of ethnic communities, a multinational empire, that makes the Soviet Union such a relevant and useful political model for certain authoritarian regimes in the Middle East. This is especially the case where the regime represents a militant but minority ethnic community, e.g., the Alawi–based regime of Hafez Assad in Syria (the Alawis represent a variation of Shiism) and the Sunni–based regime of Saddam Hussein in Iraq. In Syria, the Alawis comprise some 12 percent of the population; in Iraq, the Sunnis comprise some 45 percent. A minority regime tends to compensate for its smaller numbers of natural supporters with greater intensity of repression and terror. Such regimes are natural admirers and consumers of Soviet secret police organization, methods and advisors.[17]

The Israeli practice within the disputed territories. The Israeli policy toward the territories they acquired in 1967 is in accord with these enduring military and social realities of a Middle East of "ruling institutions" and "millet societies," but it is so in a relatively benign form.

A glance at the map quickly and clearly shows than any viable framework for military security for the land between the Mediterranean Sea and the Jordan River would have the military security border at or near the river and on the Golan Heights. As the core people in that land, the Israelis organize the military security of the area, including the disputed territories. Each core people has always had its political and even spiritual center, the center of the center, so to speak. For the Israelis, of course, this is Jerusalem, an integral part of the system we have described.

The Israelis also provide a wider range of economic and social services than normally has been provided by other core people in the Middle East. Many other political, administrative, economic, and social functions in the territories are either shared with or assumed by other authorities, such as local councils of Arab communities and even the Jordanian government.

> The policy of the Israeli government was to avoid interfering in the internal affairs of the local population, to allow them to determine their own relationships, and to recognize the municipalities and the elected institutions as the exclusive authoritative–formal bodies representing the residents of the cities and towns.[18]

Different Palestinians respond to this structure in different ways. Some Palestinians see their primary concern as economic, and their political concerns as primarily local.[19] For them, Middle Eastern practice, economic interests, and political focus converge in making communal and personal autonomy within the Israeli military security framework a viable and acceptable situation.

Other Palestinians weight concrete economic interests less and value abstract political ideas more. For them, their natural political arena could be found within Jordan, for, in large measure, Jordan has become a

Palestinian society within a Hashemite or Transjordanian state.

> By the end of the 1970s the population of Jordan on the East
> Bank was nearing the 2 million mark, while the West Bank
> population was close to what it had been thirty years earlier
> (700,000). The population of the East Bank had become more
> and more Palestinian, housing almost three times more
> Palestinian Arabs than the West Bank. Jordan was the
> demographic center of the Palestinian population.[20]

Accordingly, Amman, the capital of Jordan, is now the largest Palestinian
city in the world. The time is not far off where there could be in Jordan a
reversal of the cores, when the Palestinians themselves could organize the
state structure within Jordan.

The overall system, then, is one composed of (1) an Israeli-organized
realm composed of Jewish and Palestinian peoples and (2) a Jordanian-
(or potentially a Palestinian-) organized realm of Jordanian and
Palestinian peoples. This system, of course, is not a stable one in the sense
that nation-states, such as France, or pluralist democracies, such as the
United States, are stable (although even in the U.S. there have been times,
such as in 1968, when "stable" was not the first adjective that came to
mind). The point, however, is that this is the most stable political system
for these lands that the social realities can produce.

But what will be the consequences of this political system for Israeli
democracy? Will it change the nature and meaning of the Zionist project?
This is the question that most troubles many Israelis and many of Israel's
friends in America and Canada.

Here, it might be useful to view Israel and the territories in a
comparative perspective. Even those nations which have long established
democratic systems have been brought, by historical circumstances, to rule
other peoples which do not have the same set of rights and duties as do
the people of the majority. In the case of the United States today, Puerto
Rico and the Virgin Islands are territories whose peoples assume different
rights (e.g., they cannot vote in national elections) and duties (e.g., they do
not pay the same taxes) than Americans in the fifty states. Many other
western democracies also rule peoples with a different corpus of rights and
duties than that of the citizens in the core area. These include Canada,
Britain, France, the Netherlands, Denmark, Australia, and New Zealand.

Of course, in many of these cases, the relationship between the core
people and the associated ones is undergoing a continuous evolution, as
one would expect with any complex relationship among different peoples
in a modern, changing society. Similarly, one would expect a continuous

evolution in the relationship between Israel and its associated territories.

Still, we do not want to overemphasize the similarities between Israel's situation and that of other democracies. The scale of the disputed territories in relation to Israel obviously makes for a more difficult problem than do the analogous ratios elsewhere. And the central argument of this essay has been that western concepts of politics, including western concepts of democracy, are ill–fitted to the social realities of the Middle East.

Even if the Arabs in Israel and in the disputed territories were to assume the same set of rights and duties as the Jews, a viable democracy would not result. The history of the Middle East, down to the present day, provides no evidence and no example whatever that, in any country, there are enough people among the Muslim Arab population who share democratic norms and practices to be able to sustain a democratic political system. Conversely, if Israel were to withdraw from the West Bank, even democracy in that country would be at risk. For as Israel gave up the West Bank, it would also give up its military security, and to compensate for its loss, it would have to construct an even larger military establishment, with an even larger military expenditure than it has today. These changes would also alter the nature of Israeli democracy, moving Jerusalem further from Athens and closer to Sparta, so to speak. Indeed, the conjunction of heightened military insecurity, heightened economic strains, diminished democratic practices, and diminished quality of life would drive many Israelis out of Israel to become emigrants to the United States and Canada.

At a more fundamental level, the abstract idea of democracy, whose modern version dates only from the Enlightenment, may be too slight a foundation on which to build an enduring Israel, an Israel that will be passed on to generations yet to come.[21] An enduring Israel may have to be based upon the more ancient heritage of Jewish religion and tradition. This potentiality is already recognized and accepted in Israel by the Likud, by the various religious parties, and by many Sephardi Jews. These are not, of course, the Israelis who are most known and understood by most of Israel's friends in the West. Rather, from the conventional Western perspective, the most comprehensible and sympathetic Israelis are found in the Labor Party. But it is probably only a matter of time, perhaps only a matter of a new generation, until the necessity of building upon Jewish religion and tradition is recognized by the Labor Party, too. Gershom Schocken's account is to the point:

> The Labor Party of Israel has lost its sense of identity. Early in the century it was conceived and developed as a movement of

pioneering workers. Its mission had been to convince the bands of penniless Jewish youngsters, born in a Europe that did not want them and was about to kill them, to come to the wasteland that was Palestine in the 1920s and 1930s. The Zionist labor movement imbued these young people with the belief that they could do nothing more meaningful with their lives than to lay here, under heavy personal sacrifices, the foundations of a modern agriculture and industry, of a modern society providing basic social services to all in Palestine. And when the need arose, they even built an army--as pacified European socialists, they had not contemplated that. They also bore the main burden of providing succor for the mass immigration in the early days of the state. It was a great task, admirably performed. But it is over.[22]

In conclusion, no Israeli government can accept either a pure American or a pure European model for Israel and its territories. Pluralist democracy, American-style, would result in an Israeli state that was no longer distinctively Jewish. A nation-state, European style, one composed only or overwhelmingly of Jews, would shrink to frontiers even less viable and defensible than those before 1967. For a Jewish state in the Middle East to be secure against its enemies in the Middle East, it must have a state-community structure, Middle Eastern style.

Implications for U.S. policy. These considerations about the Middle East and millet society in general, and about Israel and the disputed territories in particular, suggest that the U.S. would be wise to develop a new policy toward the Israeli-Palestinian conflict more in accord with these Middle Eastern realities. The U.S. could contribute to a more realistic environment in the Middle East by no longer opposing and disputing the Israeli presence in the territories. It would also be sensible, although now obviously controversial, for the U.S. to better align its diplomacy with this reality by recognizing Jerusalem as the capital of Israel and by moving the U.S. embassy from Tel Aviv to Jerusalem.

In addition, a new U.S. foreign policy that recognized and accepted the realities of the territories, including the centrality of Jerusalem within them and within the wider Israeli realm, would itself liberate political and intellectual energies within the American foreign policy community. For too long, American policy-makers and policy analysts have squandered their talents in attempting to reconstruct the always-unstable and now-vanished conditions that existed before 1967, or in constructing a European or American fantasy-state among the Palestinians in the West Bank. However, if these talents and energies can be harnessed to build on the rock of reality, rather than on the sand of fantasy, the United States, Israel and the more reasonable and constructive Palestinians together can work out a political order that will be as stable, humane, and authentic as the doleful history of the Middle East can permit.

U.S. Policy Toward the Iranian–Iraqi War: the Case for a Partition of Iraq

In the past year, U.S. policy–makers have expressed concern about the potential defeat of Iraq by Iran as the final outcome of the long Iranian–Iraqi war. President Reagan and other officials have said that the defeat of Iraq would be against the national interest of the United States. This, in turn, has given rise to speculation about various kinds of military action that the U.S. might be compelled to undertake, either to contain the Iranian expansion or at least to keep the Iranians from attacking oil tankers in the Persian Gulf or closing the Strait of Hormuz.

It is possible, of course, that this issue may become a moot question. The stalemate in the war, which has already lasted more than four years, may persist, with the Iranian advantage in manpower being contained by the Iraqi advantage in materiel. A pattern seems to have developed in which Iran normally launches a "great offensive," an "Operation Jerusalem," twice a year: once in February, at the time of the anniversary of the coming to power of Khomeini and the establishment of the Islamic Republic in Iran; and once in September or October, before the onset again of winter. These battles occur in the marshland battlefields of the confluence of the Tigres and Euphrates, which, according to tradition, is not far from the site of the Garden of Eden. The Iranians achieve some initial advances and take some territory, but the Iraqis then contain the Iranians with their firepower and with their progressive escalation into more ruthless tactics, initially the bombing of Iranian ships and towns and later the use of poison gas. The Iranian offensive grinds to a halt, and the stalemate resumes again for another six months or so.[23]

If, however, the Iranians should at last be able to alter this pattern, to break through the Iraqi defenses, and to bring about the defeat and overthrow of the regime of Saddam Hussein, would it really be necessary for the United States to respond in some hostile and perhaps desperate way? Here, once again, it is useful to consider the millet society nature of Middle Eastern politics.

Iran and Iraq as multinational empires. The conventional way to look at both Iran and Iraq is to see them as nation–states; in fact, each is a multi–ethnic society, indeed a multinational empire.

Iran. Of the total population of Iran of some 40 million, about two–thirds are Farsis, the core ethnic group. Substantial minorities, each concentrated in a peripheral region, are the Azerbaijanis (5 million), Kurds (4 million), Arabs (2 million), Turkomens (1 million), and Baluchis (1 million). On the other hand, viewed from the perspective of religion, more than 90 percent of Iran's population is Shiite.

These figures suggest that the Islamic Republic may be able to spread its revolution to other Shiites in the Middle East. But they also suggest that, as the revolution spreads to additional non–Farsi ethnic groups, the government in Tehran could find itself stretched thin beyond its natural ethnic base, and that the Islamic Republic of Iran would have to be content with indirect rather than direct rule, with loyal allies rather than annexed provinces.

Further, the actual extent of the spread of the Shiite revolution may be relatively limited. Other than Iran itself, the countries in which a majority of the population is Shiite are actually only two: Iraq (55 percent) and Bahrain (70 percent). There are substantial minorities in several other countries: Kuwait (24 percent), United Arab Emirates (18 percent), Qatar (16 percent), and Lebanon (about 30 percent). In Saudi Arabia, the Shiites comprise nearly 50 percent of the 1 million population of the oil–rich Eastern Province, but only 8 percent of the population of Saudi Arabia as a whole.[24]

These figures suggest that the Shiite revolution itself would be relatively easy to contain. The waves from its overflow from Iran would first break upon, and ultimately be broken, on the rocks of more numerous ethnic communities, which provide the core peoples and the state structures in most countries in which Shiites reside.

Bahrain, with its large Shiite majority, may not be a rock against revolutionary Shiism; but it is an island, one with a small population (360,000) and with no obvious capacity to be a dynamic center of spreading Shiism. The serious territorial threat, then, actually involves only one country, Iraq.

An Iranian defeat of Iraq in the Iranian–Iraqi war might well result in a revolution among the Shiites in Iraq, located in the populous southern half of the country and including Baghdad as well as the Shiite holy cities of Najaf and Karbala. This region could then be converted into a satellite or, at least, a loyal ally of revolutionary Iran.

However, since Iraq has never been a nation–state but rather a multinational empire, a revolution among the Shiites in Iraq would not have the same impact as a revolution throughout Iraq. In particular, the Kurds in northern Iran, who are Sunni in religion and comprise some 18 percent of Iraq's total population, would resist this spread of revolutionary

Shiism and Iranian control. As they have done many times in the past, they would see in the revolutionary turmoil in the south a "window of opportunity" through which to escape from the hated control of Baghdad.[25]

At the same time, Turkey would see in the Shiite revolution in Iraq its own window of opportunity to split off an oil–rich area of Iraq (including the oil fields of Mosul and Kirkuk) and to make it an ally or even a province of Turkey, as it was in Ottoman times. And, in fact, during the past year, the Turks, with the cooperation of the Saddam Hussein regime, have sent military units into the Kurdish areas of Iraq, to undertake patrols and to provide order while the Iraqi army itself is engaged in the south.[26] An Iranian invasion of the southern region of Iraq and a Shiite revolution could detonate a Turkish occupation of the northern region of the country and the separation of Kurdistan from the rest of Iraq. There could be a partition of Iraq into an Iranian sphere and a Turkish sphere.[27]

Implications for U.S. policy. This possible outcome of the Iranian–Iraqi war could easily serve, rather than subvert, U.S. interests in the Middle East. Turkey, a traditional U.S. ally and a natural barrier to Soviet expansion, would be strengthened with the addition of revenues from the oil fields of Mosul and Kirkuk. These oil revenues, along with providing other obvious benefits, could go a long way toward financing Turkey's heavy burden of foreign debt with Western banks and governments. Iran, a current U.S. adversary, but also a natural barrier to Soviet expansion, would likewise be strengthened with the end of the military and financial hemorrhage of the war and by the addition of revenues from the oil field around Basra, should it choose to annex the areas it occupied.

Furthermore, with the revolution among the Shiites in Iraq, the Shiite revolution would have largely reached its natural limits. Of course, in the flush of enthusiasm and triumph after the Iranian victory and the overthrow of Saddam Hussein, Shiite groups scattered around the Middle East would doubtless undertake this or that violent and disruptive action, as, for example, in the oil fields of the Eastern Province of Saudi Arabia. But the natural strength of the majority communities in Middle Eastern countries would soon make its weight felt, and a new and relatively stable equilibrium would ensue.

Indeed, the new equilibrium would likely be more stable than the conditions of the recent past. The partition of Iraq, after all, would mean the partition of a state which for more than a generation, since 1958, has been one of the most *destabilizing* forces in the Middle East.[28] In its internal politics, it has been one of the most repressive and brutal. And with its disregard for the norms of international behavior--its export of assassinations, its efforts to acquire nuclear weapons, and its use of poison gas--it has been one of the most disruptive, indeed barbaric.[29]

Of course, any chain of events that would bring about benefits to Iran seems extraordinarily controversial, indeed repugnant, to most Americans at the present time. This is the country whose revolutionary regime has inflicted the humiliation of the hostage crisis upon the U.S., executed thousands of its own citizens, and sent tens of thousands of its own children to die in the marshland battlefields; whose President, Ali Khamenei, has declared, "if the Americans are prepared to sink in the depths of the Persian Gulf waters for nothing, then let them come;"[30] and whose supreme leader, Ayatollah Ruhollah Khomeini has also declared, "the Americans lack the courage to come to Iran and do something."[31]

Nevertheless, the Iranian revolution, like most other revolutions before it, will one day enter its Thermidor, a period when revolutionary enthusiasm is succeeded by bureaucratic stabilization. The Iranian revolution, too, will likely produce its Napoleon, now perhaps a young major demonstrating his prowess and his promise in those marshland battlefields at the confluence of the Tigres and the Euphrates. One day he will enter into his 18th Brumaire, that moment when a military leader seizes political power from revolutionary civilians (or mullahs).[32] At that time, the American foreign policy establishment will once more see clearly, as it did from 1945 to 1978, that the United States has a profound interest, indeed a natural ally, in an Iran whose territorial integrity is preserved by a strong central government and whose multi-ethnic ensemble is contained in a strong state structure centered in Tehran.

Notes

1. On U.S. misperceptions of Lebanon, see John Keegan, "Shedding Light in Lebanon," *The Atlantic* (April 1984), pp. 43-60; also David Ignatius, "How to Rebuild Lebanon," *Foreign Affairs* (Summer 1983), pp. 1139-1156.

2. Stephen L. Spiegel, "The U.S. and Israel: A Reassessment," in Stephen L. Spiegel, editor, *American Policy in the Middle East: Where Do We Go From Here?* (New York: Josephson Research Foundation, 1983), pp. 139-155.

3. Sasson Levi, "Local Government in the Administered Territories," in Daniel J. Elazar, editor, *Judea, Samaria, and Gaza: Views on the Present and Future* (Washington, D.C.: American Enterprise Institute for Public Policy Research, 1982), pp. 105-106.

4. Meron Benvenisti, *The West Bank Data Project: A Survey of Israel's Policies* (Washington, D.C.: American Enterprise Institute for Public Policy Research, 1984) (a summary is given in Benvenisti, "The Turning Point in Israel," *The New York Review of Books* (October 13, 1983), pp. 11–16); Arthur Hertzberg, "Israel and the West Bank: The Implications of Permanent Control," *Foreign Affairs* (Summer 1983), pp. 1063–1077; Daniel J. Elazar, "Present Realities in Judea, Samaria, and the Gaza District," in Speigel, editor, *American Policy in the Middle East*, pp. 111–122. For a comprehensive background, see the essays in Elazar, editor, *Judea, Samaria, and Gaza.*

5. Benvenisti, *West Bank Data Project*, pp. 1–2, 61.

6. *Ibid.*, p. 73 (map 1); Elisha Efrat, "Spatial Patterns of Jewish and Arab Settlements in Judea and Samaria", in Elazar, editor, *Judea, Samaria, and Gaza*, pp. 9–27.

7. This categorization is drawn from Elazar, "Present Realities in Judea, Samaria, and the Gaza District," pp. 114–117.

8. Benvenisti, *West Bank Data Project*, pp. 57–60; Walter Reich, "A Stranger in My House: Jews and Arabs in the West Bank," *The Atlantic* (June 1984), pp. 57–60.

9. Quoted in Benvenisti, *West Bank Data Project*, p. 24.

10. Gershom Shocken, "Israel in Election Year 1984", *Foreign Affairs* (Fall 1984), pp. 82–83.

11. Haim Shaked, "The U.S. and the 'Moderate Arab States' ," in Spiegel, editor, *American Policy in the Middle East*, pp. 77–83; William R. Brown, "The Dying Arab Nation," *Foreign Policy* (Spring 1984), pp. 27–41.

12. *Ibid.*; Daniel Pipes, "How Important is the PLO?" *Commentary* (April 1983), pp. 17–25; Bernard Lewis, "The Return of Islam," in Michael Curtis, editor, *Religion and Politics in the Middle East* (Boulder, Colorado: Westview Press, 1981), pp. 9–29. The fading of Arab nationalism is also discussed in several other essays in the Curtis compendium.

13. The pattern of Middle Eastern politics and society is discussed in Ernest Gellner, *Muslim Society* (Cambridge: Cambridge University Press, 1981), especially chapters 1–2; Daniel Pipes, *In the Path of God: Islam and Political Power* (New York: Basic Books, 1983), especially chapters 1, 7–9; James A. Bill and Carl Leiden, *Politics in the Middle East* (Boston: Little, Brown, 1979). Gellner reviews Pipes' book in his "Mohammed and Modernity," *The New Republic* (December 5, 1983), pp. 22–26.

14. Daniel J. Elazar, "Shared Rule: A Prerequisite for Peace," in Elazar, editor, *Judea, Samaria, and Gaza*, pp. 211–216.

15. *Ibid.*, p. 214.

16. Daniel Pipes, "The Third World Peoples of Soviet Central Asia," in W. Scott Thompson, editor, *The Third World: Premises of U.S. Policy*, revised edition (San Francisco: ICS Press, 1983), pp. 155–174.

17. Karen Dawisha, "The USSR and the Middle East," *Foreign Affairs* (Winter 1983/84), pp. 438–452.

18. Levi, "Local Government in the Administered Territories," p. 110.

19. For accounts of economic activities of Palestinians on the West Bank, see Benvenisti, *West Bank Data Project*, pp. 8–18; Shmuel. Sandler with Hillel Frisch, "The Political Economy of the Administered Territories," in Elazar, editor, *Judea, Samaria, and Gaza*, pp. 123–144.

20. Mordechai Nisan, "The Palestinian Features of Jordan," in Elazar, editor, *Judea, Samaria, and Gaza*, p. 196.

21. The complex and changing relationship between the ideas of the Enlightenment, including democracy, and the course of Jewish history is brilliantly and beautifully discussed by Shlomo Avineri, *The Making of Modern Zionism: Intellectual Origins of the Jewish State* (New York: Basic Books, 1981).

22. Schocken, "Israel in Election Year 1984," p. 90.

23. An overall account of the war is given in Michael Sterner, "The Iran–Iraq War," *Foreign Affairs* (Fall 1984), pp. 128–143.

24. James A. Bill, "Resurgent Islam in the Persian Gulf," *Foreign Affairs* (Fall 1984), p. 120; also his "Islam, Politics, and Shiism in the Gulf," *Middle East Insight* (January/February 1984), pp. 3–12.

25. Yosef Gotleib, "Sectarianism and the Iraqi State," in Curtis, editor, *Religion and Politics in the Middle East*, pp. 153–161.

26. Robert D. Kaplan, "Bloodbath in Iraq," *The New Republic* (April 9, 1984), p. 22; Mark A. Heller, "Turmoil in the Gulf," *The New Republic* (April 23, 1984), p. 19.

27. On Turkey's policies in the Middle East, see Ali L. Karaosmanoglu, "Turkey's Security and the Middle East," *Foreign Affairs* (Fall 1983), pp. 157–175. The attraction of the Kurds in Turkey to the Turkish state, as well as the nature of millet society more generally, is discussed in Jeffrey A. Ross, "Politics, Religion, and Ethnic Identity in Turkey," in Curtis, editor, *Religion and Politics in the Middle East*, pp. 323–347.

28. In past Arab–Israeli wars, Iraq has sent between a third and a half of its army as an expeditionary force to take part in battles against Israel. As a result of the Iranian–Iraqi war, the Iraqi army has doubled in size, from 10 to 20 divisions, and has obviously gained in combat experience. An undefeated post–war Iraq could become a serious threat

to Israel's security. This problem is discussed in "The Implications of the Iran–Iraq War for Israel's Security," *For Your Information*, May 7, 1984 (Philadelphia: Consulate General of Israel).

29. An informed, logical, and vigorous critique of U.S. support of Iraq has been made by my colleague at the U.S. Naval War College, Steven T. Ross, in his letter to the editor, "The Case for a Washington Tilt Toward Teheran," *The New York Times*, May 25, 1984, p. A22.

30. *The New York Times*, May 30, 1984, p. A1.

31. *The Washington Post*, May 31, 1984, p. A1.

32. The composition of the officer corps of the Iranian military after the revolution is discussed by Gregory F. Rose, "The Post–Revolutionary Purge of the Iranian Armed Forces," *Iranian Studies* (Fall/Winter 1984).

9
Evaluating Reagan's Middle East Policy: A First Term Balance Sheet

John H. Sigler

Foreign policy evaluation involves two different intellectual exercises, one analytic and the other normative. In the analytic mode, the evaluator proceeds from the goals and objectives enunciated by the authoritative decision-makers of State A and then proceeds to evaluate whether the mix of strategies and tactics chosen was the most appropriate to achieve these objectives. This involves not only an assessment of the behavior designed by the actions (and inactions) chosen to achieve the objectives, but also an assessment of the unintended consequences of these actions. A quite different intellectual task, often not made clear by the analyst, is a judgement on the proper choice of the goals and objectives of State A. In a subject area as value-laden as the conduct of foreign policy, particularly by a great power whose actions affect the fate of many beyond the citizens of that state, the two processes are often inextricably tied together. The analyst's own policy preferences can easily influence his discussion of the goals, strategies, and outcomes, dramatizing successes and minimizing problems where he agrees with the objectives, and dramatizing failures and maximizing problems where he disagrees. With a President as consciously ideological in his foreign policy rhetoric as Ronald Reagan, it is not surprising that so much of the evaluation will evoke the value preferences of the analyst as well.

Failure to make one's own biases clear can only impair the process of communication. This does not mean that we cannot learn much from analyses by persons whose policy preferences are very different from our own, but it facilitates communication if we do not spend too much of our time simply trying to figure out whether we agree or not with an author merely because his prejudices are similar to or different from our own. Such advice is particularly important in an area as controversial as the Middle East, where passionate commitments run very deep.

My interest in the Middle East was initially stimulated by work on French colonial problems while a graduate student in France. Most of my early research work was on nationalist movements and foreign policy in Arab North Africa (the Maghreb). Schooled in the realist tradition in the study of international politics, I have retained a strong normative commitment to conflict resolution and the vital role of independent third parties in facilitating negotiated solutions as the preferred outcome in protracted conflict situations. History may well record the efficacy of force in imposing one's will on resistant weakness, but in a nuclear age, such lessons of history may well be suicidal. My own reading of the past fifty years of the protracted Arab–Israeli conflict is that, on both sides, strong voices advocating violence have, at critical turning points, turned to war and prevented real opportunities for far more mutually beneficial negotiated outcomes. In the insightful comment by U.N. Undersecretary–General Brian Urquhart, "in the great museum of missed opportunities, the largest gallery is reserved for the Middle East."[1] And it is in that perspective of avoiding or contributing to the opportunities for peace that this essay will attempt to judge the Middle East policies of the Reagan Administration.

The development of the Reagan Administration's initial foreign policy strategies was heavily conditioned by the ideological tone of the political campaign. Reagan ran on a platform of a sharp break with the foreign policies of Jimmy Carter. Discontinuity became a strong conditioning factor in the early months of the Reagan Administration. In the Middle East, this meant a conscious ignoring of the Camp David process, one of Jimmy Carter's notable foreign policy successes, and an emphasis on "strategic consensus," building an alliance among the United States' friends in the area who shared a concern with deterring Soviet incursions into the region, viz., Israel, Egypt, Jordan, and Saudi Arabia. Such a task seemed even more urgent in light of the collapse of the main pillar of U.S. security policy in the Gulf region, viz., the Shah of Iran. Attention was to be shifted away from the Arab–Israeli conflict (bogged down in the impasse over the West Bank–Gaza autonomy talks between Egypt and Israel) toward the Gulf to develop a credible deterrent and war–fighting capability against international or internal threats to Gulf oil supplies.

The shift to the Gulf, and to containment of the Soviet Union, and the building up of a credible Rapid Deployment force (now called the

Central Command) was of course consistent with the policy of the last two years of the Carter Administration, the period following the collapse of the Shah in February 1979 and the Soviet invasion of Afghanistan in December 1979. Reagan's initial policy differed less with that of Carter's national security adviser, Zbigniew Brzezinski, than with the policy championed by former Secretary of State Cyrus Vance. Vance had advocated an emphasis on diplomatic and political means over military ones in the conduct of American foreign policy and a regional approach that emphasized local issues over the globalist East–West rivalry with the Soviet Union that informed the policies of both Brzezinski and the incoming principals (or "vicars") in the Reagan Administration.

In philosophical terms, the divergence here is not so much between Republicans and Democrats, as between conservatives and liberals in foreign policy. In the conservative view, the primary concepts are those of order and hierarchy. Order is a product of well–defined hierarchical relationships where the strong maintain their hegemonic role through a willingness to threaten or employ force against those who challenge the status quo. In the liberal internationalist view, the primary concepts are pluralism, accommodation, and change. There is a third major body of foreign policy opinion in the United States, viz., the non–internationalist view that the United States simply should not be heavily involved abroad.[2]

The Reagan coalition is a new one in American politics, and represents a sharp break from earlier Republican coalitions; hence the sharp divergence in policy, particularly from those of the Nixon–Ford Administrations, and their foreign policy architect, Henry Kissinger. The major disagreement was over any policy of accommodation with the Soviet Union. Reagan's challenge in the 1976 Republican primary, which forced Gerald Ford to drop the word "détente" from his political vocabulary, was a sign of things to come.

In addition to traditional conservative Republicans, the Reagan coalition is made up of three additional groups who have played activist roles in helping to define the policies of the Administration.[3] The first is the conservative Right whose anti–communism is largely a product of their conservative Roman Catholic religious beliefs. On the Middle East, they support Israel as an anti–communist force and take their distance from a militant Islam which is seen as a threat to Western civilization. The second group, the so–called New Right, consists largely of former Democrats, many Jewish, who are motivated by concern over the security of the state of Israel and are deeply anti–Soviet for many reasons including the Soviet Union's treatment of its Jewish minority. They are committed to a strong United States as a protector and guarantor of Israel's security. The third group, the Moral Majority, is Protestant and supports Israel on biblical grounds as well as in opposition to atheistic communism. All three of these groups, anchored in the main U.S. religious traditions, share the new conservative dismay over the degeneration of American morality and family values. Much of President Reagan's rhetoric has been addressed to these important groups in his coalition, although his Orlando speech in March 1983 about the Soviet "evil empire" echoed well beyond his immediate audience. As the critics at home and abroad of this rhetoric do not vote for the President or even support his policies, the White House has not been overly sensitive to these criticisms.

An ideological orientation and a loose coalition of interest groups may set the broad parameters within which a foreign policy is defined, but they do not provide specific objectives or policies to implement those objectives. Many of the Reagan Administration's problems have stemmed from the belief that the earlier failures in American foreign policy were due to wrong-headedness on the part of American leaders. But their articulation of the "right" orientation seemed too often to be a substitute for carefully defined objectives and policies.[4] At the outset, an excessively long time was spent in making sure that the new policies reflected the new ideology. Continuity, a virtue among diplomats, is deeply resisted by new political players who are committed to a change in direction.

The new Reagan foreign policy team was further plagued by problems of bureaucratic and personal rivalry, as well as limited foreign policy experience, particularly in dealing with the Middle East. Secretary of State Haig's initial effort to establish his authority, particularly in crisis management, was resisted, and control was placed in the hands of Vice-President Bush. From the outset, the White House staff established a pattern of preserving maximum White House control with particular regard for the Presidential image and domestic political concerns. Personal loyalty to the President, always important in Washington politics, took on heightened significance in the Reagan Administration. In this, Caspar Weinberger always enjoyed an advantage over Alexander Haig and even over George Shultz, who was always careful to express his belief in presidential supremacy in foreign policy, but who lacked prior close experience with the President.

The general foreign policy orientation was that the position of the United States in the world depended primarily on reasserting American power, both economic and military. Previous American foreign policy weaknesses were ascribed mainly to a decline in the United States' share of global economic and military power. Rather than accommodating to decline, as the Reagan team accused previous Administrations of doing, the Reagan team aimed at reasserting American hegemony. A closely related objective, again primarily directed inward, was to restore American pride in American power and the willingness to use that power in pursuit of American interests, ending the alleged Vietnam syndrome in which the Congress and the American public were seen as unwilling to countenance the use of military force abroad.[5]

In the Middle East, the policy of strategic consensus coincided with the build–up of American military and economic power. Arms sales and defense contracts with Saudi Arabia loomed large in the overall balance of payments, and one advantage of major sales for hard currency, as in the AWACS deal, was keeping defense production lines open and reducing unit costs of weapons systems. The continuing build–up of Israeli and Egyptian military forces, the reward for Camp David, was useful for the strategic consensus, but a drain on the Treasury. Like many in the business community, Weinberger appeared more sensitive to these commercial aspects of Saudi arms sales and less in tune with the pro–Israel elements of the Reagan coalition identified earlier.

The rapid escalation of fighting in Lebanon in the spring of 1981 appeared to catch the Reagan Administration by surprise, and a senior career diplomat, Philip Habib, was called from retirement to use his professional skills to keep a lid on the Israeli confrontation with Syrian–PLO forces in Lebanon. This pattern of delegating Middle East responsibilities from Washington to a roving ambassador was set early. This became a major handicap in that it inhibited a strong and continuing involvement in Middle East affairs by the President and his senior cabinet officials. The original tactic was probably a correct one, since the Administration did not see the Arab–Israeli conflict as one of its first priorities. When war in Lebanon eventually forced a major presidential Middle East initiative in the form of the Reagan Plan of 1 September 1982, the pattern of implementation had already been set, and the strong political will necessary to exert pressure on the parties involved was lost as the principals in the area needed only to deal with career diplomats Habib or Morris Draper, and their successors. Secretary of State Shultz long put off his visit to the Middle East, promised in the President's speech on 1 September, because he preferred to intervene only after the roving ambassadors established the basic framework, leaving merely the final sticking points to the major Washington actors.

Influence, however, is not just a matter of military and economic strength, or the willingness to use military force, as the Reagan Administration's rhetoric seemed to imply. These might work in coercing enemies, or rivals, or neutrals, but how would they be used to influence friends? By adopting the Jordanian option, preferred by the Israeli Labor opposition, President Reagan set himself on a collision course with Prime

Minister Begin who promptly rejected the Reagan Plan, and announced new West Bank settlements. Subsequent efforts to revive the plan failed to deal with King Hussein's complaint that there was no evidence of any American pressure to freeze further West Bank settlements. Reagan did intervene directly with King Hussein, promising F-16s and other arms aid for a Jordanian rapid deployment force and also future pressure on the Israelis, if Jordan would only declare its willingness to enter negotiations with Israel on the Reagan Plan.

Defenders of the Administration may well argue that the Reagan initiative was overwhelmed by events in Lebanon. Who could have anticipated the assassination of Bashir Gemayel, the scrapping of Habib's guarantees on the protection of Palestinians in West Beirut, and the massacre at Sabra and Shatila? These were precisely the events which put an end to Israeli Defense Minister Sharon's grand plan[6] for securing Israel's northern frontiers and installing a Phalange government closely tied to Israel in Lebanon. The Reagan Administration, temporarily buoyed by Habib's success in negotiating the PLO withdrawal from Beirut, now seemed to believe that it could take over the Lebanon operation and succeed where Sharon had failed.

At this point, the Reagan Administration seems to have arrived at the conclusion that the goals of the Lebanon operation were the right ones in terms of supporting pro-American friends in the region. All that was wrong was that the new government should rely on U.S. help, rather than Israel's to implement its goals of removing all foreign forces, achieving central government control over all Lebanese territory, reconciling the contending factions in Lebanon, and negotiating peaceful relations between Lebanon and Israel. Here the Reagan Administration returned to the main theme of the Kissinger era——only the United States could broker any agreement between Israel and its neighbors. The Administration's goal in Lebanon, to use President Reagan's somewhat injudicious phrase, was "to create more Egypts." The stakes were, of course, dramatically different in the two cases. Egypt was the Arab world's largest state and most significant military power. Lebanon was insignificant politically and militarily, and never a confrontation state with Israel in any event. By saying that establishing a pro-Western Lebanon was a vital interest for the United States, the Reagan Administration threw down the gauntlet to Syrian President Assad who saw this as another step in a coordinated American campaign to isolate Syria, in the Sinai II disengagement plan in 1975, at Camp David, and in the Reagan Plan to draw Jordan into a U.S.-sponsored peace plan. The U.S. obviously sought to take advantage of Syria's humiliating defeat at the hands of the Israeli Defense Forces (IDF) in the opening days of the Lebanon operation as well as the disarray in the ranks of the PLO. In power terms, it must have seemed tempting to the Administration to face down the Soviet Union's leading client in the region and bolster the image of American power in the eyes of its friends in the region. But on what power basis was this effort to face down the Syrians founded? The Administration seemed to place great reliance on the effort by the U.S. army to train and equip the Lebanese army rapidly. As a deterrent to action against the Lebanese army, the Administration relied on the visible presence of the Sixth Fleet off the Lebanese coast. Meanwhile, however, the IDF provided the only real deterrent against further outbreaks of fighting between the private Phalange–dominated militia, the Lebanese forces, and their Druze and Shiite rivals. The IDF further provided the real deterrent against any effective Syrian military threat in Lebanon.

When it became clear in April 1983 that the U.S. effort to enrol King Hussein's support for the Reagan Plan had failed, the Administration moved to support Israeli efforts to extract some advantage from the Lebanon operation by brokering the ill–fated May 17 1983 withdrawal agreement between Lebanon and Israel. In his meeting with regional U.S. ambassadors in Cairo just before putting U.S. prestige on the line in the final negotiations for the withdrawal agreement, George Shultz was told unanimously that any agreement at that time was unwise.[7] He rejected this advice and went ahead with the agreement that set the United States on collision course with Syria on the ground in Lebanon. Long–standing American diplomatic wisdom cautioned against any direct military involvement in the Lebanon quagmire. The Israelis, perhaps the world's most successful current practitioners of realpolitik, were learning their own cruel lesson about the limited efficacy of military force against highly politicized indigenous guerrilla forces, much as the U.S. had learned such a lesson earlier in Vietnam. The Israeli public seemed no more willing than the U.S. public had been in the 1970s to accept the price of continuing high casualties in such settings.

A major problem for the Americans, as it was for the Israelis, was the inability of the Lebanese government to control its own friends in the Lebanese forces who sought to even old scores and to press their advantage against the Druze and Shiite militias. This polarized the opposition against the Gemayel government and led to the formation of the pro–Syrian National Salvation Front, composed of former Maronite President Suleiman Frangieh, former Prime Minister Rashid Karami, and Druze chief Walid Jumblatt. The opposition was more broadly representative of Lebanon's divided factions than was the government.

The Administration was deeply divided on what to do next.[8] One group argued that the U.S. should go back to Syria and see what modification in the May 17 agreement might gain Syrian acceptance. The other, led by Secretary of State Shultz, who had a growing vested interest in the agreement he had brokered, argued that the United States should raise the ante with Syria by brandishing American military power and, by reinforcing relations with Israel, raise the specter of joint U.S.–Israeli military pressure on Syria. The second group won, and great efforts were made to pressure the Israelis not to go ahead with their planned withdrawal from the Chouf mountains, which was motivated by frustration over their inability to influence their Phalange allies toward a reasonable compromise with the Druze and the Shiites. The Israelis had given up hope of achieving any peace agreement with the Gemayel government and were preparing to secure southern Lebanon by developing the South Lebanon army, under Major Haddad, which would work closely with the IDF in policing the area.

When the IDF withdrew in the summer of 1983 to more secure positions behind the Awali River, full–scale war broke out in the Chouf mountains between the Lebanese army and their Phalange allies on the one hand and the Druze militia on the other. Faced with the humiliating defeat of the Lebanese army at the strategic junction at Souk al–Gharb, the new U.S. roving ambassador, Robert McFarlane, a former Marine colonel, called on the guns of the Sixth Fleet, used for the first time in the Mediterranean since the Second World War. Unlike aerial attacks, large naval guns are not very accurate and hardly qualify as "surgical strikes." Resentment against direct U.S. armed intervention in the Lebanese civil war now escalated rapidly, although neither the Druze nor the Shiites at this point were particularly anti–American or anti–Israeli. McFarlane argued that the Sixth Fleet's intervention was successful in forcing an agreement on a national reconciliation conference among Lebanon's contending factions. Coercive diplomacy appeared to be working, albeit insufficient attention was paid to the vulnerabilities of the coercing power. As the Sixth Fleet mission changed to active support of the Phalange and the Lebanese army, the Marine contingent at the Beirut airport was left in a dangerously exposed position. A suicide squad had attempted to deter Secretary of State Shultz from concluding the withdrawal agreement on 18 April by blowing up the American Embassy in West Beirut. In a climate of growing hostility to the American and French military presence, which was seen as supporting the Lebanese central government, suicide squads conducted the devastating bombings of the U.S. Marine base and of French forces in Beirut on 23 October. This was followed by a similar suicide attack on an Israeli military intelligence center in Tyre on 4 November. The Israelis and the French responded with air attacks on the dissident Shiite Islamic Amal organization's base in Baalbek, which they regarded as the base for the suicide squads.

The U.S. now moved to back up its exposed military position by closing ranks with the Israelis. National Security Decision Directive 111 of 29 October aimed at restoring close U.S.-Israeli military cooperation, and the Administration cleared the decks on all outstanding Israeli military requirements prior to the visit of Prime Minister Shamir and Defense Minister Arens to Washington in late November. The Americans now needed Israeli strength, so no quid pro quo on the West Bank and other matters was even asked for. "We had to get the Israelis out of their military cocoon," was the reported statement of one senior White House official. As a result of these new commitments, the Lebanese government expected the United States to take a strong stand against Syria. The Sixth Fleet stepped up aerial reconnaissance over Lebanon, presumably to assist in targeting retaliatory strikes similar to those of Israel and France. The reconnaissance flights provoked Syrian anti-aircraft fire. In an effort to silence the Syrian anti-aircraft position, 28 U.S. aircraft attacked Syrian positions in Lebanon on 3 December. Lacking Israeli experience against the Syrian units, the U.S. lost two aircraft and one U.S. pilot was captured by the Syrians and taken to Damascus, where he was subsequently released at the request of U.S. Democratic presidential aspirant Jesse Jackson. The U.S. was now in direct confrontation with the Syrians as the Sixth Fleet guns continued to pound Syrian and Druze positions in the mountains outside Beirut. The whole dreary drama came to an abrupt end in early February when the Shiite Amal militia took over West Beirut as Shiite soldiers deserted the Lebanese army rather than fight their co-religionists as ordered by the Gemayel government. The ever pragmatic Amin Gemayel now made his peace with Damascus in a Saudi-brokered agreement which resulted in the abrogation of the May 17 Lebanon-Israeli accord. A national unity government under Prime Minister Rashid Karami, installed on 10 May 1984, returned the situation to where it had been in 1976 when Syria emerged in the dominant position from the first round of the Lebanese civil war. Faced with the collapse of the Lebanese army and the shift in Lebanese government orientation from Washington to Damascus, the U.S. Marines departed Beirut in February 1984 as the USS New Jersey lobbed its last shells into the Lebanese mountains in a final demonstration of ineffective military power. But the situation was less than a return to the status quo ante for the United States. The U.S. had brandished its military and diplomatic power on behalf of the Lebanese government against Syria, and it had been ignominiously defeated. The Sixth Fleet, whose movements had long served as a signal of American resolve and commitment in the complex bargaining behavior of the superpowers in Middle East crises, was now exposed as being of limited utility. Rather than "standing tall **again**," the American military, in the report of the Long Commission inquiry into the Marine tragedy, took the unprecedented step of criticizing their civilian masters for "over-reliance on military options at the expense of diplomatic alternatives," and urged "a more vigorous and demanding approach to pursuing diplomatic alternatives."[9]

The Administration, in the politics of an election year, tried to shift the blame for the Lebanese debacle to the Congress. Public opinion, which had been consistently critical of the Administration's handling of the Lebanese affair, now only seemed relieved that the Marines were safe and the American part in the war was over. The Administration shifted attention in the Middle East away from Lebanon to the Gulf, where the war of attrition between Iran and Iraq moved to a new stage as Iraq tried to provoke greater U.S. efforts to stop the war through widespread attacks on tankers headed to and from Iranian ports, thus provoking Iranian attacks on Saudi and Kuwaiti vessels and a threat to close all shipping in the Gulf.

With decreased reliance on northern Gulf oil and the availability of alternative overland routes to the Red Sea for both Iraqi and Saudi oil, the Straits of Hormuz choke point came to be seen as having diminishing strategic importance. In an election year, Washington seemed to have little incentive to become involved in another Middle East adventure, and the Reagan Administration entered the election campaign with solid relations with the state of Israel, thus silencing any Democratic criticism. The revival of the issue of moving the embassy from Tel Aviv to Jerusalem can be interpreted primarily as an election effort by the Democrats to embarrass the Reagan Administration.

The failure of the Labor opposition to win a clear-cut victory in the Israeli elections of July 1984 ended any hopes that the Administration had of early efforts in 1985 to revive the Reagan Plan, which envisaged Arafat and the PLO moderates, supported by Egypt, permitting King Hussein to enter U.S.-brokered negotiations for the federation of the West Bank and Gaza with Jordan. The close association with Israel, deemed necessary for an election campaign, alienated Arab moderates, particularly after the Congress blocked weapons sales to Jordan, Saudi Arabia and Kuwait. King Hussein charged that the Reagan Administration had lost all credibility as an honest broker, and moderate Arab regimes opened new talks with the Soviet Union on arms supplies and diplomatic recognition. Egypt restored diplomatic representation with the Soviets. Rather than restricting Soviet inroads into the Middle East, the close alliance with Israel now risked a new polarization of the area and crippled American diplomacy.[10]

Both Israel and the United States may have learned some important lessons about the limits of coercive power in imposing peace in the Middle East. Whether the use of reward power can include the Syrians as well will be the challenge in the next round of U.S. Middle East diplomacy. Perhaps the Administration is hoping that political instability in Syria attendant on the ill-health of President Assad will prevent Syria from following up on its political victory in Lebanon. However, it would be a mistake to believe that the problem of Lebanon is over, as the suicide attack on the new American Embassy in East Beirut on 21 September 1984 so clearly demonstrated. The attack came in retaliation for the U.S. veto in the UN Security Council on 6 September of a Lebanese-backed resolution calling for the moderation of Israeli occupation practices in south Lebanon.

Faced with an increasingly hostile Shiite population in south Lebanon, the Israeli government decided on a withdrawal of the IDF, leaving an eight to ten kilometer "security zone" in south Lebanon to be patrolled by local militias and the remanants of the South Lebanon army under Antoine Lahad, a former Maronite general. The departure was accompanied by "iron fist" retaliation policies to deter further attacks on the departing Israeli forces. The legacy was to increase the bitterness of the Shiite population over the Israeli occupation. Ezer Weizmann, minister without portfolio in the Peres government, reportedly voted against the "security zone" plan because it would create conditions for continued Israeli military intervention in southern Lebanon.

Israel has put the Lebanese government on notice that it will not tolerate any reintroduction of PLO bases in the "security zone." Syria has little incentive to provoke further quarrels with the Israelis on this issue, and neither the Shiites nor the Druze are willing to see any re-establishment of the PLO presence in south Lebanon. But there is a bitter irony here. The Israeli withdrawal without adequate security arrangements in the region has left a vacuum in which the contending militia, many armed by the Israelis, have set off a new and bitter round in the Lebanese civil war, just as the Druze and the Phalange did when the IDF withdrew from the Chouf in 1983. By intervening in Lebanon, the Israelis have contributed to destabilization of that tragic country. The Syrian task in working with the Lebanese coalition government to try to impose order in Lebanon and keep the PLO out is now much more difficult as the traditional Lebanese warlords have lost effective control of their militia to younger, ambitious rivals, many of whom worked closely with the Israelis and with the Americans. Only the ten-nation United Nations Interim Force in Lebanon (UNIFIL) seems to offer any possibility of keeping the fragile peace in the southern part of the country. The

Israelis appear to have learned that the UN force, which they much maligned in the earlier period, was more effective in stabilizing Israel's northern frontier than the Israelis have been. Both Israel and the United States have followed "escalation and retreat" military strategies in Lebanon, which have only exacerbated tensions and instability, thus contributing to the threat to their interests in the region. U.S. Assistant Secretary of State for Near Eastern Affairs, Richard Murphy, a seasoned veteran, has now been called back to try to resume the vital diplomatic brokerage role which the Lebanese debacle has so seriously damaged.

President Reagan continues to enjoy the confidence of a majority of the American electorate, even though they remain critical of his foreign policies in Central America and the Middle East. He continues to look and act like a president, and the image buildup has managed to turn aside any fallout from such gross foreign policy failures as Lebanon. The President simply disappeared for two weeks after the Marines left Lebanon, and the story disappeared from the media. American friends in the area are used to the vicissitudes of American foreign policy. The Reagan Administration thinks its regional friends want demonstrations of U.S. power, but in reality they want some consistency in U.S. policy.[11]

In terms of the basic goals of American foreign policy in the Middle East, oil continues to flow from the Gulf, and the world is less dependent on this supply, for the near future in any event. The Soviet Union's image as a supplier of advanced military weapons systems was tarnished by the IDF success in the early days of the Lebanon war, but the Soviet Union has demonstrated its value as a patron through its rapid resupply and expansion of the Syrian forces, including important surface-to-air missile deterrent capability against any air attacks on Syrian territory. Rather than expanding influence, however, both superpowers have demonstrated in the Middle East a declining ability to influence or control regional events.

Official U.S. support for the state of Israel is at its highest level ever, and U.S. public support for Israel has only been marginally diminished by the after-effects of the Lebanon war. Administration spokesmen have neatly turned aside any criticism of Israel or American involvement in Lebanon by referring to the Palestinian "terrorists" as the cause of it all. The United States has come to rely more heavily than in the past on Israel's services as a regional policeman and anti-terrorist specialist in the Middle East, Central America and elsewhere. To bail out the severely depressed Israeli economy, the United States has been forced to increase dramatically its economic and military subsidy of the state of Israel. As they draw closer together, however, the capacity of each to influence events in the Middle East has dramatically declined. Hans Morgenthau, the most influential exponent of a realist theory of international politics, always placed major reliance on prudential diplomacy to ensure international peace and security. The impasse in Israeli politics, enshrined in the Likud–Labor coalition government, prevents Israeli diplomacy from taking any new initiatives toward a negotiated settlement of the Palestinian question. At the same time, the American–Israel Public Affairs Committee, and the myriad of Political Action Committees committed to support of the state of Israel, act as a veto group on any renewed U.S. government initiatives to act as an effective diplomatic broker in the region.[12] Faced with such an impasse, confidence in any constructive American role in moving toward a diplomatic settlement has largely disappeared among America's Atlantic allies and Japan, and seriously alienated its Arab moderate friends. Without an active diplomacy, and with its military deterrent powers in question, the United States will have great difficulty protecting its widespread interests in the region from the buffeting of the winds of change now sweeping the area.

Notes

1. Brian Urquhart, remarks to annual conference of the World Affairs Council of Northern California, Asilomar, California, 29 April 1983.

2. William Schneider,"Public Opinion," in Joseph S. Nye Jr., ed., *The Making of America's Soviet Policy* (New Haven: Yale University Press, 1984), pp. 11–36.

3. James A. Reichley, "The Reagan Coalition," *Brookings Review* (Winter 1982), pp. 6–9.

4. Raymond Aron, "Ideology in Search of a Policy," *Foreign Affairs,* Vol. 60, No. 3 (1982), pp. 503–524.

5. Kenneth Oye, "International Systems Structure and American Foreign Policy," in Keneth A. Oye, Robert J. Lieber, and Donald Rothchild, eds., *Eagle Defiant: United States Foreign Policy in the 1980s* (Boston: Little, Brown, 1983), pp. 3–32.

6. Ze'ev Schiff, "Lebanon: Motivations and Interests in Israel's Policy," *Middle East Journal,* (Spring, 1984), pp. 220–227.

7. Confidential interview.

8. William Quandt, "Reagan's Lebanon Policy: Trial and Error," *Middle East Journal,* Spring 1984, p. 246.

9. "Executive Summary of the U.S. Department of Defense Report of the DOD Commission on Beirut International Terrorist Act, October 23, 1983," in *Congressional Quarterly* 42 (January 7, 1984), p. 33.

10. Stephen Green, "Strategic Asset, Soviet Opportunity," *American–Arab Affairs*, Summer 1984, pp. 46–54.

11. Barry Rubin, "The Reagan Administration and the Middle East," in Kenneth A. Oye, Robert J. Lieber, and Donald Rothchild, eds., *Eagle Defiant: United States Foreign Policy in the 1980s*, p. 387.

12. Stephen Green, "Strategic Asset, Soviet Opportunity," *American–Arab Affairs*, Summer 1984.

Part 3

The Impact of the Great Powers

10
The Great Powers and Conflict Transformation in the Arab-Israeli Dispute

Shmuel Sandler

Introduction

The Arab–Israeli conflict, which is now almost a century old, has become one of the most important in international politics. Its salience derives not only from its longevity but also from the involvement of the superpowers in the conflict. War in the Middle East has the potential of escalating into a global confrontation and this underscores the significance of the conflict.

Although a dominant theme among scholars of the Arab–Israeli conflict is the persistence of basic unresolved issues—-notwithstanding the 1978 Egyptian–Israeli Peace Treaty—-it should be noted that the conflict has not really remained constant. One of the goals of this paper is to analyze the way in which the structure of the Arab–Jewish conflict has evolved, since the dynamics of continuity and change would seem especially pertinent for attempts at conflict termination.

In particular, we will examine the impact of the great powers on the transformation of the Arab–Israeli conflict. Dependence by regional actors on external material support, coupled with the ongoing possibility of

The author wishes to thank Dean June Chaikelson and Associate Dean Ronald Coyte of Concordia University, Montreal, for providing a grant which made possible the research for this paper. This article was written while spending a year in Canada, under the auspices of the Israel–Canada Foundation for Academic Exchanges. I would especially like to thank Blema Steinberg and Paul Marantz for helpful insights and revisions.

great power intervention, has repeatedly played a role in the decision making of the parties to the conflict as well as in their military or political interactions. In this paper we shall limit our analysis to great power impact on structural transformation. Understanding the role of the great powers in structural preservation or transformation in the past may assist us in understanding the possible future evolution of the conflict in the Middle East.

We base our analysis on a typology provided by Edward Azar *et al.* Azar distinguishes between three types of conflict: those that are clearly "international conflicts or wars," "civil wars," and a "mixture of international and civil wars."[1] On the basis of this formulation we distinguish between three types of conflicts which relate to the Arab–Israeli context.

1) Intercommunal conflict: contending communities engage in disputes within a formal centralized order where the authority and legitimacy of communal institutions surpasses that of the central government.

2) Interstate conflicts: contending sovereign polities engage in disputes which cross national–territorial boundaries.

3) Compound conflicts: contending states and communities engage in disputes over both strategic and communal issues.

The three types differ from each other not only in structure but also in process (interaction). In the intercommunal conflict, interaction is usually expressed through demonstrations, riots, revolts and terror. In interstate conflicts, violence assumes the form of insurgency, limited warfare, and war. In compound conflicts both types of interactions are prevalent. The first section of this paper discusses these characteristics of conflict during different periods of the Arab–Israeli conflict. Our basic assumption is that the conflict did not begin in 1948 but rather in the early 1920s at the point where both the Arab and the Jewish communities in Palestine started to function as political entities.[2]

Within this framework we will then examine the impact of the great powers on the evolution of the structure of conflict. The second part of this paper will focus on the role of the great powers.

Conflict Evolution in the Arab–Israeli Context

Despite its persistent nature, the Arab–Israeli conflict has not been immune to change. Although it began as a conflict between two communities under the jurisdiction of the British Mandate, the establishment of the Jewish state transformed the conflict between Jews and Arab Palestinians into an interstate conflict between Israel and the Arab states. The re-emergence of the Arab Palestinians as a community in the late 1960s and 1970s again restructured the dispute along communal lines. At the same time, the reappearance of intercommunal conflict did not eliminate the interstate conflict. Currently, the conflict can be described as being composed of two domains--interstate and intercommunal.

In line with this evolution, the Arab-Israeli conflict reflects each of the three types of conflict systems outlined above. During Mandatory Palestine, the conflict belonged to the intercommunal conflict type, between 1948 and 1967 to the interstate conflict type, and since 1967 the conflict can be characterized as a compound conflict type. We shall now examine each of these conflicts in terms of its structure and process.

The Palestinian-Jewish conflict in Mandatory Palestine was between two non-sovereign communities segregated from each other by socio-political boundaries.[3] Each community developed political institutions designed both for internal purposes and to represent the community before the British Mandate authorities. The Arab Executive replaced, subsequently by the Arab Higher committee and the Supreme Muslim Council founded in 1922 were the main communal organs on the Arab side. On the Jewish side it was the Zionist Executive, later replaced by the Jewish Agency, and the National Assembly and the National Council which came to be known as the National Institutions. Each community had political parties--constituted along family or local power bases in the Arab community and along ideological lines in the Jewish community--and paramilitary organizations. In the social structure, the Arab community was dominated by land-owning notables, while on the Jewish side it was a mixture of labor cooperatives (associated with the Histadrut) and private enterprise.[4]

Interaction between the two communities was very limited. On the political level, contact between the communities was channelled through the British Mandate. In the social and economic arenas it was limited to the market place and to land purchases, and lacked communal legitimation. Violence between the two communities broke out on several occasions (1921, 1929, and 1933) and reached a peak in 1936-1939, in what was called the Arab Revolt. The final confrontation between the two communities came in 1947-1948 when the United Nations accepted the partition resolution, followed by Britain's withdrawal and Israel's declaration of independence. The war which began with clashes between Palestinians and Jewish regular and irregular forces then turned into an interstate war. The entry into Palestine of five regular armies from the neighbouring Arab states, following Israel's declaration of independence, was accompanied by the defeat of the two Palestinian armies and the exodus of numerous Palestinians, thus terminating the intercommunal conflict. The Arab Palestinians lost their status as a communal actor by leaving Palestine and either moving to various Arab states or to the two territories of Mandatory Palestine—the Gaza strip and what later became the West Bank—occupied by Egypt and Jordan. The bulk of the Palestinians were now divided among three states, two of which (Israel and Jordan) granted them full citizenship.

An interstate conflict system replaced the intercommunal conflict system that had previously existed.[5] The collapse of the socio–political structure of the Palestinian community, the emergence of the Jewish state, and the assumption of political goals by sovereign Arab states transformed the character of the conflict into an interstate conflict. It is worth recalling that the role of the Palestinians in the Arab–Israeli conflict between 1948 and 1967 was marginal. It was largely confined to sporadic acts of insurgency against Israel, acts that were totally controlled by the host Arab states to the detriment of Palestinian political interests. Organizational and political activity in the diaspora was decentralized reflecting general Arab ideas represented by the Ba'ath, Nasserite or Communist parties and ideologies. Even the establishment of the Palestinian Liberation Organization (PLO) in 1964 was not an independent Palestinian enterprise but was rather initiated and supported by Egypt. The political and military battle over Israel's existence and legitimacy was between the Jewish state and the Arab states.

The Arab–Israeli interaction between 1948 and 1967 reflected the interstate structure of the conflict. Relations were characterized by diplomatic and economic boycott and border clashes.[6] In addition, all three wars, 1948–1949, 1956 and 1967, resulted from balance of power calculations. In 1948–1949, a coalition of five Arab states assumed that the newly established Jewish state would not pose a serious threat to their combined military power. In 1956, Israel attacked Egypt because it feared the long–term consequences of the sharp increases in Egypt's military capabilities. Finally, the 1967 war was related to a strategic threat that was taking place on Israel's borders. The positioning of the Egyptian army along Israel's southern borders, the Jordanian–Egyptian agreement permitting non–Jordanian armies to be positioned in the West Bank, and the threat of continued Syrian shelling from the Golan Heights were all actions that transformed the strategic balance of power. In order to deter or contain attacks from each direction, Israel would have had to maintain a level of mobilization that the Israeli economy and society could not sustain for any length of time. Moreover, since Israel committed itself not to allow such one–sided steps, as they constituted a challenge to its deterrence credibility, it was left with the choice of either accepting the new status quo or removing the threat by force.

Israel's decisive victory in June 1967 terminated the pure strategic conflict that characterized the previous period. It then became a conflict consisting of two domains, an interstate and an intercommunal one. In the interstate domain the issues at stake were Israel's legitimacy, and the territories which Israel captured from Egypt, Jordan and Syria-- the Sinai, the Gaza strip, the West Bank and the Golan Heights. In August 1967, the Arab leaders met in Khartoum and adopted the "three no's" resolution: no to negotiations, no to recognition and no to peace. Israel's insistence upon peace in exchange for withdrawal from the occupied territories was followed by two wars designed to push Israel back from the territories, the War of Attrition 1968-1970 and the Yom Kippur War of 1973. Another facet of the interstate interaction was the Sadat initiative of November 1977 which culminated in a peace agreement between Israel and Egypt. Under the terms of this agreement, Israel evacuated the entire Sinai Peninsula in exchange for a formal peace treaty.

Israel's acquisition of the West Bank and the Gaza strip in 1967 changed the status of the Arab Palestinians within the territories and in the diaspora.[7] Following the defeat of the regular Arab armies in the Six Day War, the Palestinians assumed a greater responsibility in the struggle against Israel, and the period after 1967 was marked by growing Palestinian self-assertion. Even though their guerrilla tactics against Israel were largely unsuccessful, the Palestinians reappeared as an actor on the international scene and within the Arab-Israeli conflict context. Institution-building took place both within the territories and the diaspora. But most important from our perspective was the fact that a new dimension in the Arab-Israeli interaction was occurring. Alongside its continued conflict interaction with Arab states, Israel as the power controlling the West Bank and the Gaza strip was also interacting with the Palestinians. It would not be accurate to describe this interaction as one between government and citizens or merely between occupying power and occupied citizens of another state but rather as one between a state and a national community. Moreover, the pattern of conflict interaction between Jews and Arabs within the occupied territories differed from that between Israel and the Arab states. It was marked by strikes, demonstrations and other hostile activities that are symptomatic of a communal conflict rather than an interstate conflict. In short, the Palestinian-Israeli relationship resembled more the patterns of the Yishuv period than the interstate period.

In summary, the Arab-Israeli conflict began as an intercommunal conflict; it was subsequently transformed into an interstate conflict and then into a compound conflict. We turn now to an examination of the role played by the great powers in the preservation or transformation of each of these three conflict structures.

The Great Powers and Conflict Transformation

The basic assumptions underlying our analysis of conflict transformation is that changes in the nature of the parties to a conflict followed by new patterns of interaction represent a new type of conflict. Hostilities in a protracted conflict do not always mean change; sometimes they may mean continuity while peace may bring change. While war, according to Azar's definition, represents a change from the "Normal Relations Range" of the behavior between two parties, it need not transform the structure of the conflict.[8] War may emanate from changes in the distribution of power, but as long as the overall equilibrium has not shifted it may result in a return to the traditional structure and to the regular patterns of interaction.[9] Our main task will be to evaluate the role of the great powers and their impact on conflict preservation or transformation. The approach will be a historical-analytical one. We shall examine the evolution of the conflict and the role of the great powers in each of the major confrontations of 1936–1939, 1947–1949, 1956, 1967, 1973 and 1982.

Since the inception of intercommunal conflict in Palestine, the balance of power shifted steadily in the favor of the Jewish community. In the period between the end of World War I and 1936, the Jewish Arab population ratio grew from 1:9 to around 1:3. The total land owned by Jews during that period almost tripled.[10] In addition, the Zionist organization moved its headquarters from the diaspora to Palestine, established an economic infrastructure, and the all-embracing Histadrut complex.[11] The creation of mobilizing national institutions such as the Jewish Agency and the Vaad Leumi, and modernizing institutions such as urban centers, political parties, elections and the press, promoted the phenomenon of a state within a state. Furthermore, the Yishuv created the Haganah—a military organization which was under the direction of the national center. Although a process of modernization and institution-building had begun among Arab Palestinians, at that time the process was no match for Jewish activities. The traditional socio-political structure of the Arab Palestinian community had not evolved to the point that it could match developments on the Jewish side.[12]

At first, Arab hostility to the Zionist enterprise expressed itself through a sociopolitical boycott and violent disturbances in 1921, 1929 and

1933; by 1936, the Arab Palestinian community initiated a major confrontation that lasted until 1939. The British government reacted by taking direct action against the Arab rebels and even cooperating with Jewish forces to defeat the rebellion. Following the Arab defeat, Britain shifted course and issued the 1939 White Paper which restricted almost totally the growth of the Jewish community.[13] At the same time, Great Britain rejected the idea of partition which had been proposed by the Peel Commission--a concept which the Yishuv accepted in principle, while the Palestinian Arabs and the Arab states rejected it. By suppressing the Arab rebellion, rejecting the Partition Plan and then accepting Arab demands, Great Britain restored the communal structure and prevented system transformation.

Between 1945 and 1947, the conflict in Palestine took place between the Yishuv and Great Britain. In this struggle, Britain tried to prevent the transformation of the communal system into a state system, as demanded by the Jewish community. But Britain could no longer play her traditional role of a great power as she began her forced "retreat from empire." The management of order in the international system shifted to the two new emerging global powers, the United States and the Soviet Union. Although the struggle in Palestine was largely determined by the distribution of power between the Yishuv and the Jewish state on the one side and the Arab Palestinians and the Arab states on the other, it was the rare joint support of the United States and the Soviet Union for the partition plan, and later for the Jewish state, that determined the transformation of the conflict.

Evidence of great power involvement in the transformation of the conflict system included the following factors: (a) American pressure on Britain between 1945-1947 which inhibited British reactions against the Yishuv; (b) U.S. and Soviet diplomatic support at the UN; (c) Soviet sponsored arms sales to the Haganah; (d) material support by Western diaspora Jews which made possible arms purchases from various sources; (e) U.S. and Soviet support for a Jewish state which inhibited British military support for Arab armies. Notwithstanding the Yishuv's decision to declare independence and its ability to overcome the Arab invasion, the policies of great powers played a central role in the process of conflict transformation. Britain's failure to counterbalance Zionist aspirations and American and Soviet support for a Jewish state promoted a new structure. It would be very hard to postulate that the Yishuv could have succeeded in its struggle with the Arab states had the great powers responded with support for the Arabs. The combination of Palestinian local resistance, an invasion by five Arab regular armies and active opposition by the great powers would have aborted the attempt of the Yishuv to achieve independence. Early recognition of the Jewish state by the United States and the Soviet Union set the tone for many in the international community.

The transformation of the intercommunal conflict into an interstate structure was reflected in patterns of interaction. Conflict was now processed through interstate behavior such as economic and diplomatic boycotts, incursion raids into Israel, and Israeli reprisals. What restrained both sides from going to war was the balance of power, which was watched very closely, especially by Israel. During the early years of the 1950s, Israel became concerned with Soviet arms supplies to Egypt and Soviet penetration of the region. Israel feared that an Egypt supplied with modern weapons and led by a charismatic leader like Gamal Abdel–Nasser would become a regional power whose first aim would be to conquer Israel. Israel therefore looked for allies to assist her in offsetting this unfavorable trend. A blow to Egypt's capabilities and the overthrow of its charsimatic leader seemed a rational policy that could serve these interests.

Israel's alliance with France and Britain, who shared some of its views regarding Nasser's regional aspirations, was designed to create a configuration of power that would favor the attacking side. But while Israel correctly calculated its policies in terms of the military balance, it miscalculated the overall political equilibrium. Notwithstanding British and French veto power at the Security Council, Washington and Moscow wielded effective political power. It was they who determined that Israel would not be allowed to keep its territorial gains and then bargain for termination of the conflict. Without the support of at least one of the two superpowers, Israel's extensive political goals could not be achieved. Indeed, American political pressure combined with Soviet military threats undercut the achievements of Israel's military victory and reinstituted the previous interstate conflict structure.

The 1956–1957 experience also provides evidence for our interpretation regarding the transformation of the conflict system in 1947–1949. If Israeli, British, and French collaboration was insufficient to implement these countries' shared goals against Soviet–American dictates, Israel, alone in 1948–1949, would have found it even more difficult to achieve statehood against the wishes of the great powers. One can only speculate that if the two major powers had divided their support between the two sides of the conflict an intercommunal conflict might not have been transformed into an interstate structure.

The restoration of the interstate conflict system during 1957 was reflected in the ensuing period. As in previous years, the Jewish state and its Arab neighbors continued their struggle over political, cultural, economic, and territorial issues. The diplomatic and economic boycott of the Jewish state by its Arab neighbors continued. Violence was constrained by a balance of power that was maintained to a large degree by arms supplies from external powers. After several years of relative calm along the border, hostilities resumed in the early 1960s, this time over the diversion of the Jordan waters and the resumption of raids into Israel by an Arab–sponsored Palestinian guerrilla group called al–Fatah. In terms of great power involvement, the West supported Israel and the conservative Arab regimes, the Soviet Union supported the Arab cause at the international level and supplied weapons to the more radical Arab regimes.

After testing her military capability vis–à–vis Egypt in the 1956 Sinai campaign, and having been assured of a supply of arms from France, and later from West Germany and the United States, Israel's attitude towards the balance of power became more relaxed. Its only concerns were Egypt's missile project assisted by German scientists and the threat of water diversion by Syria. But, in Israeli opinion, these threats did not require a preventative strike. The balance of power seemed stable until May 1967 when the Russians, fearful of the collapse of the Ba'athist regime in Syria provided false information to the Egyptians that Israel was planning a major attack on Syria. Nasser apparently seized this opportunity to shore up his prestige and regain the leadership of the Arab world by expelling the United Nations Emergency Force (UNEF) and blockading the Straits of Tiran.[14]

When the May 1967 crisis broke out, most of the West European countries and the American administration accepted Israel's view that Nasser's steps constituted a violation of international law and guarantees given to Israel in 1957, but they were not ready to take upon themselves the responsibility of restoring the status quo ante.[15] The Soviet Union, on the other hand, supported the Arab position, warning Israel and the West against unilateral action. Having guaranteed itself a sympathetic hearing in the West, Israel acted to restore the geo–strategic balance of power.

Israel's decisive victory in 1967 resulted not only in the restoration of the geo–strategic balance of power but also provided Israel with assets with which it anticipated it could demand the transformation of the conflict system. Until 1967, Israel's view was that it had no means of influencing the Arab states to accept the legitimacy of the Jewish state. Similarly, Israeli decision–makers did not believe that they possessed the means to force the Arabs to alter their stance. They saw their own military power as a means of deterring the Arab states from initiating war. Should deterrence fail, victory in war was designed to prevent the Arab goal of destroying the Jewish state. However, the acquisition of Arab territory in 1967 was perceived by Israeli policy makers as a bargaining card permitting an end to the state of war between Israel and its neighbors.

But Israel's aspirations would have been squelched without international support. A repetition of American–Soviet collaboration along the 1956–1957 model would have again forced Israel to abandon territorial assets without a significant political quid pro quo. It was the lesson of this precedent in conjunction with Soviet support of Egypt in May 1967 that caused a more sympathetic administration in Washington to support Israel's position. U.S. mobilization of votes in the United Nations General Assembly to counter the Arab–Communist bloc, and an American veto at the Security Council allowed Israel to maintain its positions.[16]

Israel's military victory in combination with American political support changed the existing equlibrium but was not sufficient to terminate the conflict system. The Soviet Union was unable to restore the status quo ante, but it possessed sufficient strength to assist the Arab states in resisting a negotiated solution to the conflict. Just as it is difficult to assume that Israel would have been able to sustain her positions without Washington's support, so too Arab hopes for regaining the lost territories without recognizing Israel would have been unrealistic without a Soviet build–up of their arms arsenal. A new structure thus emerged; the conflict instead of moving towards termination, evolved to a compound structure composed of interstate and intercommunal domains.

The main actors in the new conflict structure were states and a national community based in the diaspora, the West Bank and the Gaza strip. In the interstate domain, this structure was maintained by a new configuration of power. It consisted of several factors: 1) Israel enjoyed superiority in the existing military balance of power, but 2) not enough to dictate to the Arab states a negotiated peace agreement; 3) the potential military balance seemed stable as long as existing levels of arms supply from external sources continued to be balanced; 4) Israel enjoyed more secure borders in terms of a military threat against its existence. On the intercommunal level, what existed was a coercive balance. This balance was composed of several elements: 1) Israel enjoyed superiority in force and economic resources enabling her to maintain order in the territories, but 2) Israel lacked sufficient force to enforce Palestinian acceptance of the existing structure; 3) control of the territories did not imply a physical burden on Israel; 4) the emergence of a Palestinian state depended now on Israel. In short, there was no incentive for Israel to return territories without conflict termination.

The compound structure of the conflict was reflected in various forms of interaction: border clashes, raids, a war of attrition in the interstate domain and violent demonstrations, strikes, terror, met by a variety of governmental countermeasures in the intercommunal domain. Ultimately both domains of conflicts were reflected in war, the interstate level in 1973 and both levels in 1982.

The combined attack by Egypt and Syria on October 6, 1973 appears to have been designed to achieve at least one of two goals, and perhaps both: to undermine Israel's geo–strategic position, and to impress upon the Western powers the dangers of the status quo. In other words, the goal was to change the existing distribution of power in the absence of a negotiated settlement. There is growing evidence that during the winter of 1973, the Kremlin began actively to support a military action that would bring about a transformation of the status quo.[17] In contrast, Israel's goal was to demonstrate to the Arab states that the territories would be returned only through direct negotiations. Golda Meir's decision not to preempt was based on the calculation that a possible early set–back was preferable to alienating the United States. Nevertheless, even though the United States refrained from resupplying Israel's military arsenal during the early stages of the war, the Israeli army succeeded in containing the combined Egyptian and Syrian assault, and ultimately brought the attacking states to the verge of total defeat in the ensuing stages of the war.[18] American pressure on Israel not to destroy the Egyptian 3rd Army demonstrated to the Arab states that it was the only external power which was in a position to regain for the Arab states the territories lost in 1967. In exchange, the United States would expect progress towards peace arrangements with Israel. In effect, both the Soviet Union and the Arab states were forced to recognize their inability to alter the status quo through military means.

As a consequence, the compound structure of the Arab–Israeli conflict did not change. In fact, it became more complex following the Yom Kippur War. The resolution of the Rabat conference of 1974 which recognized the PLO as the sole representative of the inhabitants in the territories, the ascendancy of the PLO on the international scene, and the landslide victory of PLO candidates in the 1976 municipal elections in the West Bank, intensified the intercommunal conflict.[19] The political transformation that took place in the May 1977 Israeli elections added another component to this new structure. A portion of the territories was now perceived on the Israeli side not as a strategic asset or a bargaining card but as communal property of the Jewish people.[20] Another indication of the intercommunal struggle was the process of Palestinianization of the Israeli Arabs who began demanding communal rights and not just individual rights in the Israeli polity.

The acid test of the new structure was the peace process between Israel and Egypt that began in November 1977 with President Sadat's visit to Jerusalem and reached its peak in March 1979 with the signing of the first formal peace treaty between Israel and an Arab state. A pure strategic–political structure would have allowed this act to transform the conflict system. With Egypt, the most powerful Arab state out of the military equation and U.S. influence in the Middle East at an unprecedented level, the traditional Arab goal of destroying the Jewish state seemed more unrealistic than ever. However, the establishment of the Rejection Front on the interstate level, and the obstruction of Palestinian participation in negotiations over autonomy with Israel by the PLO, demonstrated the solidity of the compound conflict structure.[21]

The particular issues that were activated in Israel–Arab interactions also reflected the compound nature of the conflict system. On the interstate level, the main issues were the Golan Heights, a Palestinian state, and the question of Jerusalem. On the intercommunal level, the main issues were the nature and scope of autonomy, the authority of political institutions in the territories, settlements, water resources, land ownership, etc. The positions of the parties to the conflict were determined by whether or not they saw the ultimate solution of the Palestinian question in nation–state or communal terms. The fact that many of these issues were negotiated by Israel, Egypt and the U.S. reflected the linkage between the interstate and the intercommunal domains. By the same token, the failure of these negotiations, primarily because of the absence of the Palestinians and the disagreement between Israel and Egypt over the ultimate status of the Palestinians, reflected the new realities of a compound conflict structure.

Another facet of the compound conflict and its communal component can be seen in Israel's behavior and Palestinian reaction. To a large extent, Israel's policies under the Likud government resembled those of the Yishuv in Mandate Palestine. They were composed of settlements, land purchases, migration of Jews to the territories and infrastructure construction. The Arab Palestinian reaction included demonstrations, boycotts, strikes, and other forms of civil violence.

In June 1982, the compound conflict reached a climax. The Israeli operation in the North was designed to accomplish two main objectives: security for the Galilee and the demolition of the PLO. (Another possible objective was to transform the Lebanese political structure, thus making it possible for a second Arab country to sign a peace treaty with Israel.)

While the first objective belonged to the realm of national security, the second reflected the communal dimension of the Arab–Israeli conflict. There are many indications that some Israeli policy–makers expected that the destruction of the PLO in Lebanon would spill over into the Palestinian community in the West Bank and the Gaza strip, thus enabling

Israel to advance the autonomy process. If we take into account the erection of the civil administration in the territories less than a year before the war, and its attempt to crack down on pro–PLO power centres in the West Bank, it is possible to discern a blue–print for a unilateral solution to the intercommunal conflict. The timing for the operation was related to the interstate power relations. With Egypt out of the military equation, and Iraq bogged down in its war with Iran, Israeli policy–makers may have calculated that they had a free hand to destroy the PLO and thus break the impass of a compound conflict structure.

While Israel's calculations with regard to the Lebanese war may have been correct in terms of the regional configuration of military power, they were mistaken in estimating the overall equilibrium. Obviously, an important element in this equilibrium was the superpowers. Even if some U.S. policy–makers tacitly accepted Israel's goals, it is clear, *ex post facto*, that the American administration as a whole did not. The Reagan Plan of September 1, 1982[22] indicated that his administration may have desired a transformation of the existing structure of the Arab–Israeli conflict but not in the direction that Israeli policy–makers intended. The U.S. saw the solution to the Palestinian problem in a Jordanian framework rather than an Israeli one. With Syrian capability affected only partially––since the Soviet Union was resupplying the Syrian army––the balance of power in Lebanon swung back to the pro–Syrian coalition. Lacking American support for its broader goals, Israel had to reduce the scope of its operation and limit itself to providing security for its northern border. Thus, while the PLO base in Beirut was eradicated, the overall structure of the conflict system was not transformed.

To sum up, we have traced the role of the great powers in the evolution of the Arab–Israeli conflict. Having identified three distinct types of conflict structures and six major confrontations, we can now delineate the impact of the great powers on change and continuity in the Arab–Israeli conflict in terms of structure preservation or transformation.

In order to be able to measure the impact of the great powers, we shall compare the operational objectives of the great powers and those of the militarily victorious side on the one hand with the structural outcome on the other hand. We use the term operational objectives in order to distinguish between what may have been the ultimate goals of each great power (which we do not analyze here) and what were their objectives with regard to the existing structure. Thus, for instance, in 1948 the Soviet Union's ultimate goal was to expel Britain from the Middle East, and its operational objective with regard to Palestine was to transform the existing structure.

Our findings are summarized below in Table 10:1, but before presenting them some remarks should be made. In 1936–1939 only one great power, Great Britain, was involved because of the particular nature of a pure intercommunal conflict that was almost exclusively within its domain. We must also differentiate direct British involvement in this case from the patterns in the other cases where the great powers (the United States and the Soviet Union) were not involved directly in military operations. Since 1948 the involvement of the two superpowers has included diplomatic support, economic assistance, arms supplies, and ultimately military threats and mutual deterrence but not direct military action.

Table 10:1
Conflict Transformation and the Great Powers

Type of conflict	War	Objective of the victorious regional actor	Objective of the great powers	Outcome
Intercommunal	1936–39	T	P	P
conflict	1947–49	T	T	T
Interstate	1956	T	P	P
conflict	1967	T	TP	T
Compound	1973	P	TP	P
conflict	1982	T	P	P

T = Transformation
P = Preservation
TP = One great power supports transformation, the other preservation

Of the six confrontations, there is only one case where there was convergence between the goals of the victorious side and the objectives of both of the great powers. In 1947–1949, Israel, having won the War of Independence, supported partition as did both of the superpowers. The outcome was a transformation of the conflict from an intercommunal to an interstate one. In two cases––1967 and 1973––the goals of the military victor (Israel) were supported by one superpower (the U.S.) while the

Soviet Union had opposing objectives. In 1967 Israel's political goals, supported by the U.S., resulted in structural transformation. In 1973, Egypt and Syria, with the support of the Soviet Union, demanded a return to the pre–1967 situation. Israel, having achieved the upper hand on the battlefield in the last stages of war, and supported by the U.S., objected to transformation. The outcome was that the conflict structure remained essentially unchanged.

In three cases, there was a discrepancy between the objectives of the victorious side and those of the great powers. In 1936–1939, both the Jews and the Arabs desired change. To be sure the Yishuv preferred the status quo over a Palestinian state, but their first choice was partition, especially since at the time this idea was supported by the Peel Commission. Great Britain's balancing act between Jews and Arabs resulted in the preservation of the intercommunal conflict. Following its victory in 1956, Israel objected to a return to the status quo ante. The combined pressure of the United States and the Soviet Union resulted in an Israeli withdrawal from the Sinai and the Gaza strip, without any significant change in the interstate structure of the Arab–Israeli conflict. In 1982, Israel, despite its decisive military blow against the PLO, did not succeed in accomplishing its objective of eliminating the intercommunal domain of the Arab–Israeli conflict. Lack of American support for the Begin government's policy towards the Palestinian problem and Soviet support for the Syrian position foiled Israel's strategic goals in both the Lebanese context and vis-à-vis the Palestinian question. In these three cases, it was the will of the great powers that determined the political consequences of the military confrontation.

On the basis of this analysis the following conclusions regarding conflict system preservation and transformation can be drawn. First, the degree of congruence between the operational objections of the victorious party in a military conflict and those of the great powers determined the evolution of the conflict. Second, it was sufficient that the objectives of the victor and those of *one* of the great powers overlapped for the outcome to be determined. Third, when the objectives of the only relevant great power (1936–1939) or both superpowers (1956, 1982) differed from those of the regional victor, it was the will of the great powers that prevailed.

Conclusion

The Arab–Israeli conflict, despite the persistence of hostility and violence over a broad set of issues, has not been as static as it may seem. In the long period since its inception, both the structure and process of interaction have gone through change. An understanding of the nature of the conflict and whether it is simple (intercommunal or interstate) or compound (a mixture of intercommunal and interstate) would seem to be essential for successful conflict resolution. In its current phase, a comprehensive peace between Jews and Arabs would have to encompass both domains of the conflict, the interstate and the intercommunal.

The main concern of this paper was to explore the role of the great powers in conflict transformation. Indeed, our analysis has provided evidence that conflict evolution is related not merely to the actions of the regional players at the core of the conflict but also to the role of the great powers. The evidence suggests that the Arab–Israeli conflict has been transformed through a combination of two processes: changes in the power configuration at the core and the external support of at least one great power for a new structure. In 1947–1949, the intercommunal conflict came to an end following Israel's demonstration of military and political supremacy vis-à-vis the Palestinians and the Arab states, accompanied by U.S. and Soviet support for conflict transformation. In 1967, a new conflict structure emerged following Israel's decisive military victory accompanied by U.S. support for Israel's refusal to return to the previous conflict structure. In contrast, when the great powers objected to conflict transformation (1936–1939, 1956, and 1982), their position prevailed.

Finally, these findings may be viewed from an additional perspective. In the event of a split between the great powers, the military outcome on the battlefield does make a difference. In both the Six Day War and the Yom Kippur War, the two superpowers were divided as to their objectives, and the outcome was more supportive of the objectives of the military victor. This finding confirms two traditional Israeli maxims. First, Israel must win its wars and second, it must ensure the support of at least one great power in order to maintain its gains on the battlefield and transform them into a political victory.

Notes

1. See Edward E. Azar, Paul Jureidim and Ronald McLeurin, "Protracted Social Conflict; Theory and Practice in the Middle East," *Journal of Palestine Studies*, Vol. VIII, No. 1 (Autumn, 1978): 41–60. See also Stephen P. Cohen and Edward E. Azar, "From War to Peace, the Transition between Egypt and Israel," *Journal of Conflict Resolution*, Vol. 25 No. 1 (March, 1981): 87–114.

2. Our analysis of the Palestinian–Jewish relationship as an

intercommunal conflict is based on Dan Horowitz and Moshe Lissak, *The Origin of the Israeli Polity* (Chicago: The University of Chicago Press, 1978), ch. 2.

3. *Ibid.*

4. For a comprehensive analysis of the political and social structures of the Palestinian Arab Community during Mandatory Palestine see Yehoshua Porat, *The Emergence of the Palestinian Arab National Movement, 1918–1929* (Tel Aviv: Am Oved, 1976) and Yehoshua Porat *From Riots to Rebellion, The Palestinian Arab National Movement, 1929–1939* (Tel Aviv: Am Oved, 1978), (in Hebrew).

5. The Analysis of the Arab–Israeli Conflict between 1948–1967 is based on Nadav Safran, *From War to War* (New York: Pegasus, 1969) and Yair Evron, *The Middle East: Nations, Superpowers and Wars* (New York: Praeger, 1973).

6. For the strategic and political aspects of border clashes between Israel and its Arab neighbors see Shlomo Aronson and Dan Horowitz, "The Strategy of Controlled Retaliation: The Israeli Example," *Medina U'Memshal*, Vol. 1, No, 1 (Summer 1971): 77–100 (in Hebrew).

7. The analysis of the Israeli–Palestinian relationship since 1967 is based on Shmuel Sandler and Hillel Frisch *Israel, the Palestinians and the West Bank, A Study in Intercommunal Conflict* (Lexington, Mass.: Lexington Books, 1984).

8. Azar, *et al.*, "Protracted Social Conflict," p. 52.

9. Michael Brecher and Hemdo Ben Yehuda, "System and Crisis in International Politics," unpublished manuscript.

10. Porat, *From Riots to Rebellion, The Palestinian–Arab National Movement, 1929–1939*, p. 58 and ch. 4; and Baruch Kimmerling, *Zionism and Territory, The Socio-Territorial Dimensions of Zionist Politics* (Berkeley: Institute of International Studies, University of California, 1983), Table 2.1.

11. See Sandler and Frisch, *Israel, the Palestinians and the West Bank*, pp. 15–19.

12. Lois A. Aroian and Richard P. Mitchell, *The Modern Middle East and North Africa* (New York: MacMillan Publishing, 1984), pp. 225–229.

13. For the full text of the 1939 White Paper see *Middle East Focus*, Vol. 2 No. 6 (March, 1980): 23–27.

14. On the 1967 crisis see Robert O. Freedman, *Soviet Policy Toward the Middle East Since 1970* (New York: Praeger Publishers, 1975), pp. 22–33.

15. Peter Mangold, *Super Power Intervention in the Middle East* (London: Croom Helm, 1978), p 145.

16. On the American role following the Six Day War and its impact on Israeli policy see *ibid.*, ch. 8; and Dan Margalit, *Message from the White House* (Tel Aviv: Ot-Paz, 1971), (in Hebrew).

17. See Dina Rome Spechler, "Soviet Policy in the Middle East: The Crucial Change," in this volume.

18. On American goals and policies during the Yom Kippur War see Marvin Kalb and Bernard Kalb, *Kissinger* (London: Hutchinson, 1974), p. 479; Walter Laqueur and Edward Luttwak, "Kissinger and the Yom Kippur War," *Commentary*, September 1974; Matti Golan, *The Secret Conversations of Henry Kissinger; Step-by-Step Diplomacy in the Middle East* (London: Bantam, 1976), pp. 86–89.

19. For the text of the Rabat Conference see *Middle East Focus*, Vol. 4 No. 4 (November, 1981): 30. For an analysis of the new communal structure of the Palestinians see Sandler and Frisch, *Israel, the Palestinians and the West Bank*, chs. 4–5.

20. *Ibid.*, ch. 6.

21. Menahem Milson, "How to Make Peace with the Palestinians," *Commentary* (May, 1981): 25–35.

22. For a full text of the Reagan Plan see *Middle East Focus*, Vol. 6, Nos. 2&3 (July and September, 1983): 95–97.

11

The Dynamics of Superpower Involvement in the Middle East: Retrospect and Prospect

Blema S. Steinberg

The papers in this volume reflect a mutually shared perspective on the part of the various contributors. Irrespective of whether they focus on Soviet or American foreign policy in the region, or both, each author explores a particular dimension of policy to provide us with important insights into how the superpowers define their interests, the constraints under which they operate, and the way in which their perceptions of each other influence their behavior.

The five papers on Soviet foreign policy in the Middle East focus primarily on the constraints that limit the Soviet Union's ability to implement its objectives in the region. These include Soviet perceptions of countervailing American strength in the region, fears of a superpower confrontation arising from escalating regional conflicts, the challenges posed by Islam, the pressures of client demands and the nature of internal power struggles between competing Soviet foreign policy elites.

In his essay, "The Soviet View of the Utility of Force in the Third World," S.N. MacFarlane explores the pattern of Soviet force projection in the Third World. From a rather conservative posture during the early 1960s, Soviet analysts shifted their views in the late 1960s and early 1970s to regard intervention in Third World conflicts as a more attractive policy option. In MacFarlane's view, this change can be partially explained by the expansion of Soviet military capabilities and the process of détente itself. He suggests that, paradoxically, the Soviet pursuit of détente vis-à-vis the United States caused it to behave in a more expansionistic fashion in peripheral arenas as a way of defending its revolutionary credentials in the Third World.

At the same time, MacFarlane is careful to note that a greater Soviet propensity to project force in the Third World is accompanied by considerable caution and moderation. He sees little evidence that the Soviet leadership is prepared to become involved in offensive operations mounted by its clients. Soviet operations tend to be relatively low risk and the use of Soviet regular units is viewed as a last resort. With the single exception of Afghanistan, Soviet use of force in the Third World tends to be reactive, ad hoc in character and responsive primarily to local crises.

While the experience of the past decade provides little support for the contention that the Soviet Union is moving toward a policy of indiscriminate and aggressive use of force throughout the Third World, MacFarlane recognizes that Soviet leaders are clearly more sanguine about the utility of force. Moreover, in so far as the United States is perceived to be less willing and less able to defend its interests in the Third World, the USSR can be expected to expand its military presence, particularly as Soviet force projection capabilities continue to grow.

As Moscow expands its influence in the Middle East, it is being confronted with the need to come to terms with various constraints on its ability to project power in the region. Carol Saivetz, in her paper, "Soviet Perspectives on Islam as a Third World Political Force," focuses on the challenge posed by Islam and the militancy of the Khomeini regime. She details the way in which events in Iran and Afghanistan have produced a resurgence in Soviet academic and official analyses of Islam. Soviet orientalists have explored the causes of the Islamic awakening and are now attempting to assess its political utility for Moscow. Opinion is divided between those who see the Islamic resurgence as a useful anti-western force and those who regard it as a right-wing reactionary phenomenon.

At the policy level, Saivetz notes that the Soviet Union is attempting to appease its own Muslim population as well as their counterparts in the Middle East. At the same time, she observes that the Soviet leadership appears fully cognizant of the fact that the strength of Islamic sentiment may indeed be an obstacle to Soviet Middle East-Gulf objectives and that Soviet leaders remain uncertain in their handling of this potentially incendiary phenomenon.

Another important variable that has affected Moscow's past and present involvement in the Middle East is its perceptions of American goals in the region. In his essay, "Moscow's Perceptions of Recent American Involvement in the Middle East: Implications for Soviet Policy," Herbert L. Sawyer examines the way in which Soviet perceptions of American successes and failures influence the formulation of Soviet foreign policy. To illustrate his argument, Sawyer analyzes Moscow's interpretation of America's role in Lebanon since the summer of 1982.

Sawyer argues that the Soviet leadership had ambivalent feelings about Washington's performance in Lebanon. On the one hand, Moscow believed that the U.S. role in Lebanon lacked leadership and that the U.S. performance raised serious questions about America's credibility as a major player in the region. This in turn suggested that the Soviet Union could look forward to maximum gains in the area with minimum risks. Offsetting this perspective, however, were Soviet perceptions with regard to the establishment of a direct and permanent U.S. presence in the Middle East–Gulf region. The Soviet Union appeared to view this development as constituting a potentially important set of constraints on future Soviet freedom of maneuver.

Robert O. Freedman's examination of Soviet policy during the Lebanese crisis of 1982–84 suggests that constraints on Soviet policy were a function not only of elite perceptions of the United States but that links with client states also constituted an important explanation for Soviet behavior. In his essay, "Moscow, Damascus and the Lebanese Crisis of 1982–84," Freedman sees these constraints largely as a function of the behavior of other actors--primarily, the United States, Israel and Syria. In his view the Soviet Union's concern to avoid a military confrontation with both Israel and the United States led it to refrain from giving military assistance to Syria from June to November 1982. At the same time, Soviet unwillingness to lose its Syrian foothold in the region caused it to resupply its client with defensive surface–to–air SAM–5 missiles in the wake of Syria's military defeat at the hands of Israel.

After the September 1983 Syrian–American confrontation, the Soviet Union once again cemented its relations with Syria by providing it with offensive air–to–air SS–21 missiles. Although Moscow continues to retain the ultimate upper hand in its dealings with Syria by virtue of its ability to open and close the arms pipeline, Freedman's analysis reveals the extent to which Soviet interests in the region were frequently constrained by Syrian goals that were pursued in opposition to Moscow's wishes. President Assad's efforts to split Fatah splintered the already divided Arab world and made Moscow's long sought "anti–imperialist" Arab unity even more difficult to achieve, while Syrian attempts to destroy the PLO undermined Soviet interests in maintaining the organization as an independent actor open to continued Soviet influence.

While both the Soviet Union and Syria have tried to use each other to further their own goals, Freedman asserts that Moscow's decision to provide Damascus with two major weapons systems, the SAM–5s and the SS–21 missiles--weapons never before deployed outside the Warsaw Pact Organization--must be seen in terms of Moscow's attempts to regain some of its lost credibility in the Arab world. Soviet relations with Syria, as illustrated during the Lebanese conflict from 1982–84, suggest that the asymmetries in military power between the Soviet Union and Syria were not replicated in the patterns of influence. Given Soviet fears of being excluded from the region, Syria was able to hold the Soviet Union hostage to some of its political aspirations.

Efforts to understand the dynamics of Soviet involvement in the Middle East are frequently postulated in terms of dichotomous categories: either Soviet foreign policy is defensive and reactive, or it is offensive and aggressive. Structuring the problem in this way presumes, according to Dina Rome Spechler, that Soviet foreign policy behavior over time tends to reflect a consistent pattern of objectives and that the task of the foreign policy analyst is to marshall the evidence to support one or the other competing hypotheses.

Focusing on the critical period 1967–73, Spechler in her essay "Soviet Policy in the Middle East: The Crucial Change," argues that oscillations in Soviet Middle East policy and, most particularly, the decision taken in February 1973, "to unleash the Arabs," cannot be adequately explained by a rational actor paradigm. In her view, a bureaucratic politics model that assumes a diversity of views and conflicts over policy priorities and objectives among Soviet political elites greatly assists us in our efforts to understand Soviet behavior. More specifically, Spechler asserts that the best explanation of Soviet support for an Arab military initiative against Israel in 1973 is that the dominant voice in Soviet Middle East arms transfer policy ceased to be individuals or groups that attached high priority to confrontation avoidance and the development of détente. Elites primarily concerned with expanding Soviet power and building positions of strength in the Middle East, gained in influence.

Spechler's case study suggests that a focus on competing elites within the Soviet Union––the diversity in their images of the opposing superpower, their conflicting priorities and objectives with regard to both global and regional policy and the shifts in their respective political fortunes––is critical to our understanding of the determinants of Soviet foreign policy.

A common thread running through the four essays on American foreign policy in the Middle East is an emphasis on the faulty assumptions that have characterized that policy and which explain its failure. In particular, U.S. policy is castigated for its excessive concern with Middle Eastern oil, its inaccurate perceptions of PLO moderation, its inappropriate transfer of Western ideas of democracy and the nation–state to the Middle East and finally, its unsophisticated application of the East–West ideological struggle to the Middle East battlefield.

In his study of American foreign policy in the Middle East, David Haglund focuses on the role that American perceptions of Middle East oil have played. "Oil as a Factor in U.S. Policy Towards the Middle East" examines the salience of oil using a logical–deductive and an empirical–inductive approach. From a logical–deductive perspective, Haglund addresses the issue of why strictly economic considerations such as efficiency do not allow decision–makers to regard dependence upon foreign oil as no worse than dependence upon imported tomatoes. He suggests that enmeshed in the perception of dependence on imported oil are issues of perceived "vulnerability" and "essentiality," as well as the concentration and location of oil deposits.

Superimposed upon a logical–deductive argument for regarding access to Middle East oil as a vital strategic U.S. interest, American decision–makers have interpreted historical developments since 1920 as providing strong empirical evidence for their assumptions. In the post–World War I and World War II years, they viewed access to Middle East Oil as a "national" interest; by the early 1980s, it had become a truly "vital" interest worthy of a commitment of American military force to defend it. Haglund examines the evidence for this perspective and finds it open to serious challenge.

Even if it could be demonstrated that secure access to Middle East oil were a "vital" American interest, a position which Haglund strongly doubts, neither diplomacy nor force are likely, in his view, to be useful techniques to protect that interest. Rather than concentrating on access to Middle East oil, Haglund suggests that the United States should emphasize the adoption of vulnerability–reducing strategies such as stockpiling oil supplies, import diversification, increases in domestic oil production, substitution and conservation measures.

In his paper, "Faulty Assumptions, Failed Policy: the Arabists and the PLO During the First Reagan Administration," Martin Indyk assigns paramount responsibility for failures in America's Middle East policy--and more particularly for the stalemate over the future of the West Bank and Gaza--to the professional bureaucrats in the Near East and South Asia Bureau and their counterparts in the CIA and the Pentagon who have come to be known as Arabists. According to the Arabists, the protracted Arab–Israeli conflict and the general instability in the region are rooted in the failure to resolve the Palestinian problem. The solution they propose is the creation of a Palestinian entity in the West Bank and Gaza and American sponsorship of negotiations between Israel and Palestinian representatives including the PLO.

Indyk attacks these policy prescriptions on the grounds that the critical assumption upon which they are based--namely that the PLO is a "moderate" organization—-has no basis in fact, and he provides detailed documentation to support his contention. Given this faulty assumption which provides the basis for the way in which the Arabists structure their thinking about the PLO, it is hardly surprising, writes Indyk, that "successive American administrations have failed to persuade the PLO to moderate its position." Instead of continuing to woo the PLO, Indyk advocates the Jordanian solution in which the West Bank and Gaza would be returned to Jordan.

Like Martin Indyk, James Kurth also believes that the best explanation for the failures in America's Middle East foreign policy can be found in the faulty assumptions that characterize much of the thinking by political elites in Washington. In his paper, "American Perceptions of the Israeli–Palestinian Conflict and the Iranian–Iraqi War: The Need for a New Look," Kurth examines U.S. policy towards the Israeli–Palestinian conflict and the Iran–Iraq War under the first Reagan Administration. In the case of American policy towards the Iran–Iraq War, Kurth argues that American support for Iraq is based, in part, on the faulty assumption that the maintenance of its political and territorial integrity is a critical component in the containment of Shiite fundamentalism. In Kurth's view there are natural limits to the growth of Islamic fundamentalism which are rooted in the religious and cultural demography of the Middle East.

With regard to the Israeli–Palestinian conflict, Kurth asserts that the thinking of the American decision–making elite is characterized by two faulty assumptions. The first is that the Jewish presence on the West Bank is reversible. He underscores the fact that, for better or worse, Jewish settlements, with the exception of those located in the heartland of Judea and Samaria adjacent to Arab cities, have broadly based support from both Labour and Likud. A second faulty assumption is that the politics of the Middle East are analogous to those of the United States or Western Europe. According to Kurth, the Middle East is more accurately understood as a complex society of ethnic communities in which concepts of an American pluralist democracy or a European homogenous nation–state are simply not appropriate. Ethnic communities in the Middle East have traditionally lived under state structures organized by the dominant group and this is a reality which is unlikely to change in the forseeable future. Once this reality is acknowledged, Kurth argues that the policy implications are as follows: for the Jewish state in the Middle East to be secure, it cannot adopt either an American or a European model but must retain a state–community structure Middle Eastern style in which the West Bank Arabs will have to tolerate an Israeli monopoly of political and military power in exchange for the right to exercise local autonomy.

In his analysis of the failures of American foreign policy in the Middle East during the first Reagan Administration, John Sigler's paper, "Evaluating Reagan's Middle East Policy: A First Term Balance Sheet," ascribes them to a variety of factors: first, the strong ideological tone of the Administration which resulted in an unwarranted shift away from the Camp David process to an emphasis on deterring Soviet incursions into the region; second, the influence of a number of conservative interest groups that were either staunchly anti–communist or pro–Israel; and third, bureaucratic and personal rivalries within the foreign policy team which resulted in poorly defined objectives and policies.

More specifically, Sigler takes the Reagan Adminstration to task for investing Lebanon and a pro–Western outcome with so much importance. In so doing, he claims that the United States only succeeded in throwing down the gauntlet to Syrian President Assad who saw this endeavour as but another step in the effort to isolate Syria. Sigler also chastizes Secretary of State Shultz for brokering the ill–fated May 1983 withdrawal agreement between Lebanon and Israel after he had been told that any agreement at that time was unwise. The President's decision to use the Sixth Fleet on behalf of the Lebanese government against Syria also failed, providing a painful exposé of the limits of sea power as an effective instrument of U.S. government policy.

From Sigler's perspective, U.S. policy failed because it was based on a series of faulty assumptions. The lessons the United States should now draw from the experiences of the first Reagan Administration are three fold: there are limits to "coercive" power in imposing peace in the Middle East; military strategies of "escalation and retreat" are unwise and only exacerbate tensions and instability; and American reliance on Israel's services as regional policeman and anti–terrorist specialist will hamstring new American initiatives towards a negotiated settlement of the Palestinian question.

The concluding paper in this volume, "The Great Powers and Conflict Transformation in the Arab–Israeli Dispute," explores the impact of the great powers on the transformation of the structure of the Arab–Israeli conflict. From a theoretical perspective, Shmuel Sandler distinguishes three types of conflicts: inter–communal conflicts involving contending communities within a formal centralized order, inter–state conflicts in which contending sovereign polities engage in disputes that cross national territorial boundaries and compound conflicts which contain elements of both inter–communal and inter–state conflicts.

Sandler then examines the Arab–Israeli conflict showing how it evolved from an inter–communal conflict type (Mandatory Palestine), to an inter–state conflict type (1948–67), to a compound conflict type (1967 to the present). Central to Sandler's thesis is the neglected role that the Great Powers have played in the structural transformation of the Arab–Israeli conflict.

On the basis of evidence derived from an examination of six major Arab–Israeli confrontations, Sandler argues that structural transformations of the conflict were the function of two processes: changes in the power configuration at the core and the external support of at least one great power for a new structure. In the absence of the support of at least one great power, the wishes of the local victors were insufficient to bring about a transformation of the conflict structure. This suggests that irrespective of the magnitude of the victory that a regional protagonist could achieve in the future, it would be unlikely to be able to transform the nature of the conflict without the support of at least one of the great powers.

A retrospective view of superpower involvement in the Middle East has focused attention on a wide range of constraints, including faulty assumptions, that have prevented both the United States and the Soviet Union from successfully implementing their foreign policy objectives. Are these constraining forces likely to persist or are we dealing with phenomena whose significance can be expected to wane in the late 1980s and 1990s? The answer would seem to be mixed. Fears of escalating regional conflicts are likely to continue to produce reasonably prudent superpower behavior thus limiting the extent of their willingness to project force in the region. The existing and projected "correlation of forces" between the two superpowers makes any other strategy far too risky.

But some constraints on the behavior of the superpowers do appear to be changing. If world demand for oil continues either at present levels or in fact declines, this factor coupled with the development of new sources of supply (e.g., Mexican oil), may remove some of the perceived constraints under which American decision–making elites previously functioned. This could lead the United States to re–evaluate the overall political and strategic importance of Saudi Arabia and the Gulf States and to de–emphasize the salience of the "moderate" Arabs in their calculus of interests.

Somewhat more problematic is the role that a resurgent Islam is likely to play in the formulation of Soviet and American foreign policy in the region. At this time, it remains unclear whether we are dealing with a force that is likely to increase or decrease in importance. Much will depend upon the impact that the death of the Ayatollah Khomeini has on the Shiite community. An upsurge of Shiite factionalism could significantly reduce the necessity for either superpower to program the fundamentalist factor into their foreign policy equations; alternatively, it could provide greater opportunities for both superpowers to try and manipulate competing factions for their own ends.

A focus on external constraints such as the opponent's power capabilities, ties with client states, dependence on imported oil, and Islamic fundamentalism provides us with an understanding of some of the parameters within which American and Soviet elites structure their foreign policy options. But, as a number of contributors have cogently argued, it would be a serious error to ignore the role of internal constraints. As in the past, superpower Middle East policy will continue to be shaped in the months and years ahead by bureaucratic struggles between competing factions in the foreign policy elite, standard operating procedures of governmental agencies and, perhaps most importantly, the pervasive influence of standard operating assumptions.

About the Contributors

Robert O. Freedman is Dean of the School of Graduate Studies of the Baltimore Hebrew College and Peggy Meyerhoff Pearlstone Professor of Political Science. He is the author of *Soviet Policy Toward the Middle East Since 1970* (third revised edition, 1982). He is the editor of *World Politics and the Arab–Israeli Conflict* (1979), *Israel in the Begin Era* (1982), *Soviet Jewry in the Decisive Decade 1971–1980* (1984), and *The Middle East Since Camp David* (1984).

David G. Haglund is Director of the Center for International Relations and teaches in the Department of Political Studies at Queen's University, Kingston, Ontario. He has recently published *Latin America and the Transformation of U.S. Strategic Thought, 1936–1940*, and has written on international resource politics, U.S. foreign policy, and U.S.–Canadian relations.

Martin Indyk is Executive Director of the Washington Institute for Near East Policy. He served as Middle East Assessments Officer in the Australian Prime Minister's Office of National Assessment and as a Senior Lecturer in Political Science at Macquarie University in Sydney. Dr. Indyk has published many articles on U.S. policy in the Middle East. His latest monograph, *Sadat's Jerusalem Initiative*, was published by Harvard University's Center for Middle East Studies in 1984.

James R. Kurth is currently a visiting professor at the U.S. Naval War College, where he is Director of the Strategy and Campaign Department of the Center for Naval Warfare Studies. He also holds a permanent position as Professor of Political Science at Swarthmore College. His publications have focused on U.S. foreign and defense policies and on the politics of modernizing countries.

S. N. MacFarlane is Assistant Professor of Government and Foreign Affairs at the University of Virginia. He is the author of *Soviet Intervention in Third World Conflict* and *The Idea of National Liberation.* His recent articles have appeared in *World Politics, International Security,* and *International Affairs.*

Paul Marantz is Associate Professor of Political Science at the University of British Columbia. He is the co–editor of *Peacemaking in the Middle East* (Croom Helm, 1985). His most recent articles, dealing with Soviet foreign policy and East–West relations, have appeared in *Orbis, International Journal, Current History,* and *Canadian Slavonic Studies.*

Carol R. Saivetz has taught at Northeastern University and Simmons College and is currently an Associate Professor of Political Science at Tufts University. In addition, she is a Visiting Scholar at Harvard University's Russian Research Center. Professor Saivetz is the author of numerous articles on Soviet policy in the Third World. She is the coauthor of *Soviet–Third World Relations* (Westview Press, 1985).

Shmuel Sandler is a Senior Lecturer in the Department of Political Studies, Bar Ilan University, Israel. He is the coauthor of *Israel, the Palestinians and the West Bank* (Lexington Books, 1984) and has published articles dealing with the Arab–Israeli conflict, the West Bank, and American foreign policy.

Herbert L. Sawyer is Chairman and Professor, Department of Government, Bentley College. In addition, he is a Fellow of the Russian Research Center, Harvard University. He is the author of *Soviet Perceptions of the Oil Factor in U.S. Foreign Policy: The Middle East–Gulf Region* (Westview, 1983).

John H. Sigler is a Professor of Political Science and International Affairs at Carleton University, Ottawa. He is co–editor (with Charles Doran) of *Canada and the United States: Enduring Friendship, Persistent Stress* (Prentice–Hall, 1985). His most recent articles on American foreign policy and the Middle East have appeared in *International Journal* and *Circa, 1984–5* and in previous volumes of the Conflict Yearbook published by the Centre québécois de relations internationales.

Dina Rome Spechler is Associate Professor of Political Science at Indiana University. She is the author of *Domestic Influences on Soviet Foreign Policy; Permitted Dissent in the USSR;* and *Russian Nationalism and Political Stability in the USSR.* Her articles in journals and collected volumes have dealt with Soviet policy in the Middle East, Soviet foreign economic policy, and domestic politics and policies in the USSR.

Blema S. Steinberg is Associate Professor of Political Science at McGill University. Her research has focused on American and Soviet foreign policy and her work has appeared in such journals as *Orbis, International Interactions, Jerusalem Journal of International Relations, Études Internationales* and the *Canadian Journal of Political Science.*

Index